THE 1826 JOURNAL OF JOHN JAMES AUDUBON

Audubon at Green Bank
Almost Happy!! —
Sep.r 1826. Drawn by himself.

THE 1826 JOURNAL OF

JOHN JAMES

Audubon

An account of his journey to England and Scotland to arrange the publication of *The Birds of America*. Transcribed from the original, in the collection of Henry Bradley Martin, and with a Foreword and Notes, by **Alice Ford.**

ABBEVILLE PRESS · PUBLISHERS · NEW YORK

Editor: Walton Rawls
Designer: Howard Morris

Library of Congress Cataloging-in-Publication Data

Audubon, John James, 1785–1851.
  The 1826 journal of John James Audubon.

  "An account of his journey to England and Scotland
to arrange the publication of The birds of America."
  Bibliography: p.
  Includes index.
  1. Audubon, John James, 1785–1851—Diaries.
2. Audubon, John James, 1785–1851. Birds of America—
Diaries. 3. Ornithologists—United States—Diaries.
4. Artists—United States—Diaries. I. Ford, Alice,
1906–   . II. Title.
QL31.A9A3 1987   598.092′4 [B]   86–28813
ISBN 0–89659–689–3

Contents

Illustrations

Foreword

THE 1826 MANUSCRIPT JOURNAL, rare possession of Mr. Henry
Bradley Martin, left the hands of a descendant some years
ago. Its 428 closely penned pages and fly leaves of coarse, laid
paper lie bound within worn brown covers that have the outward
appearance of a ledger, measuring 12⅛ inches by 7¾ inches.
Audubon's frequent mention of pen knives suggests his use of a
quill but does not rule out an iron pen. He hired a scrivener to
copy into the journal some of his letters, which are scattered
throughout its pages. In this edition, all of these letters have
been introduced into the chronological sequence of entries, for
their added information on events of the day. Letters of introduction that Audubon obtained in England and Scotland were
also copied into the journal; they can be found in my earlier edition of the journal.

Except for his small, slight, now indistinct sketch of two cats
fighting over a dead squirrel, repeated in an oil on canvas that
was subsequently auctioned by his landlady and lost sight of for
a century and a half; a small, sketchy floor plan of a prison that
he visited; and some coarse Gulf Coastal lines drawn on board
the *Delos*, all of the surviving pencil sketches are reproduced in
this volume. The missing half-page may or may not have borne a

9

sketch. Since the 1967 edition of this book another deck sketch, and a last page, addressed to Lucy, have come to light. (Last page for the fateful year, that is.) They appear by courtesy of Mr. William Reese. Neither of these, nor the drawing of a "Petrel" found at Yale, appears on the microfilm of the journal at the New-York Historical Society.

The crucial, questing months covered by this journal suggest that it is the rarest and the most important of any of the many kept by the artist. That it was actually, as he wrote, his "nineteenth" is open to doubt because of his calling the one begun in 1828 his twenty-seventh (*Audubon and His Journals:* "Feb. 1, 1828") (1897). However that may be, it is by far the most fluent, graphic, spontaneous, and readable of any of the few that escaped extinction by fire at the hands of three granddaughters. It enables us to attend the momentous departure from Louisiana, to experience the long and often becalmed voyage, and to watch the first months of his mission—which was to exhibit and publish his portfolios of birds, or, that failing, to sell them outright. Finally, we witness the launching of his almost hopelessly visionary ambition to publish his drawings in the size of nature. For the first time we are here allowed to see, as Audubon himself described it, the fateful, embryonic stage of *The Birds of America*, one of the great books of all time.

The journal has made three previous appearances of sorts. Mrs. Audubon drew lightly from it for her compilation edited by Buchanan for her *Life of John James Audubon* (1868). Maria Rebecca Audubon, daughter of John Woodhouse Audubon, brought out roughly one-third in her two-volume work of 1897, *Audubon and His Journals*, reissued in 1964. She cut, censored, paraphrased, bowdlerized, and even rewrote at will, until her misguided striving for an image relieved of imperfections stripped the original manuscript of truth and many engagingly human touches. These two family works have been the stuff of fictional romance enough for several generations. The latter has also become available in paperback (Dover Press, 1960). On her work Miss Audubon imposed such reforms as "bare rock" where "naked rock" was written. The following innocuous capsule illustrates how at one point—one of many such—she watered down the substance and vitality of the original: "Mr. Rathbone is enthusiastic over my publishing plans, and I will proceed with firm resolution to attempt being an author. It is a terrible thing for me; far better am I fitted to study and delineate in the forest, than to arrange phrases with suitable grammatical skill." The journal shows Audubon's actual ebullience.

The following pages are scrupulously faithful to the original manuscript, except of course where failure to transpose a phrase or add and bracket a word would mean certain confusion for the reader. Audubon often hyphenated noun modifiers that today would appear as separate words, or be written solid. The dictates of *Webster's* were unknown to him. His "setting-room," not without its charm, prevails. "This happy 2" meant "this happy [pair]." Double negatives disappear. Incorrect spelling of proper names—such as Greg, spelled by Audubon with a double *g;* Loyd, misspelled with a double *l;* Greenbank or Green Bank, spelled with a plural *s;* Priestley, without the second *e*—seemed to the editor to serve no useful purpose, any more than would the bewildering misspelling of words at random. However, every exclamation point, every dash used strictly as a dash (and not merely as a substitute for a period, or two of them to indicate a paragraph) appears as written. Indelicate words are sometimes omitted and *XXXXXX* is substituted *by Audubon.* The date lines here become uniform in style; hours are given in numerals, without exception. "Honor" and "labor," although spelled by Audubon with and without the eighteenth-century *u,* here generally take the commoner form. Often but not always he capitalized names of birds and other creatures. He also capitalized certain words for the sake of emphasis.

A sample glossary of Audubon's coinage would run somewhat as follows: *were* for *where,* and vice versa; *otherways* for *otherwise; front* for *countenance; retrograde* for *retrogress; in* for *of; for* for *concerning; thursday* for *thirsty; engaged* for *urged; set* for *sit; raise* for *rise; raised* for *arose; hedge* for *edge; boor* for *bore; orison* for *horizon; hearth* for *earth; trachy* for *trachea; at all event* for *in any event; longgone* for *long-drawn-out; scuttlefish* for *cuttlefish; sancto* for *sanctum; so* for *saw; sparr* for *spar;* and such gallic approximations as *procured* for *fixed in a board.*   ALICE FORD

THE 1826 JOURNAL OF JOHN JAMES AUDUBON

I

Departure and Voyage

26 April [May 27th] 1826

I LEFT MY BELOVED WIFE LUCY AUDUBON and my son John Woodhouse on Tuesday the 26th of April, bound for England. Remained at Doctor Pope's at St. Francisville until Wednesday 4 o'clock P.M. [Took] the steam boat "Red River" [under] Captain Kemble, having for companions Messrs. D. Hall[1] and John Holiday. Reached New Orleans Thursday [the] 27th at 12. Visited many vessels for my passage and concluded to go in the ship "Delos" of Kennebunk, [under] Captain Joseph Hatch, bound to Liverpool, loaded with cotton entirely.

The "Red River" steam boat left on her return [voyage] on Sunday and I wrote by her to thee, My Dearest Friend [Lucy] and forwarded thee two small boxes of flowering plants.

Saw, spoke to, and walked with Charles Briggs,[2] much altered young man.

1. Sea Captain David Hall, of New Orleans. Audubon drew his portrait in chalk (Howard Corning, ed., *Journal . . . 1820–21* [Cambridge, 1929]).
2. Charles Briggs, an English-born merchant, first of Henderson, Kentucky, then of New Orleans. He was a friend of John and George Keats (Hyder Rollins, ed., *The Keats Circle* [Cambridge, 1948]).

Lived at New Orleans at G. L. Sapinot's in company with Coste.[3]

During my stay at New Orleans I saw my old and friendly acquaintances the family Pamar;[4] but the whole time spent in that city was heavy and dull. A few gentlemen called to see my drawings. I generally walked from morning until dusk, my hands behind me, paying but very partially attention to all I saw. New Orleans, to a man who does not trade in dollars or any other such stuff, is a miserable spot.

Fatigued and discovering that the ship could not be ready for sea for several days, I ascended the Mississippi again in the "Red River" and once more found myself with my wife and child. I arrived at Mrs. Percy's[5] at 3 o'clock in the morning, having had a dark ride through the magnolia woods, but the moments spent afterwards full repaid me. I remained two days and three nights, was at a wedding of Miss Virginia Chisholm with Mr. [David] Hall, &c. I left, in company with Lucy, Mrs. Percy's house at sun rise and went to breakfast at my good acquaintance Augustin Bourgeat[6] who lent me a horse to proceed to Bayou Sara again. At 8 o'clock I gave and received the farewell kiss to my beloved wife and her to me. I parted from her about two miles from home.

Arrived at New Orleans, my vessel still unready. I called on the Governor who give me a letter bearing the seal of the State, obviating the necessity of taking a passport. I received several letters of introduction from different persons, the copies of all of which will be found herein.

"Copy of a letter received from Henry Clay Esq., dated Washington, March 17th, 1823."

---

3. G. L. Sapinot was a New Orleans boardinghouse keeper. Napoleon Coste was to command the U.S. revenue cutter *Campbell* for Audubon's Gulf cruise, 1837.

4. The merchant Pamar had been bondsman for Audubon in 1819 in his case against Samuel Bowen, for payment of a boat bought in Louisville from Thomas Bakewell. Audubon drew portraits of each of the three Pamar daughters and taught them art. Governor Roman Pamar was to be his host in New Orleans in 1837.

5. Jane Middlemist Percy, widow of British Royal Navy officer Robert Percy who in 1802 settled near Bayou Sara, Louisiana, and who had helped to set up the short-lived West Florida republic, was mistress of Beech Woods plantation. There Lucy Audubon taught a neighborhood school for seven years.

6. Augustin Bourgeat, Bush Hill plantation, St. Francisville, West Feliciana, Louisiana. A favorite hunting companion.

I have known for some years the bearer hereof Mr. Audubon, a naturalized citizen of the United States, as an ingenuous, worthy and highly respectable gentleman. He resided several years in the state of Kentucky and has been engaged for some time past in exercising his fine talent for painting on objects connected with the natural history of the U. States. He purposes going to Europe, to avail himself of the artists and opportunities of that quarter, in executing some of his sketches and designs, so as to give them a wider diffusion.

I take particular satisfaction in recommending him to the good offices and kind reception of the American ministers, consuls and public agents abroad, and to the hospitality and good treatment of all other persons.

H. CLAY

Washington, 17th March 1823

"Copy of another received from the same dated Washington, 24 Feb. 1826."

Rufus King Esq.
Sir,

The bearer hereof Mr. J. J. Audubon a respectable citizen of the U. States, whom I have had the pleasure to know, has been, for some years, engaged in procuring drawings and preparing manuscripts in relation to the birds of America. He goes to England, with the purpose of completing his work, and having it published there. I shall be glad if you would procure from government any facilities (should any be necessary) that may be reasonably asked in a foreign country for the handling, & c., of his drawings and manuscripts, and that you would otherwise show him any attention in your power. I am respectfully,

Your ob. servant,

H. CLAY

"Copy of a letter from the Governor of the State of Louisiana dated New Orleans May 13th, 1826."
[At the left Audubon drew a fine facsimile of the Louisiana official seal.]

The bearer hereof, Mr. J. J. Audubon, a citizen of the United States, who has resided in this state eight years, has been for some time engaged in procuring drawings and preparing manuscripts in relation to the birds of America. He proposes going to Europe with the purpose of completing his work, and having it published there. Mr. Audubon is a gentleman of worth, and highly respected for his talents. I take particular pleasure, as Chief Magistrate of this State, in recommending him to the friendly reception of all American officers and citizens abroad, and to the kind treatment of all other persons.

H. JOHNSON

New Orleans
May 13th, 1826.

"Copy of a letter received from Mr. Vincent Nolte at New Orleans dated May 16th 1826." [To Richard Rathbone, of Liverpool, destined to befriend Audubon.]

I have ventured to put in the hands of Mr. J. J. Audubon, a gentleman of highly respectable Scientific requirements, these introductory lines for you under a persuasion that his acquaintance cannot fail to be one of extreme interest to you. Mr. A. is a native of the U.S., and has spent upwards of twenty years in all parts of them and devoted most of his time to ornithological pursuits. He carries with him a collection of upwards of 400 Drawings, which far surpass anything of the kind I have yet seen, and afford the best evidence of his skill and of the perfection to which he has carried his researches. His object is to find a purchaser, at any rate a publisher for them, and if you can aid him in this, and introduce him either in person or by letters to men of distinction in arts and sciences, you will confer much of a favour on me. He has a crowd of letters for England, amongst others very particular ones from Mr. Clay, Mr. De Witt Clinton and others, which will do much for him, but your introduction to Mr. Roscoe and others may do more. His collection of ornithological drawings would prove a most valuable acquisition to any Museum, or any monied patron of the arts, and I should think convey a far better idea of American Birds than all the stuffed birds of all the museums put together.

Permit me likewise to recommend Mr. Audubon to your hospitable attentions. The respectability of his life and of his family connections entitles him to the good wishes of any gentleman, and you will derive much gratification from his conversation. I am, Dear Sir, with very sincere regards,

Yours most truly,
VINCENT NOLTE

"from the same and same dated————"
Adam Hodgson, Esq., Liverpool

May 16, 1826

MY DEAR SIR:
Permit me to make you acquainted with the bearer Mr. J. J. A., an European by birth, but upwards of 20 years a resident and citizen of the U.S. He has devoted most of that time to ornithological researches of various kinds, and of the pitch and perfection to which he has carried them, the beautiful collection of drawings from his own pencil, with which he now proceeds to England, may afford the best evidence. These drawings, or pictures, are *unique* in their kind—something like *tableaux*

de famille of birds (if birds lived in families), and Mr. A.'s object is to find a purchaser for these fruits of his exertions, assiduity and perseverance. You will, on seeing them, be able to judge for yourself how valuable a collection they form, and that they cannot fail to prove a desirable acquisition to any museum or to a wealthy person of the arts and sciences. If, either by letters of introduction, or personal recommendation, you can bring Mr. A. in contact with men of that description, you will sincerely oblige him as well as myself.

I have known Mr. Audubon for many years, and can truly say that the respectability of his life and that of his family entitle him to the particular notice and good wishes of every *"homme de bien."*

Mr. Clay, Mr. De Witt Clinton and other men of distinction on this side of the waters have supplied Mr. A. with letters of introduction and ample testimonials of the merit of his performances.

Excuse the freedom of my applications and believe me always and most sincerely devoted to you.

I am, my dear Sir,

Yours most sincerely,

VINCENT NOLTE

"Copy of a Letter from Mr. Edward Holden, New Orleans, May 16th, 1826."

George Ramsden Esq.
DEAR SIR.

The present will be handed to you by Mr. J. A. A. of this city, whom most respectfully I beg to introduce to you. The principal object of Mr. A.'s visit to England is to make arrangements for the publication of an extensive and very valuable collection of his drawings in Natural History—chiefly, if not wholly, of American birds, and he takes them with him for that purpose. Can you be of any assistance to him by letters to Manchester and London? If you can, I have no doubt that my introduction of him will insure your best attention and services. Mr. A. is afraid of having to pay heavy duties upon his drawings; he will describe them to you, and, if in getting them entered low at the Custom House, or if in any other respect you can further his views, I shall consider your aid as an obligation conferred upon myself. Pray introduce him particularily to Mr. Booth, who, I am sure, will feel great interest in being acquainted with him, were it only on account of the desire he has always expressed to be of service to the new Manchester Institution—to which Mr. A.'s drawings would be an invaluable acquisition.

I am Dʳ Sir,

Yours Truly

EDWARD HOLDEN

On the 17th day my baggage was put on board. I had written two letters to my wife, [and] one to my son Victor [in Kentucky] to whom I sent as present my pencil case with a handsome knife—and also to Charles Bonaparte,[7] apprising him of the box of bird skins forwarded to him through Mr. Currell. The steamboat "Hercules" came alongside at 7 P.M., and in ten hours put the "Delos" to sea. I wrote from here another letter to Lucy, and in a few minutes found myself severely affected with sea sickness. This lasted, however, but a short time; I remained on deck constantly, eating and drinking without inclination and forcing myself to exercise. We calculated our day of departure from the 18th May, at 12 o'clock, when we first made an observation.

[Here appears Audubon's rendition of the seal of the state of Louisiana. See page 21.]

We are now [at] the 27th, and having nought else to do I put down the little incidents that have taken place between these two dates.

The weather has generally been fair with light winds, and the first objects that had any weight, like diverting my ideas from the objects left behind me, was the number of beautiful Dolphins that glided by the side of the vessel like burnished gold during day and bright meteors by night. Our captain and mates all proved expert at alluring them with baited hooks, or dextrous at piercing them with a five-prong instrument generally called by seamen "grains." If hooked, the Dolphin flounces desperately, slides off with all natural swiftness, oftentimes raises perpendicularly out of his element several feet, shakes off the hook and escapes partially hurt. If, however, the Dolphin is well hooked, he is played about for a while, soon drowned, and hauled into the vessel. Some persons prefer pulling them in at once and are seldom successful, the great vigor with which the fish shakes sideways, as he ascends, generally being quite suffi-

7. Charles Lucien Bonaparte (1803–57), second Prince of Canino, son of Lucien, nephew and son-in-law of Joseph Bonaparte (the erstwhile King of Spain) and nephew of the Emperor Napoleon I, became an outstanding zoologist in Philadelphia. *American Ornithology*, a work in four volumes, was published in Philadelphia in 1825–32.

Audubon's drawing of the seal of the state of Louisiana.

cient to extricate him. Their flesh is firm, perhaps rather dry, yet quite acceptable at sea. They differ very much in their sizes, being, agreeably to age, smaller or larger. I saw some four and a half feet long, but a fair average could reduce them to three. The paunch of all we caught contained more or less small fishes of various species, amongst which the Flying Fish is prevalent. The latter is apparently their congenial food, and is well adapted to exercise their physical powers. Dolphins move in companies of four or five and sometimes of twenty or more. [They] chase the Flying Fish that, with astonishing rapidity, after having avoided his sharp pursuer a while in the water, emerges and goes through the air with the swiftness of an arrow—sometimes in a straight course and sometimes deviating by forming part of a circle. Yet frequently the whole is unavailing. The Dolphin raises out of the sea in bounds of ten, fifteen or twenty feet, and so rapidly moves toward his prey, that oftentimes the little fish just falls, to be swallowed by his antagonist.

You must not suppose that the Dolphin can, however, move through the seas without risk or danger to himself. He has, as well as others, valiant and powerful enemies. One is the Barracuda, in shape much like a Pike, growing sometimes to a large size. One of these cut off upwards of a foot in length of the tail of a Dolphin, as if with an axe, as this latter made for a baited hook; and I may say that we about divided the bounty. There is a degree of sympathy between Dolphins quite remarkable. The moment one of them is hooked or grained, all those in company immediately make up towards him, and remain there until the unfortunate one is hoisted, and generally then all move off and seldom will bite. When small, and in large schools, they then bite and are caught, perhaps to the last. The skin of this fish is a tissue of small scales, softer in substance than generally seen in scaley fishes of such size. The skin is tough, and torn off from their bodies when cleaned.

We also caught a Porpoise about seven feet in length. This feat took place during the night when the moon gave me a full view of all that happened. The fish, contrary to custom, was *grained* instead of being harpooned, but grained in such a way and so effectually, through the forehead, that he was thus held and suffered to flounce and beat about the bow of the ship, until the very person that had secured it at first gave the line holding the grain to our Captain, and slid down along the bobstay with a rope. Then, after some little time and perhaps some difficulties, the fish was secured immediately above its tail; and, hoisted with that part upwards, it arrived on deck, gave a deep groan, much like the last from a large dying hog, flapped silently on the deck, and died. I had never before seen one of these animals at hand; and the duck-bill-like snout, along with the horizontal disposition of the tail with the body, were new matters of observation. Their large, black, sleek body, the quantity of warm, black blood issuing from the wound, the blowing aperture placed over the forehead, all attracted my attention. I requested that it should remain untouched until the next morning, and this was granted. On opening it, the intestines were still warm (say eight hours after death) and resembled very much those of a hog. They filled all the under cavity. The paunch contained several cuttle fish, partly decayed. The carcass was cleaned of its flesh, and left the central bone supported on its sides (after the abdomen) by two horizontal bones and one perpendicular, giving the appearance of a four-edged cutting instrument. The lower jaw, or, as I prefer to style it, the mandible, exceeds the upper by about three-quarters of an inch. Both were furnished with single jaws of divided conical teeth, about ½ inch in length, just so parted as to admit those of the upper jaw between each of those of the lower. The fish might weigh about 200. The eyes were small, proportionally speaking, and the fish, having a breathing aperture above, of course had no gills. Porpoises move in large company; and generally, during spring and early summer, close by pairs, coming on top to breathe and playfully exhibit themselves about vessels. I have seen a parcel of them leap perpendicularly about twenty feet and fall with a heavy dash on the sea. Our captain told us that small boats had been sometimes sunk [near] our ship, fishes falling into [them] in one of these frisks.

While I am engaged with the finny tribe I may as well tell you that one morning, when moving gently two miles per hour, the captain called me to shew me some pretty fishes just caught

Dolphin. May 28th 1826. Latitude 24. 27. Gulph of Florida.

total length 4 feet 2/12
upper fin Dark blue
from hence a Dark Blue to azure-blue
Lower part Gold with deep blue Spots.

from our cabin windows. Those measured about three inches, [were] thin and broad of shape, and very quick through the water. We had a pin hook and with this caught 370 in about two hours. They were sweet food. They are named generally *Rudder Fish* and always keep to the lee side of the rudder, as it affords a strong eddy to support them and enable them to follow the vessel in that situation when going doubly fast. When the sea becomes calm they disperse themselves about the sides and bow, and then will not bite. The least breeze brings them all into a company body astern again, where they seize the baited hook the instant it reaches the water—by this time we have caught and eat about 500.

We also have caught two sharks, one a female about seven feet that had ten young alive and able to swim well. One of them was thrown overboard and made off as if accustomed to take care of himself for some time. Another was cut in two, and the head half swam off out of our sight. The remainder was cut to pieces, as well as the parent, for bait for Dolphins that are extremely partial to that meat. However, it is to be remarked that these fishes, being viviparous, consequently never leave the water unless fully formed. Of course I concluded that the young here spoken of had never left the dame, being yet fastened to the womb by the feeding conduit. The weather being calm and pleasant, I felt anxious to have a view of the ship from off her, and Captain Hatch politely took me in the yawl and had it rowed all around the "Delos." This was a sight I had not enjoyed for nearly twenty years, and was made pleased with it. Afterwards, having occasion to go out to try the bearings of the current, I again accompanied him and bathed in the sea, not without, however, feeling some fears. To try the bearings of the current, we took an iron pot fastened to a line of 120 fathoms and made a log board out of a barrel's head laden on one edge to sink it perpendicularly on its edge. We tried the velocity of the current with it fixed to a line by the help of a second glass, whilst our iron pot, sunk at the end of our line, acted as an anchor.

I must now change for a moment my theme and speak of birds awhile. Mother Carey's Chickens (*Procellaria*) came about us, and I longed to have at least one in my possession. I had watched their evolutions, their gentle patting of the sea when on the wing with their legs hanging and webbs expanded. I had seen them take large and long ranges in search of food, and return repeatedly for the bits of fat thrown overboard and for them intended. I had often looked at different figures given by scientific men, but all this could not diminish for a moment the long-wished-for pleasure of possessing one in nature *fideli:* I loaded a piece and dropped the first one that came after alongside; and the captain, again desirous of pleasing, went for it. I made two drawings of it. It proved a female with eggs, numerous but not larger than grains of fine powder, inducing me to think that these birds must either breed earlier, or much later, than any other in our Southern latitude. I would be inclined to think that the specimen I inspected had not laid this season, although I am well satisfied that it was an old bird.

During many weeks following this date I discovered that many flew mated, side by side, and, occasionally, particularly in calm pleasant weather, caressed each other as Ducks are known to do.

About this time we saw a small vessel with all sails set toward us. We were becalmed and the unknown had a light breeze. It approached gradually; suspicions were entertained that it might be a pirate, as we, that same day, had undoubtedly heard reports of cannon from the very course she was coming. We were well manned, tolerably armed, and yet uneasiness was perceptible on every face, more or less—yet we were all bent on resistance, knowing well that such gentry gave no quarter—to purses, at least. Night arrived, a small squally breeze struck us and off we moved, were out of sight in a short time, and resumed the mirth and good mien that had existed amongst us. Two days afterwards a brig that had been in our wake came near us, was hailed and found to be the "Gleaner" of Portland, commanded by an acquaintance of our commander and bound also to Liverpool. This vessel had left the city of New Orleans five days before us. We kept close together, and the next day Captain Hatch and myself boarded her and were kindly received; after a short stay, her captain, called Jefferson, came with us and remained the day. I opened my drawings and shewed a few of them. Mr. Swift[8] was anxious to see some, and I wanted to examine in what state they kept. The weather being dry and clear I feared nothing. It was agreed that both vessels should keep company until through the Gulf Stream, for security sake against pirates.

So fine has the weather been so far that all belonging to the cabin have constantly slept on deck, over which an awning had been extended to keep the heat of the sun and dampness of the atmosphere at night from us.

When full one hundred leagues at sea, a female Rice Bunting came aboard and remained with us overnight and part of next day. A Warbler also came but remained only a few minutes and made for the land we had left. It moved, whilst on board, with great activity and sprightliness; the Bunting to the contrary was exhausted, panted, and, I have no doubt, died of inanition. Many Sooty Terns were in sight during several days. I saw one Frigate Pelican high in the air, and could only judge it to be such through the help of the telescope. Flocks of unknown birds were also about the ship during a whole day. They swam well and preferred the water to the air. They resembled large Phalaropes, but could not be certain. A small Alligator that I had purchased for one dollar at New Orleans died at the end of nine days, through the want of knowledge that salt water was poisonous to him. In two days he swelled to nearly double his natural size, breathed hard and died. In Latitude 24.17' a Green Heron came on board and remained until frightened by me, then flew toward the brig "Gleaner." It did not appear in the least fatigued.

The captain of the "Gleaner" told me that on a preceding voyage from Europe to New Orleans, when [his vessel] was about fifty leagues from Balize, a full grown *Whooping Crane* came on board during the night. Passing over the length of the deck close over his head, and over that of the helmsman, [it] fell in the yawl, and the next morning the bird was found there completely exhausted, [after] everyone on board supposed that it had passed on. A cage was made for it. It refused food and lingered a few

8. John Swift, son of Benjamin Swift, of St. Francisville, Louisiana, was bound for Dublin, to join his parents on a visit.

"John Swift, Esqr., Asleep."

days, then died. When plucked [it] was found sound, free from any wound, and in good case, a very singular case in birds of this kind, which are inured to extensive journeys, and of course liable to spend much time without food.

I have not written since the 27th for reasons as natural as can be; I had fewer if any new incidents to relate. Now, however, that it is the fourth of June, and now that at 12 o'clock I find myself a few miles south of the line[9] for the second time in my life, I feel rather an inclination to write. I am thinking daily, and I might say almost constantly of my wife, of my family, and my hopes, all in *the breeze* (which bye and bye is quite contrary). My times goes on dully—lying on the deck on my mattress which is a hard bale of cotton, having no one, scarcely, to talk to, and only a few books and but indifferent fare to engage me even to raise from that situation to feed myself. But to the purpose—I am really south of the line. What ideas it conveys to me, of my birth, of the expectations of my younger days, &c., &c.

[Full-page drawing, annotated, of a dolphin, appears at this point. See page 25.]

Since I wrote last we have parted from our companion the "Gleaner," have had the wind constantly ahead, and are yet in the Gulf of Mexico. Here permit me to give advice that might have been given to me. Never, if you can do otherwise, sail from New Orleans for Europe, in June, July or August, as, if you do, you may calculate on delays incalculable in the Gulf, such as calms, powerful currents all contrary and worst of all the *Trade Winds* so prevalent during these months and indeed much later—so much so that if I had this day to sail from New Orleans again (and as I said before, I believe, on the 4th June), I would wait until late in October. But better say abandon the thoughts, and go through to New York and there take passage.

I have been at sea three Sundays and yet have not made the shore of Cuba, and have scarcely doubled the Florida cape—but it is not worthwhile experiencing.

---

9. "South of the line" means south of the Equator, a reference to passage from Haiti in childhood. Audubon (?) inked out a few lines at this point.

I have seen, since my last date, a large *Sword Fish*, but only *saw* it; two Gannets; killed a *Great-footed Hawk*; caught alive a nondescript warbler which I named the *Cape Florida Songster*; saw two Frigate Pelicans at a great height, and a large species of Petrel entirely unknown to me. We had a severe squall (as I call it) and plenty of dull times withal. Read Byron's poems, "The Corsair," &c., &c., &c., &c. And now—I will shut my book. [*Referring to the hawk, Audubon later added this note in pencil:* "This bird, having alighted several times on our yards, made a dash at a Warbler, feeding on the flies about the vessel, seized it, and eat it in our sight on the wing, much like a Mississippi Kite devouring the Red-throated Lizards."]

[Pencil sketch of a "Rudder Fish," natural size, measuring four and three-fourths inches, length, appears here. See page 33.]

[Opposite sketch of the rudderfish is a full-page pencil drawing, measuring six inches by five and one-half inches, over all, entitled, "A Swift to be made at Sheffield," picturing the needlework article, and annotated beneath. See page 73.]

The seventh of this month [June] a brig bound to Boston called the "Andromache" came alongside, and my heart rejoiced that letters could be carried by her to America to furnish thee with intelligence of our passage thus far. I fell to and wrote to thee and Nicholas Berthoud. The weather, however, altered suddenly. We had a light squall that separated us, and it was not until June 9th that we boarded her. Fond of all such expeditions, I went with our captain. The sea ran high and the tossing of our light yawl was extremely disagreeable to my feelings. The brig "Andromache" was covered with cotton and extremely filthy, and I was glad to discover that with all our disagreeables and disappointments we were quite comfortable on the "Delos," comparatively. The passengers there were extremely polite, offered us wine, &c. The captain had our letters put in the post bag and after half an hour's chat we pushed for our vessel again. The sea was extremely rough then. We took in more or less water from every wave that came toward us. I was glad when I found myself on the deck of the "Delos."

The Rudder Fish.

Delicate, fine eating when well fryed—

> **Rudder Fish**—*have seen some specimens*
>   *double this size—*
> *300 of these were caught in about two hours,*
>   *are fine eating.*

These little fellows
leave the ship as soon as
our soundings and also during gales.

Delicate, fine eating When cold fry &c —

Rudder Fish

from form down the
300 of them were caught in
about 2 hours we fine eating

Two days elapsed and the "Andromache" was out of our sight, having ran a different tack. On June 11th we still are on the same latitude and but a few miles different in longitude. I catch Dolphins, Porpoises, draw a little, read some, sleep a good deal, and withal find the time extremely fatiguing.

[Here occurs a faint pencil drawing, hardly more than a vignette, of a fish measuring two and three-fourths inches in length. No name is given.]

[Here occurs a full-page pencil drawing of the northwest end of Cuba. It consists of four coastal lines, at the left lettered H, F, D, B, and at the right G, E, O, A, and E. The letters D, B, O, and A apply to water, the others to land. Underneath are the words: "NORTH WEST END OF THE ISLAND OF CUBA. Ship Delos June 15th at 5 P.M. by sea, account of the bears and distance of the principal head lands were taken 10 miles. Bearings by compass."]

[At this point a page was cut from the journal, so that on the following page one reads lines which represent only the close of the partly missing entry:]
    . . . Having come into the company of a brig bound to Havana from Liverpool, called the "Howard," under Captain Joseph Birney, I wrote to thee, Mr. Currell and [Napoleon] Coste, to give thee again an account of our slow movements. It was the 16th instant and I hoped that my letter might reach thee in two weeks.
    We have been in sight of Cuba these last four days. The heat is excessive. I saw three beautiful White-headed Pigeons or Doves flying about our ship, but after several rounds they shaped their course towards the Floridas and disappeared. The Dolphins we catch here are suspected to be poisonous; and to ascertain if they are so or not, a piece is boiled along with a dollar until quite cooked, when, if the piece of silver coin is not tarnished either black or green, the fish is good and safe eating. I found bathing in sea water extremely refreshing, and therefore enjoy this luxury every night before lying down on my mattress. We

have had in sight, and almost in company, four or five sails of vessels for several days.

[On opposite side of the preceding page is a charming pencil drawing of First Mate Samuel L. Bragdon. See page 67.]

[The next page is given over to an admirable pencil drawing of the "Balacuda Fish" (Barracuda). See page 53.]

[Full-page drawing of a shark, twelve and one-fourth inches by five inches, over all, accompanied by the annotation, "Sailors sometimes eat of this, yet it has a very unflavorable flavor—." See page 63.]

[On the other side of the page that bears the second of two Nolte letters Audubon wrote the name of the bird drawn life-size on the next facing page: "DUSKY PETREL—Lath. Puffinus obscurus." See page 39.]

[The following entry is from a long missing page of the journal and identified as such in May, 1961, by Alice Ford. The "Petrel" (*Audubon's Shearwater, Puffinus lherminieri*) was previously published as a random sketch with observations on the verso (Yale University Library). See page 37.]

At Sea   June 20th   Off Florida Coast
"The Birds that at different times during my passage thus far towards England I had taken for a Specie of Large Phalaropes, were about our vessel in great numbers and our Mate was so fortunate as to kill four at one Shot that were all picked up by the yawl at my request. I was surprised and pleased at finding them belonging to the Genus *Procellarias,* or Petrel, made a sketch as usual Size of Life and Preserved the Skins of all of them.
"These Birds skim very low over the Sea in search of the bunches of floating sea weeds that abound over this Gulph, flapping their wings 6 or 7 times in quick succession and then sailing an equal intermediate length of time, say 3 or 4 seconds,

with great apparent ease, carrying their tail much spread and long wings squarely angular with the body. Raising and falling with such beautiful ease to motions of the waves that one might suppose they receive a special power to that effect from the Element below them.

"On approaching a bunch of weeds they raise their wings obliquely, dip their legs and feet, run apparently on the water, and rest at last on the sea where they swim with all the ease of the Genus Anas [duck], dive freely, at times several feet in pursuit of the fishes that at their approach of the weeds leave for safety and seize them with great agility as well as voraciousness—four or five and sometimes fifteen to twenty will then alight on and about one bunch of Weeds and during their stay about it, diving, fluttering and swimming all in a heap present quite agreeable groups—during this period many gulls of different kinds are hovering over and about the same spot, vociferating their anger, disappointment at not being quite so well able to furnish themselves with the delicate fare.

"No sooner have all the fishes being taken or chased than all the birds, raise [rise], diffuse, and extend their flight in search of more.

"I heard no sound issuing from them although many came within 20 paces of us; consequently I suppose them endowed with excellent quick power of sight, as at the very moment that our individual lighted many immediately made for the spot and reached it in an instant.

"At times and as if by way of reposing" [end of journal page; next page missing].

Capes of Florida   June 22nd, 1826

Whilst sailing under a gentle breeze last night the bird outlined on this sheet, commonly called by Seamen the *Noddy*, alighted on the boom of the vessel and a few minutes afterwards was caught by the mate. It then uttered a rough cry, not unlike that of a young Common Crow when taken from the rest. It bit severely, and with quickly renewed movements of the bill, which, when it missed the object in view, snapped like that of our larger flycatchers. I found it one of the same species that hovered

At Sea June 20th 1826 off Florida Coast.

The Birds that at different times during my Passage they
fore towards England, that I had taken for a Specie
of Large Phaleropes, were about us in great
Numbers and our Mate was so fortunate as to Kill
four at one Shot that were picked up by the
Yawl at My Request — I was surprised and pleased at
finding them belonging to the Genus Procellarias
or Petrel, made a Sketch as usual one of Life and
Preserved the Skins of all of them.

These Birds skim very low over the Sea in Search
of the Bunches of Floating sea Weeds that abound over
this Gulph, flapping their Wings several times in quick
Succession and then sailing an equal intermediate
length of time say 3 or 4 Yards with great apparent
ease, Carrying their tail much spread and Long wings
Squarely angular with their body — on approaching a
Bunch of Weeds they raise their Wing Obliquely, Drop
their legs Expand, run apparently on the water, and rest
as last on the Sea where they swim with all the ease
of the Genus Anas, Dive freely, at times several feet
in pursuit of the Fishes that at their approach of the
Weeds leave for Safety and seize them with great agility
as well as Voraciousness — 4 or 5 and Sometimes
from 15 to 20 will thus alight on and about one
Bunch of Weed and during this stay about it, Diving,
Fluttering and swiming all in a heap present quite
a great groupess — during this Period many Gulls of
different kinds are hovering over and about the same
Spots, Vociferating their anger and Disappointment at
Not being quite so well able to furnish themselves with
the delicate food — No Sooner have all the Fishes being
taken or chased, that all the Birds, Raise, Disperse, and
extend their flight in search of More —

I heard no sound issuing from them although many
came within 20 yards of us, consequently I Suppose
them endowed with excellent quick power of Sight,
as at the very moment that one Individual lighted and
many Immediately made for the Spot and each if in one
Instant — At times and as if by way of reposing

Audubon's Shearwater, **Puffinus lherminieri,** *life-size drawing of a "Petrel," identified as a missing page of the Journal. Audubon redrew the species from this sketch for its portrait in* **The Birds of America,** *Plate CCLXXXXIX. The outlines are identical.*

Presented fresh killed by Cap^r Joseph Hatch of Kennebunk.
4. specimen
June 20th
off Florida coast
4 [?] killed at 1 discharge

A a mere nail

Total length. 11 Inches—
Tail extent beyond wings closed ⅟₁₂
Legs nearly even
Breadth 2 feet 2½/12
Tarsus outside dark indigo mixed to black
Tarsus inside and webbs, pale yellowish flesh
Nails blue black

Tongue short & fleshy—
Inside of mouth and bill light blue as cold flesh.
General colour sooty black above snowy white below.
The above Size of Life—

Eye dark blue nearly black

Eyelids light blue
Bill   Do. Do. ends black above and under [?] nostrils to the head—

over the seaweeds in company with the Large Petrel, that I thought then had a wholly white head. Having kept it alive during the whole night, I took it in hand to draw it. It was dull-looking and silent. I know nothing more of this bird than what our sailors say—that it is a Noddy and frequently alights about vessels in this latitude, particularly in the neighborhood of the Florida Keys. The bird was in beautiful plumage, but poor. The gullet was greatly extended, the paunch was empty, the heart large for the bird, the liver was uncommonly so. A short time before the Noddy's capture, a ship came between us and the "Thalia." We all supposed it to be a South American Republican or Columbian. The vessel of war was detained for some time by the "Thalia," which fired a gun at a distance of about half a mile from our stern. The probable reason was that the "Thalia's" passengers [were] Spaniards and the cargo Spanish. However, this morning both vessels were in view, making along on different routes. The man-of-war deigned not come to us, and none of us on board was much vexed at this mark of inattention.

This day was calm. After my drawing finished I caught four Dolphins. How much I have gazed on these beautiful creatures, watching their changing hue in twenty varieties of richest arrangements of tints, from burnished gold to bright silver, mixed with touches of ultramarine, spots of red, bronze and green, [seeing them] shivering and quivering to death on our hard, broiling deck. And yet I felt, but a few moments before, a peculiar share of pleasure in seizing them with a sharp hook, lured by false provision.

Two more Noddys were shot by our mate this day. They resembled in all particulars the specimens I have drawn. We saw about twenty.

We at last entered the Atlantic Ocean this morning, June 23rd, with a propitious breeze. The land birds have left us and, I—I leave my Beloved America, my Wife, Children and acquaintances. The purpose of this voyage is to visit not only England but all Europe, with the intention of publishing my work of the Birds of America. If not sadly disappointed, my return to these happy shores will be the brightest birthday I shall have ever enjoyed: Oh America, Wife, Children and acquaintances, Farewell!

[Here Audubon listed hastily, in pencil, items, reminders, etc., which later on he checked and struck off, drawing a line through them:]

Large Petrel, taken the 26th June.
When near the Grand Banks saw large flocks of the above.
Their flight, swimming & c.
Weather here much altered, being a Foggy Mist, cold enough to wear
    Clothes; ran in 12 days 1713 miles.
The motion of the vessel when sailing 9 Nots extremely fatiguing.
Read Thomson's Seasons.
The Dullness of the 4th of July with us.
Change of clouds.
Our cook, singular free man of colour from Martinique.
History of our hen. Capt. Jefferson's mate for her.
Explanatory Description of Belle's Letters by a Friend.
Employment of time on boat by the Crew.
Our young boat passengers—Dick & c.
Three vessels in sight, our Sailing—Whales—My Studying Navigation.

[The following entries, dated June 26 and June 29, are Maria R. Audubon's edited version of an entry that she apparently removed from the original 1826 Journal. (From *Audubon and His Journals* [2 vols., Scribner, New York], I, 89–90.) The originals are missing.]

June 26, 1826

We have been becalmed many days, and I should be dull indeed were it not for the fishes and birds, and my pen and pencil. I have been much interested in the Dusky Petrel; the mate killed four at one shot, so plentiful were they about our vessel, and I have made several drawings from these, which were brought on board for that purpose. They skim over the sea in search of what is here called Gulf Weed, of which there are large patches, perhaps half an acre in extent. They flap the wings six or seven times, then soar for three or four seconds, the tail spread, the wings extended. Four or five of these birds, indeed sometimes as many as fifteen or twenty, will alight on

Noddy Tern, Anoüs stolidus, *drawn life-size.*

Size of Life

Bill Glossy Black
Nostrils pervious
A: Breadth of the Mouth.
On the junction of
the mandibles.

Tail Feathers
The 3 on each outside cuneiform
& midle ones even and about 12 inches
longer than the rest.

Legs feet & Webbs purplish
lead.
Claws black.
22 June Cape Florida
1826

General color Dark Chocolate
Total length 15 inches. Tail & wings
even at their extremity when closed.

Called by Seamen Noddy

Tail extends beyond the nails or claws 2¾ Inches when flying.
Breadth 2 feet ¹/12.

Bill 2 1/4
Black
North America

[A]

A bird of the Month
of the Junction
of the Man & July ✝

22 June Cape Florida
1826 —
Caught by Common
Noddy

Egg 1 for 2 Nearly purplish Ash —
Claws Black —

Size of Life —

Tail feathers
12 on each outside curvature
6 Middle ones even and along 18 below
Longer than the rest —

General Color Dark Chocolate
Total Length 16 Body Tail Longer even of
Bin extending out in claws —
Feet extend beyond the Body or claws 2 3/4 Inches
when flying —
Breadth of feet 1 1/2 —

this weed, dive, flutter, and swim with all the gaiety of ducks on a pond, which they have reached after a weary journey. I heard no note from any of them. No sooner have the Petrels eaten or dispersed the fish than they rise and extend their wings for flight, in search of more. At times, probably to rest themselves, they alighted, swam lightly, dipping their bills frequently in the water as Mergansers and fishy Ducks do when trying, by tasting, if the water contains much fish. On inspection of the body I found the wings powerfully muscular and strong for the size of the bird, a natural requisite for individuals that have such an extent of water to traverse, and frequently heavy squalls to encounter and fight against. The stomach, or pouch, resembled a leather purse of four inches in length and was much distended by the contents, which were a compound of fishes of different kinds, some almost entire, others more or less digested. The gullet was capable of great extension. Fishes two and a half inches by one inch were found nearly fresh. The flesh of these Petrels smelt strong, and was tough and not fit to eat. I tasted some, and found it to resemble the flesh of the Porpoise. There was no difference in the sexes, either in size or color; they are sooty black above, and snowy white below. The exact measurements are in my memorandum book.

June 29, 1826

This morning we came up with the ship "Thalia," of Philadelphia, Captain John R. Butler, from Havana to Minorca up the Mediterranean, with many passengers, Spaniards, on board. The captain very politely offered us some fruit, which was gladly accepted, and in return we sent them a large Dolphin, they having caught none. I sent a Petrel, stuffed some days previously, as the captain asked for it for the Philadelphia Society of Sciences.[10]

At Sea   July 9th, 1826

My leaving the United States had for some time the appearance and feelings of a dream. I could scarce make up my mind fixedly on the subject. I thought continually that I still saw my

---

10. Academy of Natural Sciences, Philadelphia, Pennsylvania.

beloved friend [Lucy] and my dear children. I still believed, when every morning I awaked, that the land of America was beneath me, that I would in a moment throw myself into her shady woods, and watch for and listen to the voice of her many lovely warblers. But now that I have positively been at sea since *fifty-one days*, tossing to and fro, without the sight nor the touch of those objects so dear to me, I feel fully convinced, and look forward with anxiety that I do not believe ever ruffled my mind. When I calculate that not less than four months (a third of a year) must elapse before my friend [Lucy] and her children can receive any tidings of my arrival on the distant shores that now soon will divide us, when I think that many more months allotted to my existence from life's sandglass must run out, and that the time of my returning to my country and friends is yet an unfolded and unknown event, my body and face feel a sudden glow of apprehension that I can neither describe nor represent. I know only the acuteness of the feeling that acts through my whole frame like an electric shock. I immediately feel chilled, and suddenly throw my body on my mattress and cast my eyes towards the azure canopy of heaven, scarce able to hold the tears from flowing.

Our Fourth of July was passed near the Grand Banks—how differently from my last one, and how differently from any that I can recollect ever having spent! The weather was thick, foggy and as dull as myself. Not a sound of rejoicing did reach my ear, not once did I hear the sublime "Hail Columbia, happy land!" No, nothing—perhaps nothing could have so forcibly awakened me from my dozing than the like of a pleasure so powerfully felt by me at home. It was then that I suddenly arose from my lethargy and remarked the reality of my absence and of my present situation. The day passed as I conceive one might be spent by a General who has lost a great advantage over an enemy. I complained of my loss and I attributed all my disappointment to my want of foresight, but I complained to no one else. I felt sorrowful in the extreme, as if America had lost much this day.

My companion passengers lay strewn about the deck and on the cotton bales, basking like Crocodiles during all the intervals granted to the sun to peep at them through the smoky haziness that accompanied us. Yet the breeze was strong, the waves moved majestically, and thousands of Large Petrels displayed their elegant aerial movements to me. How much I envied their power of flight to enable me to be here, there, and all over the globe, comparatively speaking, in a moment, throwing themselves edgeways against the breeze as if a well sharpened arrow, shot with the strength and grace of one sprung from the bow of an Apollo.

I had remarked a singular increase in the number of these Petrels ever since the capes of Florida, but here they were so numerous for part of a day, flew in such succession towards the West and Southwest, that I concluded they were migrating to some well-known shore to deposit their eggs, or perhaps leading their young. They very seldom alighted. They were full the size of a Common Gull, and, as they flew, they shewed in quick alternations the whole upper and under part of their body, sometimes skimming low, at other [times] forming immense curves, then dashing along the deep trough of the sea, going round our vessel (always out of gun-shot reach as if she had been at anchor). Their lower parts are white; [there is] a broad white patch on the rump; the head [is] apparently all white, and the upper parts of the body and wings above [are] spotty brown. I would conceive that one of these petrels fly over as much distance in one hour as the little black petrels in our wake do in twelve.

Since we have left the neighborhood of the Banks, these birds have gradually disappeared; and now, in Latitude 44.53, I see none. Our sailors and captain speak of them as companions in storms as much as their little relations, the Mother Carey's Chickens.

As suddenly as if we had just turned the summit of a mountain dividing a country south of the Equator from Iceland, the weather altered in the present latitude and longitude. My light summer clothing was not sufficient. Indeed a cloth coat felt light and scanty, and the dews that fell during the night rendered the deck, where I always slept, too damp to be comfortable. This, however, of two evils, I preferred, for I could not withstand the more disagreeable odor of the cabin, where, now, the captain, officers and Mr. Swift eat their meals daily.

Sitting during the day as I am now, with my book in my lap on a parcel of coiled cables near the helmsman, (who, bye the bye, gazes at me as much as he looks at his compass), I spend nearly all my time, or part of it, reading; thoughtfully leaning over the railing, looking on the noisy breaking waves that urge us on, and again thinking of America. As the sun inclines her eyes to my reposing place, I am forced to make a better choice of situation, and perhaps will go and lie on the starboard side of the long boat, where our cook, ready at trying to please, will talk to me until, wearied of this, I remove from this spot again. Night gradually coming on, the *wish to repose in sleep* after a few stories told, and each gradually leaves the spot and goes and lays down, either in the hammock, his berth, or the harder chicken coop that lines both sides of our companionway. Here the days have increased astonishingly. At 9 o'clock I can easily read large print. The day opens at 2 A.M., and twenty-five minutes after 4 Phoebus enlivens the globe and promises a fair, prosperous sixteen hours.

Our unconcerned, happy mariners set to their daily labor at 6 o'clock of the morn, and cheerily spend the day improving the appearance of all about our ship, rendering her the more secure the while. Their joviality, their industry, their witticisms, would enable probably any other than a friend away from a friend, to pass the time away. I have told you that I sat frequently on a parcel of coiled cables, but you are still ignorant that since I left New Orleans I have sheared my beard but once. It now profusedly expands from each ear, and from out my chin and neck, around like a crowd of stiffened bristles, which, along with the tawny acquired hue of my skin since I came aboard this floating prison, renders me as unlike the daughter of Titian as Satan is to God.

We had for several days a stiff propitious breeze that wafted us over the briny deep [at] full nine miles per hour. This was congenial to my wishes, but not to my feelings. The vessel felt

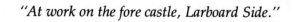

"At work on the fore castle, Larboard Side."

at work on the fore Castle
Larboard Side

the motion before me and shifted my body to and fro too soon or unwarily, and caused me violent headaches far more distressful than any seasickness feeling ever experienced. During that period I found food highly seasoned and spirituous liquors of great benefit. Here, for the third or fourth time, I read Thomson's "The Four Seasons," and I believe enjoyed them better than ever. When I came to his "Castle of Indolence" I felt the all powerful extent of his genius operating on me as a cathartic, swallowed when well aware that my body was not in fit condition (through situation) to be benefited by it.

As we drew nearer the shores of the far-famed spot, even the clouds seem to proffer a difference of consistency and shape. No longer did the vivifying orb set, with her globular flame all afire, beyond the deep. It shewed dull, pale, sickly, and as if sorry that, *because of differences that must forever exist*, the light refulgent was not to be extended over the globe until the omnipotent God had granted to each, of all, its portion of that real hope of freedom better experienced in the Western hemisphere. Here fog succeeded fog. The Englishmen on board pronounced it the *"clear weather of England,"* but I named it the atmosphere that blasts comfort.

I would continue now but the dampness is so powerful, (although the sun still streaks through the haze), that my paper is damp and receives the ink quite too finely. Dear friend, adieu.

Amongst the inmates composing our amount of livestock we have had a large hen. This bird was quite familiar and allowed the privileges of the decks. She had been hatched on board at New Orleans, and our cook who claimed her as private property was much attached to her, as well as our mates. One morning she imprudently flew overboard when [we] were running about three miles per hour. The yawl was immediately lowered, and four men rowed her swiftly from us towards the floating bird that anxiously looked at her place of abode until picked up out of the sea. Her return on board appeared to please everyone, and I was much gratified to discover that such kind treatment was used towards a bird. It assured me that all possible exertions would be made to save the lives of any of our seamen should they fall overboard. Our hen, however, ended her life most distressfully, a few weeks after this narrow escape. She again made over the side of the vessel, then moving at nine knots. The sea being high and rough with squally weather, the captain thought it imprudent to risk his men for the bird, and we lost sight of her in a few moments.

We have had our long boat lashed fast to the deck as usual, but instead of being filled with lumber and cargo, as is usually the case, it contained three passengers, all bound to Europe to visit their friends, with the intention of returning the same autumn to America. One, named Vowles, has several books which he politely offered me. He blows sweetly on the flute, and is a man superior to his apparent situation. We have a tailor also; this personage is called a deck passenger, but the fact is that full two thirds of his time is spent sleeping on the windlass. This man, however, like all others in the world, is useful in his ways; he works whenever called on, and would with much good will put a button or a patch on anyone's clothing. His name is Crow. He lives on biscuit and raw bacon the whole voyage.

At noon one beautiful day, we discovered two sails ahead of our ship, and our captain renewed his exertions to overtake them. The masts were frequently greased, all our sails brought to a nice bearing, and the helmsman ordered to be wary and exact. At the break of the next day we were just between them. We had not, however, the contemplated pleasure of speaking to them. I discovered that as soon as the breeze became lighter, they gained away from us and vice versa.

We now see no fish except now and then a school of porpoises; and I frequently long for one of the hundreds of dolphins that we caught in the Gulf of Mexico. Some Whales were seen by the sailors, but I saw nothing of them.

I frequently sit during this tedious voyage, watching our captain at his work. I do not remember having seen many more industrious, and apt at doing almost everything that he needed himself. He is a good and nice carpenter, turner, cooper, black-and-white smith, excellent tailor, &c. I saw him making a pair of pantaloons of fine cloth with all the neatness that a city brother of the cross-legged faculty could have used. He made a handsome patent swift for his wife. He can also plait straws in all

The "Balacuda" Fish.

Balacuda Fish. Good eating—
32 inches long—2 inches ½ thick, 4½ deep.
Fishes of this species are caught as long as 10 feet.—
Off Cuba   Latitude 23.7   June 17th 1826.

Barracuda. Pike. Fish Esox —
32 inches Long. 2 inches th thick 4½ thick —
Fishes of N. America are caught in Long 10 feet.
off Cuba Havana 23.9. Jan 17 1826

sorts of ways and make excellent bearded fishhooks out of common needles. At this very moment he is employed at finishing a handsome smoothing plane for his own use, manufactured out of a piece of beech wood that probably grew on the banks of the Ohio, as I perceived it had belonged to some part of a flatboat, and brought on board here to be used for fuel. I think him an excellent sailor. The more equally it blows, the gayer he generally would be—and frequently, during such times, when drenched to the skin, he laughs and says, "Who wouldn't sell a handsome plantation and go to sea!" I became anxious to understand the means of ascertaining the latitude on land, and also to find the true rising of the sun whilst travelling in the uninhabited parts of America. This he shewed me with pleasure, and I calculate our latitudes and longitude from this time.

I find it necessary to employ all my time as much as possible. Therefore, I frequently go about the deck, a pencil in hand, viewing the different attitudes of the sailors at work, and I made many sketches. They frequently caused a general laugh, and passed a moment agreeably.

Our mates exhibited a kindness towards me that I would not suffer to remain unnoticed under any consideration. They [have been] all alertness at meeting all my wishes. Indeed I often feel vexed that they should exert themselves so much when I am quite able to help myself. Yet frequently before I am aware of it, should I be walking either to the bow or to the stern, I would find my mattress, books, &c., all carefully removed into my bunk. The first mate [is] named S. L. Bragdon, from Wells, the second William Hobart, from Kennebunk.

Now I expect you will ask what sort of machine my *bunk* [is]. The question would be natural enough, and before you [ask] it I will try, like our mates, to surprise you. Imagine (and that I know you can easily do) a flat box without a bed, measuring six and a half by three feet in breadth, and nine inches deep, made of white pine. Again imagine two pieces of the same wood rising about two and a half feet from the center of each end, notched at the tops to receive a light pole lengthwise, over which a pair of my sheets, sewed together, [are] fixed to cover the elongated tent wherein are my mattress, pillows, shoes, books, &c., &c., all snugly fitted, free from the rays of the sun and nearly so from the water during the rain. This is what the sailors call my bunk and so I shall call it that myself.

Every sailor or set of sailors has a deity at sea on whom they call more or less frequently for fair wind as the case may require. By all, from our captain to the cook (or, for courtesy's sake, I will call the latter a steward), this relation of Eolus was called on many times every day during our long stay in the Gulf. It was a saint of great renown, one who, bye the bye, I believe has *stranded* as many poor devils as any other saint or saintess ever did. He was hailed St. Anthony. The prayers of all our crew, those of our captain, of our steward, nay even those of Mr. Swift and mine, proved unavailing. Not a breath of fair wind would he entice his Master to send us. Indeed I became so disgusted with the personage that I proposed, one morning, when nature seemed all asleep and our vessel was so becalmed that a feather, dropped from our masthead, would scarce have deviated in its easy fall to the deck, to abandon this renowned, fattened saint and call on one or more in need of our regards. The proposition was unanimously accepted. St. Mark [was] appointed Chief Director of the Breezes intended and much longed for, to carry our vessel to the shores of England. Will you believe it (yes you will, as it is I that writes it)—St. Mark came to our calling under an easy gait. The "Delos" moved at three miles per hour. All on board begged of [the saint] to come near us, and in three days he helped us on full 400 miles.

I had heard in my youth that saints, as well as men, would accept light gifts, not to be unfashionable. I conceived it my duty to try the experiment. What do you think of my offering? It was not a bull, snowy white, resembling Jupiter in his pranks, no. Neither was it an heifer, snowy white, for the fairest are seldom without spots.

"What then? What, my dear?" [thee wonders]

It was a ram's head, yes a ram's head I promised to this godly saint for a continuance of fair winds until we are safely landed in Liverpool in England. I promised more. I assured the Great

"Our Capt. Making Powder flasks."

Left: *"Mr. Hobart, 2nd Mate."*
Right: *"our carpenter."*
Center: *Captain Joseph Hatch.*

Mr Hobart
2d Mate —

mr Carpenter

our Capt Making
Pudding flasket

Unknown that it would be served up to his appetite either raw, boiled, toasted, roasted or pickled, or fried or tarred and feathered. I have had no answer from this Genie. Polite genies, I am told, never thank one no matter how much they get when in need. This, however, does not signify [anything]. The fact is that I am well convinced he has not despised the promised boon, for, since eighteen days, he has procured fair winds for us to the amount of 2,475 miles. St. Mark, I do hereby bind myself (but no other member of my family, recollect) to think of thee whenever I am in need, and that's enough.

[Below this entry Audubon penciled these notes:]

Larger Petrels—Northern Gale & Cold Weather
Spoke Brig Albion bound to Quebec
Sea sickness
Mother Cary's Chickens Left in Latitude 44.53 probably on account of the Cold Weather—

[Half of the page which follows was cleanly cut off; the verso is blank.]

Here we came in with a new set and species of Petrels resembling those killed in the Gulf of Mexico, but considerably larger—between fifty and sixty were at one time close to the vessel, catching small fishes that we supposed to be herrings. The birds then flew swiftly over the water, their wings partly raised, now and then diving and dipping after the "fry." They flew heavily and with apparent reluctance, and alighted as soon as we passed them.

We spoke to the brig "Albion," bound to Quebec with many passengers.

The little petrels had left us two days [ago]. I thought that probably the cold weather had drove them away. I was satisfied that several in our wake had followed us ever since the Gulf of Mexico. Of course the sudden difference of the weather must have been seriously felt by them. Or, perhaps, do they not [come nearer] the European coast?

I had a beautiful view of a whale, about 500 yards from the vessel when we first perceived it. The water it threw from [its] valve had the appearance of a small thick cloud in the horizon when it was near us. It dove, and exhibited its tail, and appeared about twelve or fourteen feet wide. Never do I recollect having felt the weather so cold in July. Wrapped in our cloaks we felt chilly [in] the drizzle of rain.

Wednesday, May 17th at 7 o'clock P.M. Left New Orleans:

Friday—19th		Latitude			Latitude	
Sat.	19	28.24	Sun.	18	23.12	
Sunday	20	27.28	Mon.	19	23.45	
Monday	21	26.56	Tues.	20	24.45	
Tuesday	22	25.47		*—ran up to this day*		
Wednesday	23	25.		*2079 miles*		
Thurs.	24	24.21				
Fri.	25	24.19	Wed.	21	26.11	
Sat.	26	24.21	Thurs.	22	28.	
Sunday	28	24.27	Fri.	23	28.25	
Mon.	29	24.42	Sat.	24	29.25	86
Tues.	30	25.21	Sun.	25	30.57	137
Wed.	31		Mon.	26		180
[June]			Tues.	27	33.53	152
Thurs.	1	24.38	Wed.	28	34.44	80
Fri.	2	24.24	Thurs.	29	35.16	60
Thurs.	3	23.51	Fri.	30	36.24	134
Sun.	4	23.27	[July]			
Mon.	5	23.37	Sat.	1	37.26	155
Tues.	6	24.18	Sun.	2	38.45	190
Wed.	7	23.38	Mon.	3	39.90	177
Thurs.	8	23.39	Tues.	4	40.09	192
Fri.	9	24.57	Wed.	5	40.38	170
Sat.	10	24.09	Thurs.	6	41.26	150
Sun.	11	23.48	Fri.	7	42.37	130
Mon.	12	24.36	Sat.	8	43.41	161
Tues.	13		Sun.	9	44.53	133
Wed.	14	23.08	Mon.	10	46.08	136
Thurs.	15	23.20	Tues.	11	47.25	131
Fri.	16		Wed.	12	48.50	141
Sat.	17	23.09	Thurs.	13	50.09	161

Fri.	14	51.05	133	Wed.19	128
Sat.	15	51.07	125	Thurs.20	128
Sun.	16	51.03	61	Fri.21	
Mon.	17	51.09	66	Sat.	
Tues.18		51.16: off cape Char.	102	Sunday	

At Sea   July 15th, 1826

The same dull, cold, damp weather still prevails. Still the wind is northwest and propitious as can be. On a passage like this, how much a man may find to think upon! I am pretty sure that few memorable events of my life, (if I dare call any of them memorable), have not been recalled to memory, weighed, disarranged, and improved (in thought only, not, unfortunately, in action), until the whole of my life has been surveyed with scrutiny, and all the lines, landmarks, beacons, branding places, &c., &c., have been examined fairly or unfairly. The days have been brought before my sight and bodily feelings. Yes, I have had time enough, I assure thee, to consult on all points. There can exist no doubt that had I been fortunate enough whenever I have erred, (and I have no doubt erred enough), had I had an equal opportunity to think before I acted, I would have committed but few errors, and probably never a sin.

These are a curious fit of thoughts, thou wilt say. Yes, I acknowledge in return that these thoughts contain much truth. Thus [are] my brains distracted or amused with past recollections when, all of a sudden, I recollect that I [am] still at sea, on board the "Delos"—in the very cabin of the "Delos." Very naturally, it made me cast my eyes around, and they suddenly stopped their flighty course [and rested] on the looking glass opposite me. I stopped short all further inquiry about myself, and determined to copy with my pen (which by the way is very poor when compared to my pencil) a strict picture, from life, of all the objects surrounding me. I had already cut the goose quill afresh [and] set all my intentions on this picture when I turned disgusted from the thoughts, and thought of thee. Ah, my dearest friend [Lucy] art thou well? Art thou happy? The confusedness of ideas that suddenly rushed across my mind was indescribable. I felt as if I were travelling through a dismal, heavy snowstorm without a compass. I could only hope to reach the desired spot. I sighed, my pen dropped, I raised my eyes, and the confounded looking glass reverberating my coarse image destroyed thine and again forced me, unwillingly, to a wish of beginning the picture.

Mr. Swift just left me. We just emptied a bottle of American porter (which, bye the bye, is equal to any in the known world). [This accounts for the erratic writing, and for what follows.] Mr. Swift went on deck to try to see the land of his forefathers and father, and where, I can swear, not a potato will be raised this season should this cold weather continue. Firm as a Florida live oak I then dip my pen in the inkstand and swear that I would describe this cabin of the "Delos."

The looking glass is from American merchandise, and I hold it more sacred because it was made, I am sure, where tea was abhorred in a goodly time.[11] The picture or frontispiece exemplifies the bountifullness of God on our favored land, *as it shews the powers of man.* "Now My dear husband, what are you going to say?"—to say that the picture on the Boston-made looking glass exhibits American fair, viewing the fair American. Here I had a wish to immortalize My Beloved country (was it not already so?) with powerful arguments. But I stop to mend my pen again.

Like an able painter I have begun by the upper and distant part of my picture as Claude Lorrain[12] would have—lightly and more inimitably I am sure—thrown an azure sky over his better prepared canvas. I might have brought objects after objects schoolboylike to my very book (the nearest object to me), when following my usual habits I flew at once to those behind me. And what were they? Six splendid muskets, American born, from Harper's Ferry, all as bright as the sun that sets this night over Louisiana, all in a row and ready to defend the fair flag that now, &c. (I was going to enter a train of politics that probably might have strained all my nerves to no purpose when I recollected the promise made mutually between us never to open our

11. An allusion to the Boston Tea Party, December 16, 1773.
12. Claude Gellée or Gelée (1600–82). French painter called Claude Lorrain.

Shark.

7 feet long.   Off Cuba.
June 18th. 1826

[Detail]
Inferior front view of the head.
Seen with mouth closed.

19

lips (or write) either on religion or the above). Very well then, the muskets are behind me. *My bunk,* now well known, is on my left, my trunk—the very one I purchased from Captain Cummings in 1820[13]—on the seat that forms a half moon facing the hatchway, over which I can see into Mr. Swift's cabin, formerly mine, where now it is so dark that nothing could be remarked in it of darker hue than the jaw bones of a large shark that are hanging at the foot of it. As I look up to see if the sun shines or not, I perceive the reversed compass, and the tin lamp moves both to and fro with each motion of the ship. The bottle that contained the porter is at my right, and the tumblers and basket too. The mate's cabin [is] still further on my right. Several mice are running about the floor, picking the scanty fare. The cockroaches begin to issue from their daily retreat. My bottom is sore from sitting on the mate's hard chest. I look at the sea through the two windows, and shut this book. Why? Because the last object on which my eyes rested was the captain's hammock, swinging so immediately over my bunk that it reminded me most painfully of the many hurried times I have been obliged to put my nostrils between my thumb and index, for safekeeping from winds neither from the Southwest nor Northwest but from—. Ah My Dears, what strange incidents happen at sea.

"A whale! A whale! Run, Mr. Audubon, there's a Whale close alongside." The pen, the book, were abandoned, the mice frightened. I ran up, and lo! there rolled most majestically the wonder of the oceans. It was of immense magnitude. Its dark auburn body fully overgrew the vessel in size. One might have thought it was the God of the Seas beckoning us to the shores of Europe. I saw it and therefore believed its existence.

Yesterday night ended the ninth Sunday spent at sea. The weather was as usual, but the breeze was very light. Each person, anxious to reach the shores, conceived a difference in the appearance of the water. Indeed I once thought and said that I smelt the putrid weeds on the shore. Several who had not as sensitive nostrils thought it probable. During the afternoon all

---

13. Samuel Cummings, in 1820 a fellow passenger on an "ark" on the Ohio and Mississippi, was author of a standard work, *The Western Pilot, Containing Charts of the Ohio . . . and Mississippi . . .* (Cincinnati, 1825).

the noses were up and pointed toward Clear Cape (which might, with more propriety, have been named Foggy) when suddenly our captain smelt something new. It had become stronger, gradually, ever since the morning as the imagined land smell had made its escape from the slush barrel lashed to the [camhouse]. And when the real cause was ascertained (which now required scarce a moment) a horse laugh was raised for a while, when a good share of dejection showed on all the visages and turned nearly all the company's noses blue. We had many whales near us during the day and an immense number of porpoises. Our captain who prefers their flesh to the best of veal, beef, or mutton, said he would give $5 for one. But our harpoon was now broken, and although several were fastened for a while to the grains, those proved too light, and the fishes regularly, after a few bounces, made their escape, probably to go and die in misery. Two European Hawks were seen, and also two Curlews. This gave me some hopes that we might see the desired object shortly.

How uncomfortable the motions of a vessel are to a man unused to them, when writing as I am now, all crank-sided with one half of my bottom wearing fast, while the other in vain is seeking for support. This is not all—one, as I said before, unused to this disagreeable movement, may now and then slide off his feet and go and throw down a person peaceably reading three feet off. (I wish I could have said three yards but our cabin is hardly that wide, and as I sit immediately in the center of the baseline it could not be so.) This person might conceive it as an intended insult, indeed might say so. Words might arise and perhaps blows might fall, when, after much trouble and hard labour on both sides to hold fast [and] to attack and defend, another heavy roll of the sea might come and force each adversary to seek a retreat in different ways.

Many people speak lightly of leaving America to go and visit Europe. Many indeed, when returned, who have not found Europe what they wished, speak lightly of the whole. I cannot touch the subject so superficially. I spoke for many years of this, my present voyage, always dreaded it before I undertook it; and after being swung about, rolled, heaved, bruised and shifted around probably around half a million times within the first

*"Our First Mate Mr. Sam'l L. Bragdon Reading on the Booby
Hatch—Off Cuba—"*

our first Mate Mr. Saml T. Bragdon
Reading on the Booby Hatch —
off Cuba —

sixty days of a voyage that I moderately calculated to last full fifteen months, have I not good substantial reasons for thinking of
it *rationally?* Just as I wrote the word rationally—which, bye the
bye, means much more than many rationals conceive—our second mate entered the cabin and repeated the last words of the
man at the helm at the same time that he called Mr. Bragdon
(who, you recollect, is first mate), saying "Seven bells!"

Had it not been for this happening this very moment, I probably would have forgotten to tell you that we had a bell on board.
It is not the curfew or *couvre-feu;* it is the sounding instrument of
joy to each man at the helm, as it is the sorrowful token to the
sleeping one in the foc'sle that he must arise, to go to the relief,
and gaze on the sails within half an hour and the compass for
full two hours. Yes, we have a bell, it sounds four sharp strokes,
or four times twice, at four in the morning, or at twelve the Meridian. I was going to describe all its useful properties when the
steward said, *"Sir, permettez moi de preparer la table pour diner."*
I looked at him, remarked his large flattened nose, staring black
eyes, beautiful teeth and swarthy slick complexion until I felt a
desire to laugh, when I shook the ink from my pen and again
bid farewell to my book.

Ah!!! Dinner is at last over, and I can return to *this faithful* un-
complaining friend; How estimable are *such qualifications. How
noble!!!* The steward, God bless him, has cleared (using a sea
phrase *à propos*) the table, and I have had a full opportunity, as
he was thus employed, to remark and examine and scrutinize
the whole of his person, from his old, clean, red flannel shirt
rolled up to his sinewy arm joints with the shoulder blades,
down to where the same red flannel shirt shews again distinctly
through a very small apperture, looking somewhat—though
very miniaturely—like the sun setting in our Western prairies
during *the Indian summer evenings,* just at the junction of the two
stout pillars that support his body. Good honest fellow, how
little he thought or believed that I was thus looking at his better
parts. The bell that I had again forgotten has just struck four. It
is of course 2 o'clock. Now let me tell you how this very bell
saved the lives of several seamen, a vessel, and cargo. All these

things I would have omitted, probably, had not the second mate entered the cabin so *à point,* just as I would have omitted many other incidents less alarming, had I not written at the very moment they took place. Advice I would regularly give to any person anxious to employ his time as much as I am by writing down all *he sees, all he thinks,* or all—yes, out with it—*all he does.*

A few minutes before 12, during a dark squally night when our vessel was running swiftly, close to the wind in the warmer latitudes of the Gulf of Mexico, the man at the helm cried out, "Sail oh!—close to windward." I jumped from my bunk, when I had been thinking of thee, my dearest friend, and started toward the spot like a wild man. The captain had leaped to the deck from below in an instant. The vessel was small. It was a schooner running full below the wind, and the thoughts of a pirate approaching to board us filled all my veins with fear and apprehension. All was silent, all dreadful suspense, when the thundering voice of our commandant reached my ears and, I have no doubt, those of everyone on board with, "Strike the bell there." This was done; of a sudden the little stranger hauled to and passed so close to our stern that an active man might have leaped from our vessel to it. Had our bell struck one minute later, the schooner would have struck our heavy, strong, broad side and sunk in an instant. Moving as fast as both ships then did, we had just time enough to gather from the breeze a few heavy vociferations of the captain of the unknown to the man at his helm, to whom he promised a good *whaling.* In a few minutes we were far apart, and thanking God that matters thus so happily ended.

The steward is come again, and is now asking if I want *"quelque chose,"* which he is now too apt to do, because I gave him, when the weather turned cold, my *Cold Breeches,* a poor gift for such an emergency. I was ready to answer him with his own question when I thought it would be unkind to treat him that rudely. A blush raised to my face and I said, "No, my good fellow." Yet, as these words issued from my lips, I could not help looking at the little portion of red shirt issuing from and looking like——
—— [*sic*].

At Sea   July 1826

Our captain is again turning. We have a brig in sight and not very far, but we have not the land in sight. No! and God knows when we will have it. My time is really dull, not a book on board that I have not read twice since here—I mean, on board this ship—and, I believe, twice before. Thought, as I said yesterday, of everything I can well remember through the mist of time, and feel as dull as ever. I move from the deck here, from here to the deck; lay there a little, and down here longer. It is all alike, dull, uncomfortable. Nay, was it uncomfortable only, I do not believe I would complain, but it is all idle time I spend here—all dreary, idle time: the most miserable, pitiful, sinful way of spending even one moment.

I have this very instant cut the quill afresh. Now how much could be said about this goose quill, but I will not pretend to philosophize on—a goose quill. I would rather weigh the *pros* and *cons* of the Genus Anas. Yet who knows but that this single quill, now cut and sharpened to a very acute angle, did or did not, belong to the offspring of an egg laid as near the North Pole as geese dare go. I can safely say that John Hotchkiss, a handsome youth, of the firm of Hotchkiss & Co. of New Orleans, and I believe of New York, and I believe of New England, sold me this very quill for four cents lawful money of the United States—more or less, &c., &c. Now do you think, all at once, that I am merry because we are nearing land. No, by heavens!! Never in my life would I feel less concerned about land than I do now, did not my knees ache so dreadfully, and did I not long as much as I do for a large bowl of milk and a full pound of fresh bread. Ah yes, even such a loaf as our Franklin discovered in our Philadelphia market, when somewhat in my situation. For if *I* have not ran off from my mother and friends and farm, I have from the country that has nourished me and brought me up with all the feelings I now profess. What was I about when this soliloquy was begun? Let me think. I began about a quill, and this very quill reminds me that I saw a few minutes since when I ran on deck for the purpose of disposing of a certain portion——a bird that always resides near soundings. It looked like a small Merganser, birds that you well know are used to diving.

The first mate called it a *Mure!!!* Linnaeus never described this bird. Neither have I, nor any of my predecessors—not even the very highly celebrated and most conspicuous Mr. Ord[14] of the city of Philadelphia, state of Pennsylvania, member of all the societies, &c., &c., &c.—the perfect *academician* that laughed because [I said] a turkey could swim!

"Now where the devil are you running to, Audubon?" Running?—Why, towards the shores of that England that gave birth to a Milton!! To a Shakespeare!!—To a Dryden—[that England] that raised [Benjamin] West; that enabled Thomson to prove his merits,[—]that called Goldsmith by a well deserved name——where Johnson flourished——that gazed with admiration on the pencil of Hogarth.——laughed with Smollett—might have cried with Young——was delighted of late with Scott, and shed tears for her Byron. Oh England, renowned isle! How shall I enter thee? Good God, what have I pronounced—am I fit to enter her dominions at all? My heart swells. The bird seized when sitting on her nest could not be more terrified. I look up— yes, for mercy—I look up, and yet how much I dread it! How far I would thus have gone I know not, when Captain Hatch called out and said the brig "Homer" was close to us. The preliminary greetings of "Brig oh! Ship hi!" were returned, "Whence came you?" &c., &c., had been all interchanged with a few hundred of *et ceteras* besides. I reached the rail way and saw the brig, which was twenty-six days less than we were from New Orleans, a more normal calculation. *She looked well*, although her sails were lashed with *Russia duck* [canvas] to save on importation.

[Audubon's handwriting in this entry was by now powerfully under the influence of porter.]

Ah England! Is it possible that thou shouldst be untroubled by thy own sons? I can scarce believe it. Thy hoary head, used and connected with all kinds of tricks, ought not to suffer this. Now again, what strange itching will prevail and lead a poor

14. George Ord (1781–1866) was among the founders of the Academy of Natural Sciences, Philadelphia. He edited the *American Ornithology* of Alexander Wilson, to which he added a ninth volume. He was largely responsible for the failure of Audubon to publish in America. Later he joined with Charles Waterton to prejudice Great Britain, also, against his *The Birds of America* and to belittle his knowledge of birds.

"A Swift, to be made at Sheffield."

12 pieces 15¾ inches
entering 6 at top and 6 at bottom intersected in each center by a
loose rivet.
12 others the same length crossing the formers at their points at square
angles, and confined at their points with thread to enable the whole
to open and close like an umbrella.
The distance from the center of each working on the upright staff—
equal to the length of the 24 sticks excepting that part of them neces-
sary to confine them through the wire that holds them on their axis.

12

12 being 15 ¾ Inches
entering 6 at Top & 6 at Bottom intersected in each center
by a loose rivet —

12 others the same length crossing the formers at their points
at Square angles, and confined at their points with Threads
to enable the whole to open & Close like an Umbrella —

The Distance from the center of each working on the
upright Staff to be equal to the length of No 24 Sticks
excepting that part of them necessary to confine them
through the Wire that holds them on their Axis —

A Swift — to be made of Sheffield

devil to think on matters entirely unconnected with him? It is almost dark. I will drink the residue of my glass and write perhaps again tomorrow. The word perhaps brings a thousand and one recollections to mind. I recollect just now that when I first knew thee, Dearest Friend [Lucy], frequently I was asked if this passion of mine would be of lasting duration. Help, I am now entering on a sacred subject. "Husband, shut thy book, pray."

At Sea   July 18th, 1826

The sun is now shining clear over Ireland. That land was seen at 3 o'clock this morning by our sailor at the helm, and our mate with a stentorian voice announced us the news. I cannot conceive why I felt no particular pleasure, not even a difference of sensation from my feelings of yesterday, or the day previous, or three weeks ago. What can be the reason? When I have landed in France, or America, I always bounced with joy. Now I look indifferently on the shore, although it looks well. Indeed I feel so mortified that I can scarce write, for the want of better spirits. My Dear Friend, oh it is thee that concerns me, it is our dear children, that fill all my thoughts, the immense ocean that divides us, and the time that must be spent far from thee. I cannot write—oh may God preserve you and bless you all!

[Later]:

I have come again to the cabin. We have had Irish *fishermen* alongside. I would call them beggars but as they are much like me, *brothers in blood*, I would be shocked to say so, although they acted, *through a current of actual misfortunes*, as if they had been conceived and formed of inferior materials to *men American*.[15] Shall I tell you how they acted? "Yes do, my dear friend." Well, as·we neared the Irish Coast a small boat neared us, and bye and bye came close under our lea. It looked somewhat like those boats employed in fetching large or heavy provisions to New Orleans. Her sails were more tattered but her men were more fair. (I mean to say they were *fairer*). They hailed us fairly too, wished to know if we wished for fresh fish, or new potatoes, or fresh eggs. Good fellows, they might as well have

---

15. Audubon alludes to his Celtic Breton blood from his mother Jeanne Rabine's ancestry.

asked a set of miserable sinners if they would accept a drink of salvation. All was acceptable I assure thee, and I will prove it in the sequel. They came alongside, and most dexterously threw a light line to us. Presently they were all busy congratulating us on the beauty of the vessel, her sailing, &c., &c., fishermenlike. However, fish, potatoes, eggs, were passed from them to us, and in return we passed whisky, porter, beef, bread and tobacco to them—probably as acceptable on their side as their goods were to us. I thought the exchange a fair one. I expected that they were satisfied, but no—used to different ways, they called for more brandy, whisky, more of everything, until I really believe that if we had not ordered them to let go our line they would have been following us until now, and begging all the while. Their expressions struck me with wonder. It was as if they put the liquor to their mouths, "Here is to your Honor's health! Long life to your Honor! God bless your Honor!" And honors followed with such rapidity that I became quite unable to look at them any more, and turned away in disgust.

Reflexions followed reflexions, until I was lost and perplexed so much I——— will drop my pen and say no more.

[Later:]

However, another and another [reflexion] successively came. To see distressed beings is really distressful. When in thought I compared these starved beggars with Irish gentlemen, I could hardly conceive them as if at all appertaining to the same race. My God, why are they not independent, and able to scorn this miserable way of attaining a pittance? Oh!

The breeze has freshened. We are proceeding fast towards the emporium of commerce of England. Perhaps tomorrow may see me safe on land again, but tomorrow may see us all stranded, perishing where the beautiful "Albion" went ashore. Incidents relative to many dull days spent on board this ship will be seen by you when I write again.

It was my intention to commit here, on this second-rate paper, the incidents alluded to above, but as I neither dined on eggs today nor am likely to sup on fish this evening, I feel a certain emptiness, produced by habit, that forces me to extinguish thought. Perhaps tomorrow, or tomorrow after, when equal in disposition, if not in power, to a sergeant or lieutenant. Perhaps you have not read Pike's[16] journal but I have and found that during [his] expedition up the Mississippi rialto and across the Missouri river, and further Southwest to the Colorado in Mexico, [one of his men] refused to obey orders on a cold morning. When the lieutenant, surprised to find his best cable (recollect I am speaking on a ship) giving way, spoke and remonstrated, [one of the] full-blooded American soldiers said, "Lieutenant Pike, feed me and I will follow you to hell." The expression was powerful, I must allow, and the case is so connected with my present situation that I would freely repeat the same words to our———[captain]. We are becalmed—I mean the "Delos" is. Not so my bowels! No, by heavens, my bowels are crying, "Help, help, for God's sake save us, take pity on us, for God's sake!"

I have opened a new thread and must, for your sake my dears, proceed to save *you* perhaps, at a future time, from being in *durance vile* as I now find myself.

Although our———[captain] would willingly, a few days since, have given five dollars for a sea hog he would not, to save our lives, have killed either of the two *dear little pigs* that we have on board (so heavily fat that they cannot stand up) for ten dollars each! One would suppose that at any rate Mr. Swift and I, lowering ourselves, even in the eyes of the world, to the lowest minimum, were worth full half that amount each. It is all fudge, my dear. Mr. Swift would go to hell, as you remember the sergeant was willing to do for his lieutenant, and I might also go there before our———[captain] would disturb one of the bristles of these innocent, lovely swains! "Indeed, why is it possible that your Captain Hatch should have brought two pigs across the Atlantic and yet fed you on wretched beef, and half a pound of chocolate for seventeen men's breakfast, and grudged you whisky enough to save a few small fishes in a small bottle when Mr. Swift brought eleven gallons (the greatest portion of which was drank by all hands)? When you had syrup and he had porter, when you had vinegar and oil and he a good cheese? When you had lime juice and gin! Why father, this is

---

16. Zebulon Montgomery Pike (1779–1813), American military officer and explorer. In 1806 his expedition scaled a Colorado peak, named for him Pike's Peak.

most wonderfully strange!" [My sons exclaim.] Yes my Dears, it is the strangeness of it that renders the whole situation wonderful. But in America, my boys, we have, yes even in our own dearly beloved land, men of all sorts—men, of course, uncommon of their sort, and our————[captain] is one of them.

[Handwriting is almost illegible from here to end of entry.]

I could now relates tales of wonder. Yes wonderful tales! I did tell you precisely the truth when I said two pigs. No, I mistook. We positively had three. Ah yes, three! Ah, poor things. The youngest brother of them died one morning for want of Indian corn or other food, but he was good, yes he was. He was murdered at the very instant that his soul————for I believe they have souls as well as lives————heaved out between his nearly clenched jaws like a spirit. Some of it was roasted, some boiled, some was put inside when brought on the table. Now do you not think the dead pig was in fault, no, no. When an animal is dead he is inactive, and I defy inactives either to act right or wrong. The weather is at fault. The thermometer might have raised to 90°. The poor dead pig could not stand the like, and, during one night and a whole day of consideration, its flesh at last gave way to Natural impulse—and stunk.

Do you prefer maggots to cheese? Now maggots, with me, have an irresistible, irritating, repulsive power, and to see two armies of them issuing from two opposite parts of a cheese so much revolutionizes my stomach, particularly at sea, that this same stomach revolts against them. I feel inclined, with a different instrument bye the bye, to exterminate both the "nations" with the broad side of a knife blade. I am not thinking of the maggots that eat the cheese that was intended to go to Kennebunk again, had not the maggots, like overwhelming armies on friendly land, devoured, unaware, the whole, except the crust. A. B. Well, the crust is something. We can look at it whenever the same story flies on the table. Do you understand the allusion? It is a query. But tomorrow (and I will not say precisely the day following this one), I may explain it. What a beautiful, true, ah faithful, idea of a man as unaware of the worth of time as is the worthy Maria, [servant girl] of Ireland, given to us. Now it is because I have no inclination to write. It is not because I feel much perplexed. No, it is because I will not write any more to-day.

I have a wish to allude here to the most sanctified and most holy alliance (with my food, the larvae in the cheese) called France!!!

Ireland is still along our side. [We are] perhaps fifteen miles from shore. The newspapers given to us yesterday by the first fishing smack that boarded us speak of Irish ways of election-eering. I have now to regret that I am *by oath* no politician, or I might or would have argued over the contents of the papers we received. But I, without further Irishmen—in the paper at least—seem very———.

St. George's Channel   July 20th, 1826   Thursday

I am approaching very fast the shores of England. Indeed Wales is abreast our ship, and we can plainly distinguish the hedges that divide the fields of grain. But what nakedness the country exhibits, with scarce a patch of timber to be seen. Our fine forests of pine, of oak, of heavy walnut trees, of magnificent magnolias, of hickory, or ash, or sugar trees, are represented here by a diminutive growth named *furze*. Come, come, no criticism—I have not seen the country. I have not visited any of the nobles' castles, nor any of their renowned parts. No, I never was in England, except when I turned *page over page* with a pleasure that I hope I may feel again. The animating, natural, and therefore the criticizing Scott! Well then, I will look on, and think a while.

Yesterday morning we passed the "Tuskar," a handsome light-house on a naked rock. This morning we saw *Holyhead*, and now we are not exceeding twenty-five miles from Liverpool. I feel no pleasure, dearest friend; no, and was it not for *Thy* sake and the sake of *our children*, as God Almighty was the maker of the sun, I would readily, ah and most willingly, embark to-morrow to reach America's shores and ———so my Dearest Friend!

The pilot boat that came to us this morning contained several men, all dressed in blue, with overcoats of oiled linen, all good, hearty, healthy men but rather too much shaped like their boat that undoubtedly was very clumsy and a miserable sailor compared to our New York and Philadelphia. I will hold my pen and————go on deck to see if it rains still.

[Later:]

Now it does not rain, and I may safely say without being rash that the sight now in sight is truly beautiful. Fifty-six vessels with spreading sails are in view on our lea, and mountain after mountain fading into the horizon are on our right. Lucy, I have now cast my eyes on the land of England. From the bow it is plainly distinguishable. My dull thoughts have all abandoned me; my heart is elated. I see the Dear Country that gave thee birth and I *love it*, because I Love Thee!!!!

What a picture could here be painted or *imagined*. I am not very much surprised that English artists excell landscapes in our day. The weather, the sea, the shipping, the land, would have given to Vernet the long wished-for view. Tomorrow, yes tomorrow, depend upon it, I shall not go to the swamps below Philadelphia to listen to the croaking of frogs. No indeed. I shall have a listen to the sounds of [a] different animal. What, I wonder, ah what! I will go on deck again.

[Later:]

What a wildness of thoughts prevails on me! I wonder if anything like the same ever prevails on men approaching land? For my part, I am really struck with astonishment at myself. I stare with my eyes on this good pilot's face of ours, and stare again at his words (with my ears) so much so that I fear he remarks me in the act, as the very Honourable Mrs. XXXXXX once remarked me at—where was it? I have very nearly forgotten her and the spot where she remarked me so conspicuously that—hush, no more. Mrs. XXXXXX is thy sister [Ann Bakewell Gordon][17] and for thy sake I will hush.

---

17. Alexander Gordon, husband of Mrs. Audubon's sister Ann Bakewell, headed the mercantile house of Gordon & Forstall (later Gordon, Forstall & Berthoud). Aware of a business dispute between Audubon and George Keats, whose wife was visiting Liverpool, the Gordons were indifferent—at first—to the arrival of their brother-in-law.

Tomorrow, *happy day of our Mind*, it is said will see us safely landed in the city of Liverpool, and happy it may be but with me I doubt it. Custom houseofficers—acceptance of bills—hunting up lodgings, down one street and up another, looking at all things about me, will, I know, so perplex *me* that *I* shall scarce know what position to lay myself in, when I go to bed *tomorrow* in Liverpool. I must [go] on deck again.

Mersey River opposite Liverpool   July 20th, 1826

It is now half an hour after 9. The night is cloudy and my heart is—aching. Ah! I sigh, really involuntarily. And yet we are at anchor, yes positively at anchor opposite Liverpool—not exceeding 200 yards. The lights along the city shewed bright to my eyes a minute ago.

But let me tell you. About three hours since, a pilot boat came along our side and left on our deck full forty pilots that had left Liverpool this morning, each of them in a ship bound out. They were all decent looking men, all dressed in blue, and all, I believe, thy countrymen. As soon as our anchor was dropped, boats came along the vessel and three good loads of them delivered us of that extra crew. Now, My Dearest Friend, I am in England. With what success I shall go through my undertaking I shall be sure to inform Thee. Now I shall conclude with the tide here this day and at this hour runs up the Mersey full 6 miles and raises 30 feet spring tide and 18 feet night tide. God bless thee, good night!

II

Liverpool

Liverpool   July 21st, 1826

WHEN I LANDED IT WAS RAINING. Yet the outward appearance of the city was agreeable. But no sooner had I entered it than the smoke from coal fires was so oppressive on my lungs that I could scarcely breathe. I felt the same affecting my eyes also. All was nearly new to me.

After a breakfast taken at an inn for two shillings sixpence, Mr. Swift accompanied me to the Exchange Building, to the countinghouse of Gordon & Forstall. I was anxious to deliver the letters that I had for Mr. Gordon from Mr. Briggs. After a few moments Mr. Gordon made his appearance but did not recollect my countenance (although I am sure it has always been of the odd order) until I opened my lips to pronounce my name. I was coldly received (I think). I would be sorry to say that it was *à l'anglaise,* yet it bordered on something as *new* to me as England is this very moment. I was asked, when I took my leave (which was not long, I assure thee, after our meeting) if I would not call there again!!!! [Gordon did not then invite Audubon to call at his home; hence the remarks that follow.] Where is that sweet sister of thine who almost grew [up] by my side, Ann Bakewell [Gordon] that I knew when [she was] a child? She is here in Liverpool, and I shall not see her. It is severe, but it must be endured. Yet what have I done? Ah, that is no riddle, my friend, *I have grown poor.*

During the morning I presented my bill of exchange for acceptance and was *somewhat mortified* that, although several vessels had arrived from New Orleans that had all left since the "Delos," Mr. Charles Briggs had not forwarded the one I left in his charge at *his* particular request. The rest of the day was merely spent gazing about and clearing my brains (as much as possible) from a multiplicity of confused ideas that filled them alternately in the early part of it. I went to the Museum. I tried to see Mr. Richard Rathbone[1] and some other persons, but was unfortunate in all this.

How lonely I feel—not a soul to speak to freely. When Mr. Swift leaves me to go to his parents in Ireland I shall then be

1. William Rathbone IV (1787–1868), scion of a prominent family of Liverpool cotton merchants and civic reformers, and his brother Richard were great-grandsons of William Rathbone I (1696–1746), founder of the firm and owner of ships trading in the West Indies, the Baltic, and North America. William II (1726–89) left the established Church to become a Quaker and abolitionist. William III (1757–1809) married Hannah Mary Reynolds (1761–1839) daughter of Bristol philanthropist Richard Reynolds; both were Friends and abolitionists. At the age of sixteen their son William IV quit his Oxford tutor; although he never matched his father in brilliance, he became mayor of Liverpool in 1837. He also headed distribution of New England relief funds during the Irish Famine of 1846–47, favored Roman Catholic emancipation, and befriended Daniel O'Connell and the controversial Father Theobald Mathew. From 1829, upon expulsion from the Society of Friends for vociferousness, he was a convinced Unitarian and correspondent of William Ellery Channing, who helped to establish Unitarianism in America. Statues memorialize him in Sefton Park and Renshaw Street Chapel, Liverpool. He married Elizabeth Greg (d. 1882). His daughter Elizabeth married writer and London magistrate John Paget; his daughter Hannah Mary married John H. Thom; his son William (1819–1902) was once M.P. at North Carnarvonshire. His father, an ornithology enthusiast, collected an outstanding library of scientific and literary works. His brother Richard married Hannah Mary Reynolds. His sister Hannah Mary married her cousin Dr. William Reynolds in 1831, after the period of this journal.

Vincent Nolte, whose letters introduced Audubon to the Rathbones and Hodgson, helped them and their cousin Adam Hodgson to head off a wildcat cotton market. Nolte described his meeting with Audubon at Juniata Falls, Pennsylvania, in 1811, but without awareness that the artist played fast and loose with the facts of his birth (*Fifty Years . . . Reminiscences . . .* [London, 1854]). See also Bibliography, *Dictionary of National Biography* (Oxford, 1960); Eleanor F. Rathbone, *William Rathbone* [IV] (London, 1905); Eustace Greg, *Reynolds–Rathbone Diaries (1753–1809)* (Privately printed, University of Edinburgh Press, 1905); and Norris MSS V, Box Y, Rathbone Family, Friends Library, London, England.

William Rathbone (1787–1868).
From a portrait drawn some years
after he befriended Audubon.

entirely destitute. Ah my Victor, where art thou? What a blessing it would be for me to have thy company whilst travelling through this world, but that is denied me and that also I must endure.

We took lodgings and board at the Commercial Inn not far from the Exchange Buildings. We are well fed and well attended, although, to my surprise altogether, so far by females, neatly dressed and tolerably modest. I found today the persons of whom I inquired for different directions remarkably kind and indeed so polite that even to a man like—me—it was real politeness. I examined several watches at Mr. Roskell's and his politeness was most agreeable.

I shall try to keep Mr. Swift here until I have seen *all* that *I* can see of Liverpool. His going to London with me will be very acceptable, I assure thee.

Liverpool, England   July 22nd, 1826

The lark that sings so sweetly and that now awakened me from a happy set of slumbers is nearly opposite my table, prisoner in a cage hanging by a window where, from time to time, a young person comes to look on the world below. *I look to the world above,* and think of the world of the West, and—larks really sing very sweetly, delightful creatures!!

The Custom House officers suddenly entered my head, and after a very considerable delay there, I gradually returned to larks again and thought of those [in drawings] I brought from America. I concluded after looking at the thousands of columns of dark smoke that arise, always in contrast with distant objects beyond them (many of which I longed to see), to call again on Mr. Gordon, and follow the principles specified between men of business, i.e., to take advantage of circumstances (even with reluctance). I saw Mr. G. again. He was much the same. He gave me *his card,* and I now can go to see thy sister, if I feel inclined or think it proper. Mr. G.'s young gentleman accompanied me to the Custom House; (I could here write six full pages). My drawings went through a *regular, strict,* and *complete examination.* The officers were all of the opinion that they were free of Duty, but *the Law* was looked at because it is not every day, it seems, that such portfolios as mine are presented at the Custom House, and I was obliged to pay two pence on each, [these] being water-coloured *Drawings*. My book being American, I paid fourteen pence per pound weight. After the regular formality of procuring a *Certificate* of *my* landing was over, I took my baggage and drawings to my lodgings.

The noise of pattens [on the flagstones] startles me very frequently. Indeed I generally turn my head (of course when the noise comes from behind), expecting to see a horse [running] full speed, with open mouth, intent on taking my head for fresh grass. I am sure my eyes are then quite full, but the moment that they meet those of a neat, plump-looking maid tripping as briskly by as a Killdeer, they soon compose again to their regular size, and—Lucy, thy countrywomen are very beautiful! Yes indeed, they are to my eyes very beautiful! It is not only the freshness of their complexions, nor, added to this, their lovely rosy hue, nor (continuing to add) their well shaped forms but it is——*all about them* I admire so much. I received a polite note from Mr. Richard Rathbone this morning, inviting me to go next Wednesday to dine with him and Mr. Roscoe. I shall not forget the appointment, I assure thee.

Mr. Swift took me to dinner to Mr. Lyons', and there I spent a most agreeable afternoon, or say evening rather, for it was 5 P.M. when we dined and nearly 10 when we left. Good Night.

Sunday:

Yes, it is Sunday: therefore, I must expect a long dull day. Thou wouldst again say, "Ah my Dear Friend, how canst thou say so?" And I would reply as I have done frequently before with——but Lucy, I am now too far from thee to be improved by thy maxims and rendered as happy as I have when—nearer to thee. Therefore the day has been dull. Yes, my Dearest Friend, very *Dull*.

I leaped from the downy bed at dawn of day. I had, then, impatiently been longing (for a long time) for!!!—the sweet voice of the lark at the window nearly opposite mine. Its mellow throat reached my ear and followed the rotary movements of my system with electric swiftness. I thought immediately of England, but wished myself in America. I would have wrote *heaven*, but some of my friends having once told me I was nearing the bombastic, I did not—"a word to the wise." Now [to] the dullness of the day.—I needed shaving but I did not shave—no!—why? Because it was Sunday. Sunday is a sacred day with me. I like to spend it dully—soberly and—I will not say another word. Oh! that oath of mine, never to tell a politician, or a priest, no, [that] I am—what? What? [Illegitimate.] No one knows, not even my poor self. I have frequently believed myself a fool; but the opinion has been variously received, and it was Sunday, this very morning, when I thought so again as much as I ever did in my life.

The weather [is] beautiful for English weather, [with] the thermometer 65° in the sun. In the shade (and there is plenty of this about my body) [it is,] say 41°. (I would have wrote 40° but I love odd numbers. I have been told that they are the fortunate ones at lotteries, or at making a choice among a set of females for a wife,—&c.) The fact, however, is this: that my teeth *clattered* as I exerted myself toward promoting reaction in my blood vessels by walking fast, as I was fasting, this clear, beautiful, English morning before the door of the Commercial Inn.

Dost thou remember the wife of George Keats, Esq., of London, &c., &c., &c.? (I will write no more *et ceteras*, these dull my German quill.)

"Remember her? I am surprised thou shouldst put fresh questions to me," thou sayest.

Well if I did not see Mrs. Keats, the wife of George Keats of London, &c., &c. (confound the &c.'s, I say) I saw, undoubtedly, her ghost in Wales this afternoon.

"Why, is it possible?" thee asks. Yes it is possible, and I will answer thee *why* with, "Because it was Sunday." Formerly ghosts walked at night. Now they walk on *Sun*-day. Pho! Pho!—what a poor pun. I do acknowledge that if I did not see Mrs. George Keats, the wife of George Keats, Esq., of London, &c., (damn the &c's), I undoubtedly saw her ghost, or a ghost very much like her ghost.

"Come, no more of this." I am again intruding on—what?—ah, religion! Must I put thee aside again, when thou art the leader of all and every one of my movements, either mental or physical, vertical or horizontal? Sterne, yes Sterne said, I believe (it was either Sterne or some other merry-inclined gentleman writer of *his age*) that horizontal patterns were most congenial for all descriptions of feelings whatever. The last word, *whatever*, is (in my mind) very strenuous. Indeed it becomes important for persons *conceived*. But I will return to my Sunday, and may God bless the merry Sterne, or the *learned* Sterne, ah Sterne!!! I am not, no, (never can I write with a worse pen than I do now, and yet I feel now as anxious as ever I did to help to keep up his *memory's monument until the expiring times of ages will raise it again* with his immortal resurrection *forever, yes forever!!!* [The preceding lines denote inebriation, not only by their contents but by their extremely erratic handwriting and explosive punctuation.]

I was in Wales and thereby missed my dinner. And why? Because it was Sunday. My forenoon was spent as my afternoon was yesterday (*say last Saturday*) most agreeably, in the company of Mr. Lyons. He sat with me, and *stood up* looking at my drawings for a good while, then was kind enough to introduce Mr. Swift and myself in the Commercial reading room of the Exchange Buildings where, believe me, many men read of the distress now generally felt in England without caring a f——. Well, this pen of mine continues to move as much astray from the direct course as a crab does from the unacquainted pursuer of that naturally sideways moving animal. I am no conchologist, (although I am fond of eating good crabs *out of the sea*). None of our Florida fiddler [crabs] for me, I say. I know you blushed a little when the single letter F [above], came to your sight, unaccompanied. I will soon relieve you. Do not dread any explosion from Mount Vesuvius, for instance, or any mountains that now and then do explode most tremendously. I intended to write *Fig* in full but my rascally pen was not supplied with material sufficient. As I was walking very slowly toward the Mersey, for my feet are most confoundedly sore, I saw Mr. Swift passing on the opposite side of the street, looking at me between the edge of his cheek and that of his spectacles. (He does not know how often I have looked at hawks. I made direct for him as if a hawk myself.) But he spoke so much like a *renard* that I made immediately, *poste de velour*, and I went over the Mersey, Lucy. Ah my Dearest Friend! Beloved wife! How many contrary winds we are apt to meet in our passage through life, or at sea, or a steamboat going only over the Mersey for only three pence each. Upon my word, I do know what I can fairly or appropriately call our species. The country was dull on Wales shores opposite Liverpool and duller the further we proceeded from Liverpool. Why? It was Sunday. Every object looked dull. The larks, as they sprung from the earth, felt the powerful effect of this unaccountable talisman, and dropped, with powers *unused*, to the soil again as if—[but] not one more word.

We returned, eat supper, drank some *claret* called here *port*, heard of politics in the travellers room, drank our glass of *pousse coffee* and—God bless thee—must to bed, wishing thee, my children and my country well. Ah yes, Dearest Lucy, fare thee well.

Liverpool   July 24th, 1826

Who would have thought it? I was [still] in bed at 10 o'clock this morning, yet I was in full health. This is an occurrence in a man's life who, generally has been quite *awake* before the diurnals of the feathered tribe retire to their rest. Here inquiry is requested? "What could the reason be?" What indeed. [It is] the influence of the climate on vegetables and animals so much adhered to by that great French naturalist who puzzled his brains to discover impossibilities, who often repeated that American productions were *all* objects degenerated from the European original. I wish I had known the Count de Buffon[2]—*what an original he was*, and is yet. What a model to copy from! What lights!! Yes, what lights!—and what shades he has cast over Nature's grand tableau.

Did you expect that the beginning of the last paragraph was going to trail from my raising at 10 o'clock out of my bed after Owls, climates, anatomical parts, impossibilities, the Count de Buffon, and almost all other objects wanted to illustrate Nature's great works? No, you did not. This is not my fault, but—I shaved quickly, was dressed in a twinkling. I bustled about briskly,

---

2. Comte Georges Louis Leclerc de Buffon (1707–81), a noted French naturalist and writer.

locking my trunk, took my cane, my hat, my gloves—all in a hurry—ran downstairs, swallowed my breakfast without mastication, and made as directly as I could through the sinuous streets of Liverpool to *No.* 87 Duke Street, where the polite English gentleman Richard Rathbone resides. My locks flew freely from under my hat, and every *lady* that I met looked at them and then at me until—she could see no more.

The kind gentleman was not in. I almost ran to his counting-house at the salt dock, down Duke Street, &c., &c., &c. A full dozen of clerks were at their separate desks. The ledgers, day books, &c., were all under full sail—royals, royals, extra, [studding] sails, &c. An immense letter bag belonging to the packet that sailed this day for the shores where I hope thou art happy, Dearest Friend, was near the entrance. My name was taken to the special room of Mr. Rathbone, and in a moment I was met by one who acted towards me *as a brother ought to do!* How truly kind and really polite. *He* did not give *his card* to poor Audubon. He gave the most polite invitation to call at *his house* at 2 [P.M.] that I ever received since I left America. What an immense distance I had to walk to reach *No.* 6 Norton Street, the house of Mr. Noble, where thy sister resides with *thy* brother-in-law Mr. Gordon, in the road leading to London, full one and a half miles, over a pavement composed of *one pebble* to each toe. Thou knowest my feet and their author's are not extravagantly large. No, neither are the pebbles here, but how much harder are my toes? Good God, if my toes could write as well as those of a woman now exhibited here, called Mrs. (I rather suspect through mistake) XXXXXX, what a scientific description the mineralogists of America would have, when I return there, of these same, small, hard pebbles that my toes have *assured me* were of the hardest texture they have felt since they—let me think a moment, [for] 'tis best not to be too rash—since they were, ah where?—in Liverpool! [More signs of drinking appear in the tipsy handwriting.]

Well, I trotted like a horse that is string-halt, street after street, through alleys and gutters of streets until I reached—no, I did not reach the desired object. "Oh, how is this? What? Could not find Norton Street?" Damn Norton Street. I could not find the sisterly lips of Ann [Bakewell Gordon], to imprint on them an affectionate, purest kind of kiss. The bird that once sung so sweetly into my ears and down to my heart's vitals, had flown; and I looked on the empty nest with more melancholy, believe me, than ever I did when in full expectation that a pair of doves well known to me might be seen once more. Ah, delusion. I can swear that I was at the appointed moment at the house of Mr. Noble. No more. I did a brother's part, and I ambled off back again to Mr. Rathbone in Duke Street.

See me leaning against a window from the inside of a handsome dining-room, melancholy, thought after thought rolling like a tormented stream over rocks all sharply angular, from my head downwards, until I felt positively feverish over all my body. Le Brun[3] could not have had a better subject to illustrate that passion. I leaned heavily until my thoughts suddenly turned to the happy years that I have spent with thee. Then my life was alive again!!! Mr. Rathbone entered the room. With both arms extended he advanced towards me with, "My dear Sir, I regret that I suffered you to wait thus." I dined—but no, I did not dine, I feasted my eyes and heart on the delightful picture before me, the mellow picture of a happy family, the Rathbones. Oh sweet children, oh amiable woman, oh hospitable man! What a sublime subject. Who could not study when Nature is at her best?

The table was left. I had the pleasure to walk [beside] this happy pair, slowly, composedly, to a powerful exemplification of the powers of genius, the night [showing] of the [panorama painting of the] Chapel of Holyrood. Ah marvelous science, to what sublimity thou art thus raised. I hope Richard Rathbone lost nothing more by the trouble I gave him to-day than the money that he paid for my entrance at the exhibition of the holy Chapel. I was wishfully inclined to copy its situation. Mrs. Rathbone is, my dearest Lucy, as amiable a lady and as learned a one as—but come, what shall I say? Well then, as thy sweet self!!!!!

I have wrote two full sides of my poor book in the current account of this day's transactions, and in that respect it is only

---

3. Marie Anne Elisabeth Vigée-Lebrun (1775–1842), French painter.

Mrs. Richard Rathbone, drawn by Thomas Hargreaves. To Audubon, she and her husband were "Philemon and Baucis."

about half past 3 with me here. But it is 11 A.M. by the clocks that all sound for fifteen minutes, one following another, (like the sea captain unacquainted with the soundings of an harbour). And I have not [yet] reached the Exchange Building where I am going to take you through this writing medium, in company with Mr. Rathbone, walking fast arm-in-arm in order to see the American Consul, James Maury, Esq., and others.

Introduction followed introduction. Then I was taken through all the Exchange, the Mayor's public dining hall, &c. I gazed on the [oil portraits] of the royal family [and] pictures of the English landscape by Thomas Lawrence and others, mounted to the Dome and there gazed on the picture composed of Liverpool city, with the harbour that nature formed for her. Far, far, my eyes took my senses. I could see the Irish Channel, a steamboat issuing from the river Dee in Wales, the Mersey filling the interior with the world's produce, and the heavens bounding the scene divinely.

It was past 5. I ran to my appointment with Mr. Swift, and then went to purchase a black chalk to make a sketch of his phiz tomorrow. I have wrote a great deal, have I not? "Pretty well I think." I could write more, but I am so distracted by the noise of all sorts of people below that I will bid thee Good Night, wish thee blessed; and God preserve thee, Lucy.

Liverpool   July 25th, 1826

Burst my brains, burst my coarse skull, and give the whole of *your* slender powers to enable me to describe my feelings this day! I must begin slowly, gradually warm my powers, and—oh, poor head, never can I express through thee the extent of all I saw in the beautiful picture surveyed.

"Stop," [thou sayest], "take time, consider and proceed gradually. No rashness. Recollect thou art now going to attempt a very difficult task. I advise thee, wait."

My beloved friend, I will follow thee [accordingly]—yes, through future worlds as well—and receive thy affectionate advice with loyal pleasure!!!"

I waited fully dressed nearly fifteen minutes before the sweet lark, my *reveille matin*, had turned his head from [his] soft pil-

low towards the orb of Apollo. I waited anxiously. I felt gay and
—no, not happy. But the sweet tingling melody of the lark
helped my spirits much. Mr. Swift rose and dressed in a moment, and my black chalk once more touched the paper to ani-
mate it. Ah yes, I have drawn in England! Ah, how much I have
drawn in my America!! I finished early, so much so, indeed, that
when 7 struck my ear from the clock, we were on the pavement
bound toward the West, to near thee a step.

Naked streets look dull. We soon returned and eat a bountiful repast. I issued forth again. My dear Lucy, I bought a beautiful watch for thee from Mr. Roskell & Son, Church Street, and
one also for me from the same polite gentleman. Ten of the
morning was positively past, and I felt much ashamed when,
after reaching Dale Street, where our lodgings are, [I found] a
note from Mr. Rathbone, for it had been there some time, waiting for me. I dreaded that this should be.

A hackney coach was produced in a moment. I entered it
with my Portfolio Number Two, and ordered Duke Street quickly.
The Rathbones were gone to Mr. Rathbone's mother. I inquired
the way, but before my sentence was finished I saw their carriage turning back, making for me. And I had once more the
pleasure of being near these kind persons. Their youngest sweet
little son Basil looked at me, and I wished him well. Mr. James
Pyke was introduced to me. We proceeded slowly and I thought
of my situation in England, in the carriage of a man generous
and noble of heart. [I myself was] dressed, although perhaps
queerly to them, in clothing very different from the Indian garb
which, with gun cocked, I dashed through the deep swamps of
lower Louisiana after the Wood Ibises in the company of my
good friend [Augustin] Bourgeat.

The country opened gradually to our view, and after we had
passed beneath a cool arbor of English trees I entered the habitation of "Philemon and Baucis."[4] Yes, a venerable happy pair
who received their children with kisses bid me welcome with all
kindness and with natural ease that I thought had deserted this

---

4. Lucy Audubon often read aloud to Audubon, and may have introduced him
to the poem of Jonathan Swift, "Philemon and Baucis." Philemon and Baucis were
the Phrygians who offered hospitality to Zeus and Hermes.

earth with the Golden Age. I felt painfully awkward (as I always do in new company) for a while, but so much truth was about me that I became calmer, and the good venerable couple walked me round a garden transplanted from abroad. And my portfolio was opened in the presence of several females and a younger Rathbone. I am always in too great haste. I saw as I entered this happy dwelling a beautiful collection of the birds of England, well prepared. Yes, well prepared. What sensations I had whilst I helped to untie the fastening of my [Birds] Folio Book![5] I knew, by all around me, that all was full of best taste and strong judgment, but I did not know if I would at all please. A small book was opened. I was panting like the winged pheasant that dreads the well taught friend of man that may perhaps prove him too weak to proceed in full sight of his learned eye.

Ah Lucy, these *friends* praised my Birds, and I felt the praise, yes breathed as if some celestial being succored me in Elysium. Praises are of many kinds, but kindly praises are true, and these good friends praised me kindly!!!

Farewell, venerable double one. Ah yes, you will, you must, *fare well* in the Heavenly Gardens above. Tender embraces were again exchanged. Again I was held by those sacred hands, again in the seat next to Richard Rathbone, and moved through the avenue the same way to Liverpool.

I am now leaping out of the carriage. I have bid farewell to all my friends. And—Lucy—Richard Rathbone stepped towards me, and in a low tone said, "Mr. Audubon, the coachman has been satisfied." My blood ran high, then cold. I felt, yes, much abashed then, myself, in the vehicle that brought me to Dale Street again. Could such incidents ever be forgotten? No. Give my life the lasting solidity of the adamant, and the deep touches of the keenest engraver will [sooner] be effaced from the rock than from my heart.

The good American Consul had called on me. I must thank him tomorrow.

The Reverend W. Goddard, the Rector of Liverpool, and sev-

---

5. The Misses Audubon presented the covers to the American Museum of Natural History in New York City in 1909. They have since joined the original drawings for *The Birds of America* at the New-York Historical Society, New York City.

eral ladies called on me and saw some drawings. All praised them.

Oh what can I hope?

Beloved wife, Good Night.

[Below this entry Audubon lightly penciled these notes, the first included later in text:]

An Orange Woman
  Shall I describe her.
She sells sweets during day and poisons at night.

My cards.
Called on Mr. Maury [the American Consul].

Liverpool   July 26th, 1826

As my business increases here so much, the more must my exertions and industry be called on and employed to meet all demands.

It is very late, my beloved wife. It is past 12 o'clock. The watchman below announced it some minutes ago. I hope thou art reposing calmly with health and happiness on each side thy pillow. May it be God's will.

I feel fatigued and would soon join thee again in sleep, but the maxim that never will cease to be good is present, and I will not put until tomorrow what can yet be performed to-day.

The morning was beautiful and serene. I enjoyed it in its prime. But no sooner had the thousands of noisy wheels began to shake the pavement than my heart swelled and involuntarily bursted with acute sensations of unknown sorrows accumulating so mistily fast before my imagination that I could not refrain from shedding an abundance of tears. I felt as if some great misfortune was neared. I felt how much I need thee! Yes, I recollected that the venerable [Consul,] Mr. Maury, must not be neglected. Then I saw him. Mr. Swift left for Dublin. I called in vain at the Post Office for news from America, put in the letters Mrs. Percy had charged me with, and returned to my little room, where my heart again was forced to discharge its burthen, and I cried. Oh——. The soreness this brought on to my eyelids forced me to recollect that I was engaged to dine with

Mr. Richard Rathbone, that I had already too much against me to enable me to go through this ceremonial trial, and I washed my eyes, prepared my person, and waited patiently. The good gentleman called on me with his brother William. The latter invited me to dine on Friday next with him. I accepted, and promised the former to be punctual with him also.

It is half past 6. The coach is at 87 Duke Street. The coachman has rung the bell and my heart fails me. Now this is, very simply, very foolish. As yes, it is all this and more: it is a most painful action on my faculties.

I am in the corridor, my hat is taken civilly from my hand, and my name humbly requested. I am pointed the way above and—bear me on my legs—I am in the setting-room of Mr. Rathbone. It was time I met his eye, his lively mien! What a relief it gave me[!]

With all this, I have frequently thought it strange that my *observatory nerves* never gave way. I remarked immediately the more polite way of introduction; i.e., I remarked that no one shook hands unless they thought fit. This pleased me. Many pictures embellished the room, and they also helped remove this misery of my life, this *mauvaise honte*.

Mr. Roscoe[6] came in, tall, with a good eye under a good eyebrow, all mildness. He shook hands with me.

"Indeed!! Hast thou already seen and touched that renowned citizen?" [thou asks.]

Yes Lucy, and talked with him!

Dinner is announced. Mr. Rathbone locks his tutor in arm. Mr. Roscoe locks thy husband in arm. I saw not the remainder of this friendly procession.

We descended to the room where I had leaned against the window some days ago, and I was conducted to the seat of honor. Mr. Roscoe sat on my left next me; Mr. Barclay, London

6. William Roscoe (1753–1831), English historian, was the foremost Liverpool art patron. His *Life of Lorenzo de' Medici* (1796) and his *Life and Pontificate of Leo the Tenth* (1805) became classics. Besides being a writer and poet of note in his time, he was politician, abolitionist, republican, attorney, agriculturist, and, finally, banker whose failure in 1816 had brought the Rathbone circle to his aid. Roscoe is mentioned by De Quincey in his *Autobiographical-Sketches* and by Washington Irving in *The Sketch Book*.

William Roscoe (1756–1831).

banker, next; Mr. [André, var. Andrew] Melly,[7] Swiss entomologist, beyond. On my right [sat] Richard Rathbone next, and opposite me the Honorable American Consul, James Maury, Mr. Arnault, &c., until the friends formed a circle round the table.

Conviviality wafted her gentle wings, full spread, over the whole. I was soon less observed, and this gave me the means of observing more. With pleasure infinite I listened to the mirth and *bons sens* that always preside in such company.

This was a good lesson much needed. I was glad to be assured that *bon ton* no longer required me to drink unwillingly! The practice of XXXXX was, however, resorted to as we rose from the table and in mixed company reascended to the parlour, where Mrs. Rathbone appeared like a diamond well set in the circle formed about [her]. It is no wonder her husband is amiable; they grow together. I had the pleasure of holding her hand for a moment whilst she bid me welcome!!

But my dear friend, thou hast not seen the beautiful set of boxes Mr. Rathbone possesses?

"No."

I have. During the latter part of dinner he shewed me several, all chosen by taste and all chosen to improve the taste.

The lights are arranged. I am moving a table. The company is all expectation and I, oh I——. Mr. Roscoe, seeing my drawings, does not give me any hopes, but neither can he destroy a hopeful feeling. I must return to [your maxim]: "Expect not too much and thou shalt not be disappointed." Yes, it is better so.

The tissue paper is turning, and one drawing after another [is inspected]. The style is examined, questions [are] answered, and Mr. Roscoe is—yes, I believe—rather surprised. I sincerely hope so. The attracting rays of my sight prove to me that my very own head is looked at, and I shrink again. Good Mr. Rathbone is all intent on procuring my desires. He has retired from the group and is in close [conversation] with Mr. Roscoe, infusing his generous heart into the mind of the great man. I am invited to see Mr. Roscoe at his seat tomorrow and to attend him at the Botanical Garden. "Good night my dear sir," [he says]. Thus Mr.

7. André (Andrew) Melly was soon to marry Ellen Greg, sister of Mrs. William Rathbone IV. His papers are in the Linnaean Society, London.

Roscoe is just gone and has left me with the Intelligent Swiss [Mr. A. Melly], the [other] kind guests, and my thoughts.

I see that I was not self-deceived when first I saw Mrs. Rathbone at table with her lovely flock, a pleasure not felt this day. Some of her drawings are before me, and talent has put his undeniable stamp on each touch! I am positively a little proud of my judgment on this subject. Excuse me, dearest friend. I must leave yon happy two, "Farewell!" It is now dark. The Intelligent Swiss leads me swiftly towards Dale Street. We chat very brotherly-like. We arrive. We part. I walk faster. I would write more but I am now safely lodged. I have bid thee again good night, and I will not, no, will not soil my paper with details of the last objects I saw [prostitutes on the street].

Liverpool   July 27th, 1826

It is now 12 tonight, my Dear Lucy, but it is thrice that Mr. Rathbone has suspected me [of tipping] the coachman. Yes, Mr. Rathbone, I begin to think, has made some private bargain with all those fellows, for as soon as I say, "How much?" they reply, "Sir, I have been paid." This is extraordinary. What a misrepresentation of things Mr. Leacock[8] gave us at our little mansion in Natchez when he said it would require five or six years for such a man as me to be noticed in England! I believe that was the substance of his speech when he observed how much I longed to issue into the world.

I have been only a few days in thy country, and all smile a welcome to me. Ah yes, I assure thee, a welcome. Read and judge.

I walked to Duke Street at fifteen past 1, and as I entered the house of this real friend, Mrs. Rathbone met me. I followed her upstairs to the parlour above and sat there a few moments. Some *English* grapes were presented to me, refreshments were offered, and I was told that I might trust my portfolio to the driver, who would certainly return it safely. I had not the pleasure of seeing Mr. Rathbone, but I saw his sweet miniature, [Basil], and tapped his fat little round arm in gratitude as much

8. "Mr. Leacock" appears in 1823 diary notes as a visiting English naturalist (Lucy Audubon, *The Life of John James Audubon* [London, 1868; New York, 1869]). Leacock had urged a mission to England but predicted slow progress.

as I did for pleasure's sake. Thou knowest best how fond I am of children.

I soon reach Mr. Roscoe's place[9] about one and a half miles distant, and was welcomed at the door. I entered a little drawing room where all was Nature. This gentleman was drawing a very handsome plant very handsomely. The cabinet was ornamented with many other shrubs receiving from his hands the care that Nature had insured them in their native climes, for I believe they were principally exotics from many distant and different parts of the world. The youngest daughter, the next, and the next, were alternately introduced to me. As it was too early to dine; it was proposed that we go to the Botanic Garden and the proposition was accepted immediately. Mr. Roscoe and I rode there, and I was shewn the whole with great attention. A gentle-botanist guided us and called name [after] name, [telling us] all we asked. The hot-houses were in fine order, and I saw here many of my country's growths. This Garden is level, well drawn, and well kept. The season is rather advanced to say that I saw it with all its advantages.

Now Mr. Roscoe is driving me in what he calls his little car, but the horse is so much less than what I conceived needed to pull it along with his master in [it] that I was quite surprised to see the pony trot with both of us with apparent ease. Mr. Roscoe is, my dear Lucy, one of those come-at-able persons that are just what is necessary for me to have to talk to. He is plain, kind, and prompt at bringing ease in his company.

Again in his charming *laboratoire* I look through windows that encompassed one full third of the oval, into a neat little garden. A glass of good wine is offered. It is drank, and my large portfolio is again on view. I am not going to trouble thee again by enumerating the numbers, generas, species, varieties or sexes. No, I will put all that aside. But I will remark to thee that one of the daughters[10] is an artist herself, and I thought that she exam-

---

9. Lodge Lane. Roscoe wrote and illustrated *Monandrian Plants* (1828), as well as papers published by the Linnaean Society, London.

10. Actually a daughter-in-law, Mrs. Edward Roscoe, noted for *Floral Illustrations of the Seasons*, paintings by Mrs. Roscoe, engraved by R. Havell (London, 1829–31). This folio is No. 266 in the classic by Gordon Dunthorne, *Flower and Fruit Prints of the*

ined the form of my poor head more closely than did Dr. Harlan[11] when he wished to convince me that I was by no means a fool. It is rather an uncomfortable situation for a man to be anatomized by a handsome young lady that has two eyes that say more, at sight, than all the books I ever read put together. However, I found her extremely amiable and full of the wish to improve. Now do not think I am going to be rude. I neither mean to say improve her person nor her manners. No, merely her manner of painting flowers. She asked many advices and I gave them to her with all my heart.

Mr. Roscoe is anxious I should do well. I handed a packet of letters that he patiently read. He says that he will try to introduce me to Lord Stanley.

"Indeed!"

Ah yes, Lucy, this is nearing the "Equator" fast. In a word, he assured me that nothing would be left untried to meet my wishes. "But," said the venerable good gentleman, "Lord Stanley is rather shy—*however!*"

It was near 9 o'clock when I left my drawings at his house, and him also. I spent there what I denominate an agreeable day. The lady assisted [with] all their power to bring me somewhat at home, and thou knowest well how powerful *ladies* are. The old gentleman was left alone. The youngest daughters went forth, and the eldest, her husband, and I talked of America—localities, improvements, politics, &c. Presently I am in Dale Street again, where I find the following polite note from Mr. Martin: "Mr. Martin, from the Liverpool Royal Institution, will do himself the pleasure to wait upon Mr. Ambro tomorrow at 11 o'clock." If that gentleman had not missed one letter, or if he, by putting an "i" between the "r" and the "o," had made my name Ambrio [embryo], it would have been *almost correct*, and very much more appropriate I am sure. But no matter, I excuse the gentleman. He meant well. And I, my beloved, dearest friend, wish thee well also.

18th and 19th Centuries (Washington, D.C., 1938). Mrs. Roscoe is listed in the *Dictionary of National Biography*.

11. Richard Harlan (1796–1843), American physician, wrote *Fauna* and various zoological papers; he was called more a compiler than an observer. He became agent for the American edition of Audubon's *Ornithological Biography*.

Liverpool   July 28th, 1826

Dearest friend, I left my lodgings this morning to ransack this city in search of *pastels*. I have a great wish to present the hospitable and amiable Mrs. Rathbone with a small drawing, as a small token of the gratitude that I shall forever hence feel for them. I had walked the principal busy streets, and inquired at all the booksellers I saw, for the materials wanted. [I] had visited even what is called here the "Artist's Repository" and was returning full of disappointment when I met——Mr. Gordon again. I was on the point of passing by, so shy am I of those who do not meet me with open heart and friendship. But the thought that Ann Gordon was thy sister—that once she resembled thee in kindness—that I had passed the happiest portion of my life with ye all when we were all children—vibrated my heart-strings, and I presented my hand to him. I related my having called, my disappointment, and, no, I did not say surprise—the word might have been irritation—but I repeated the great anxiety I felt to see Mrs. Gordon. I did not say, as I always was wont to say, "*sweet sister Ann.*" And when and where could I meet her, I asked—tomorrow? Ah, why did I say tomorrow? She is engaged to go out and so am I. Shall I, then, see her again, and look at her fair heart through her glowing eyes? Oh yes, I hope so.

A full-grown man with a scarlet vest and breeches, black stockings and shoes to match the coloring of his front, a blue long-coat covering his shoulders, back, &c., reminded me somewhat of our *Summer Red Bird* (*Tanagra rubra*) as I passed him. Both species attract the eye, and since I have been here my eye has been frequently attracted by them. It is probable they are Tanagers, but the scientific appellation is yet unknown to me.

There are many orange women in this city. I will describe one of them as quickly as possible: *They* sell sweets during the day, and poison during the night.

At 11 or thereabouts Mr. [F. J.] Martin (who, I expect, is Secretary to the Royal Institution) called and arranged in my presence a notice directed to the members of the Institution, announcing that I would exhibit my drawings to them there next

Monday, Tuesday and Wednesday morning for two hours.

The time felt heavy. I took the liberty of calling on Mrs. Rathbone. I knew her husband was much engaged with his business; and for me to have gone to his countinghouse would have been absurd. I paid my respects to his lady. I found her engaged at putting away, in a little square box the parts of a dissected map with which, [Maria] Edgeworth-like,[12] she had been transmitting knowledge with pleasure. The calmness of her countenance proved the ease she possesses in thus educating her children. I thought of thee, in thy days at Henderson [in Kentucky]. Upon talk of art Mrs. R. immediately produced some new paintings. A portfolio of prints was examined, but I often raised my eyes to the pictures on the walls, hung by chains from the ceiling. This was also new. I saw her portrait when she was younger, and that of her good husband, mother and father. I saw her children coming one by one into the room, and I kissed the youngest.

"This is a minute description," thee remarks. "However, I could not expect one, more so, of a nondescript bird of thine." [*Nondescript* means birds not yet named and described ornithologically.]

This one is not a nondescript. It belongs rather to that rare genus, *Amiability real.* I would have remained longer but ——.

I returned by a great roundabout way to this little room and found on my table the following note:

"Mr. Rathbone presents his compliments to Mr. Audubon, and begs leave to remind him of his engagement to dine with him today at six o'clock. He has made another effort for Dr. Traill,[13] and has a brother-in-law dining with him who resides in London, and who, he hopes, may be useful to Mr. Audubon there. He ventures therefore to request Mr. A. to bring a *few* of his drawings with him. Bedford Street, Abercromby Square, Friday morning."

So it seems that I must feel awkward once more? Well, it is for my friend's and my children's sakes. From the tenor of the note, I took for granted that *only a few* drawings were wished, to be

---

12. The reference is to Maria Edgeworth (1767–1849), a popular novelist.
13. Thomas Stewart Traill (1781–1862) was a physician and naturalist, Royal Institution officer, and editor of the eighth edition of *Encyclopaedia Britannica*.

looked at, and fearing to act amiss, I packed up only a few.

I am rolling in a hackney coach towards Abercromby Square. The weather is pleasant and warm for this country. I have entered a parlour and find at work a very handsome daughter of William Rathbone perhaps thirteen years of age, and another much younger. I peep at the heat garden and at prints beautifully framed with oak borders. I cast my eyes from a picture of the "Declaration" of our *Independence* to one of the good face of Charles Fox[14] [that now faces me] on the chimney mantle. Mrs. Rathbone enters as if she had known me for years, with "Sit down, Mr. Rathbone will be here directly [she tells me]; how do you like our country," &c., &c. She sets at her needlework. How extremely kind and polite she is. I suspect that good Richard Rathbone has told them all of my *mauvaise honte,* and she wishes to save me from the feeling. I thank them both. The conversation opens on America and my travels. Gentlemen gradually accumulated. Mr. Rathbone is very kind; and once more, Lucy, there are my drawings.

The dinner is announced. Mrs. Rathbone presents her hand to me; (and it was fortunate that she was this kind, for I was standing like an ass). We walk to dinner. The gentlemen did not reach the dining room for some moments and I blushed, thinking that they had remained to comment on poor me.

The conversation was a long time kept up on the subject of *Hunter,* who says, (and it may be true), that he has spent nearly all his life with the Indians. The *pros* and *cons* were debated gently, but I felt very uncomfortable during the while, as I dreaded that the suspicion that I might prove an imposter was at hand.[15]

---

14. Charles James Fox (1749–1806), an English statesman and orator who supported the American Revolution.

15. Audubon dreaded the epithet "imposter," hurled at him in Philadelphia in 1824 by Scots-born engraver Alexander Lawson who had discovered Alexander Wilson, "father of American ornithology," and taught him to draw birds. Accused of ignorance, Audubon replied impulsively that he had studied for "seven years" under Jacques-Louis David, artist to the Napoleonic court (William Dunlap, *Diary* [3 vols. New York, 1830]). Thus began a transparent legend, to this day treated with awe even by some scholars. The fact is that even if Audubon had risked conscription—after having failed to become a Republican Navy candidate at Rochefort-sur-Mer, 1796–1800—by visiting Paris between late 1800 and June, 1803, before sailing for America, his stay would have been fleeting. Moreover, Charles Bonaparte alleged that David had denied having had Audubon as a pupil (Alice Ford, *John James*

Mr. Hodgson,[16] to whom I had a letter from Mr. Nolte, was particularly kind to me, and when the dinner was over he took me aside, asked for the letter, and spoke of doing all in his power for me. He wished me to see Lord Stanley, &c., &c. The young Swiss [A. Melly], whom I now wish thee to know by the name of the "Intelligent Swiss," came. The English company appeared desirous that I should succeed in England. The "Intelligent Swiss" wishes me not to lose time here but to proceed to Paris immediately. Whilst this was going on, a number of prints, paintings and books were laid on the table. Charles Bonaparte's work was "much admired" until, or so I was politely told, my own work came in sight.[17] Every person was kind to me, particularly those who had visited America.

I heard the house clock count 10, (for I dreaded to pull out my watch). My *portfeuille* was taken by a servant. Mr. James Pyke and me were soon moving from Mount Pleasant towards Dale Street. Mr. Pyke is a gentleman of merit, I am sure; he speaks well, and is altogether [of] good breeding.

I pulled a shilling for the servant, took my *portfeuille*, walked three flights of stairs, and here I am. What reflections [crowd upon] my mind! Would it be possible that I should not in any degree succeed? I can scarcely think so. Ah delusive hope, how much further wilt thou lead me?

Farewell, friend of my heart, and ye my dear sons, all good night. How I long to hear of you all.

Audubon [Norman, 1964]). Actually, Audubon was in Nantes on October 23, 1800, for his deferred baptism. His *Ornithological Biography* invites the inference that he studied with David in 1805 during a return visit to France, an interval of scarcely thirteen months; his drawings of that interval, though haphazardly marked, often bear "near Nantes," precluding a Paris visit of any length. A letter in the Princeton University Library proves how he feared to venture out of the house to hunt. His crude draftsmanship gives no hint of Paris training by 1805–1806. The papers of David in the *Bibliothèque Nationale* and in the *Institut de Beaux-Arts*, Paris, abound in names of pupils, but Audubon's name is not to be found. The claim denotes the same uneasiness which in later years led Audubon to claim La Rochelle as his birthplace, then Paris and Louisiana, as well as—on occasion—Saint-Domingue, where he was born on April 26, 1785.

16. Adam Hodgson, cousin and partner of the Rathbone brothers, received one of the two most crucial letters of introduction—both written by Nolte, whose part in the triumphal American tour of Lafayette had increased the prestige of the quixotic merchant.

17. The Bonaparte work was a continuation, supposedly, of the Alexander Wilson ornithological classic of the same title, *American Ornithology*, already cited.

Liverpool, England   July 29th, 1826

I arose this morning full of the hope that I would receive a sweet kiss from thy sister, and—no—I was not altogether disappointed. I walked about the city a while, and visited Mr. Hunt,[18] the best landscape painter of this city. I examined much of his work and found some beautiful pieces, representations of Wales scenery. I visited the Royal Institution to judge of the lights, anxious to have all the advantages necessary to a man of my humility of powers. And by a great roundabout way (to come at the precise, appointed hour, say 12), I reached Mr. Noble's house [in] Norton Street, London Road, and knocked. A coarse female answered, to my question, that Mrs. Gordon was *in*. Ah!!! at last I am again within a few paces of—yes—of a kind of likeness of thee. I sat a while below stairs; and, for time ripens all things, I saw and kissed thy sister, Ann——Gordon. I kissed her, I thought, more than she wished; at all events *she* did not kiss me. (I was going to write *never*, but that would have been as false as anything could possibly be.) However, she became more sensible that I was yet Audubon; perhaps, too, recollected that I never injured her; perhaps, indeed, she might have recollected that I always loved her as *my sister*. Whatever might be her present reasons, she *returned* to old times with more familiarity than I expected. She talked a good deal, and I did also. Still, I thought and think still, and perhaps may think forever, that she had acquired a great deal of the Scotch stiffness, so well exhibited *toward me* at *a particular house in Louisiana* and that I daresay thou knowest as well as *I do* [Mrs. Robert Percy]. "Yes indeed a hundred times better," [sayest thou.] I heard a great deal that I will not mention now. I believe thy sister, or my sister, or our sister (I am a poor one at discriminating) was *rather* surprised that I should have been so well treated by Messrs. Rathbone, Roscoe, and Hodgson. We talked altogether of *my concerns*, but I watched my slippery tongue that Doctor Pascalis[19] called *candid*, but the word is very unfashionable I am assured.

18. William Henry Hunt (1790–1864).

19. Dr. Felix Pascalis-Ouvière (1750–1833). Noted Philadelphia (later New York City) specialist in yellow fever, of which Audubon nearly died in 1803; but Pascalis is not known to have treated him. He appears on page 159 of Lucy's life of Audubon, London edition, 1869.

Indeed to be candid is quite *burlesque, I am also told,* so that I tried to be somewhat fashionable also—much, I assure thee, against my heart. But the world dictates, and man must follow the mandate.

We had in [our] company a Miss Donathan.

"Very like our Jonathan, is it not?" [thee asks.]

No indeed, this was a good looking young woman. Her hair was beautifully clean, well put up to attract, and of a fine, light tint much esteemed by Thomas Sully's[20] pencil.

"Now what is all this stuff about Sully's pencil?" thee asks.

Stuff! It is hair I am speaking of, [and] of light silky hue. The sun is just going down beyond a church that breaks my view most disagreeably, yet the clouds about the sunset are much like the young Miss Donathan's hair in coloring. I cannot give any other description, the sun dazzles me so.

Now do not stare nor start. There's no snake in the way. I am merely invited to dine with Mr. Alexander Gordon and sister Ann; (yes I will call her so). I have been nine days in England, slept each night within half a mile of thy sister, and this day I first saw her. Yet Mr. A. Gordon knew well where I reside. But the Scotch character does not admit *Friendship Free.* No. I can swear it by a long course of circumstances too tedious to be repeated (but well known to thee in my 19th number of this my poor work [a reference to his nineteenth journal]); I left after a good long visit of one and a half hours, and I am again gazing to the right and left in the streets of Liverpool. Two tall men are walking just before me, both wearing black epaulets made, I believe, of coarse cotton yarn. They both have round hats and a cockade of the same materials that dance about their shoulders. Each is tightly buttoned from the chin to the abdomen in a *surtout,* all black, that nearly reaches their heels. To what corps do they belong? Ah, here is one of the same make, dressed like [them], holding the door of a fine carriage open whilst two handsome females are getting out of it, helped by a gentleman. Now I know the regiment. The carriages here are generally handsome and drawn by well made, fat horses. It is not rare to see, setting by the side of the coachman, a waiting-maid full as

---

20. Thomas Sully (1783–1872) instructed Audubon in the use of oils in 1824.

handsome as any portion of the whole establishment, and two waiters or valets behind the carriage in a chaise, attached to it.

I was shocked this very morning to see in the barouche of a wealthy banker a young lady tormenting a beautiful goldfinch in chains. How different the feelings of that young lady, or the feelings of her parents, must be from the noble sentiments of Tristam Shandy's Uncle Toby![21]

I have not found the population of Liverpool as dense as I expected, and, except during the evenings (that do not commence before 8 at this season), I have not been at all annoyed by the elbowings of the greater numbers that I still remember having seen in my youth in the largest cities of France. Some shops here are beautifully supplied. They are generally lined with two sets of purchasers, mostly ladies, seated and choosing the articles wanted. I counted in one of these shops sixteen gentleman attendants behind the counters.

The new market is, in my opinion, an object worth the attention of all traveller strangers. It is thus far the finest I ever have seen. It is a large, high and long building divided into five spacious avenues, each containing their specific commodities. I saw here viands of all descriptions—fishes, vegetables, game, fruits both indigenous and imported from all quarters of the world, bird sellers with even little collections of stuffed specimens, cheese of enormous sizes, butter in full abundance—superior freshness and quality—along with immense crates of hen's eggs laying upon and between layers of oat straw, imported from Ireland—twenty-five for one shilling. This market is so well lighted with gas that at 10 o'clock this evening I could plainly see the colors of the [irises] of living pigeons in cages.

The whole city is lighted with gas. Each shop has one of those brilliantly illuminating fires in each window and many about the room. Fine cambrics can be looked at by good judges.

Mr. Adam Hodgson called on me this day and I am to dine with him Monday. He has written to Lord Stanley about me.[22]

---

21. Laurence Sterne, *The Life and Opinions of Tristram Shandy* (9 vols., 1760–67).

22. Lord Stanley was Edward George Geoffrey Smith Stanley, fourteenth Earl of Derby (1799–1869). He was an M.P., naturalist responsible in part for the later fame of the delineator Edward Lear, Chief Secretary of Ireland, Secretary for the Colonies, Prime Minister, orator, writer, and translator of the *Iliad*.

He very kindly asked if my time passed heavily, gave me a note of admittance for the Atheneum and told me that he would do all in his power for me. I saw Mr. William Rathbone and he was unchanged.

I dined at the Inn to-day, for the second time, only, since my arrival here. But I immediately remarked that almost every individual at table knew me and I was treated with attention and respect. An American gentleman told me this evening that, when I retired, the principal number evinced a great desire of seeing my work, and that they would go to the Royal Institution every day during my exhibition there.

I was peaceably writing all this when a knock at my door required my raising to go and unfasten it, (a precaution I take always when I retire for the night), and [I] saw Captain Joseph Hatch of the "Delos." This reminded me immediately of my having walked to the vessel this afternoon and given some silver change to the honest crew to drank freely of the good ale of England. But Captain Hatch told me a sad piece of news. He has lost his pocketbook this morning with about £30, the register of his vessel, and sundry papers besides. He appeared much afflicted, but I could do nothing for him. He left me at 11 o'clock. Mrs. Brown of Natchez[23] arrived this day in the "Hugh Valace." The noise in the street is rather subsiding. Good night, Lucy, God bless thee, good night.

Liverpool, England   July 30, 1826

It is Sunday again, but not a dull one, no. There are certainly exceptions to all rules. I have become better acquainted here. [I] do not look on every object about me with the stranger's stare.

I went to the Church of the Asylum of the Blind. I have just returned and I write because it is a pleasant Sunday altogether with me.

Follow Dale Street, northeast, all its length, keep inclining to the right until you come opposite the Islington Market and continue to where you see the asylum itself. The church is there near you. Ascend a few steps of cut stones after passing the iron-barred gates, walk under the colonnade, pay whatever you

---

23. An acquaintance of Natchez days, 1822?

pledge *over* a sixpence to either of the collectors at the inner door, and if you are *a man* pull off your hat. Then look at the large picture of Christ freeing the blind. It is a copy of the great original, "Charity." Follow an assistant down the middle aisle. He opens a pew and you sit on a clean, well-stuffed serge cushion, under which [you] place your "cover-head," and look around before the service begins. The general structure is a well proportioned, oblong square. A niche contains the picture of Christ. Ten light columns support the flat ceiling imitation of marble. A fine organ with brass barrels is placed over the entrance in a kind of upper lobby that also contains the blind musicians. The windows are large; the glass of each pane is ground rough [so as] not to distract the mind by admitting [sight] of outward objects. Congregational attendants gradually fill the whole. All is silent, yes silent.

The mind is filled with heavenly subjects and thoughts (I mean, of course, the mind of non-sinners). The two pulpits garnished with purple velvet seem to be all that is lukewarm here. Hark!!!! Angelically the sound [in] imitation of music sublime and heavenly gradually glides into your whole composition, until, by the exertions of accord, a general chorus is produced, imbibing an idea of the sounds of the trumpets of Resurrection. My frame shakes; not with fear, no, but with a wish that I might feel the sensation oftener.

The rites proceed, and divine female voices open an anthem entrusted by the Creator to Haydn!! Oh celestial sounds!!! No, it is impossible for me to describe them. A good, excellent service is mixed with this to entice the mind and imagination to refrain from evil doings. Prayers are read and musically echoed by the blind, and each person gently rises, walks out lightly, and not until entirely out the colonnade do you hear the sound of a single voice.

I give it here, as my opinion or my best recollection, that I never before this day saw *such devotion in a Church*. I know *thou* understands me well.

The Reverend Wm. Goddard took me to some institutions of children, [run on] the Lancastrian system, where the whole appeared well dressed, clean, and completely systematic.

During this morning I saw long files of youths of both sexes, marching the streets on their return from devotion. Nothing except the tread of the feet on the pavement could be heard.

I reached Norton Street at half past three in a coach, and found Mr. Gordon in the setting-room upstairs. I [was] met very differently, I am sure. He praised my work and said that he was glad that I came to England, &c.

I was struck with Ann Gordon asking me if thou wert as fond as ever of Doctor [Dowe]. Our conversation, however, was principally on science; (that is, their conversation). Miss Donathan reminded me much of the eldest daughter of Thomas Sully. We had a comfortable family dinner. Walked to the Botanic Garden with thy sister under my arm. How little did I expect, when at thy [girlhood] home in America, "Fatland Ford," that I should ever be in this situation. Mr. Gordon asked me many questions about Charles Bonaparte, and Joseph Bonaparte[24] also. He offered me some letters for London and we parted more as I wished than I expected. Ann recommended my hair to be cut and a coat cut fashionably. Mr. G. and Miss D. appeared *brotherly* and *sisterly* kind to *each other.*

Liverpool, England   July 31, 1826

This day, Lucy, was one of trial to me, believe thy friend. This was Monday, and it was appointed to exhibit my collection partially to the public and my kind Liverpool friends. At 9 this morning I was quite busy, arranging and disposing in sets my drawings to be fairly inspected by the public, the connoisseurs, the critics. This last word has something very savage in its nature, as well as in its orthography or its pronunciation. I know not why. Yet I know that I dread this very casting askance of a single eye of those dangerous personages of whom I have so much heard, but whom, fortunately, thus far, I have only met in scanty form, and of little value.

I drew my new watch and in five minutes, by its regular movements, it proved to be at the meridian. The doors of the Royal Institution were thrown open and the ladies flocked in; I, however, saw but one: Mrs. Rathbone. Then I was in view of the

---

24. Joseph Bonaparte had an estate, Point Breeze, near Bordentown, New Jersey.

world. How many glances to meet—questions to answer and repeat! *"La, that's beautiful,"* again and again repeated, made me wish to be in the forests of America, to be able myself to say at meeting a new specimen, *"Ah, how beautiful!!"* The time passed, however. My drawings were on the floor and a gentleman, walking up directly toward me, said, "Sir, did you ever reside in New York?" I answered, "Yes, Sir." "Pray, Sir, did you marry a Miss Bakewell?" Now to this, [Lucy], answer thy own self? This proved to be a Mr. Jackson who lived at Bloomingdale near Mr. Thomas Kinder,[25] and who knew thee well, for he said, *"Your lady was very handsome."* Yes, he might say that, but he said immediately, "Your drawings are charming." I could have slapped the man for bringing [up] my paltry pictures with thy face, all of a breath. But it is past 2 o'clock; the doors are closed, and I run to my chamber to dress a little and wait for Mr. Adam Hodgson. Four o'clock. Half past 4. I am looking from my window for his gig. Is it here? Let me see. Aye, that it is! My portfolio is under my arm and, three-by-three, I leap down the stairs, shake the friendly hand, and am seated on [Mr. Hodgson's] left, moving towards his cottage. I am sorry I cannot paint portraits. I would represent to thee the meekness of his blue eyes, his sweetness of language, his comely movements. But my dear Lucy, thou knowest in all my attempts I never yet reached the original.

We are going, talking about me, thee, and ours. The little pony has stopped. I am out of the little chair, and conducted into a neat *English* setting-room. Wert thou not an English-born lady thyself, I would describe this one as being considered by myself a fair specimen, really scientifically. But, I will merely say: It was beautifully snug and had gothic windows, through which the eye was freely permitted to extend its [range] over an uncommon extent of picturesque scenery.

"Mrs. Hodgson, Mr. Audubon, my dear"—a fairly tall young female with the freshness of spring entered the room and wished me welcome with an air of plain contentedness, [which] not *even my eye* would [mistake for that], letter for letter, as well as what was spoken.

---

25. On Bloomingdale Road, which later formed Upper Broadway, New York City, where Benjamin Bakewell, uncle of Lucy, had a summer place. Arthur Kinder was once a Bakewell business associate.

We dined!—Lucy, like at home. These good people gave me, in perfect friendship, lessons of English politeness. I spoke plainly about the different conditions of my past to Mr. H., and moved from the dining-room into the setting-room, rather after the setting of the sun.

We had four visitors, a Captain somebody, his lady and son, and a pert young woman, the names of whom I do not care half so much about as I do for those of the others. But I must let them all go by, as my poor head will not remember names, unless they chance to be the names of friends.

The calmness of the countryside soon reached my heart, and soon did I contemplate [American] scenery in imagination. I thought of an evening when we were walking, gently arm-in-arm together, towards the waters of the Bayou Sara, and I watched thee bathe thy gentle form in its current. I thought of the happiness [we] have enjoyed while [I] gazed on the happy couple before me. I thought—ah, my dearest friend—!

Mr. Hodgson asks if I will retire to rest or listen to his usual habit of reading prayers to his little flock and servants. I preferred the latter; and, silently mute, each bent on devotion, prayed with this good man.

Liverpool   *August 1, 1826*

The "good night" [was] expressed and a sweeter *good night* I never listened to, except when———. Wouldst thou like to see the little room where I am going to spend my few hours of bodily rest? It also has a gothic window. My kind host opens it at my request. Before it [stands] a table covered with all the implements necessary to render the body clean and comfortable. And I can see the particular shape of my poor head fully in a large mirror before me. The bed was made as if by thyself. I do not remember the rest, for I went to sleep thinking of thee.

I arose to listen to the sound of an English Black-bird, perhaps just as the day broke. It was a little after 3 of the morning. I dressed, and silently as in my power, carrying my boots in one hand and the house key in another, I moved down the stairs, and out of the cottage, and pushed off toward the fields and meadows. I walked a good deal—went to the sea shore; saw a hare; and returned to Mr. A. Hodgson's to breakfast, after which, and [with] many kind invitations to make it my home, I bid them farewell; and, drove beside their servant in the little carriage drawn by the little pony. I reached Dale Street a little after 8 [o'clock].

I immediately went to the Institution. [By] 12 the assemblage was great. I saw Dr. Traill and many other persons of distinction. Several persons who, I believe, are attached to that Institution wished that I should be remunerated by exhibiting for money and [also that] an offer of the room [be] proposed to me *gratis*. But my heart revolted at the thought, and although I am poor enough, God knows, I could not think of doing such a thing consistently, with the station I wish to preserve, one forwarded, I may say, from America, by letters of our most eminent men, to eminent and kind persons in this country, who all have received and honoured me highly by personal attentions. I could not, I repeat, think it consistent to become a mere *show man* and give up the title of *J. J. Audubon, Naturalist*. Many were in favor of my principles, but more [were] against them. I called on Mr. Gordon and was glad to see that he thought as I did. The "Intelligent Swiss" [Melly], was also on my side. I saw at the Institution some ladies from Natchez [who] had known us there, but I did not [speak with them]. I spent the evening with thy sister and Mr. Gordon. I felt extremely fatigued both [in] the head and body, and at 10 o'clock bid thee good night.

August 2nd, 1826

I put up, this day, 235 of my drawings and the *coup d'oeil* was not bad. The room was crowded. Old Mr. Roscoe did me the honor to come, and presented me to Mr. Sismondi[26] of Geneva. I was introduced to Mr. Barclay, Dr. Traill, Mr. Martin, the Misses Hodgson (Quakeresses); and I daresay one hundred besides. Ann, Mr. Gordon and Miss Donathan came. I had sent a note to Mrs. Rathbone to acquaint her [with] the extra number of drawings on view, but she had removed to "Green Bank," and sent me a note. I consulted her good husband about the

26. Jean Charles Léonard de Sismondi (1773–1842), a Swiss historian and economist.

[paid] exhibition. He was against it, Dr. Traill in favor, Mr. Roscoe in favor. I consulted Mr. A. Hodgson, [who was] against it. I now concluded to drop the idea entirely, collect my letters for London, and go there as quick as possible. I remitted my letter to Mr. Ramsden of this city, and saw Mr. Booth of Manchester who promised me all his assistance.

I went to Mr. Roscoe's cottage during a heavy drizzle, and returned by 7. An American gentleman of Charleston, South Carolina, asked me to go to the theatre, and I went. I was anxious to see the renowned Miss Foote. We had been seated for some time [and] the piece had begun when who should enter the box—ah yes, who should enter the box, Ann, sweet sister Ann, Mr. G. and Miss D. Miss Foote[27] *has been* pretty, nay handsome, nay beautiful!—but she *has been*. The play was good, the playhouse very bad. My sister, Miss Donathan, and Mr. G. shook hands with me and my companion, and I moved toward our lodgings. I feel very wearied. It is past 12 o'clock. God bless thee, good night.

Liverpool   August 4th, 1826

My head is very much like a distracted hornet's nest. I am fatigued, nay harassed, and with all satisfied and *almost* happy.

Thou seest that I was not at my usual lodgings last night by the very date above. No indeed, I was not. My night was spent much more agreeably, I assure thee. But before I speak of the night, it may be proper to write down an account of the day. It is long, my dearest friend, but not tedious, for I assure thee I shall say nought but of friendship-like manners.

My morning rolled off at the Institution. The room was crowded. Four hundred and thirteen persons entered during two hours. I was broke down bowing and scraping to all the new faces I was introduced to. It was, in a word, *a business to bow.* A certain somebody took it into its head to draw a copy of one of my nondescripts, but the doorkeeper, an alert Scotchman, baffled him in his attempt, and tore his sketch!

Mr. A. Hodgson called on me, to invite me to dine with Lord Stanley *tomorrow* in company [with] Mr. William Roscoe, Sr. The

27. Maria Foote (1797?–1867) was to become the Countess of Harrington in 1831.

"Intelligent Swiss" gave me a letter to the Baron von Humboldt,[28] from Mr. Sismondi, and shewed me a valuable set of insects received from Thibet. This young gentleman, [A. Melly,] Lucy, is interesting beyond description. He repeated the polite invitation of Mr. Rathbone to go to "Green Bank" to spend the night, &c. I was engaged to take tea at Mr. Roscoe's and I went. Mr. Hodgson has invited me to breakfast with him *this morning,* so I am under the guard of three promises.

I had the pleasure of seeing Mrs. William Rathbone at the Institution. Perhaps never was a woman better able to please, and more disposed to do so than this very Mrs. Rathbone. I looked at her dark eyes, sparkling with all the good sense a *man* can possess, with a sensation felt stronger as I was fully persuaded of the candor that existed about her.

Well, I went (I mean in the afternoon); for during [noon] dinner Mr. A. Hodgson came to me with two letters of recommendation to *two* noblemen,[29] copies of which will be inserted here. [I started to say] I went to Mr. Edward Roscoe's to drank tea.[30]

"How didst thou go?" [thee asks].

A young son of Mr. Roscoe called in a car at the Institution. I put up a few drawings and off we went to—I have forgot the name of the street, and, almost, the situation of the house. But, Lucy, Mr. Edward Roscoe is a *handsome,* agreeable man, and his lady—but come, I dread to say too much about the ladies of a foreign country, and yet it is very hard for my slippery tongue not to say *amiable,* after its having turned and twisted itself more than three times, I am sure, within my mouth, anxiously bent on giving that word. There was there much company, generally ladies that draw well, also two famous botanists who knew at once every plant or flower I exhibited to them.

Having to walk to "Green Bank" (the habitation, recollect of old Mr. [William, Sr.] Rathbone)[31] I left Mr. Roscoe at sunset, which, by the way, was beautiful.

28. Baron Friedrich Heinrich Alexander von Humboldt (1769–1854), a noted scientist.

29. See Letters of Introduction, reprinted in author's earlier edition of 1826 Journal.

30. William Roscoe had seven sons, among them Henry, his biographer; Edward, husband of the painter of *Floral Illustrations* (cited); and William S. Roscoe. His daughter Jane is mentioned in this journal.

31. Green Bank (sometimes Greenbank) was built soon after the birth of Au-

I was conducted by the young son again, and was soon put on the road. We parted. The evening was calm and pleasant. As I advanced into the country, groups of persons, exercising leisurely, met me. Some turned their heads to remark that "Original," me. However, I passed again under the avenue of trees leading to "Green Bank" and gently knocked at one of the inner doors, my hat and cane in one hand. Between the raps that I gave I passed my handkerchief over my face to take away the moisture occasioned by a brisk walk. I could easily hear the mirth of many whom I supposed were on the green, fronting the buildings. I rapped with stronger blows and the Mother Rathbone met me with, "Oh, I am glad to see you."

I was not mistaken. The green was covered with beauty, good sense, and pleasure. I was attracted mostly, however, by the sight of ladies with bows and arrows, shooting at a target perhaps twenty-five paces off.

Presently it grew darker. I was seated between the two brothers Rathbone, sorry that my little friend Basil had retired to repose. I would have liked to kiss him very much. The father of Mrs. Rathbone asked many questions respecting the religious inclinations and rites of Indians. We spoke a good deal about American trees, things quite unknown here where there are none larger than common Louisiana saplings. The good Richard brings me a glass of wine. Miss Hannah Maria Rathbone has just entered the salon and comes towards me with open hand, and I press that hand with pleasure, I assure thee, yes the hospitable hand out to be pressed.

The table was covered with a profusion of fruits and refreshments and everyone amicably helped themselves. Ah! I hear the clock strike 10. The company leave for their own habitation, and I am with the family only. I wish to see the new work on the *Birds of England*.[32] I was guided into a drawing-room and shewn it. Mr. Richard R. asked if I am a musician. I answered that I am fond of music. And in a moment my ear is pleased.

---

dubon's benefactor William Rathbone IV. Today it is within the city limits and is used as a student annex near Rathbone Hall, University of Liverpool.

32. Prideaux John Selby (1788–1867). His was the first attempt to portray British birds in natural size (Plates to Selby's *Illustrations of British Ornithology*, 2 vols., 218 plates of birds [earliest state]), some of which were drawn by Albert Mitford (later admiral), brother-in-law of Selby. Engraved by William Home Lizars, who was to

Now Lucy, what thinks thou of all this? Is it not delightfully kind in this good people to treat me so? Oh my beloved wife, my eyes were often on the eve of shedding tears of gratitude and pleasure the purest!

I did not like the work I saw on birds. I prefer Thomas Bewick greatly. Bewick, Lucy, is the [Alexander] Wilson of England. I do not know how to call the other. Indeed, I find no name for him yet. It is late; we all return to the parlour or salon. We are standing up when a servant comes and offers to pull my boots——draw my boots—yes. I could no more have suffered it than I could have restrained myself from esteeming the family Rathbone—not because I had holey stockings on, no. My stockings were not holey, but I thought rude in their presence. "Good night, good night"—to each and from each. Richard Rathbone precedes me and I follow the gentle flights of stairs to a chamber where I am again shewn comfort. Mr. R. takes me by both hands, desires me to make myself at home, and bids me good night. I wished to return his adieu with "God bless thee, good man," but the word[s] did not reach my lips in time. He was gone, and my heart felt the value of my wish, as the wish returned to it to rest there forever. Farewell, Dearest Friend. To thee also [Lucy], I send from my heart, a "God Bless thee."

I hear the clattering of rain against my window. I am up, dressed, and walking through the wet fields anywhere, everywhere. I see the Mersey; I reach it. The carriage is to be ready for me by 8, to go to A. Hodgson. I return, and the first object I see in the walk is the elder Mrs. Rathbone reading a pamphlet of Sismondi on religion. I accost her and she smiles happiness.

---

aquatint the first ten plates of Audubon's *The Birds of America*. [Nineteen Parts in Quarto, Edinburgh, 1821–34.]

Reissued in octavo under title: *Illustrations of British Ornithology*, 2 vols. (Vol. I was revised and republished with Vol. II in 1833) (Edinburgh, 1825–33). The Henry Bradley Martin Collection, New York City, has 306 of the double-elephant watercolor original studies—four volumes and portfolio—or 88 more than were engraved; 26 are by Mitford and the remainder by Selby and, perhaps, Mrs. Selby who, according to Audubon's 1827 journal, drew birds superbly (Maria R. Audubon, *Audubon and His Journals*, 2 vols. [New York, 1897]).

Simultaneously, Selby collaborated with Sir William Jardine (1800–74) on *Illustrations of Ornithology*, 3 vols. Quarto. 150 plates (Edinburgh, 1825–39). Second series: one volume of 53 plates (Edinburgh, 1843). The first wife of Jardine was Jane Home, niece of William Home Lizars.

I could have had a hundred breakfasts had I accepted one half of what was offered to me.

The carriage is at the door. I bid farewell and [hear], "Mr. Audubon, my daughter [Hannah] will be glad of the pleasure of accompanying you, if you have no objection?" Objections! In a moment I see her dark eyes through her veil, give her my hand, and we are both seated in the little carriage called her own. Two little Welsh ponies that two common men could take up on their backs draw us beautifully. They are beautifully grey and very well matched. I examine the large buttons on the livery coat of the driver, but I soon [turn] from them to remark the brilliance of Miss Rathbone's eyes. She is a very amiable indeed. "Now LaForest, I never knew thee to say that a lady was not admirable" [I hear thee say]. No. Oh, I beg thy pardon—recollect Miss XX, Miss XX, Miss XX, &c., &c. "Ah yes," [thee answers,] "I now remember well—what of Miss Rathbone?"

She inquires after thee and our children, talks of America again and again; and, having reached the house of A. Hodgson, I press her hand again and she returns to "Green Bank," whilst I proceed into the cottage. (I speak, recollect, as in England.) In a few minutes I see my kind friends again, enter the breakfast room, and find Mr. Hodgson reading prayers. Breakfasted. Wrote a note to William Roscoe, Esq., about meeting Lord Stanley, headed towards Liverpool. We are rattling at about a rate of seven miles per hour. It rains a little. I hold the umbrella, [and we say] "good bye, good bye." I have arrived and Mr. H. goes to his compting-house. He will call for me at the Institution tomorrow at 12 precisely.

I dined today with sister Ann and Miss Donathan. The time there quite agreeable. Ann dislikes England, and I like it. I saw Dr. Traill at his house. I also saw Mr. Hinks and perhaps 200 persons at the Institution; bought an umbrella for sixteen shillings; saw a boxing match; and good night, My Lucy—God bless thee, good night.

Liverpool   August 5th, 1826

Fine clear morning, weather somewhat resembling the 10th of March with us. Took my beneficial walk and breakfasted as usual before everyone at the Inn, say 8 o'clock—two hours later than we were in the habit of doing at Natchez, when the good old Doctors Dowe and Provan were pleased to drank of our coffee and eat of *thy* toast. Ah, America!

From the time I was up this morning until the moment I reached the Institution, my head was full of Lord Stanley, and indeed so much so that I believe thy sweet name did not come forth to my senses for perhaps an hour at a time. I am a very poor fool, to be sure—to be troubled and disturbed in mind at the idea of meeting an *English gentleman* called, *moreover, a Lord!* Yes, and particularly the bigger fool am I, as the English lords are not only more like others but are superior men—in manners, in interests, in kindness—to strangers, and generally the upholders of science in their country. But that confounded feeling is too deeply rooted ever to be extricated from my nature; and with a sense of pity towards myself I must get more and more accustomed to the disagreeable thoughts of dying with it.

The Misses Roscoe were at the Institution. I tell thee that because they have spent two, or perhaps three hours, looking at my drawings every day, I believe, since [the] exhibiting. How differently they view them from what I do! I wish to do more drawings and am sick of those already made.

Lucy, a lady came in (I mean at the Institution) her younger self at her side, and handed me a parcel directed [on the] outside to "Mr. Audubon." Her eyes sparkled, dark and yet mild. "Ah there, it was Mrs. William Rathbone," [thee guesses]. Yes Lucy, it really was, is, could be, no other with such looks, believe me. I received the packet with thanks, for she told me it contained letters from her husband for persons in Manchester and other parts. I put it up and bid her farewell for the present, took a few rounds around the room, and thought of opening the parcel to read the name[s] of the persons to whom the letters were directed. The parcel is opened. A pocketbook! My heart shook and the slenderest tendrils of it filled my frame and judgment with apprehensions. I trembled as I examined each compartment, lest it should contain more than letters. Gradually those feelings subsided and others warmed me again. I looked on this kindly token with affectionate regard, and kissed it in devotion! Ah England, 'tis no wonder thy renown is spread afar, possessed as thou art of such real, intrinsic worth. Lucy, I kissed the token again, and I hope thou shalt do the same.

Those are the moments of my life, Dearest Friend, when filled with reciprocating desire to please that I suffer so violently through want of means. I would have given all I had to be so situated as to be able to return something as kind to this amiable, accomplished lady. There was *a note* in the book—yes, Lucy—a note, beautifully written, well lettered, and dearer to me at that moment than all the notes on the bank of England! I looked at the book again, and twice again; and now that I am writing, it is so fixed on the table before me that I can easily see it and guide my pen.

Twelve o'clock came. I was dressed according to my means; i.e., cleanly decent. Mr. A. Hodgson is come, the portfolio is packed up, and not one drawing is to be publicly seen at Liverpool. We are off towards the cottage again, [and I am] filled again with the idea of meeting a lord. (I would rather have been engaged in a bear hunt.) I asked many questions to Mr. H., to enable me not to be too rude to Lord Stanley. He very kindly gave me all the information requisite and required. I am again sitting just opposite his sweet consort and he is tapping her rosy cheek amourously. Thou knowest how, does thou not? "Ah now my dear LaForest, proceed," [thee commands me]. I wish I could but—. Well, I will proceed. Mr. H. requests me to drank two glasses of wine. This good man enters into my feelings and down goes the wine. "Sir Lord Stanley," [is announced]. I have not the least doubt that if my head had been looked at, it would have been thought the body—globularly closed [or rolled in a ball]—of one of our largest porcupines. All my hair (and I have enough) stood straight on end. Here he comes—tall, well formed, formed for activity, simply dressed, well dressed. "Sir, I am glad to see you," [he begins]. Believe me I was gladder of the two to hear Lord Stanley thus address poor Audubon. [The] drawings [are shown] again. Lord Stanley is a good naturalist, and it is Audubon who says it.

"Fine," he remarks. "That is beautiful."

I saw Lord Stanley on his knees, looking at my work! There's

[one] for you, my countrymen!! What an erroneous stupid idea
we have of an English lord in America. Lucy, Lord Stanley is
very like Thomas Sully. I mean, he spoke the truth. He remarked *a fault* in one of my drawings and I thanked him for
that. He praised my drawings highly and I bowed to him.

We are at dinner and I look at him closely, depend upon it.
His large, uncovered forehead would have suited Dr. Harlan
precisely, [in order] to assure the Philadelphia Academy of
[Natural] Sciences (of which I never will be a member)[33] that a
conceptive natural power existed within that cranium. The acquired protuberance over his eyebrows would also have proved
to those academicians (if they are not what I fear they are) the
extent of his readings, speculative scientific powers, and powers
of exertion to acquire knowledge. I was friendlily requested to
call on him in Grosvenor Street in *town* (thus he refers to London). He shook hands in a friendly way twice, and, mounting
an elegant hunter, moved off at the rate of twelve miles an hour.
[My eyes] followed the rider. The horse was lost from view
[because of] the height of the hedges. I lost sight of his white
hat. The servant was entirely lost to view.

My dear friends, the Hodgsons, I must lose sight of also. I
gaze upon them, feel the pressure of their warmhearted hands,
and walk toward Liverpool. I reached a new city street and inquired if it would lead me toward Abercromby Square. "Yes,
Sir," [I hear]. There I go, anxious as I am to thank Mrs. William
Rathbone for her letters and the pocketbook. I reached her
house, but having found her employed with her handsome
daughter [Hannah], my powers proved inadequate, and I stood
or sat just like a fool again. Oh that I had been flogged out of
this miserable way of feeling and acting when young!

Mr. Rathbone came. Tea was on the table. Captain Kirkland
was announced. I looked at the sweet children gamboling
through their little garden. Here entered the *Intelligent Swiss*,
Melly. I took a full pinch of his improved snuff and we all talked
about interesting subjects. (*Of course not all at once, as is done in
some countries in Latitude 31°; I will not mention the longitude because from where I am it would require some calculation.*)

---

33. Audubon was eventually elected to membership.

"I must leave you all," I said. "Yes I must. I must call on sweet sister Ann. Good night." Down Mount Pleasant, down Rodney Street, down Norton Street. It is dark; I am obliged to walk up to the door and seek with my eye for the numbers. "Four." Two doors below—here it is—I knock. I know nothing about the proper way of knocking, but I knock as properly as I know how. I found sweet sister Ann and her sweet companion busily engaged at *Saturday night's work*. Lucy, Dear Friend, guess like a Yankee what they are at. Cannot, hey! Indeed! Well, let it go.

I left them. Went home. Found my bird [drawings] in my room, sent [back] from A. Hodgson. Found my eyelids drooping fast. Wrote this in a hurry. And wish thee good night.

Liverpool   August 6th, Sunday, 1826

When I arrived in this city I felt dejected, yes miserably so. The uncertainty of being kindly received, of having my work approved, were all acting on both my physical and mental powers. I felt as if nutritive food within my sight was not to be touched. Now how different my sensations! I am well received wherever I am known. Every object known to me smiles as I meet it, and my poor heart is at last relieved the great anxiety that has for so many years agitated it, by [the feeling that] I have not worked altogether in vain: that I may no longer be positively ashamed of the production of my pencil (whatever may become of those of my pen, as yet very far in the distant ground of the future, and I dread will never produce an effect unless, indeed, it be a bad one, and then I doubt if, speaking like an artist, it would be effective at all).

"Well my dear LaForest, these thoughts of thine have been known to me these eleven years at least. Give me, pray, thy day's expenditure," [I hear thee say].

Ah, expenditure—let us see. Bed last night, one shilling; breakfast, two; dinner, three; boot, sixpence; maid, sixpence; waiter, nothing this day; wine extra, three shillings; and sixpence at the Blind Asylum Church. That makes ten shillings sixpence—within sixpence sterling of two dollars. I will manage differently when I reach *town*, (speaking as Lord Stanley did [of London], and as I dare venture to say many more lords do, without ennumerating the gentlemen that do so also). It is rather a high way of living for *a naturalist;* nay, let me fully write, *an author.* However, it is about the rate we pay at the Mansion-house in Philadelphia, and the City Hotel in New York. It is indeed less than in Washington City. But to return to the true meaning of thy question (for which I would give half my authorship to have *in natura personalis*) I will say: up early as usual, and will not mention it again. Indeed I must beg thy pardon for thus miserably tormenting thy kind patience. I went to church, as thou seest in the bill annexed [above]. Now there's mercantile stuff for thee! *Bill annexed.* 'Tis many ["Bills"] I could bring forward as *living specimens,* I assure thee. But let's go to church.

It was filled to a cranny. I had dropped my sixpence in the silver plate, and had walked with that natural awkwardness, that I possess so eminently, smack into the middle of the central aisle, when so many female constellations flashed on my staring eyes that I stopped, dropped my head, and waited patiently for events. Do not believe that I was thoughtless—no indeed. I really thought then of thee, Dearest Wife, and wished thee at my elbow to urge me and to————. The conductor walks up, takes hold of my soiled glove with his snow-white hand, and leads me politely [to] the pew next to the priest. The music was exquisitely fine. I am rather a judge, thou knowest that, by my ears. But the sermon was not so. It was delivered by a *closet priest;* I mean, by one who had not studied *Nature herself,* beautiful Nature devoid of art. However, I understood that he was a young man of great promise.

I called on sister Ann and chatted some there. I understood she was writing to sister Eliza [Bakewell] Berthoud[34] and it gave me a desire to write also. She had evinced a wish to see thy watch, and I gratified her in that. The more I see of Miss Donathan, the more I like her. She is very amiable, and not ugly, believe me. Mr. Gordon had my Bonaparte's *Birds* carried to Dr. Traill to whom I had promised a view of it.

I dined, as thou has already been informed, by bill of fare, at 2 o'clock, in company with the American gentleman of Charles-

---

34. Mrs. Nicholas Berthoud, of Shippingport, Kentucky, was the former Eliza Bakewell, younger sister of Mrs. Audubon.

ton. I remained too long at table. I dressed afterward, packed up Harlan's *"Fauna"* neatly for Mrs. E. Rathbone [Mrs. William Rathbone IV], and, having taken my cane, pushed for the Institution. [There] Mr. Munro was to be, to escort me to Mr. William Roscoe, Sr.'s., where I was to take tea. No Mr. Munro.[35] But I found his wife and some little children, clean and pretty enough to be kissed, so I kissed them. Fatigued of waiting I am under way, have delivered the packet for Mrs. Rathbone to a servant at her door. Passed the Botanic Garden; entered *Lodge Lane* and Mr. Roscoe's habitation. It was full of ladies and gentlemen, all of his *own family*, and, as I knew almost the whole I was soon at my ease.

A great deal was said about Lord Stanley, his bird [drawings], and my Birds. I was asked to imitate the Wild Turkey call, and I did, to the surprise of all the circle. Hooted like a Barred Owl, and cooed like the doves. I am glad, really, that I was not desired to bray! "Why?" Why! Because an ass is an ass and it would have been rude even in an ass to bray in such company. Lucy, remark my position. I sat, rather reclining, my legs extended before me at the upper end of the room between Mr. William Roscoe and his son Edward, facing the whole of the amiable circle before me, and having to answer to question, as fast as I dare answer. Mrs. Edward Roscoe has rose from her seat twenty times, to come and ask me questions about my style of drawing.

The good old gentleman and myself retire from the group into the dining-room to talk about my plans. He strongly advises me not to exhibit my work without remuneration. He repeats his wish that I may succeed, and desires that I should take tea on Tuesday evening with him, when he will give me letters for London. Tea is presented, and I take one cup of *coffee!*

A beautiful young lady, called here a *Miss*, is at my side, and asks with the volubility of interesting youth and enthusiasm many, many questions about America. But they all appear very much surprised that I have no wonderful tale to relate; that, for instance, *I*, so much in the woods, have not been devoured at least six times by tigers, bears, wolves, foxes, or—a rat. No, I never was troubled in the woods by any animals larger than

---

35. Munro was on the staff of the Royal Institution, Liverpool.

ticks and mosquitoes; and that is quite enough, is it not, Dearest Lucy?

I must acknowledge, however, that I would like to have rode a few hundred miles on a Wild Elk or a Unicorn—or an Alligator. "Alligator!!!!! Who in the known world ever heard of such things?" [thee exclaims.] Heard, Lucy? I do not know; but I am sure hundreds of persons have *read* of the like having been performed by a man just about the size of common men. "Come, come." But indeed it is a fact the ride was taken by an Englishman.[36] Now I am sure thy wonder has vanished, for thou knowest as well as myself, and much better too, how many, many wonders and wonderful things *they* have performed.

Well, it is late. Son after son, each with a sweet wife under his care, bids me and their venerable father *good night*.

Lucy, the well bred society of England is sublimity of manners. Such tone of voice I never heard in America except when with thee, my wife! The gentlemen are—no, it is impossible to be more truly polite than they are. A gentleman at church this morning who knew me for a stranger, handed me book after book, the book that contained the hymns then [being] sung. With the page open and with a gentle bow, he pointed to the verse with a finger which was covered with a beautiful white glove. Have I not reason to like England thus far? Indeed I have.

I myself bid Mr. Roscoe good night, and, accompanied by a young man, come all the way to Norton Street where I stopped to rest and talk to Mr. Gordon about my views of the exhibition of my drawings *for Nothing*. He is of my way of thinking. We talked also about the relations in England, &c., &c., &c.

And now, it being six minutes past 12, I will bid thee Good Night, my love!!!!

Liverpool   August 7th, 1826

I am just now from the learned Doctor Traill's, and have enjoyed two hours of his interesting company!! To what perfection men like him can rise on this soil of instruction!

I have had a great deal to do this day in the way of exercise, I

---

36. Charles Waterton (1782–1865) wrote *Wanderings in South America* (1828); *Essays in Natural History* (1838, 1844, 1857); and papers communicated to *Loudon's Magazine*, several of them harshly critical of Audubon.

Audubon in buckskin, drawn for the Rathbone family in 1826.

assure thee. I visited first the "Panorama of Venice,"[37] a fine painting but not to be compared with the "Chapel of Holyrood." Then I called on a great amateur, and promised him a view of some of my drawings tomorrow. He told me that a Mr. Thornely of his acquaintance knew me well in New York twenty years ago, so that I am rapidly improving toward being acknowledged a *true one*. I ran to our good Consul Maury's office, saw him, and promised to call tomorrow for letters to London. Ran to my room and wrote to thee and to N. Berthoud. I had the letters copied for me by a young man recommended to me, to save time. I dined and ran to the Institution for a guide to Mr. Edward Roscoe, to whose lady I wished to shew my way of drawing. Mr. Munro politely offered his services and we reached the park where they live. I soon prepared everything and drew a flower for her and a Miss Dale, a fine artist. Talked a good deal of Bayou Sara, St. Francisville, and the country around thee, as well as of thyself and our children. Walked to Liverpool with Edward Roscoe, Miss Lace, and Miss Roscoe.[38]

I admired this afternoon very much the daughter of Edward Roscoe. She is a Roscoe, complete, to the fine nose, the fine eyes, the fine mouth, the fine form. Aye, sentiment of her grand father exists throughout her expressions, her look, her movement! She is a beautiful child! Now some sad critic who might fall upon my journal might say, "Why that poor fool praises every individual he meets," but then the critic would be mistaken. For I would try to [change] him for his vile heart, [for] art resides whilst I would continue with pleasure to write of Nature, naturally—i.e., as I meet it!

We passed through a kind of mound thrown up artfully and with taste, from which a fine extensive view of the city and the country around may be had.

Called [on] Doctor Traill, and his absence threw me towards my lodgings, where I was anxious to see how my copyist performed. I am satisfied with his handwriting but he writes per-

---

37. The panorama was an oil painting that was unfolded on a drum, forerunner of cinema.

38. Probably Jane Roscoe, who later wrote a sonnet to Audubon, published in *The Winter's Wreath* (1832). MS letter and poem (American Philosophical Society). For poem, see Ford, *John James Audubon* (Norman, 1964).

Jane Roscoe, daughter of William Roscoe,
remembered for a sonnet she wrote to Audubon.
Pencil drawing by Thomas Hargreaves.

haps too slow. Again to Dr. Traill, and, as I told thee before, met him and his lovely children. Two sweet daughters, perhaps thirteen and fourteen years old, sat with us whilst we talked *natural history* over. Tomorrow I am to receive what he calls a budget of letters from him.

I feel grieved that I have not been able to reach "Green Bank" tonight, to enjoy the company of my good friend Rathbone and the company of the peaceable country. I hope they will not think me rude. William Rathbone, Esq., [gave] me several letters of introduction, which I received at dinner. I would like to write more, but indeed I am wearied. I must have battered the pavements this day full twenty miles, and that is equal to forty-five walking through the woods. Sweet friend, Good Night.

[These personal letters and certain others Audubon entered in the back of his journal:]

LIVERPOOL, August 7th, 1826

MY DEAREST BELOVED FRIEND,

It is now three long months since I pressed thy form to my bosom. It is now three long months since thy voice vibrated in my ear with sound that none but a wife can utter. Absence from thee, my Lucy, is painful, believe me, and was I not living in hope to be approaching the long wished for moment of being at last well received in the learned world, and of being also likely to be remunerated for my labours, I could not stand it much longer. No really, Lucy, I could not. I am fonder of thee than ever in my life. The reason is simply this, that I hope shortly to gain the full cup of thy esteem and affection. God bless thee.

My voyage was long and painful in the extreme. It lasted sixty-five days. I wrote to thee twice during the time, by way of Havana and Boston, from the Gulf of Mexico. Yet I arrived safely. Was seasick at times, yet drew four nondescripts. Thus, my Lucy, I am in England, thy native country. Oh England, continue to be prosperous! I have been received here in a manner not to be expected during my highest enthusiastic hopes. I am now acquainted—I will say cherished—by the most prominent persons of distinction in and near Liverpool. I have been feasted, day [upon] day, in a manner truly astonishing. The more [so] as it has been done in that refined amiable manner that alone can reconcile me to society.

The letters of Vincent Nolte have proved of extreme benefit, and I owe him much. Clay and Clinton have insured me a respect due to our greatest men. The famous William Roscoe, Sismondi of Geneva, and hundreds of persons have been kind to me. Indeed I cannot describe my feelings to thee. I feel elevated from my painful former situation, and no longer have about me that dread felt in the company of some of those ostentatious persons with whom I have been obliged, through my will to follow my pursuits on the other side of the ocean, *to live*. But Lucy, how is my dear, dear son John Woodhouse Audubon,[39] and what a space divides us. May God grant our meeting again, and his will be done.

My drawings have been exhibited at the Royal Institution here, and 413 persons rushed in, [in] two hours. My fame reached distant places so quickly that [on] the third day persons of wealth arrived from Manchester to view them. I have been presented to one of the noblest and oldest peers of England, *Lord Stanley*. He, Lucy, knelt down on the rich carpet to examine my style closely. This renowned scientific man received me as if [he were] a school-mate, shook hands with me with the warmth of friend-ship, and wished me kindly to visit him often in Grosvenor Street, London. I dined with him and he spent five hours looking at my drawings, and said, "Mr. Audubon, I assure you this work of yours is unique, and deserves the patron-age of the Crown."

My plans are now as follows. I leave this [city] in a few days for Manchester, where I may remain four days; [on] to Derbyshire, [to remain] eight days to be presented to dif-ferent noblemen; to Birmingham; to Oxford; to London [for] three weeks; to Edinburgh [for] a week; then back to London, or perhaps at once to France—to Paris, [for] two

---

39. Born in 1812.

weeks there; and to my venerable kind mother[40] [for] two weeks. From thence [I] return to England by way of Valenciennes and Brussels.

I am advised to do so by men of learning and better judgment, who say that my work must be known quickly and in a masterly way. This will enable me to find where it will, or may be, published with greatest advantage. I have many comfortable nights at gentlemen's [country] seats in the neighbourhood, and the style of living is beyond all description. Coaches call for me and waiters in livery are obedient to me as if I myself was a lord of England. I hope this may continue, and that the end of all this may be plenty of the needful.

Now my beloved wife, thy watch—ah, thy watch—is as good and as handsomely trimmed as any dutchess's watch in the three kingdoms. Accept it from thy husband, Lucy, and wear for my sake the brooch that is with it. I will speak of the price another time. Mr. Roskell, the maker, a man of real worth to whom I was presented by a particular person, assured me no better watch was made in England. I send thee four changes of glasses. I shall not send thee anything more from Liverpool, but will fill thy lists in London and Paris.

Thy sister Ann Gordon is well. She exclaimed on seeing thy watch and mine, "Oh how beautiful, Mr. Audubon— this is rather extravagant." Mine, Lucy, cost 80 guineas. My seal has three engraved faces, and cost 15 guineas. Mr. Swift bought one from Mr. Roskell also, of lesser value yet very good. He saw thine and mine. He is now in Ireland. He was well—[do thou] let his friends know this. He was very good to me during the passage.

I will have from this place letters of great importance for me, amongst which will be [to] the Baron de Humbolt [sic], General Lafayette, Sir Walter Scott, Sir Thomas Lawrence, Sir Humphrey Davy, Robert Bakewell, Maria Edgeworth, Hannah Moore, &c. [(1778–1829), noted chemist]. &c. &c.

40. Audubon did not yet know of the death of his mother in 1821. He was her son by adoption.

I wish my Victor could have been with me. What an opportunity, for him, of seeing the highest circles of the
learned and the nobility of this island and of the Continent. Perhaps no ordinary individual ever enjoyed the
same reception. If I was not dreading to become proud, I
would say that I am, in Liverpool, a shadow of Lafayette
and his welcome in America.

I would have wrote sooner, but I disliked to do so until
something was done that might in some degree be worthy
of thy attention. It was not, thou knowest well, through
want either of inclination or affection. I found, at the Royal
Institution, persons who knew me well and knew [of] the
existence of my work, particularly the president, the famous Doctor Traill of this city.

I hope Louisiana has been healthy. Present my best regard to Mrs. Percy and the family, with my sincere thanks
for her kindness—also to [her brother] Charles Middlemist, and tell him that he may judge of what can be done
with the *Flora Americansis.*[41]

Should I succeed, my Lucy will be expected as early as
possible in either England or Ireland. My style of drawing
is so admired here that many ladies of distinction have
begged lessons of me. I could get one guinea for an hour's
attendance, [and] drive to and fro in the employers' carriages. My drawing of the Dove is worth 25 guineas, as
well as a dozen of eggs or, with you, sixpence.

Remember me to my good friend Bourgeat and wife,
and the whole of their connections at Pointe Coupée; to
that amiable young man, R. Stirling; to Judge Randolph
and General [Joove], to Dr. Pope, Virginia Hall, and her
husband. I expect to see his mother shortly. I like England
better than he did. If thou wert fond of kissing *young ladies,*
I would request thee to do so with my best love to all thy
sweet pupils, particularly my little woman Christianna,
whom I so hope is quite well recovered. If thou shouldst

---

41. Charles Middlemist, of London, visiting brother of Jane Middlemist Percy,
the mistress of Beech Woods plantation where Lucy Audubon taught school, hoped
to publish a *Flora Americanensis* but died before its true inception.

prefer doing the like with my friend Robert Percy [Jr.][42] do so, and present him [with] my best wishes for his happiness. I have forwarded all the letters I had [for mailing] from Mrs. Percy by mail except those for Mrs. Middlemist, on whom I shall call soon after I reach London.

The ladies here wear their watches out of sight, merely shewing the chain, but they have an exquisite way of looking [to see] what the time is; and in doing this [they] often exhibit the whole. I have been astonished at beholding the plainness of dress in large circles. No first-rate ladies wear any *fandangos*. I am as usual admitted free at all public institutions and exhibitions.

I am at one of the finest hotels in Dale Street, called the Commercial. I have wrote to N. Berthoud and requested him to send thee either [this] letter, or the copy, by our Victor.

Farewell, sweet beloved Friend and Wife, farewell. Believe [me] forever thine, most truly thine,

J. J. AUDUBON

LIVERPOOL, August 7th, 1826

MY DEAR NICHOLAS,[43]

The interest I have known you to take towards my welfare prompts me to write to you from this renowned isle. I hope it may reach you and find you and all yours well and happy. More than two months at sea, uncomfortable of thoughts as well as body, rendered me almost disconsolate, and I approached England with a heavy heart, on the eve of bowing to the world with my humble performances in my hand and a few friendly letters.

I reached the shore and felt it underfoot with a sensation too difficult for me to describe, beyond saying that it was painfully acute. I have been in Liverpool two weeks, and although not a scrap from my Lucy has yet reached me,

---

42. Son of Mrs. Percy of Beech Woods.
43. Nicholas Berthoud, merchant of Shippingport, Kentucky, husband of Mrs. Audubon's sister Eliza Bakewell. Victor Audubon, son of the painter, was apprenticed to Berthoud. Audubon took a defensive tone because Berthoud, who in 1819 bought him out in his bankruptcy, now ignored his aims.

my feelings this day are as bright, light and comfortable as they were—at my arrival—dark and gloomy. I have been most kindly treated by all respectable persons, and honored beyond the most sanguine expectations I had ever pictured to myself in those moments of peace and quietness that, like ancient dreams of happiness, have sometimes during my life touched my heart. I will approach the truth still nearer and say that I have been feasted on kindness. The second day after my landing, I presented some letters of Vincent Nolte of New Orleans, De Witt Clinton of New York, Clay of Kentucky, C. Bonaparte in Philadelphia, [all of whom] threw the doors of the first persons of distinction in this busy city open for my reception.

The families Rathbone and Hodgson and Roscoe, so renowned through Europe and America, procured for me all my heart desires connected with my views in visiting England. Two hundred and fifty of my drawings were exhibited at the Royal Institution, and my fame as an ornithologist and artist has flown from mouth to mouth with a rapidity that has quite astounded me. Persons have come from Manchester to view these collections of mine, undertaken in my youthful, playful moments of contentedness, and completed with a heart almost broken down by deepest sorrows. Nay, they have already had compliments paid them by one of the most learned peers of England. I have had the pleasure of being presented to Lord Stanley, an eminent naturalist and most amiable man, who kneeled on the carpet to examine my work. I dined with this influential man and am to see more of him in town; (this means, throughout England, the famous city of London).

I have, my dear Nicholas, some hopes of success at last; and should I not succeed I will return to my beloved America, my wife, and children with the conviction that no man will hereafter succeed. To give you an idea of the crowd that rushed to the Institution during the six hours (two hours each day for three days) that my drawings were in view, (about half the 450), at one sight, hung on a purple cloth ground for the purpose of exhibiting paintings of greater merits, I will tell you that 413 persons entered the hall in two hours. And I had to stand on view and listen to the plaudits of each individual. At the request of very many of my acquaintances here, I suffered the exhibition to be general, and [to be] opened from 10 until dusk; and it has been kept crowded. I will proceed slowly towards and to London, Edinburgh, and most of the principal cities of this improved garden of Europe, and proceed to Paris to show them there also. My wish is to publish them in London if possible, if not in Paris; and should I, through the stupendousness of the enterprise and publication of so large a work, be forced to abandon its being engraved, I will follow a general round of remunerating exhibitions and take the proceeds home.

I have seen sister Ann Gordon and her husband. They are well. I have purchasd a watch for Lucy that I have given to Mr. Gordon to forward to her. Be so kind as to send her either this, or a copy of this letter, by my dear beloved son. Assure him that I will take an early opportunity of writing him, and forward to him some music; and be so good also as to request him to draw, at his leisure hours, in my style as much as possible, and on that subject to read a long letter I sent him from Louisiana.

Now my dear Nicholas, kiss thy sweet family for me, my beloved sister Eliza, and believe me to be sincerely and truly

Thy friend,
JOHN J. AUDUBON

When you write direct to the care of the American Minister, London, he will always know where I am. Mr. [Albert] Gallatin is the present one.

P.S. As you may wish to know whom I am likely to become acquainted with shortly, I will say: the Baron von Humboldt, Sir Walter Scott, Sir Thomas Lawrence, Sir Humphrey Davie; and, as the venerable Roscoe was pleased to say, "it would not be a wonder, Mr. Audubon, if our King might wish to take a peep at the *Birds of America*; and it would do no harm." Should my Lucy receive this, May God grant her health and happiness. Yes, may she fare well until we meet again. Lucy, God bless thee.

I had no difficulty worth mentioning at the Custom House.

Liverpool   August 8th, 1826

Although I am extremely fatigued and it is past 12 o'clock, I will write.

This day I forwarded one letter for thee and one for Nicholas Berthoud via packet, copies of which are annexed here. Called on Mr. James Maury and received two letters of recommendation, for Mr. Albert Gallatin[44] and Mr. Welles of Paris. Shewed my drawings to several persons, and saw Mr. Thornely who knew me well in New York twenty-three years ago. I wrote a note to Mrs. Rathbone of "Green Bank" to beg her pardon for not having called to see her and family. I walked to Lodge Lane to take tea at William Roscoe's, but stopped at the Botanic Garden, where I drank the botanist's health in a glass of excellent port wine, it being his birthday. He presented me with a bottle of gooseberries for thee. I found at Mr. Roscoe's, besides himself an artist of merit in the landscape way called Austin,[45] and shortly afterward in came Mr. [Chester] Harding[46] of Kentucky, the renowned painter!!!! Three sons of Mr. Roscoe, and a lady besides Mr. Roscoe's daughter, were there.

Mr. R. spoke a great deal about my exhibiting my drawings for money, and advised me so earnestly and fatherly-like to do so that I Promised to see Mr. Gordon on the subject this night, and [said] that, if he thought well of it also, I should decline any further opposition. Mr. R. drew a draft to be inserted in the papers, and after my having spent a very agreeable afternoon there, I went to see Mr. Gordon.

But I must not forget to tell thee that Mr. Yates met me at the Institution and gave me several letters.

44. Albert Gallatin (1761–1849), Swiss-born American statesman, financier, Congressman, and diplomat.

45. J. G. Austin was a Liverpool architect.

46. Chester Harding (1792–1866) was a New England portraitist who visited Kentucky in 1820 to paint Daniel Boone and others.

Mr. Gordon has removed three doors from the corner of High Street near Hedge Hill Church, where I found the trio at tea. I shewed them the [gift] that Mr. Roscoe kindly presented me with—thy gooseberries. And I opened *the* subject—my subject. Then it was decided that I should follow the advice of Mr. Roscoe. Mr. Gordon accompanied me some distance toward Liverpool, and I reached my lodgings, where I found my clerk just about going, and Mr. Munro waiting patiently for me. He handed me a kind note from Dr. Traill, who had been so exceedingly careful of my Bonaparte [bird] book that he requested Mr. Munro not to deliver it to anyone but me!

I talked a good deal to Mr. Munro and read a little to him. Drank some ale with him and he left, quite pleased that my drawings were to be up again, and that I might do well with them.

I never had any desire not to be remunerated, quite to the contrary, but I wished it done in a most honourable manner. And as Mr. Roscoe says that it is by no means disgraceful, I will now shew them for a shilling, heart and purse are open, and may I be so fortunate as to receive plenty. My eyes positively give way. Farewell. Good night.

August 9th, 1826

William Roscoe, Esq., Lodge Lane, Liverpool
My Dear Sir:

I called on my friend A. Gordon, Esq., last evening after I left your house, and, having shewn to him the drafts you had made to announce the re-exhibition of some of my drawings, I also begged for his opinion, when the following was as near as possible his answer: "Mr. Audubon, no person, in my opinion, can advise you better than Mr. Roscoe, and his polite attentions to you prove the great desire he has that you should succeed, and I think that all different advice ought to fall before his!"—so that my dear sir, I hesitate no longer, and will now exhibit my drawings, if I receive permission from this day's committee at the Royal Institution, with a feeling entirely cleared of the clouds, that I dreaded before now, might have thickened and put a stop to my career.

Can I beg of you to be present at the Committee this

morning? Your influence is such you know that all difficulties would be levelled before you! Permit me to be forever your much obliged and obedient servant.

J. J. A.

Liverpool   August 9th, 1826

"So, poor Audubon, thy Birds will be seen by the shilling's
worth, and criticized no doubt by the pound. The fruits of thy
life's labour ought now to ripen fast, or the winter may yet be
spent without fresh embers, as thou has been used to during
thy happy youthful days. I am almost sorry for it. Indeed I have
more than once felt vexation at heart on the occasion, and yet
perhaps withal it may prove best. As for me, rest forever assured that it will never in the least diminish the affectionate regards and esteem that has been felt by me ever since I found
thee for the first time reclining at the foot of a magnolia, thine
eyes humid with the waters of admiration cast on the beauties of
thy resplendent friend, Nature! No Audubon, whatever may become of thee (speaking in a physical way), will never [keep] me
from speaking of thee, and thinking of thee, as I consider thee
to be, ever since then, and now!!—forever thine."

My beloved wife, the above note, (the hand-writing of which,
as well as the conception, thou knowest well), acquaints thee as
quickly as all the Liverpool papers that my Birds of America
(about one half, bye the bye, for the Portfolio No. 1 is yet sacred)
will be seen next Monday at the Royal Institution, not *pro bono
publico* but for the benefit of *E Pluribus Unum*.

So much is to be said on the subject that I will mend my pen
and write slow, although it be now half past 11. How many at
this moment, with a heart differently framed, are carousing,
cheating, cheated—ah, perhaps a thousand times more disappointed, after all, than I ever yet have been in my humble life.

I put the pen on my right thumb, and nipped it with the knife
thou hast given me. [J. J. A. was ambidextrous.] The pen is not
very good yet in some hands how well it would write. Oh venerable Roscoe, that I possessed thy sublime powers and could ani-
mate the coldest sense of feeling as well as thou art able! Lucy,
this exhortation has almost congealed the black fluid, and my

quill works now as if I had done wrong in attempting to express my opinion of that great man. I have daubed a canvas that nought but a Milton was ever fitted to outline [or,] the God of the sacred mount to finish!

I was forced to resort to my sixteen shilling umbrella this morning to take my walk. The sky and my heart were much troubled alike. The clouds [came] and went as my thoughts contraried and agreed. To be engaged is a useful [thing] on such occasions, and I went full six miles [round] about to my breakfast at my lodgings again. Wrote a note to William Roscoe, Esq., Lodge Lane, walked fast to the Institution, and Mr. Munro took it to be delivered. Fast to Dr. Traill, [only to learn] "Sir, the Doctor is not in." Fast to Mr. Hinks: "Sir, Mr. Hinks is not at home." However, having given my name, I was told letters were ready for me, and Mr. Hinks politely (thou mayest be sure) gave me three. I went as if in pursuit of a new specimen about the street, pulling out my watch and looking on its dial to see it mark 10, with much impatience.

It is 10, and I am in the entry room of Dr. Traill. A lady begs that I will wait, and taking from the shelf *La Beauté des Champs*, I try to be for a moment in the forests! Another lady, ah it is Mrs. Traill, [enters]. My eyes naturally fall. The lady with an English lady's voice asks that I put my name on a book she gives me, and, whilst [I am] doing this, her mouth pays me a compliment. I bow, Lucy. It is, unfortunately, all I can do tolerably. She disappears. I open the folio—a poem! William Roscoe's name. Oh my heart, support me! Had it not been a lady who handed me the book, like Mrs. Rathbone or [Mrs.] Hodgson or Roscoe's lady, I would have felt miserably vexed, but I remember immediately that I was in England, and that all here is genuine and with good heart and amiable sublimity. I at once scratched the following lines and closed the album with a blush:

> If my wanderings through America so dear!
> If my warmest desires to offer to others in an humble
>   manner the pleasures of viewing Nature's warbling brood!
> If the gratitude my heart feels toward the friendly hands, so kindly
>   inclined to guide me on, can entitle me to write, on this paper, my
>   name? Then I do it with all my Heart.

Had Byron, the famous, been near me (and I wish he had), what a slap he would have administered my hot cheek for three successive "If's" that I wrote there. As indeed he might have given me three blows, and I would no doubt have undergone the evolutions of right, left, front. However, Byron was not there (although he was in the house and close by), and I did not study the tactics from under his hand.[47]

Rap, rap. How is Dr. Traill? What a fine, friendly head—ah!—and heart, too!! "Here is the budget for you," [he says]. "Have you breakfasted—come in and set with us, do." Lucy, our most hospitable Kentuckians such as our friends General William Clark's daughter and Major Croghan [his son-in-law] were almost as kind.[48] I see two daughters, a son with hair of the color I admire in men most, and Dr. Traill breakfasting. My eyes view the whole, my heart feels more. I am shewn many curiosities. Having opened the subject of my exhibition to the doctor, [and] having told him that the situation of a naturalist at heart is very different to that of an exhibitor of drawings, he shook his head and said, "It is unfortunately too true, my dear Sir."

[Next] I am at the Institution, and find the following note:

My Dear Sir,
   I am glad Mr. Gordon agrees with me in the opinion as to the expediency of exhibiting your drawings to the public, and [I] will endeavor to be at the Committee this morning in order to promote that measure. Believe me,

Most faithfully yours,
W. Roscoe

Lodge Lane, Wednesday Morn: J. J. Audubon, Esq.

My good friend Richard Rathbone enters, and as usual asks me to go to "Green Bank," [and] is so kind as to apologize for his not having seen me. Now Lucy, who is the debtor, thinkest thou?

The trial is approaching. I am walking about the rooms. The Committee is setting. The keeper of the Institution says, "Sir,

---

47. Lord Byron (1788–1824), the poet.
48. General William Clark (1770–1838) was the father-in-law of Audubon's hunting companion in Henderson, Major George Croghan; General Clark was the brother of George Rogers Clark, military leader.

the gentlemen of the Committee wish to see you." I am in their presence, and all eye me with kindness.

It is resolved that the Committee pass an order to request me to exhibit my work. This, I am sure, will and must take off all discredit attached to the whole of this tormenting endurance of thought; and as it comes under such a commanding, honourable view of the subject, I agree to do so.

William Roscoe shakes my hand, appears not very well. He announces the illness of his son Edward, and leaves me all wonderment. Then I shall not go to dine at Mr. Roscoe's. Mr. Lyons, who so politely invited me this morning, I hope will know that I did not refuse him without a true reason, should he meet me in the street.

The secretary is busy instructing Mr. Munro [that] the reading rooms, steam packets, hotels, and newspapers must now all be acquainted with my bird creations and [my] entrance into this busy world. And *I* must try to visit Wales whilst the gentlemen and ladies of Liverpool visit the Institution next week.

As I returned to Dale Street I already thought that most of the people I met pointed at me with a sneer as they looked at my poor head and broad pantaloons. What a fool I am!

"My dear husband, thou art not a fool, and all who know thee at all will agree with me there. It is true that the want of a regular classical education is much against thee, as thy nature has induced thee to admire Nature. But thy heart is good, and, believe me, many learned men have very little of that to boast of. Give me a kiss and be satisfied."

Ah Lucy, thy kindness renews my faculties. Thanks, my Beloved Wife, thanks to thee!!!

Harassed as I was, I walked to sister Ann's. Saw Mr. Gordon off to London. Walked again to this my room, found my young man [the copyist,] at work. Dismissed him for the day. Have wrote this, looked on the moon as she silently inclines toward the Western world.———Good Night, God bless thee!!

Liverpool   *August 10th, 1826*

Why should my feelings be so dampened tonight? Why, because it rains, and I have just reached the Commercial with a wet coat, wet waistcoat, shirt and skin. Had it not been for this natural incident in a country where I was told I never would see the sun shine, not a portion of my *tout ensemble* would have been in the least moist.

However, this rain was not a deluge such as we often experience in our warmer latitude. It does not stop a man from walking on. Quite to the contrary, it invites one to walk faster, unless he is provided with a sixteen shilling umbrella, in his hand and open, when he may take it leisurely—not like me and mine. Tonight [my umbrella] was dozing silently in the corner of my room, close by the washing stand. I walked fast, believe me!

The morning was beautiful, clear, pleasant. I was on the mound betimes, and saw the city plainly and the country beyond the Mersey quite plain also. When first I left the Inn the watchmen watched me, and perhaps thought that I was an owl caught out by the day, as I moved not like a meteor but like a man either in a hurry, or a flurry, or crazy. The fact is that I thought of nothing but the exhibition. Nothing else could have entered my brains.

The wind mills are very different here from the few I have seen in America, and so are the watchmen. Both, I think, are taller and fuller about the waist. I do not like four square angles breaking on the foreground of a landscape, and yet I was forced twice today to submit to that mortification. But to counterpoise this, I had the satisfaction of setting on the grass, to watch four truant boys rolling marbles with great spirit for a good full half hour. How they laughed, how briskly they moved, how much they brought from afar again my younger days. I would have liked them better still, at this innocent avocation, had they been decently clean, but they were not so, and I arose after giving them enough to purchase a shilling's worth of marbles.

I had, and have still, some idea of leaving Dale Street and removing nearer to the Institution. Mr. Munro conducted me to examine a house and a *landlord* that I liked well enough. The price was just about suitable to my means, and I only requested to be suffered to think of it until tomorrow.

I began to feel most powerfully the want of occupation at drawing, and studying the habits of the birds that I saw about me; and the little sparrows that hopped in the streets, although very sooty-tinged by the coal smoke, attracted my attention greatly. Indeed I watched one of them throwing about him the manure of the street with as much pleasure today as, I recollect, in far distant places, I watched the jingling of the mellow thrush so clear. All this enticed me to prepare myself. I bought water colors and brushes of Mr. Hunt and paid dearer than in America. I made a note for pastels and give it to William Rathbone, Esq., to forward [colors] to London. I saw him, the "Intelligent Swiss," and Richard Rathbone there. I must say that I felt sorry that the eye of the Swiss convinced me that *he* was not pleased with the exhibition; I was the more sorry because I thought so much of his talents and amiability of character.

I am [next] strolling away towards the Park because I received the following when I returned to the Inn.

PARK, Thursday morning.

DEAR SIR,

It will give us much pleasure if you will dine with us—today at 4. I am sorry we were prevented seeing you yesterday. Believe me yours truly,

EDWARD ROSCOE

Lucy, as you go to Park place the view up and over the Mersey is extensive and rather interesting, although it is not formed with any of those gigantic dashes of extraordinary mountains, cataracts and dark valleys to be met with in the Alps. Yet this afternoon it afforded a calm moment of repose, to the eye, from the bustle of the street on the silent, faint, faraway mountains of Wales. Steam vessels moved swiftly in all directions on the Mersey, but they are not to be compared with ours of the [one and] only Ohio! No. They look like smoky floating dungeons, and I turn my sight from them. Almost immediately opposite the dwelling of Edward Roscoe is a small pond, and as I neither have seen nor heard of a frog in England, I surveyed its banks and its waters as closely perhaps as a winter Falcon might have done had he been *here* also. But not a frog, no. [There is] none of that grand wildness that surrounds our swamps and marshes, no imitation of the surly bull's bellowing to be heard here, no moccasin, nor copper-headed snake; not even a dozen of the snowy White Heron to be seen stretching their necks through the grasses, and watching the intruder's motions; not a garfish basking on the surface, nor an alligator dozing in the rays of the sun. No! The rose-colored Ibis and her friend the Roseate Spatula[49] never were[50] here, wild and charming. The sprightly trout was not seen shooting arrowlike from her grassy retreat towards the silvery fry. No, no vulture soared over my head, waiting for the spoils of my hunt; not an eagle was seen, perched in gloomy silence on the dreary aspiring top of the decaying, mournful cypress. No, the warblers attracted not my senses with their Notes, to me so pleasing. The minute Humming-bird crossed not my eye. Ah, my Lucy, I was in England, not in America!

Yet, Lucy, England has its charms! Yes, the Creator in his matchless works had bountifully granted to each portion, as he has given to each atom of his creation a full share of sweets. We only, through our errors, misconstrue his meanings and understand him not!

I am received by the beautiful daughter of Edward Roscoe. How lovely and lively also, her hair light and airy, naturally divided and in playful curls, some falling on her neck whilst others are vieing the beauty of her circling eyebrows. She touches the ivory of her piano. Her fingers move as if accidentally, and the hands reach my ears and my heart! Lucy, I merely told her that I liked music, and like a sylph she moved toward the musical instrument. How pleasing when compared to the absurd "Sir, I don't play—I can't play," and all those *sordid inclined ways* of the coquette's affected disposition. A moment with such an angel can never be forgotten.

Her mother comes. She is all amiability, and the chat is all of drawings. Her husband comes, and his graceful looks fill me with admiration. Lucy, there is really *un certain je ne sais quoi* in the Roscoe family!!!!!

Our dinner is simple, consequently healthful. So the dessert, so the wine. Two females enter the room and a young gentleman also. Some receive kisses, some do not, and I am of that unfortunate number, Lucy. I say unfortunate because, was I even to ask thy sister Ann to accept of a brother's gift, she would blush like a rose and say—nothing, Lucy.

---

49. *Roseate Spoonbill* (*The Birds of America*, Folio Plate CCCXXI).
50. Audubon often wrote "where" for "were" at this stage.

Ladies' riding habits are quite strange in appearance to me. They are so cumbersome (I speak of those I saw) that the wearer must be completely occupied in holding the superfluous cloth up with both hands to save the [rider] from inevitable falls, and give to the fair sex of England a good deal of what I *conceive* to be the walk of a Chinese belle; for I never was in China, that thou knowest well, and the little knowledge I have of that country has been through the perusal of *Lord McCartney's Faux Pas*.[51]

The ladies of whom I here speak are sisters of Mrs. Roscoe, and thou knowest as well as myself that *sometimes* sisters are alike.

Tea is announced. It is a singular fact that, in England, dinner, dessert, wine, chat, along with the wine and tea drinking, follow each other so quickly that was it not necessary to partake of that last—to remove from one room to another, it would be a constant repast. No matter, it is very agreeable, and I am coming round fast, I assure thee, to the good English way of living. [From these pages] I read to the matched pair [concerning] a pair of my Liverpool days, bid them good night, [am] accompanied by the husband toward High Street a good ways, and listen to musical sounds from the Botanical Garden. Before I proceed let me say how shocking it was to my eyes, whilst running across the fields, to see: "Any person trespassing on these grounds will be pursued with all the rigour of the law." This must be a mistake certainly. This cannot be English liberty and freedom surely. Of this I intend to know more hereafter, but after I saw the printing on the board there is really no doubt. But let us return to the musical sound from the Botanical Garden—flutes, hautboys, clarinets and horns, drums, bassoons and cymbals, all in perfect unison, gave to my understanding, "God Save the King." Aye, I say so, and more than so—God save every good man besides the King!!! The sound is fainting and indeed I myself have very nearly fainted, walking too fast toward Hedge Hill Church. But I have reached the third door from the corner of High Street, and see the interesting Miss Donathan through the windows, have walked up the stairs, and am resting opposite

51. George Macartney (Earl) (1737–1806), diplomat, colonial governor, and first British envoy to China, 1792–94.

her eyes. In comes sweet sister Ann. I drank two tumblers of water; and a distant relation of thine, perhaps no relation at all, comes in. Ah, the man has talent for painting! It is imprinted just over his eyebrows. His name, Lucy, is [Bakewell,] the same that thou wert so kind to abandon for mine. [No relation; not identifiable.]

Ten o'clock: pears and plums and wine have been tasted, but none of the nectar that flows on thy sweet sister's lips. No, I would not kiss her, Lucy, for all the world. "Ah indeed, and why, pray—thou wert fond of kissing her formerly. I have many a time seen her on thy knee, looking at thee with a kind eye," [thou sayest]. Yes, 'tis all true, but Lucy, time effaces time, and those times of yore are, I fear, never to be felt again.

Mr. Bakewell, as we walk along, speaks artist-like, and I know must be like an artist in many other ways. But good, my friend, Good night.

Liverpool   August 13th, 1826

Thou wilst not call me either lazy or careless for my not having wrote as usual every night the poor journal when thou knowest the fact that effectively prevented me last night, and the night before last, when I entered my room full intent on doing so. After throwing my coat off, opening my watch to judge of the time, and hanging my cravat on the armed chair on which I always sit to write this pitiful book, my ideas flew suddenly to America so forcibly that I saw thee, dearest friend!!— ah, yes, saw thee covered with such an attire as completely destroyed all my powers. The terror that ran through my blood was chilling, and I was like stupefied for a full hour. No, I could not have moved a pen had the Universe been at stake.

Both nights I undressed slowly, mournfully, and bedewed my pillow with bitterest tears. It is not strange. Not a line from thy pen has yet reached me. Vessels, one after [another], have arrived from the dear country that bears thee and not a consolatory word has yet reached my ear to assure that [thou art] well and happy. The further distant, my Lucy, the more I need this consolatory cup of friendship and of love. Oh do write, or *I will not be able to write at all.*

To one less fixed on distant objects, these days would have been quite pleasant—nay, days [of] happiness in a land of strangers! But although I felt happiness, it [is] now like the lash of a sharp whip striking the slaves in irons on distant shores, who, thoughtless about all but his far-gone country and friends, feels not the blows.

Even now tonight, after having been before my God to pray for thy sake, and for happiness and salvation, at the Blind Asylum's Church, [I feel so].

I spent the remainder of the day at my old and kind friend's, William Roscoe. Seen thy sister well and the sun setting cloudless. Still I cannot write and am forced to drop my pen. Ah my Lucy, how art thou? Does superstition prey on me, now, as it did on the fourth of July last, when so dull did I feel at sea that I believed, then, some great and dismal event was taking place on our Eastern shores. Oh may God preserve thee still, and may he——. Oh my Lucy, the death of Jefferson[52] and his friend [John Quincy Adams on the same day] have filled me with dire apprehension. Do write to me?

Liverpool   August 14, 1826

Now that my spleen is gone with the breeze (and I can hardly tell where, for the wind does not take it toward America), I can set and write and think of thee, hoping thee well. I have spent a good, nay a happy half day at the "Green Bank" of Mr. Rathbone. It is, however, a fact that although I was well aware that it was the place most congenial to my feelings at all times, when far away from thee, I felt that shameful bashfulness that so much distracts my life, although I was anxious to go there. Reluctantly, and without positively knowing why, I put it off day after day, glad to have a tolerable, true excuse to offer any one of the members of that hospitable and friendly habitation.

But yesterday, Lucy, I dined with Mr. Roscoe, Sr., with part of his family, and spent the day well there also. I merely say this now because I was too miserable last night to write it, or indeed write anything else. "But why, my dear LaForest, shouldst thou

---

52. Died July 4, 1826, on day when Audubon had a presentiment of evil while aboard the *Delos*. Adams died the same day.

be so low spirited, when so kindly treated?" [thee wonders]. Indeed Lucy, to thee I can make no other apology than this. I thought—I dreaded—this exhibition of my poor Birds. And now that they were to be positively pointed at with the finger of the venomous critic, who "critics" merely for the worth of his shilling, I dreaded to encounter even my best friends, and wished myself in the depths of our most gloomy and retired cypress swamps.

But now that I have, this day, reconciled, I hope, those good friends of mine, and have seen benevolence, charity, hospitality and comfort, all hand in hand wishing me welcome, I feel differently. So does the soldier that is urged by the true spirit of his command to meet even death with a meek countenance and a heart free of reproach!

It is best, however, to tell the truth. When I reached the avenue leading to my good friends I felt as if suffocating, doubted if I should proceed or retrograde, or indeed if I should sink down on the spot. Anyone but thyself would think me pusillanimous, and all would wrong me. Have I not met and defeated the wild, voracious Panther, and the active Bear, attacked the Wolves during their slaughter, and defied the Wild Cat's anger. Ah yes, and again and again, for such deeds, I feel myself fit; but Lucy, to wound the heart of *Man* is beyond my courage, and more I acknowledge myself vanquished and outdone!

Well, my Lucy, I at last went forward, and met a female angel [at] the door, the eldest daughter of Richard Rathbone, beautiful in all her purity, perhaps ten years of age. Oh how I did wish to kiss her, but I did not, and do not know why unless indeed it was fear that she might blush and feel worse than I. The venerable *Baucis* received me, her son Richard, but both, although kindly, said that they had almost given me up. I trembled lest it might prove so. But no, they are still kind, and the gloomy sky, instead of sinking my spirits, raised my gratitude. Ah oh yes, my Beloved Wife, I prayed God to bless thee to the full edge of the Golden Cup.

There I am happy! I am seated with Bewick's book on *Quadrupeds* in my hands, one eye viewing that friendly creature the dog, and the other that lovely child, my little friend Basil, at his

play. "Pray, what did the sweet child play at?" [thee asks]. Our
[son] Woodhouse, my Lucy, under thy care and affection did
study the first elements of Nature's beautiful arrangement. The
same with the little friend Basil. The mother, with an eye just as
blue as thine, has a book of insects before her, and although intent on another book she cautiously attends her "fruit," anxious
that it should grow full of suavity.

The sister is writing a letter, I believe, the nephew is examining the minute pistils of a floweret. *Baucis* has her heart set on a
book full of true religion, and another nephew negligently reclining on his seat is also engaged on a work beyond my comprehension. Lucy, thou knowest with what pleasure I enjoy
these scenes of entire peace and quiet. Thou knowest also how
quietsome they are to the mind. The busy world of Liverpool,
like the troubled, muddy waters of the Missouri with its whirl-
pools and contrary currents, is probably at this moment [the
scene of] individuals encroaching, each on each; and like the
greedy current, undermining each contiguous object to force an
unfairly obtained course, whilst *I* am gazing on the placitude of
"Green Bank," and from its green position trying to produce a
high idea of its greenness on the paper before me. Wert thou to
see the kindness of thy fair country men again, Lucy, thou
wouldst return to thy native land with a heart filled with de-
votedness *toward them.*

I neither can write, nor sketch, or draw, or paint to my liking,
but I am sure I can easily say that Mrs. Rathbone is looking over
my work and fastening, with the brooch that a moment since
fastened the gauze over her fair bosom, the paper before me to
stop the breeze from disturbing my black lead touches, whilst I
make a light sketch of the scenery.

How I have gazed on these *green banks!* How much I have
thought of English hospitality and compared it with that of our
independent, brave, full-hearted Kentuckians and Virginians
and every other member of our happy Union, and said to myself, with a wish that the world might proclaim it to the universe, that never ever existed the Britons in reality! [In such ec-
static lines Audubon sometimes lost his train of thought, as he
appears to have done here.]

We have dined. I have rambled through the grounds, the

greenhouse and *jardin potager*, led by the amiable and compla-
cent nephew. I express my wish to return to Liverpool again,
and Lucy I am walking most happily, bearing the quiet frame of
Miss [Hannah] Rathbone through and across the field and along
the road that ultimately leads us to William Roscoe. I see the
learned portion of his head, and conducting Miss Rathbone
to Miss Benson's, return to William Roscoe and discover that
Miss Jane is taking her Greek lesson. Ladies here are learned
and amiable; that is a word more than the ladies of our Continent are entitled to. Yet I will acknowledge that all our ladies are
fully provided with either the one or the second qualification. I
am moving six miles per hour until I meet Richard Rathbone.
We walk. We part—I, never to part with him in my heart, believe me!

The wind blows quite a cold blast. It is quite like November all
around me except at my heart. That is not cold. I hope to receive
a letter from thee. Vessels have arrived from my America. I
hope soon to kiss thy signet and—oh, my wife, Lucy, Dearest
Friend, God bless thee! Ah yes. Good Night.

[Later:]

I arose suddenly, thinking that Mr. Munro had just left my
room, when he kindly came to give me an account of the
exhibition.

I must go to sleep with the thought that I am debtor to the
Liverpool people [by] fourteen shillings. Now Good Night.

"Green Bank," three miles from Liverpool
Tuesday, August 15th, 1826

This morning, Lucy, I ought to have been at the dwelling of
the venerable Roscoe by 5 o'clock. I had, last evening, promised
to do so, and to leave at his door a dozen of *sword beans* that I
had also promised to that good, generous gentleman. But judge
of my surprise when, after having ransacked my trunk and
thrown out of it all my chattels and apparel on the carpet, I had
the mortification to discover that I had parted with all of them. I
have given perhaps a dozen to that friendly man, but I regret
very much he has had no more, as he appeared quite pleased
with the idea of rendering them indigenous to this country.

No letters from thee, Dearest Friend, no not one word. The wind blew quite a breeze. It rained during the early part of the morning, and it was not until 12 o'clock that I reached this *enchanted spot*. Mrs. Rathbone, the benevolent mother, the Queen Bee of this honeyed mansion, received me alone, and I had the pleasure of contemplating her mien and of listening to the heavenly gifts of her heart through her conversation. How gratifying it is to be able to believe that not all our species has yet felt of the fault conferred on man at the Creation, that there yet exist spotless, matchless, divine beings to adore, to venerate, to look up to as the resemblance of the Omnipotent God that gave them breath!! Yes, dearest Lucy, such are the heavenly gifts that are to be seen under this roof, and so warming with purity are the powers of this happy being that all around [her] glows with calm contentedness and truly parental affection.

I [had] been here perhaps one hour, perhaps more, perhaps less. I felt not the time passing. I panted for more, to enable myself to bring my understanding under the rays of her whom I never can cease to admire and respect! I saw the family gradually enter, and I feared not this day to kiss all the sweet children of my friend's wife. How pleasing it was for me to contemplate these dear little ones, peaceably engaged in reaping the benefits of a good education, seated on their little benches in different parts of the room. Each held a book, and each held their eyes on the book before them.

The botanist is in [our presence], and also Miss Hannah Maria. We are all employed again, for I myself have taken my Bewick and am looking on the careful Saragoy [opossum] nursing, guarding, her tender young. How tranquil even my heart in such situation. We dined as yesterday. The afternoon is blustery, windy, and altogether fit to deepen the feelings of the American visitor that is now within. Yet it is well known that I am fond of much exercise and of Nature's contemplation. Then a walk is proposed. The dog that came from Kamchatka shores is [unleashed] for me to look at. Miss Rathbone is ready, and, accompanied by the nephew, we three depart. Ah, how I did wish that *I* could have conducted them towards the "Beech Woods" rendered by thee so dear, and shewn them our wild scenery of the woods of America! But no, it could not be, and we walked between dreary walls, contenting ourselves with the distant objects without the sweet privilege of moving freely to and fro, to right and left, or without advancing toward any particular object that might, [for the] wish, attract our eye. Thus we reached the Mersey, and I saw the free gull floating on the breeze, checking her course, falling on the waters and seizing her prey. I saw the busy, brisk little Sanderling searching cautiously the lesser bivalves. I saw the same objects on the shores of my distant country's streams [in my mind's eye], and wished to be possessed, for a while, of the powers of the eagle's nervous pinions that I might at one flight sail to thee, Dearest Friend, and acquaint thee of these English friends that every moment become dearer to me.

We are seated and feasting our lungs on the rarified breeze— our eyes on the distant scenery. Now we proceed on our return.

Is it not very shocking that whilst, in England, all is hospitality within, all is aristocratic without, no one dares *trespass*, as it is called, one foot on the grass. *Signs of large dogs* are put up to [warn] that further you must not advance. Steel traps and spring guns are set to destroy you, should you prove foolhardy. And to finish our exercise we were forced to walk [single] file on the narrow portion of a wall, fearing the rebuke of the landlord around whose grounds we had a desire to ramble. But my Lucy, this is all a trifle—read on. Beggars in England are like our ticks of Louisiana; they stick to one, and sting our better feelings every moment. England is now rich with poverty, gaping, aghast, every way you may look. Good honest people are forced here to beg not for money, Lucy, but—as yes—bread. "Bread," the beggar says, "not for me—I am strong yet—but for my poor famished little one."

[Do I hear thee say,] "Strike not my heart thus, my dear husband, do [not], pray; thou certainly is not aware how thou grievest me." No more then, but only join in this prayer, *May our Heavenly Father have Mercy on them!!!*

Lucy, look at Richard Rathbone seated with his mother on the same chair, look at them; dost thou feel the heavenly power that acts around us? Dost thou hear the suavity of their reciprocal proofs of adoration? Dost thou see the group improving with daughters, friends, and nephew, and younger children, almost clinging around her? Lucy, my heart is bursting with delight. I also will adore her!!

Gradually the day has vanished. The stormy night seems to rally all friends together, and I am, Lucy, going to open my heart to these good people. I am going to read [, from my journal,] of thee and myself and of our dear children, and of my feelings—! Lucy, *Honi soit qui mal y pense!!!* I am astounded. Mr. Richard Rathbone, who was reposing on a sofa, has approached the table. All are listening to me. My eyes are burning. Then conceive the situation of my heart! But Dearest Friend, they call my tottering essays, at giving thee the thoughts that act upon my absence from thee, quite agreeable to them. I am not now so much choked. I drink, and I read on—perhaps [about] half a dozen of my days. Ah Lucy, could they hear of my nights, at this distance from America and from all that God gave me to render life dear! But no, I will not make *thee* miserable— read on.

A portfolio [of verses] has been brought [to] the table by the mother who will not, through her kind affection, suffer either son or daughter to go for it. And out of it emerged [William] Roscoe's soul!! I read. I listen. Alas, I can but admire [these poems.] Ah I do more, I live with the surety that Roscoe will never die!!!

Friends, dear friends, Good Night. May our God bless us! Lucy, thank them for the good health they just now all wished thee and my friends here and in America. My enemies if I have any, to all Good Night! Good night to my own venerable mother, to my children Good Night, to thee the soul of my powers, Good Night. I have reached the same chamber where I rested before. I have in my hands both Richard Rathbone's hands, and we feel mutual pressure of hands. He talks of his mother as I wish every son would do, gives me, with his blessing, a letter, and we part to meet again. Lucy, Good Night.

"Green Bank"   August 16th, 1826

Well, my Sweet Friend, I am for once again writing in the chamber where I have slept, free from the bustling noise of the city.

Green Bank.

I walked early to Liverpool. I was anxious to see if my happiness might be improved by reading a letter from thy hand. I reached there so that my breakfast was over by 7 o'clock, and I took a long walk again along the different docks to pass the time and employ my mind and judgment. I saw a vessel undergoing the reinforcing action of coppering. The weather being very beautiful, I looked with pleasure on the active scenery about me, remarked the enormous size of the horses that here can singly, in one cart, draw as many as sixteen bales of cotton. They looked well, fat, sleek, and sufficiently active for the purpose intended for them to perform. I called at the Post Office, but no letter.

I went to the Institution and wrote there again a good deal. Saw Dr. Traill and we spoke much of my plans. I found the doctor highly scientific. We examined three Egyptian mummies. Many persons peeped at my Birds as I peeped at *them*. However, how many English shillings were received I cannot tell. I did not inquire.

I took tea at Mr. Edward Roscoe's, and rode in Mrs. Lace's carriage close to this place, [near] where I descended from it and walked the remainder of the way.

I felt happier tonight than I have done for months. The good ladies were at work when I made my entrance, and the time passed away very agreeably. I read again to them. My friend Richard and others were absent. The moon shone beautifully, and I hoped that thou might be gazing on its silvery robe as I was, with my eye bent that way. We walked and chatted, all [at] ease. The remainder of the friends all arrived, and found us all seated [facing] the timid yet brightest [star?] of the night. How pleasing music would have been to me then, ah music from thee! We returned home, and I am just finishing a day not too complex with incident, but one very happily spent. All I longed for was for thee. Miss [Hannah] Rathbone presented me with William Roscoe's poems. Lucy, God bless thee. I have just shook my friend's hand. Good night.

Liverpool   August 17th, 1826

My spirits are low tonight, Lucy. I am in Dale Street, not at "Green Bank." My eyes are cast—indeed perhaps sullenly—on the angry-looking clouds that chafe the full moon—not as they were last evening when seated in the rocky alcove of my friends' grounds and [my eyes] were cast on the same sublime object, [but] with different thoughts. My spirits, my dear wife, are indeed very low. The winds impart dismal tokens in their howlings; and the voice of a public crier at an auction room, not far enough distant from me, finishes the very uninteresting foreground of this evening's miserable picture. But let me return to "Green Bank" and start like a Lark from my nest at the dawn this morning, and rove through the dews and watch the timid bird's motion that flies from bush to bush before me.

Let us return to the Mersey and look on the country in Wales, on the calm, serene sky, and listen to the voice of the Quail here so shy. Ah yes, walk with me on the tide-beaten beach, and watch the Solan Goose in search of a retreat from the cruel destroyer, Man.

Seest thou the smuggler, how he runs away? How little he suspected that Goldsmith's Burchell[53] was after him! Yet I must acknowledge he made me pant before I reached him. I have regretted, all day, my adventure of this morning, and I am sorry to think now how cruel it was in me to frighten the poor fellow so. Lucy, I had my sword-cane, and the moment the stranger dropped his bag and ran from me, that moment I drew the dangerous blade and, crying unmercifully, "*Stop thief!*," made my way towards him in a style that I am sure he never had seen used by the gentlemen of the Customs that no doubt were rather drowsy. Poor fellow, had he known me as I know thee and as I am known to thee, his eyes would not have started from his head as they did, nor his heart have swelled with apprehension. There he was, begging for mercy—said it was the first time, and only for some rotten leaves of tobacco. I positively did wish he had had all that I once purchased for Richard Atkinson of Richmond. The boat that had landed him quite in my view fled by rowing off like cowards instead of landing and defending their companion who was no longer visible to the smugglers on board.

I was astonished at such conduct from Englishmen. I told this

---

53. "Mr. Burchell" was the pseudonym of Sir William Thornhill, a character in *The Vicar of Wakefield*, by Oliver Goldsmith. He believed that care and grief came from another sphere. His famous ejaculation, "Fudge!" was a favorite of Audubon's.

poor being to arise and bring the bag. He did so. No Lucy, much
is said here about the abject state of slavery in our truly United
States, but I never beheld there a thing shaped like a man so
completely subdued by fear of punishment. He walked to the
bag and brought it. I told him that a smuggler was an enemy to
his country, and that he deserved severe punishment. (Recollect
my sword was already to defend me.) He cried and said, "Oh,
for God's sake save me—take the tobacco." Poor fellow, I never
even smoked a single cigar, and that thou knowest well. I could
stand this no longer. I was [in dread lest] some real officer of the
Customs might appear and interfere in a very different manner.
I told him to clean himself and to be careful he never should do
such an outrage again. I had one of my pockets disagreeably
laden with copper stuff that the shopkeepers give here and call
pennies. I gave them all to him, told him to look at my face well,
and go. He did look, Lucy, with eyes that I cannot describe or
understand. He prayed aloud for my salvation and made for a
thick hedge, where he disappeared from my view.

I looked on the river. The boat was out of my sight. I would
say that this poor fellow had perhaps fifty or sixty pounds of
fine Virginia clean-leaf tobacco in the bag and two pistols which
he said were not loaded. Of this I am not quite sure. But can-
nons in the hands of he who fears either the laws of his country
whilst acting against them, fears not God but fears men!

I thought as I scraped the mud from my boots that I had been
rather too rash, and also that if the man had been an accustomed
villain he might have shot me dead on the spot. I have thought
of this event all day. I thought for a while that I had seen this
very man amongst the crowds of pilots that boarded the "Delos"
in the Irish Channel. He was dressed precisely like them, and
so, as well as I could see, was everyone on board the yawl that
plied away from me, a single man against five had they landed.
What a pretty figure I would have made with my small sword,
against men that were apparently full as stout as myself!

I am neither a Canning[54] nor a Gallatin. But Lucy I cannot
think that Canning, with all his cunning, is equal to our Gal-

---

54. George Channing (1770–1827): "Foremost man in the highest Parliament
after the death of George Fox" (*Dictionary of National Biography*). Foreign minister

latin. "Hush, my husband—come, no politics, I pray." Well, be it so.

I walked toward the "Green Bank" again, thinking of the smuggler until I saw, over a wall, a man digging potatoes. They were small and indifferently formed. The season has been uncommonly dry—and hot also—the English say. For my part, I am almost freezing.

I have done a great deal this morning, and yet it is only 7 o'clock. I reach "Green Bank," and as nobody is up I start again another way, not at all anxious to imitate the trusty officers of his Britannic Majesty. I have laid on the grass and am listening to the rough, rude voice of the Magpie. It is not the same bird, I am quite [sure], that we have in America's Northwest portion, but this I will detail when my Arkansas Magpie comes to view through my publication.[55]

I see that it is 8 o'clock, and toward the house I make again. I now enter. The domestics are cleaning. I open a small book, "Elements of Botanical Instruction." Miss Hannah Maria is come, dressed in a Greenfield riding habit. Lucy, she is a very kind, good girl, quite the child of Mrs. Rathbone. [Presently] she is writing. A stranger had he looked on would say, "What! The man cannot be reading with attention, certainly." But I would answer that I was, and prove it. For [the letter the girl is writing] is directed to "Constance from 'Hann'ia.'" It is the mother's wish that the daughter should study botany during her sister's absence, &c., &c. But thou, Lucy, knows as well as Mrs. Rathbone what an observer I am with the use of only one eye.

I hear, I see, I kiss the sweet children. The breakfast bell is ringing and we are seated round the table. To town Mrs. Rathbone and I are going, but before this, Lucy, look at my friend and how he kisses his wife. Happy pair, ah happy family all! Never, never have I seen such regularity of kind dispositions and feelings. But Lucy, look at thy friend, I am now really rolling in the little carriage with the *Queen Bee* of "Green Bank." And now I am presenting my respects to Mrs. William Rathbone, who, thou knowest well, has auburn hair and black, learned eyebrows. The lady of the [gift to me] of the pocketbook.

---

55. Presumably *Columbian Jay* (American Magpie: Folio Plate XCI).

I heard that my pastels have not come yet, and [so] am rolling in the little carriage again to the Institution. There, have I not done a good day's work, before the seven-eighths of the good rich people of Liverpool have opened either their eyes or their hearts on the poor that, in great patience, are waiting at the door?

I shewed thy "face" today, Lucy, to all my friends, and [the younger] Mrs. William Rathbone is, she says, just thy age. Then she is not old, nor thee, nor any amiable woman besides ye both, had each of you twice doubled each day you have spent in this world.

I received the following note from Mr. Austin, and three letters from Edward Roscoe, Esqr., who was so kind to call on me here. I answered Mr. Austin and this afternoon began a painting of the "Trapped Otter" [56] with the intention to present it to my good friend's [R. Rathbone's] wife, if well done.

I then proceeded to William Rathbone and spent a most agreeable, peaceable evening. A Quaker Lady named Abigail [Dockray], [57] a cousin of Richard Rathbone, and, I believe, from Manchester, made me straighten myself a little at first glance. But it was only momentary. *She* spoke so plainly that my understanding was not embarrassed. We talked mostly on the present situation of England—her poor, her institutions, &c. It grieved me to hear [her] say that non-intercourse had taken place between the U.S. and the British West [Indies]. I should now conclude that this government has really a wish to emancipate both white and black slaves. Here for the want of bread, and there also, where all will arise *en masse*, and exhibit to the world again

---

56. *Otter in a Trap,* oil on canvas, 42 inches by 28 inches, is identical with *Canada Otter,* which forms Plate LI in *The Viviparous Quadrupeds of North America.* Audubon first painted it in watercolor in Henderson in 1812. He rendered it in oil at least seven times. Contrary to a declaration published in 1965 that this was his first American mammal study, we have it on his own authority that he drew a mink at Mill Grove, 1803–5. His sketch *Myself* compels the inference that he drew both birds and quadrupeds in Henderson. Audubon presented the oil to Mrs. Richard Rathbone, an artist of some talent whose husband later presented it to the Royal Institution in her behalf. She felt a strong aversion to the plight of the otter. For the Audubon presentation letter, see pages 170–71.

57. Abigail Dockray (1783–1842) married David Dockray in 1805. Her mother, Sarah Benson, was a cousin of Mrs. William Rathbone III, who named her fourth son Benson. Mrs. Dockray was a Quaker minister and prison reformer.

Otter in a Trap. *Oil on canvas, life size. Audubon finished this painting of his "favorite" subject in less than a week and presented it to Mrs. Richard Rathbone. Several copies exist. This is the first made by Audubon in England.*

the horrors of a revolution.[58] But bless me, I have trespassed, have entered a wrong [conversational] path—one that I have neither a wish nor right to follow.

The "Intelligent Swiss" [A. Melly] I thought extremely kindly, invited me to dine with him and some young French gentlemen Saturday next at half past 5. I said *particularly kindly*, because I think that he perceived how low spirited I felt; consequently he was doubly kind.

This evening, rather singularly, I discovered the benevolent action of Mrs. Rathbone. Mrs. Abigail [Dockray] told her that her husband had lost very little indeed by lending to honest poor at Manchester sums not exceeding ten pounds sterling. Mrs. Rathbone repeated this to her husband, and the truth came out that Mrs. Rathbone herself followed this same principle, and had lent out, on the same terms, between 50 and 100 pounds.

Children here are forced by their parents to collect during the course of one day a certain amount by begging or stealing, or perhaps by murder, or undergo a severe punishment on the return home. There is "Home Sweet Home," but a hell it must surely be. The tricks resorted to by these miserable wretches are numberless and in some instances very curious. The newspapers abound with them, and are mostly filled with accounts of murders, hangings, thefts, and more abominable acts. I can scarce look at them.

A person followed me three squares to tempt me to purchase a watch worth four shillings for eight pounds. A neat young girl stopped me in the middle of a principal street and delivered a paper to me of a most extraordinary nature. I cannot, really, mention its contents to thee. And Lucy, two children watch me going to the Institution every day. For some time I gave them pence, but finding them more troublesome, the more I gave, I took it into my head to carry some bread and meat to them and was shocked to discover that they were not hungry. Since then I pay no attention to them, and their calling me "Good Captain" does not steer their vessel into my port.

58. While a planter in Haiti, Audubon's father trafficked in slaves. Audubon himself owned slaves in Henderson. At Beech Woods Lucy Audubon had a slave, Cecilia, whom she turned over to William Brand, of New Orleans, when she left the South.

I reached my lodgings, and My dear wife, the number of most abandoned and daring prostitutes is wonderful. What a world! Good God! Good Night: half past 1.

Liverpool   August 18th, 1826

I told thee that I had began a painting of the "Trapped Otter." I had outlined it, and today nearly completed it. Of course I have nothing much to say until I reach sister Ann's house on Hedge Hill. She is well. Miss Donathan is well. Mr. Gordon has not returned. Ah, there are two extra females. "Misses Duff, Mr. Audubon" [comes the introduction]. A dark-complected face and a negative face are in view. The first is possessed of eyes and eyebrows and an understanding of superior cast. The second, I discover, is anxious to reach the merits of her sister. The conversation is good. The music is good and pleasing to me, thou knowest well. Miss Duff sings and plays quite decently. I accompanied them—not on the piano, but to their house in Great George Square, full one and a half miles, I think my legs called it. But my mental faculties were quite refreshed by the controversy that arose between Miss Duff and thy husband about that "Lazy Horse, Genius." The Miss was against thy husband but thy husband was against her. Of course we parted as we had met, very good friends I hope.

I am now again in Dale Street. I have been three times to the Post Office in vain today, and I go now to my bed in no pleasing mood, I assure thee. My Beloved Wife, do write to me. Forever thine, Good Night.

"Green Bank"   August 19th, 1826

The days, the nights, the time all pass away, and I am still as destitute, desolate, and alone as if *thou* hadst never existed. Must I then bear sorrows forever and feel the pangs of absence still severer? Am I to live without ever hearing from thee, Lucy? Ah no. No. No. In a few minutes I will be down on a bed intended for me to repose, but it can only be to bear my body until the morning's dawn—no, there is naught without thee, and sleep but in eternity.

Unfortunate, this day, *by trade*—or better say yesterday—I committed another error to add to the thousand that have so mottled my life that, did I not believe in God, I would scarce care now if I lived or died.

"Ah my LaForest, thy unfortunate mood again. Do for my sake drop those gloomy ideas and think of my love for thee, of our dear children, of the exertions that at thy hands we need, yes, that—!!!"

Well my Lucy, I needed but a sentence from thee. My heart is lighter, my spirits are also *bon*, and I will merely relate facts.

I painted this morning until I could paint no more. My work was too wet to proceed, and I put it aside. Yesterday Mrs. Rathbone's nephew went into Wales, supposing—or rather let me say expecting—that I had gone also. It was through kindness for me and mere complacence that led him. This want of neglect in me vexed me [more] than if I had lost fifty pounds [sterling]. I will make no apology. I must only repent. I remained, much of my time, at the Institution. *I* expected to [see] there sister Ann and her companion with the Misses Duff, but after having waited until past five I was obliged to go to my appointment [for] dinner with Mr. A. Melly, and I wrote the following note to Ann:

> MY DEAR SISTER,
> You must excuse the paper, the pen and the writer. The fact, however is this. My painting was not sufficiently dry to proceed towards its achievement. Of course you will not see it to-day. But it will not go beyond Hedge Hill without your viewing it. Then, my dear Ann, try to content your friends and yourself with a small portion of *American produce*. Remember me, pray, to your amiable companion, and believe me sincerely yours forever,
>
> J. J. A.

I reached Mr. A. Melly's house in Greenville Street rather before him. He came, pulled off his wig, and made me at home in a moment. I had quite a pleasant time there. The guests were Swiss, Genevese, Italians and Germans. The *moor sauce*, however, was highly tainted, the true flavour for the lords of England. Common people, or persons who have no *hereditary* title, those who are not *heretics by birth*, have to write a very particular note of thanks for any pair of rotten grouse they receive from a fattened friend. Now in America, *freedom is hereditary!!!* Grouse and Turkey, the Elk, the Buffalo, or the Venison, reach the palate of all individuals without a sign of oppression.

"Politics again. I would be inclined to believe that thou hast a tendency toward such matters."

No, my Dear Wife, I merely wish the world well.

Our dinner was quite *à la française,* all gaiety, witticisms and good cheer. Mr. Melly drove me in his gig to bid good evening to my "Otter," and afterwards to "Green Bank." It was then that Richard Rathbone asked me if I had seen anything of his cousin that had gone to Wales, that I felt so mortified with myself.

We had much music on the piano and two flutes. I did wish to take part, but dared not, fearing the making of a false note or losing the [tempo] by losing my senses through fear. But I listened with pleasure and turned the leaves for the performers.

At 11 o'clock the moon, nearly full, was inviting for a walk, and the good old lady took a long one with me under my arm, purposely to give me pleasure. Miss Hannah walked some distance behind us with her cousin, and I assure thee, my Lucy, I heard not a word of *their* conversation. Mrs. Rathbone spoke of the Heavens, of the power of our actions, of the sources of those powers, of the deep curtain that forever must lay between our understanding and faculties, whilst we view and feel but cannot conceive. It was Sunday morning when we returned. I felt the want of rest and was conducted by my friend to a new chamber, where, again and again, I was asked to come and stay. Good people. My Lucy, Good Night.

Liverpool   Sunday   August 20th, 1826

I remained in bed four hours. How much I slept must not be known. I was at the Mersey before sunrise, when Nature was as calm as if yet asleep. So calm was all about Nature herself the noise of the paddles of a steamboat running down the River Dee, then eight miles distant, could be heard distinctly. "I know by the smoke that so gracefully curled" that a steamboat was the cause producing the sound. This morning I was quite surprised to see persons out so early. I saw two men hunting with a dog, without guns. The dog was a shabby looking setter, but moved well. I thought the men [drew back] as I approached them, but they stood still and saw me go by. Another man was catching Linnets with bird lime. Others were searching clams and other shellfish along the shores. I also examined some large baskets with mouths upstream to catch fish as the river flows toward the sea.

I walked a great distance to "Green Bank" again. It was 8 o'clock, but no sound was heard; all were yet reposing. I read on the grass. And the sweet children soon came to me to be kissed and to wish me well.

Mr. Melly took me to town again and I breakfasted with him at 10 o'clock, with six young gentlemen like those of yesterday. Afterwards he read to the whole an excellent sermon. Then I went to the Blinds' Church; then I ran to my lodgings to dress, and off to Russell Street *No*. 60, to dine with Mr. Austin, the artist. And there I am, looking at water color paintings done in a style altogether new to me, possessing rich effects without the least finishing. The imagination must supply that and conceive hands, faces, feet, dogs or horses, as the case may be. (Lucy, I have said this to be ahead of all the critics around me; I assure thee they *finish*, with a vengeance, all they begin.)

We dined well, although I could have drawn a line two miles long between this dinner and such as I have partaken of at the Rathbones', or Roscoes'. How much there is in the breed, particularly in England! I saw there a Doctor Cooke, a man of much information.

I went to the Blinds' Church again with the music master of that establishment, and was placed close by the organ. It is really surprising how well the blind do perform. The one that touched the keys was an excellent musician, and talked to me as if he saw in my eyes how much I loved good music. I saw one of the female performers gently pressing the arm of another female, and then pressing her more, to direct her tone of voice and keep in time as she sang a solo. I have had three sermons this day. They were not from a scolding wife, my dear Lucy; of course they all did me good.

I went to bed early, not however without wishing thee well and bidding thee Good Night.

Liverpool   August 21st, 1826

I painted a good deal this day, finished my "Otter" or rather Mrs. Richard Rathbone's otter. It was viewed by many, and admired. I received a gross of pastels from London for which I was charged more than double what they cost in New York, and all entirely too soft. I was invited to remove to "Green Bank" altogether, during the time that I may stay here, but I declined going until I have painted the Wild Turkey Cock for the Royal Institution—say, three days. I retired early to my room, began a letter to thee, and laid down in my bed at half past 10. Went to sleep after wishing thee well, but really do not know when.

Not having been able to write for many days, I am now obliged to resume, without date, to overtake the present date, able to write only the principal facts that have taken place, few of which indeed are worth relating. But still, here they come like a set of beggars, each anxious to be served first.

I think that as a good supper is a good thing, I will serve that first. I had it at Doctor Traill's in company of the French Consul and two other French gentlemen. The conversation, *of course*, was ornithological, and I learned a good deal. I was much encouraged and was requested to visit France immediately. A young lady then gave me some delightful music, and Mrs. Traill some excellent conversation along with good wine.

As suppers are such nice things, let us have another. "Well, no objection." I received a polite note from Mr. Molineaux [the French Consul] and I reached his house at 8 in the evening. In a few minutes seventeen persons were assembled in a chorus. Until 12 my ears were indeed feasted. I do not recollect, ever before in my whole life, having listened to so many men's voices so truly well managed. The diversity was as great as it was agreeable. Messrs. Clementi[59] and Tomlinson from London were present. At half past 1, when supper was just finished (and it was a very fine one), each person at table being told to turn his plate over, saw on doing, the Lord's Prayer printed on the back. And Mr. Molineaux having began to sing it, each person in succession entered into action, and that chorus was divinely true.

---

59. Muzio Clementi (1752–1832) was a composer and pianist.

Mr. Austin came in a moment, but having seen only two brothers of the brush I saw he was not at ease. [This] proved so, and
he soon retired. It being very late, and perceiving that the streets
had more ladies of ranks than watchmen watching, I took the
first of the latter and begged for his company to my lodgings.
He acquiesced at once and we walked safer from the apprehension of being carried off by force of *arms*. On knocking at the
Commercial Inn's door, a voice from above inquired who was
there. The watchman answered, "Number 11," the number of
my room which I previously gave him as we walked the streets,
listening to the many curious night occurrences of the streets of
Liverpool. "Number 11" was admitted, and I went to sleep for a
few hours. By 6 the next morning I was at work on my painting
of the "Wild Turkey Cock," [60] my neck uncovered as usual, my
sleeves up to my shoulders, my hair all flowing and the colors
also—on canvas measuring 4'8⁄12" by 5'8⁄12", [which] I covered
completely in twenty-three hours time. Mr. Melly, Dr. Traill,
Mr. William Rathbone, and many other persons were in my
painting room the while, talking, and wondering how I managed
to conceive and finish [so] fast; and I believe their presence made
me work still faster and better. The fact is that on the two days
after I began this large and beautiful painting, it was framed and
hung in the Exhibition Room. I call it beautiful, Lucy, because
everybody called it so before me, and thou knowest well *que la
voix du peuple est la voie de Dieu*.

At last I removed to "Green Bank," the delightful "Green
Bank," and was hailed with the same kind reception. The Good
Lady requested that I should conceive myself at home, and the
many nice attentions that I received there were convincing proofs
that I was truly welcome. I had the study of Mr. Theodore
Rathbone allotted me for my drawing room. I cannot tell how
much knowledge the gentleman took with him to the Continent, where he is now traveling with *his* Lucy, but I found an
astonishing quantity all around me in his library—portfolios,
casts of antique works, &c., &c., &c. Now this is not at all what

---

60. *Wild Turkey Cock.* The oil on canvas is identical with Folio Plate I, and with
oils at the American Museum of Natural History in New York City and the Thomas
Gilcrease Institute of Early American History and Art in Tulsa, Oklahoma. The British Museum also has an oil the same size as that of the Gilcrease.

troubled me. No. I am not, indeed, troubled by knowledge myself but very much so by the idea that Mrs. Richard Rathbone should refuse to accept my "Otter." I took the opportunity of her being absent, and, having wrote a line to Mr. Munro of the Institution, the picture was varnished and taken to her house with a note from me. She soon saw it and sent her brother to bring me in his carriage. But as I well knew that either thanks or compliments or both would be the fruits of such an early visit, I declined it and begged to be excused. I felt happy that the piece deserved the acceptance, and this relieved me of a heavy burden. When, afterwards, I saw her, she appeared more amiable than ever. Her sweet little Basil lay on her bosom and presented a picture fit for the gods to study and for men to wonder at. Her good husband, two days after, wrote me a most kind letter of thanks, worth twenty such paintings as I gave his lady.

Drawing every day, and dining every Sunday at Mr. Roscoe's.

I gave a lesson of drawing to Mrs. Rathbone, and one to Mrs. Edward Roscoe. Was really busy.

I wrote to thee, to Nicolas Berthoud, to Victor, to Charles Bonaparte, and forwarded thee *thy watch* by the packet ship "Canada," bound to New York through the care of the Messrs. Rathbone & Company.

I made a drawing for Miss Hannah Maria Rathbone, another for Mrs. William Rathbone, another for my venerable and most kind friend Mrs. Rathbone the Mother Bee, another for Mrs. Roscoe, and another for young Henry Chorley, an amiable fellow who plays on the piano delightfully.[61]

My time was in fact most happily spent. I needed only thee, my Dear Friend.

All my Sundays have been alike, breakfasting with Mr. Melly

---

61. Henry Fothergill Chorley (1808–72). His papers afford glimpses of the Rathbones but none of Audubon (Henry G. Hewlett, ed., *Autobiography, Memoirs and Letters of H. F. Chorley* [London, 1873]). Carlyle called Chorley his best read, best informed friend. John Rutter Chorley (1807–67) was a poet of minor gifts. Both Chorleys became friends of such celebrities as Mendelssohn, Carlyle, De Vigny, and actress Rachel. Henry became a music and drama critic of passing fame. Their uncle John Rutter (1762–1838) was a physician who established the Liverpool Athenaeum and served as Botanic Garden Committee treasurer. He subscribed for *The Birds of America*. The first wife of William Rathbone II was Rachel Rutter. Mrs. William Rathbone III, at the age of fifty-eight, took the Chorleys and their two sisters into her home.

and friends, and going to church [of] the Blind Asylum. Everyone is surprised at my habits of early rising, and all also say that I eat nothing. I raise very early to be sure, and eat very much also, I am quite sure. My exhibition at the Institution continues and pays well. I visit there occasionally. A few days since, Mr. Roscoe dined here with his daughter Jane. I had just finished a drawing for Mrs. Rathbone. Young [John Rutter] Chorley, the brother of Henry Chorley, a most interesting and amiable young man [and] a classical scholar, was so kind as to transmit my thoughts into verse in a delightful manner; I wrote [his] twenty well matched lines under my work. Mr. Roscoe's eyes grew larger than ever, and so did the fairer eyes of Miss Jane. They both believed, I believe, that I was the composer. But alas, no. My poor brains never measured time appropriately yet, nor ever will. But I wished to have a piece of Mr. Roscoe's poetry, and I thought that this might tantalize him to set to. He frequently repeated that the lines were beautiful, and I was glad of this as I thought so myself. The young gentlemen that visited the house were desirous of taking early walks with me, and I had them up with the lark whenever they requested it. But it was only for a day, and the next I walked alone, with only my thoughts about me.

My receiving no letters from thee rendered me very sullen at times; and every night when I [have gone] to try to rest, I prayed more fervently for thy safety, health and happiness than ever. One night I awakened suddenly, praying thee quite aloud, and dreaded to have been heard and taken for a maniac.

Vincent Nolte arrived from the U.S., but I was so unfortunate as not to see him, although I tried much. I have all my journal copied for thy sake to send it thee. I forwarded thee and N. Berthoud each a bundle of newspapers, and wrote again to thee. Mr. Gordon, who had absented to London, made some inquiries for letters for me, but none were to be found.

GREEN BANK, August, 1826
Tuesday morning

[To Mrs. Richard Rathbone]
Woodcroft,
MY DEAR MADAM,

At offering you a specimen of my humble powers of painting, I feel two-fold embarrassed. I dread to torment your better taste, and still more lest you should receive it merely through that power of amiability and natural kindness of heart so plainly observable in all your actions. Yet I feel the desire of presenting to you this *amiable Otter*, because I feel a wish of proving to you my gratitude and the high respect with which I hope you will permit me to remain, my dear Madam,

Your most humble, obedient servant,
JOHN J. AUDUBON

"Green Bank"   September 6th, 1826

I forwarded thee this morning a full copy of this book via the brig "Isabella," bound to New Orleans, with it all the papers that I could procure. May thou receive all in goodly, happy mood!

When I came to "Green Bank" this last time, I had been breakfasting with Mrs. Edward Roscoe and daughter, to whom I gave advice about drawing. I walked fast, and had a little basket lent me by Mr. Munro that contained some clean linens, a small red portfolio, my journal, and the drawing for Mrs. Rathbone framed in an oak frame as plain as could be—all under my arm and hands. The family were still at breakfast. As usual each individual rose to come and meet me. All were well. I was told that Lady Isabella Douglas,[62] the sister of Lord Selkirk, former governor of Canada, was in the house as a visitor. I was told that she was unable to walk, and that consequently she moved about in a rolling chair from spot to spot, confined, however, to a very small area for daily exercise. The name of Lady Douglas startled me considerably.

I had found Lord Stanley an extremely polite, kind, unassuming man, but what differences might there be between him and Lady Isabella were quite matters of conjecture. I concluded

---

62. Alice Jaynes Tyler used this passage to implement her thesis that Audubon was "the lost Dauphin" of King Louis XVI and Marie-Antoinette (*I Who Should Command All* [New Haven, 1937]). Francis H. Herrick identified him as the natural son of Jean Audubon, of Nantes and Les Cayes, Haiti, and one "Mademoiselle Rabin" (*Audubon the Naturalist*. Foreword of second and last edition [New York, 1938]). Alice Ford identified his mother as Jeanne Rabine, native of Les Mazures (Les Touches), Nort-sur-Erdre, Nantes vicinity, France (*John James Audubon*).

that, as she was a friend of Mrs. Rathbone, *she could not* be very unmerciful because of her being Lady Douglas.

I went to my work, and drew a very short time. I could not work to my wish. The weather was inviting. I therefore invited John Chorley, Esq., to ramble with me a while. On returning to "Green Bank" I found and met Lady Isabella. Her features are regularly formed, her complexion fair, and her countenance of a happy disposition. I looked at her well, and although she spoke not to me after being introduced, I *guessed* that she knew pretty well who was the man with the long hair and sheepish aspect.

"Shame, my LaForest, how canst thou speak of thyself in such words. I really do not like it. Few men are better formed, nay handsomer than thou art, and I am sure thy aspect (if aspect it must be called) is quite favorable in all points of view."

Well, my beloved wife, I "owe *thee* one."

Lady Douglas, sat next me at dinner, and I between her and the *Lady* Rathbone. She spoke but seldom, and I chewed my food as rapidly as if I had stolen it.

In the afternoon I had again the opportunity of seeing her ladyship, and, after some conversation, was much pleased with her acquaintance. She was apparently always in good spirits, and as I did not call her Lady D. or "my lady," I felt quite reprieved [privileged]. She admired my drawings on account of the novelty of the style. I found her possessed of excellent taste and regularly *clever*. The broad Scotch accent that accompanies each word she speaks sounds agreeable to my ear and soon sends my ideas awandering. Mrs. Rathbone wished her to see more of my work, but Lady Douglas, disliking to appear in public, *I* went to the Institution in Mrs. Rathbone's carriage and brought upwards of twenty drawings for her to gaze at. She liked them.

Dr. Traill gave me a singular drawing to make this morning. It was neither more nor less than a *pebble* about the size of a large pigeon egg that had been extracted from an unfortunate sufferer of that terrible disease, the gravel.[63] I made it during the absence of the family and returned it with the drawing the same evening.

---

63. Fate of drawing unknown.

In returning to "Green Bank" from Liverpool, I stopped at "Woodcroft," the country seat of Mr. Richard Rathbone, to take the good old lady[64] who had [wished to] stop there. [I] started my young [porter] on to wait for the portfolio of my Birds, to take it back to the Institution again. There I found Mr. Shepherd of the Botanic Garden, engaged at plotting some grounds in good taste for my friend Richard Rathbone. Mrs. Rathbone wished to take him [to his] home, and we had him in the carriage in a short time and at his house at the public garden. He promised me some letters for Manchester. Now we positively return to "Green Bank." The postilion rises with each trotting step the horse he rides. I can see the landscape as his XXXX escapes the bounce it would receive was he to ride solidly between his saddle and his well-rounded, well formed, and buff-leather-covered XXXX. We are at the outer gate. Mrs. Rathbone desires to see a servant immediately. He immediately comes. *I* hear her say, "Have something for him to eat, quickly." *I* hear no more, but I *guess* again that I discovered the wish of this wonderfully kind lady. It was for my young [porter] expressly. She heard me say that he had walked, and [she] took the hint. I heard her speak of eating quickly and took the hint also. Lucy, this gives thee an idea of the nicety of care that moves with each step of this wonder [among] females. And wert thou to see her daughter Hannah, who has undoubtedly the most brilliant and yet mild black eyes I ever beheld, with a contemplative smile over her visage, rising from table ten times during the repast to offer a nice morsel to her *Mamma*, or to see her peel an apple or a pear or a peach and hand it to her, or to see her with a vase of wine, begging of her *Mamma* to take a little more, and wert thou

---

64. Mrs. Richard Rathbone (*née* Hannah Mary Reynolds), 1798–1878, daughter of Joseph Reynolds and Deborah Dearman, of Shropshire, and granddaughter of Richard Reynolds, of Bristol, married her half-cousin. Her few lessons with Audubon are of interest because of the twenty-one plates of her bird drawings that illustrate her book of selected verse, a charming and exceedingly rare volume (*The Poetry of Birds . . . With Coloured* [*sic*] *Illustrations*. By a Lady [anonymous] [Liverpool, George Smith, 1833], quarto, 6 [1] 136). Mrs. Rathbone also published, anonymously, the supposed seventeenth-century *Diary of Lady Willoughby* (1846), a popular work that created a furor of doubt but ran through several editions. In 1852 she published her paternal grandfather's *Letters* (Richard Rathbone) with a memoir; and in 1858, a book of verse entitled *The Strawberry Girl*. The *DNB* errs concerning the date of her first work. The fact that she, her mother-in-law, sister-in-law, and daughter bore the Christian name of Hannah Mary sometimes proves confusing.

to see her blush as ingenuously as I have seen her do when she thinks that she is remarked, thou wouldst admire her. [Long, inked-out sentence, followed by:]—I am quite sure, perhaps still more than I do, and I believe it would be a puzzler for any person other than myself to do.

The day has been uncommonly disagreeable out of doors. It is quite winterlike. The blast comes from East, and the rain that accompanies it is quite cold. Fortunately, I procured a bird to draw, and drew nearly two to-day. Lady Isabella kept me company in my *laboratoire* and promised me a letter for Edinburgh [to] a nephew of hers, and politely invited me to call and breakfast at her country seat five miles from London when I reach that city—[and] as often as I may make it conveniently.

Today I gave my journal to Miss Hannah to read, and [she also read] it to her mother. They read from [the point of] my arrival at Liverpool. Do not be alarmed, my Lucy. They are *safe persons*, I assure thee. They will not make ill use of the favor.

Lucy, now that I have been a good while in this delightful family, let me tell thee the cause of my particular attachment to its members. The very first day that I visited "Green Bank," thou recollects that I was brought here by Mr. Richard Rathbone and lady, in company with Mr. Pyke. Whilst here and moving from the library or setting-room into the lobby or entry, to examine the collection of stuffed birds there, *I* heard Richard Rathbone say (to some one whom I did not see then but whom I now believe was Mr. Reynolds, Sr.) that *I* was "simple intelligent." I was struck with the power of the truth. I was quite sure that what was then said was really [his] thoughts, and as I know myself to be positively very *simple* and yet somewhat intelligent, I was delighted; and [I] thought of Richard Rathbone from that moment as I would of an excellent kind brother. Every circumstance since then [strengthened] my conclusions, and now I feel the wish that either he, or his brother, or his wife or his sister, or his mother or all of them, could judge for a moment how much I esteem, admire and venerate them all, individually and as the most truly parentally inclined alliance I ever saw, and probably ever will again.

Once more, my Dearest Friend, I must bid thee good night, far, far away from thy sweet form and sound of voice.

The sun rose beautifully fair this morning, and the birds all chirruped to its appearance with delight. Now all nature is angry. It is a night fit for hobgoblins and believers to enjoy. How long must it be before I can again press thee to my bosom and with a kiss bid thee Good Night?

"Green Bank"   September 7th, 1826

I have drawn all day and finished the "Intelligent Swiss's" piece. It consists of two water Wagtails and three butterflies.[65] I hope he will like it.

Lady Douglas expressed some anxiety yesterday to see the whole of one bird drawn in her presence. Therefore, to-day, I drew butterflies until the lady issued from her chamber. It was nearly 2 o'clock. The ladies of the house had returned from meeting. I had been with Mr. Chorley, taking a little exercise on the pond, and dinner was served. When dessert was served, a beautiful white pitcher containing cream was handed me. I admired it very much. It reminded me of thee, Lucy, young and beautifully modest, all the flowers of virginity about thee, and, I might—ah yes I *will*—say, all sweetness, like the cream in the little pitcher that now is thine. Yes, my Lucy, Hannah Rathbone gave it to me, and it shall go to America!!

After dinner [Miss Ellen] Greg, the sister of Mrs. William Rathbone (the latter of whom I presented a drawing on her birthday, the 30th of August, with a few lines from John Chorley under the little Robin of the Red Bosom) followed me into my little *laboratoire*. [This room] might be styled the "Academy of Fine Arts" as was mine at Percys' "Beech Woods" [Louisiana]. Lady Douglas came in next, and next Mrs. Rathbone with a cup of coffee in one hand and a sugar basin in the other. The first was for thy husband. [Miss] Greg sweetened it. Lady Douglas, as a lady is wont to do, heard me ask for India rubber, sent for her desk, and presented me with two nice bits inserted in a

---

65. The drawing is inscribed: "Presented to A. Melly Esqr. by his Sincerely Obliged Friend John J. Audubon Sepr 1826." Published in *Country Life Magazine* (April 6, 1951); and in *Bibliotheca Bibliographici* [Catalogue of the Collection of Sir Geoffrey Keynes] (1964).

tube. My drawing finished, Miss Hannah, hearing that I was going to Liverpool, met me with a glass of white wine (the name here for madeira). I looked at her eyes, drank the wine, and thought of thee. Off to Liverpool, walking, however, very slowly part of the way, having young Chorley with me. When we parted I put forth my powers and moved at my usual rate of five miles.

Mr. Munro was not at the Institution. Mr. Melly was not at home. My trunk was not in my room in Dale Street! No, the room was given to some other purpose, and my baggage was in the entry. I walked to "Green Bank" again, and found there the additional source of pleasure, Richard Rathbone and lady. I read a letter on my Birds, the title "The Chimney Swallow."[66]

Again, Lucy, read and be surprised. Richard Rathbone wishes me to paint a large picture, to bring my talents to public view in a more forcible, stronger light. He wishes more—he wishes that I should remove to his house, with brushes, canvas and colors, and men to sit for me, and men to prepare my tints!! It will, he says, give great pleasure both to him and to his wife. Mrs. Rathbone herself repeats the invitation. Lucy, what shall I do? It is easy to paint the picture, and be *blasted to the roots* and *mortified to the marrow of my bones* when exhibited. It may be laughed at. But to remain perhaps more than thirty days at a house where nothing besides peace and tranquillity resides, daubing a picture that could not go out of it without being distended and of course perfectly dried, a thing that might take months at the rate I put on colors, would not do. No Lucy, it would not do. The picture shall be painted, but I do not well yet know where. The generous man speaks of my talent in a way that positively renders me quite uncomfortable, and yet I forbid saying so to him, because I am quite sure that he speaks his thoughts and wishes me really well.

The weather this evening is beautiful. The carriage of Richard Rathbone has taken him and his beautiful wife away. Lady Douglas, without bidding good night, has rolled herself off [in] her chair. I have shook hands with all, rather more *brotherly* than usual with kind Hannah, and now God bless thee, good night.

---

66. *Ornithological Biography*, II, 329: *Chimney Swallow.*

GREEN BANK, Sept. 8th, 1826

William Roscoe, Esq.
Lodge Lane [Liverpool]
MY DEAR SIR,

I have taken the liberty to roll up a little drawing made by me, with the wish that it may not be disagreeable to you to receive it. I wish sincerely that it was more deserving of your attention. My fate will force me, on Sunday morning, to leave Liverpool and all the kind persons with whom I have had the honor of becoming acquainted, but I hope it will also be my good fortune to be enabled not to forget them as long as I live! Please present my remembrances to your amiable daughter. Please to believe me also and forever your most devotedly attached friend.

J. J. A.

[The first portion of this letter copy apparently summed up Audubon's journey from Liverpool to Manchester and his first experiences on arrival. Missing from manuscript journal.]

"Green Bank" September 9th, 1826

I must now tell thee that tomorrow I will positively leave this enchanted spot and move towards Manchester. My heart feels heavy. I am about leaving good friends. It reminds me of parting with my own family again. When I left America I did not feel worse.

Yesterday I drew a good deal, and had the company of Lady Douglas by my side. I was obliged to copy my own face for Miss Hannah.[67]

In the afternoon three carriages left "Green Bank" and moved toward Liverpool to pay a visit to my drawings at the Royal Institution. We arrived there about 5. Lady D. was carried up the stairs and remained in the large room for upward of two hours, and was apparently very much pleased. She complimented me very considerably.

---

67. "Audubon at Green Bank, Almost Happy!!—Sep.r 1826." Self-portrait in pencil, presented to Miss Hannah Mary Rathbone, not to her mother, as stated in the catalog of the Pierpont Morgan Library exhibition, *Audubon Watercolors and Drawings* (1965), B. L. Rathbone Collection.

At 6 o'clock I was dressed and in Abercromby Square at the house of William Rathbone, where I dined in the company of Dr. Traill, A. Melly, Mr. Foster, &c., and several ladies. It was late when we retired. I remained for [the] night at William Rathbone's, [and] presented him with a copy of Fairman's engraving of the [New Jersey] bank note plate [which bears my drawing of a grouse.][68]

Mr. Foster furnished me a letter that would procure me a personal introduction to Sir Thomas Lawrence. I slept in the same [chamber] with a young Mr. Greg, and left him in the morning long before he had any thought of awakening, and walked to "Green Bank," where I made a small drawing for Mr. J. G. Austin before breakfast.[69] Afterward I visited Mrs. Edward Roscoe, who had finished a beautiful drawing in my style. She presented me with a copy of Cowper's poems. I felt a very great pleasure at this as I really knew very little about him.

I called on Mr. Roskell and settled my bank business with him. Paid my debts to Mr. Hunt, and my bill at the Inn in Dale Street, where they charged for every day as if I had been living there. It made only a difference of £3 in the quantum of my purse. I wrote a letter of thanks to both the brothers Rathbone, and enclosed a ten pound note to pay for the chalks they had purchased for me, and the residue to pay for postage, &c.

I returned to "Green Bank" once more, dined there, made a likeness of John Chorley, and walked to see Mr. Roscoe in Lodge Lane in company of Miss Hannah Rathbone. She was so kind to give me a very beautiful pen knife, and a piece of poetry copied by her hand. I found Mr. Roscoe at home with his son and daughter. He gave me four letters of introduction, one to Miss Edgeworth particularly beautiful.[70] He was quite astonished to see me eat some raw tomatoes. So were the ladies. And yet how simple was the act. I had bid farewell to all in town, and al-

---

68. Gideon Fairman, of Philadelphia, engraved the bank note with "grous" (quail?), sketched by Audubon for gentleman farmer Edward Harris, who by his generosity helped redeem the failure of the quest for a publisher in Philadelphia in 1824. For the search for an authentic example, see *Princeton University Library Chronicle*, Vol. XXI (1959–60), 36–37.

69. Fate of sketch made for Austin unknown.

70. Audubon is not known to have met Maria Edgeworth.

most all in the country. I called on Richard Rathbone, but he was absent. I was met cheerfully by his sweet little flock of children and his beautiful lady. She requested that I should write to her when absent, and I promised to do so with inexpressible pleasure.

The evening was quite stormy. It lightened some, and I could see the effect on the features of the sweet female in whose company I was setting. I at last reached "Green Bank" and thought that I had finished my day's work. But no, a note from Mr. Austin came and announced me that Mr. Munro was distracted at the Institution; and I wrote Mr. Munro a very rude, rough note, and now am pining and repenting about my conduct toward that good man. Mr. Joseph Chorley has copied my letters of introduction [into these pages]. We have had our cheerful supper, drank thy health, sweet wife, and now I must go, and bid thee Good Night.

III

Manchester

Manchester,
County of Lancaster, England   Sept. 10th, 1826

B EFORE I MENTION MY ARRIVAL AT THIS PLACE I cannot help, my Beloved Wife, speaking more of "Green Bank" to thee. I had bid my adieu last evening to each member of the family, and calculated on leaving that sweet spot by 8 o'clock with Hannah Maria Rathbone who proposed walking with me to Liverpool. But when 8 o'clock came, the weather was blustery and inclined to rain. Therefore it was arranged that we should go in a carriage. Mrs. Rathbone sent me an invitation to see her in her own room, and I did so. I thought I saw her eyes wetted by a tear. She requested that I should write often to her and others of her family. I saw her husband's portrait, that of her father and brother, and also that of Lord Selkirk, with whom it appears the family has long been intimately acquainted.

The little Robin that she calls her own, and that she particularly requested I should not kill when shooting, was hopping about the room and flying in and out perfectly free from either fear or danger. I saw there a gem of painting; it was a small vase of flowers, all white. Her table, her books, everything about this

181

repository exhibited the tendency toward studying the best works by the owner. I took a cup of chocolate, handed Hannah Maria into the carriage, and bid my good old friend [Mrs. Rathbone] farewell.

Mr. Austin came with us. I stopped a few minutes at "Woodcroft" and had the pleasure of meeting Richard Rathbone and his beautiful wife at breakfast. I bid them adieu also. Mrs. Rathbone said, "Mr. Audubon, you must write to us womankind." Ah yes, my heart desired no more agreeable favor—yes, to womankind I will write when I have written to the kindest, to thee my wife!

Miss Hannah Maria had me deposited at Mr. Melly's where I had an agreeable enough breakfast, but my head was all full of the Rathbones, and the "Intelligent Swiss's" companions all appeared dull to me this morning. Mr. Melly proposed that we should go in a postchaise together and divide expenses. I agreed to do so, as some difficulty had been made about taking my Number Two Portfolio in the public coach. However, the arrangement proved useless, as thou wilt see by the sequel. I reached the Institution about 11 o'clock, made my peace with good Munro in a moment, and walked with him to Dr. Traill's. Met Mr. William Lawson, the treasurer of the Royal Institution. Dr. Traill gave me, with a letter for Heywood, Esq., of Manchester, the [privilege] of taking Mr. Munro for two days. I returned by way of Dale Street to the Institution. I mention Dale, because the waiter at the Commercial had refused to give up my linen, saying that the servants must each be paid something. I felt rather [incensed], and, having proved the lady that I had done quite enough for the servants, she positively begged [pardon and] denied having heard of the transaction, and I marched off with my goods. Dr. Traill told me never to give the waiters anything until I leave an inn or hotel. I shall remember it, believe me.

My seats were [secured] at the stage office. My portfolio [was] managed, and I was closing the drawings and packing my trunk by 1 o'clock. I went to bid adieu to thy sister Ann, and, shamefully as it is for me to say it, she refused for several minutes to kiss me. My mortification was extreme. I cannot bear prudery.

To be *simple*, natural, *truthfully kind*, is my motto, and I cannot well bear any other conduct. However, I took a glass of wine and drank to the health of *her sister* in America. I had the great pleasure of hearing of thy being well on the 24th of July last, by a letter of thy little friend [Charles] Briggs to Mr. Gordon. I met this latter gentleman in the street and perhaps may see him in Manchester tomorrow.

Returned to the Institution, saw Mr. Melly, and wrote the following note to my venerable, hospitable, kind friend Mrs. Rathbone of "Green Bank":

My DEAR MADAM,

The very particular interest that you have so evidently proved to have towards my future happiness prompts me to inform [you] that, during this morning's visit to Mrs. Gordon, I received *regular* intelligence that my Lucy and my dear boys were quite well on the 24th of July last, that letters had been forwarded to the care of the American minister at London, and that some must be *there now!* Will you please ask the favour of your sons here to forward them with all the speed that a *husband* needs after so long a lapse without news from those he holds so dear to his heart[.] I leave in the coach for Manchester, accompanied by Mr. Munro (whom Dr. Traill has been so good as to let me have) at 5 o'clock this afternoon.

Please present my humblest respects to Lady Isabella Douglas, to all and each of your family circle, and believe me forever, my dear madam, most truly your devoted, respectful, obedient servant,

J. J. AUDUBON

This note was taken to "Green Bank" by the "Intelligent Swiss," whom I saw at the Institution where he comes, accompanied by his cousin, to study entomology, and arranged his beautiful collection of subjects connected with that interesting science.

Mr. Munro and I went to the coach office, arranged the portfolio snug in the carriage. I paid one pound sterling for our inside seats. No charge for baggage, [because] I left my trunk at the Institution to be forwarded to me by Mr. Munroe via steam-boat packet. I took another view of the shipping on the Mersey. With anxiety and with thoughts of Louisiana, of thee my kind wife, and our dear children, I looked on the vessels bound [for] America. A minute before the appointed time for our departure we entered the coach, arranged our two selves copiously at ease, being alone. The instant that the words "all right" issued from the clerk attending the department of Coach Number 11335, off we moved briskly over the pavement.

The pleasure that in many other travellers would have been anticipated with [the] idea of visiting Manchester, one of the principal manufacturing towns of England and perhaps of Europe, had no effect on me. I wished some accident might take place that would detain me in Liverpool and enable me to go once more to "Green Bank," to view from that enchanted seat the sun about to set that was really magnificent this evening. But no, it was not to be. I saw the sun setting from the coach, and the idea that I had no one to participate with in thinking about and admiring the resplendent orb, as it made way to the placid silvery enchanter of the night, was far from giving me either animation or spirit to gaze on the landscape that was fading from my eye with the light of day. Yet Mr. Munro did all in his power to interest me. He made me remark Lord Stanley's domains, and I looked on the Hares, the Partridges and other game with a thought of apprehension that the apparent freedom and security they enjoyed was very transient. I thought it more cruel to permit them to grow gentle, nay quite tame, and suddenly and by tricks murder them by thousands, than to give them the fair play that our game has with us in our [American] forests [where] [they are] free—ah yes, free—and as wild as Nature made them, exciting and active, healthful pursuer to search after [them] and pay for them through the pleasure of hunting them down against all difficulties.

My astonishment was great and I was aroused from my sullenness at the sight of a lad, perhaps twelve years of age, [who] ran swiftly along the side of the coach and suddenly tumbled five or six times repeatedly, heels over head, exhibiting this feat to procure a few half pence. I amply rewarded him, and I was glad that my coppers made their way from the passenger's pockets onto the top of the ground, where they were picked up with alertness by the little mendicant. Mr. Munro assured me that these boys are frequently [seen], and that a letter thrown out of the coach with a few pence is taken by them and conveyed to its directed office or house with great security.

We passed through a small village called Prescot. The streets [were] extremely narrow. The coach stopped, I thought, frequently to renew the horses. We travelled about seven miles per hour. Wherever we stopped, a neatly dressed maid, sometimes quite handsome and with a side glance, would come and offer cakes, ale or other refreshment with a good English grace— grace equal, in my opinion, to any I have yet seen.

Mr. Munro and I drank some brandy and water. I was made to remark little shrubs growing in many parts of the meadows that concealed traps for Moles and served as beacons to the persons who caught these animals. The Hares that sometimes were not more than twenty steps from the coach paid no attention to us, and fed as if confident of their security.

The road was good but narrow. The country, as much as we could see of it, handsome and in a high degree of improved cultivation. We crossed a canal [running] from Liverpool here. The sails moving through the meadows cut to form the canal brought me quickly, [in thought] to Rochester in New York. I saw the falls of the Genesee again in my imagination. I thought of De Witt Clinton[1] and at last again of thee. Ah, how much of my blood would I suffer myself to be deprived of, to have thee with me, and also my dear sons—ah, when will we meet, *never to part again*.

I am, then, at Manchester, thirty-eight miles from Liverpool and nearly 6,000 from thee—with a pocketbook containing a pack of letters of recommendation. And tomorrow a new set of faces must see mine. And I feel awkward again. It is really terrible for me, and yet as I came from America for thy sake, for

---

1. De Witt Clinton (1769–1828) presided over the Masonic knighting of Lafayette in New York. Beside him and the Marquis stood Robert Bakewell Atterbury, first cousin of Mrs. Audubon. Clinton was governor of New York in 1817–23 and 1825–28.

thy sake I will suffer these difficulties and wait with patience for the only reward I long for—a sweet kiss from thy lips, my Lucy!

I paid two shillings to the coachman (a [matter] of course in this country, where the traveller must conceive them destitute of any other remuneration than [his] generosity, for the trouble they have driving and waiting on all passengers). In a few minutes I was lodged in the little room where I am now setting, writing this, and disturbed only by the watchman's cry of "Past 12 o'clock." The moon shines yet. Ah my Lucy, God bless thee, Good Night.

Manchester   September 11th, 1826   Monday

I was up early enough, I assure thee, this fair morning. After I had closed, with my habitual good night to thee, the noise in the streets last night increased but did not improve. It was most disagreeable to say the least of it, and I doubt if I was permitted to close my eyes. I am rather inclined to think that I did not.

Well, we had our breakfast. It was neither such as I was used to at my father's, or thy father's, or at Henderson, or New Orleans, or Natchez—ah, not even such a breakfast as the "Beech Woods" of Louisiana afforded me. And to compare it with the breakfast of Hannah Rathbone or my good friend the "Intelligent Swiss" would be absurd. Yes, we had enough of beefsteak, of coffee, tea and toast and buttered bread. But my Lucy, I eat it alone, yes quite so, in thoughts, and I remarked several times that Mr. Munro perceived that *something was wanted.*

My letter gives thee an account of how the day was spent. I visited, however, the Academy of Natural Sciences. Paid my three guineas for a week's rent of the Exhibition Room, and was accompanied a great portion of the day by one of those uncomfortable busy bodies that think of all other persons' affairs in preference to their own, a Mr. [W. H.] Bentley,[2] a dealer in stuffed specimens, and there ends his history. I wished him at Hanover, or in [the] Congo, or New Zealand, or at Bombay, or in a bomb-shell on his route to Eternity. But turn over [the page] and I will tell thee two curious occurrences differing broadly from each other.

---

2. Walter Horton Bentley, of St. Mary's Gate, Manchester, was a taxidermist and dealer in skins; he became an ally.

As I walked the streets with Mr. Munro in search of the house of the Reverend James Taylor in Faulkner Street, Mr. Munro inquired of a man where it was. The stranger said he would accompany us, and whilst I entered the house to deliver my letter the stranger asked Munro if he knew who I was. Mr. Munro said no. (I know not why.) The other man then told him that I was a most *eminent artist* and a most *extraordinary man.* It does not take much to compose and form the latter, but the *eminent artist* "discomboburated" my nerves very much, and although I tried for some minutes to imagine that I might be the one, I gradually fell back to my real ideas of myself and walked on briskly again.

THE MISTRESS AND HER SERVANT,
A True Story [of Green Bank]

The environs of Liverpool are adorned by numerous [country] seats wherein many persons of the highest distinction reside—of good manners, of benevolent dispositions, and good heart. The traveller who retires for a few hours from the tumult of the city, and reaches one of those seats laying about two and a half miles southeast, (as one would say if he were going by [water]) cannot help remarking a sweet delectable mansion, all appearances secluded from the world, and yet filled with a world of generous beings. The building is gothic. Evergreens run along its walls and seem to hide from public view remarkable instances of hospitality and of actions worthy the admiration of the universe. A small piece of water slowly moves across the foot of the gentle slope on which it stands. Many trees embellish the grounds around, and I recollect having seen a few sheep grazing peaceably in their shade. There, my Lucy, the mistress lives! And her servant has also lived there thirty-five years! They are both rising toward heaven as they are both growing old!!

One day the mistress (cannot tell when) called for her maid and told her that her wages must now be augmented, that her work must now be diminished!! The maid wept, trembled, feared that her lady wished her off from under her roof, and begged to know the true meaning. Then the mistress explained, and the servant refused to [*illegible*] any such alterations, indeed saying that if her wages were augmented she would positively depart. The lady insisted on keeping her on her own terms. The servant left the rooms and was taken violently ill immediately. Her mistress ran to assist with her care, and having ascertained that the indisposition was the effect of her intended generosity, abandoned the idea of doing more than good, and begged of the servant to remain with her. All is well again, and I have no doubt all will be well between them forever!!!!

Such, my beloved Lucy, are the acts of my kind friend Mrs. Rathbone of "Green Bank." I was told this by a young friend who esteems her with all those who know her—not as much as she deserves, but as much as is in our power to do.

Mr. Gordon had promised me to be at Manchester, and to give me letters of recommendation. But Mr. Munro hunted every public house of note, and of course I concluded he came not.

Three of the sons of Mr. Greg[3] called on me at the Exchange, and were extremely polite. They were anxious that I should have gone to their country seat, but my business would not allow it.

About twenty persons came to see my Birds, of course called them very beautiful, &c., &c. I had to stand the brunt of all this; and the eyes of the ladies were again, I perceived, searching the lines of my face and the undulations of my locks.

But my style puzzles all. Not a soul can ever guess how I proceed—a great proof that a simplicity of a thing proves the difficulty of its discovery.

I gave good Mr. Munro three pounds ten shillings for his trouble. Good fellow, he deserved more but I am not rich and I gave accordingly. I paid our bill at the tavern and removed to a

---

3. Samuel Greg (b. *c.* 1758, Belfast, Ireland) founded Quarry Bank mills and estate near Manchester in 1784. He was converted from Presbyterianism to the Unitarianism of Priestley. Among his thirteen children were: Elizabeth, who married William Rathbone IV; Ellen, who married André Melly, "the Intelligent Swiss"; William Rathbone Greg (1809–81), whom Audubon often mentions and who became a noted free tradist; and Robert Hyde Greg (1795–1875), who was an outstanding economist and antiquary. His papers are at Quarry Bank and the University of Manchester; Friends Library, London, has a file that quotes John Morley's *Miscellanies* and contains a note on Greg.

Mrs. Hedge in King Street, where she keeps a circulating library. Here I have more quietness, and pay twelve shillings per week for the use of the parlour and a neat bedroom. Mr. Munro left me at 10 o'clock this evening, and took with him my letters for thee and Mrs. Rathbone. He gave me his basket, hammer and foot rule. He goes in the 5 o'clock coach tomorrow morning. I sent a blank album by him to receive the names of my Liverpool friends.

MANCHESTER, [September 11th, 1826]
[Mrs. Rathbone Sr.]
[Liverpool] [Only this paragraph remains.]
. . . The above, my dear Mrs. Rathbone, gives you an account of my progress since I left you. I had the pleasure of seeing to-day several members of the Greg family, and I am very happy to be enabled to inform you that they were all well. To have had also the satisfaction of shaking the hand of the "Intelligent Swiss" [Mr. A. Melly] was a great relief from my hard labours. I have taken the liberty of forwarding a blank book to Mr. Roscoe and my other kind friends. Do me the honor, pray, to write your own name on one of its sheets. Beg for me of each member of your family to do the same, and believe me most truly and devotedly,

J. J. A.

September 12th

I engaged a man well recommended, named Crookes, to attend as money receiver at the door of the Exhibition Room. I pay him fifteen shillings per week. He finds himself [with time,] and copies letters for me.

Mr. A. Melly, whom I had the pleasure of seeing twice, gave me the following kind letter. Before I copy the letter I will say that I deposited in Mr. Heywood's Bank £244, for which he gave me a receipt.

George Murray, Esqr., MANCHESTER, SEPTR. 12th, 1826.
My Dear Sir,
These lines will be presented to you by my friend Mr. Audubon of Louisiana, of whom I spoke to you this morning. I need not say much on his account, having no doubt but that when you have had an oppor-

tunity of speaking with him you will thank me to have procured you his acquaintance.

The talent with which he has delineated the different specimens of natural history which he will exhibit in your town is so far superior to what I have yet met with, that I shall only desire you to judge for yourself, and add that Mr. Audubon's intelligence, information in natural sciences, and mind, do not fall short of his talent. I will be much obliged by the attentions you will show him, and have no doubt but that you will not find fault with me for having given you a farther opportunity of conferring other obligations on, my dear Sir, yours very truly,

A. MELLY

During the day two men came to the exhibition and inquired if I wished for a band of music to entertain the visitors. They were Italians, by their noses and large mouths. I thanked them. My exhibition being neither Egyptian mummies or deathly-looking wax figures, I do not conceive it necessary in the company of so many songsters as I have; and if my songsters will not sing or be agreeable by themselves, other music would only diminish their worth. I made some difference here in my mode of shewing my birds. I exhibited them at once to the public for money, and will depend more on their real value here than I did in Liverpool, where I *know* I was supported by very numerous and particular friends.

[The following entry, for September 12, is missing from the original 1826 journal MS, but appears in Maria R. Audubon's edited and published version (*Aududon and His Journals*, I, 117–18):]

Manchester   [September] 12th, 1826

Yesterday was spent in delivering my letters to the different persons to whom I was recommended. The American consul, Mr. Brookes, with whom I shall dine tomorrow, received me as an American gentleman receives another, most cordially. The principal banker here, Arthur Heywood, Esq., was equally kind. Indeed *everywhere* I meet a most amiable reception. I procured, through these gentlemen, a good room to exhibit my pictures, in the Exchange Building, had it cleared, cleaned and made ready by night. At 5 this morning Mr. Munro (the curator of the Institution at Liverpool and a most competent help) with several assistants and myself began putting up, and by eleven all was ready. Manchester, as I have seen it in my walks, seems a miserably laid out place, and the smokiest I ever was in. I think I ought not to use the words "laid out" at all. It is composed of an astonishing number of small, dirty, narrow, crooked lanes, where one cart can scarce pass another. It is full of noise and tumult; I thought last night not one person could have enjoyed repose. The postilion's horns, joined to the cry of the watchmen, kept my eyelids asunder till daylight again gave me leave to issue from the King's Arms. The population appears denser and worse off than in Liverpool. The vast number of youth of both sexes, with sallow complexions, ragged apparel, and downcast looks made me feel they were not as happy as the slaves of Louisiana. Trade is slowly improving, but the times are dull. I have heard the *times* abused ever since my earliest recollections. I saw today several members of the Greg family. [End of entry in *Audubon and His Journals;* the original passage was removed and apparently destroyed by Maria R. Audubon and her sisters when they destroyed other journals.]

Manchester   September 13th, 1826   Wednesday

It is 11 o'clock and I have this moment returned from the American Consul Brookes's dinner. The company was principally composed of Mr. Loyd,[4] the wealthy banker, Mr. Garnett,[5] &c., &c. Judge of my surprise when on the third removal of the plates I saw on the table a mass of good Indian corn, nicely boiled purposely to please me. [That] I ate it buttered and salted, held by my two hands as if I intended gagging myself with the ear, I took [to be] a matter of much wonder to the English gentlemen, [who] did not even like the vegetable in any way.

I found the Consul, who is from Boston, an intelligent, agreeable, and very polite man. We had an English dinner, Americanized, and the profusion of wine drank was rather uncomfort-

---

4. Thomas Loyd (not Lloyd) was a financier of the well-known Manchester family of financiers.

5. Jeremiah Garnett (1793–1870) and John Edward Taylor established *The Manchester Guardian* in 1821.

able to me. The gentlem[a]n who sat next below me proved to be a good naturalist and observer of my sort. (I mean, not of the closet [variety].) I am satisfied that he studies Nature properly, not *à la Waterton*. Much was said, of course, of my work and Charles Bonaparte's also. The conversation was mixed with many good jests and smart repartee; some politics was introduced, and Mr. Brookes and myself (the only two Americans present) ranged ourselves, and toasted the company with, "*Our enemies in war, but our friends in peace!*" I am particularly fond of a man who speaks well of his country, and the peculiar warmth of Englishmen on the subject is quite admirable.

During the day I saw a gentleman who said that Lord de Tabelay was extremely anxious to see both my drawings and myself, and that I must go to his domains fourteen miles distant on my way to Birmingham.

I perceived the family Touchet coming up the stairs of the Exhibition Room and I hid myself and made my escape. I had just a glance at Mrs. Touchet (I suppose), and saw her very beautiful. I could not bear meeting that family in such a place for the first time.

Mr. George W. Wood invited me to dinner for tomorrow, two miles [from here], and he will call for me in his carriage at 4. I remarked that many persons who visited the exhibition investigated my style more closely than at Liverpool, and the surface of the work was nearly properly understood by a young Quakeress that had eyes much like those of my kind friend Hannah Rathbone. A Dr. Holme[6] spent several hours yesterday and today looking at them. Four different times I was [asked] if they were on sale.

When at Liverpool I found the streets full of annoyances, but compared with Manchester it is nothing. I thought that the gentleman that accompanied me from Piccadilly to King Street and myself would be carried by force off the pavement. Groups of those abandoned females of from twenty to thirty stood watching for prey at all the corners we passed. The appearance of the feminine sex is not so prepossessing here as it is at Liver-

6. Edward Holme (1770–1847), physician, was founder and first president of the Manchester Natural History Society and a founder of the Chetham Society.

pool. The women in the streets have none of that freshness of coloring nor the fullness of breasts that I remarked at the seaport. I conceive this is the result of the confinement they have to [undergo] in the manufactories.

I walked to S. Brookes's along the turnpike about two miles from the Exchange. The country is not, however, verdant nor the seats immediately around the town so elegant and clean-looking as "Green Bank" for instance. The funnels raised to carry off the smoke of the manufactories appear in hundreds in all directions, and as you walk the streets the whirring sound of the jennies is constant on the ear.

Now my Lucy, Good Night. I hope to receive some letters from thee in a day or two, and I hope that thou art on the eve of hearing of me also. God bless thee, Good Night.

[Here J. J. A. entered the following thoughts, without date, under a copy of a letter to Lucy Audubon.]

When walking the streets I have been much amused with the appearance of young men wearing the uniform of footmen, mounted on fine horses, and going at the full rate of ten miles per hour as if the safety of their necks depended on the speed of their horses. I would think that the reverse might be expected. But their epaulets looking like two brass stewing pans, and a bonnet that might save the purchasing of an umbrella, a red jacket tightly buttoned, pantaloons more than double the width of mine, whiter than snow, spurs full four inches in length, and a black leather strap holding the chin from falling in action, give the best idea of all that must be as disagreeable to the comfort of the bearer as it shocks the eye of the unaccustomed stranger. However, I am informed that many of these youths, being the descendants of the lords of the nation, can live without paying their debts, either to the tailor or shoemaker, or the tavern-keeper or the XXXXXX. I have no doubt that *they* are quite happy.

Manchester   September 14th, 1826   Thursday

To-day, for the first time since here, I had the pleasure of touching a female's hand. During the morning one of the Misses Greg came with a brother and chatted a long time with me. I feel the want, however, of a family introduction, extremely. Without female society I am like a herring on a griddle. The only family [with whom] I expected to enjoy ease of conversation is out of town; [I refer to] the Touchets. I have seen nothing of Mr. Heywood's sister.

I visited the Academy. Dr. Holme was extremely polite. At four Mr. Wood drove me in his carriage, in company [with] four [other] persons all strangers to England, to his house about three miles from Manchester. Mrs. Wood is extremely tall, but cannot be called handsome. Her conversation seemed chosen and without the freedom of that of her husband, who is certainly a superior man. A very severe cold that I [am] now enjoying in all its glory rendered me dull, and the time passed, but passed heavily. One of the visitors was from Mexico and well acquainted with the country. He spoke of the mines in a very entertaining manner. Another was [from] La Guayra, another from Constantinople, the last from Sumatra. They were all men of information, visiting England for their pleasure, apparently.

The door where the tea was handed round resembled a bookseller's shop so much that anyone unacquainted with Mr. Wood would have supposed him deeply engaged in the business. This evening had the appearance of frost, yet Mrs. Wood had just made one hundred bags of black gauze [to cover the same number of] bunches of grapes, [to] enable them to ripen without being destroyed by wasps.

A controversy arose as to the benefit of black over any other color as a conductor or retainer of heat. It ended as it began, each defendant fixed forever on his own opinion.

The changes in the weather here are really remarkable. At daylight this morning it rained hard. At [noon] it was fair. And tonight it has the appearance of a very severe frost, [which] may yet melt away. And was the sun to shine [in] one hour (which would be 12 o'clock midnight), I would not think it extremely wonderful after [Charles] Waterton has performed.

I believe that I have forgot to say to thee that I have engaged a lad of about twelve years of age to receive the tickets at the exhibition for ten shillings per week. His name is John Wilson. [He is] the son of George Wilson, late of T. Kearsley's, Fustian Manufacturer, Riding Court, St. Mary's Gate, Manchester. I am quite sure that, shouldst thou meet either the father or the son or the ghost of either of them, thou shouldst know no more about them or their condition than I did before I left America.

My cold is so bad that I can hardly hold up my head. God bless thee, good night.

I cannot sleep, and I have got out of my bed, dressed and washed myself, and walked the room for upwards of one hour to try to be benefited by Franklin's advice.[7] But all this won't do. I cannot sleep. A man awake and alone in a bed is a most stupid animal in creation. What the feelings of females are on such occasions, it will be best for thee to say. I am writing again. For although I am lodging at a circulating library, the books below will not come by themselves to my assistance, and I cannot, in good conscience, [rouse] the house because I alone in it cannot sleep.

I will give thee an account of true business inclinations of almost all individuals at Manchester. A man whose name I know not advised me yesterday morning, in a very cordial manner, to have a large sign painted with birds, &c., to be affixed at the street door of the Exchange to attract the eye of the passersby. Was I to paint a sign, no doubt the Manchester gentry would stop to look at it. Moreover, I fear that [if] the sign was painted by thy husband they would gaze at it so long that they would forget that 200 drawings are waiting to be examined for the mere trifle of one shilling. This [persuades] me to have no sign.

It is half past 2, and, sure enough, the rain is battering my window. It is a sound that always operates kindly on me when wakeful. I will try to sleep now. And now my Lucy, as I hope thou art happy and composedly enjoying rest, God bless and preserve thee.

---

7. Audubon *père* apparently introduced his son early to *The Disappointed Pendulum*.

MANCHESTER, Septr. 14, 1826

To Lucy Audubon
MY DEAREST FRIEND,

Although I wrote to thee only the evening before last, I set at it again. I will not say much. I am quite well, and well doing. I am received here as kindly as at Liverpool, putting between as differences those existing from individuals in trade and those who are not. I dined with the American Consul yesterday. He entertained a fine company. The famous banker Loyd, one of the wealthiest in England, was introduced to me. I dine out again to-day two miles out of the town with a Mr. George W. Wood. I only know him thus far through letters of recommendation. I will copy the letter from Mr. Roscoe to Miss Edgeworth, and a sonnet[8] of [Jane Roscoe] the daughter of that great man, wrote to my praise. I hope it will give thee pleasure. Do write, my Lucy, do write. It is all I can enjoy when far from thee. Not a word have I yet received. Kiss our Johnny. Tell him that he must exert himself at drawing. I wish he would begin a collection, himself, of drawings in my style—birds, plants, &c.; everything is valuable here that is *correctly true*. It may prove to him of immense benefit, as I am opening such a fine road for him here. God bless thee, and all about thee,

Forever thine most faithfully,

JOHN JAMES AUDUBON

Manchester   Sept. 15th, 1826

Well, my Lucy, the weather is just as I represented it. I slept about two hours this morning, and at 5 o'clock the houses were covered with frost, and I felt uncommonly cold and disagreeable.

My exhibition was ill-attended, but those persons who came were highly pleased. A Mr. Hoyle, a very eminent chemist, brought with him four daughters with little grey satin bonnets, grey satin spencers,[9] and beautifully plain white petticoats. Their eyes searched my mode of work, but, I am sure, would reach the heart of any man sooner.

8. *See* Chapter II, page 128, note 38.
9. Coats.

I became acquainted with a Mr. Freeman,[10] miniature artist, and his lady, both Americans, the latter truly beautiful with all the coloring of the fair sex here.

I saw also a personage battered by much travelling, who had been with Baron [von] Humboldt two years in America.

Mr. Heywood,[11] the banker, came also, and invited me to dine with him on Sunday next. But the most curious incident was that I received a note drawn in the style of a puffing paragraph, anonymous, merely saying at the end of the preamble that Mr. Audubon might make use of it or destroy it. The American Consul being with me, I showed it to him and he simply assured me that it must be some friend of science that felt it too much to pay for [the advertisement], and yet wished me to have it inserted in tomorrow's paper. Singular act of courtesy, this.

Another no less curious incident took place. I received a few lines from my good friend William Rathbone, informing me that the last letter I enclosed to him, for thee, was undirected. I answered him immediately with the [reply] thou seest [Audubon copied it here].

My time passes very dully. I have not yet a family where I can go and chat in a friendly manner. Manchester feels very different indeed, so far, from Liverpool. I spent my evening at the Reverend James J. Taylor in the company of his wife and two gentlemen, one a Parisian. I cannot help expressing again to thee my surprise at finding the people of England generally speaking, so unacquainted with the customs, habits and localities of our country. The principal conversation about it always turns [to] Indians and their ways, as if the land produced nothing else. Mrs. Taylor, having visited that portion of the European continent that is, amongst this nation, called fashionable, is extremely agreeable of conversation, not handsome yet quite interesting by her polite manners. The Parisian is well versed in the knowledge of his country. The other gentleman was, and is yet I daresay, an entomologist.

Almost every lady draws well in England in water colors— very many much better than I ever will do, and yet few of them

10. Freeman, a miniaturist, enjoyed passing fame.

11. B. A. Heywood (1793–1865), the banker, was knighted in 1838. For a later generation of Heywoods, see Joseph S. Leatherbarrow, *Victorian Period Piece* (London, 1954).

dare shew me their productions. It is perhaps because I have such a quantity of my own against one or two pieces of theirs.

I retired at half past 10, the evening beautiful. What the morning of tomorrow may be, I cannot tell. I cannot imagine why no letters from thee have reached me yet. God bless thee, good night.

MANCHESTER, September 15th, 1826
[William Rathbone, Liverpool]
MY DEAR SIR,

I was as happy at receiving your short letter of yesterday as I am surprised [to] read that I had omitted writing the direction on my wife's letter. To a man of business it would appear, no doubt, bordering on the wonderful. To me it proves for the thousand and one time that I was not intended to be one. A former occurrence, of the like want of strict care, is now forced on my recollection, and if you will permit me, I will restate it.

During my desired apprenticeship at the mercantile business in New York (about twenty-five years ago, I think), I was in the employ of an agent of the house of Guest & Banker of London, and was the cashier. A remittance being ordered to be made to the house in Philadelphia, I drew a check, had it signed, received the amount ($10,000) [in *Myself* he said $6,000] at the Manhattan Bank, and, having enclosed all in a letter that I did not *forget to direct*, I put it in the Post Office *unsealed*. Having occasion to go to Philadelphia the next day, Mr. Banker or Mr. Guest (I really do not now recollect which) spoke of the error in such kind terms that I felt the mortification of having acted wrong tenfold, and thought frequently that I would try during my future life to think of only one thing at a time.

No, my excuse to you can only be this: the letter, although wrote for my wife with good intent, was *so far from the object I thought of* when finishing it, that the true object made me forget the letter. Now should I ever err thus again, please always direct to Mrs. Audubon, St. Francisville, Bayou Sara, Louisiana.

Hoping that all is well in Abercromby [Street], "Woodcroft," "Green Bank," Great George Street, Lodge Lane, St. Anne Street &c., &c., &c., permit me to remain, my dear Mr. Rathbone, forever your obliged, obedient servant,

J. J. AUDUBON

[The following letter to Hannah Rathbone appears here, and shows how Audubon was thinking and feeling after his departure from the Rathbones.]

MANCHESTER, Sept. 16th, 1826.

Miss Rathbone, Green Bank, Near Liverpool

MY DEAR MISS HANNAH,

If Manchester is a dull town of itself, I can now boast that it contains at least one happy individual at present! This morning I had the pleasure and comfort of reading two long letters from my beloved wife. My family was all well thirty days after my departure.

I have been longing to write to you ever since I left your delightful "Green Bank," but my spirits were low, and even the beautiful sharp, neat little knife that was so kindly given me by a particular friend that I hope is now quite well, under your roof, would not cut a pen to my liking until now.

I cannot bear Manchester. With the exception of two of the Misses Greg, I have not seen any ladies yet with whom I have been able to chat without either blushing, or trembling as awkwardly as ever. I am sorry to say that Mrs. Touchet's family is absent and that I fear *my visiting* your friends, the Greg family, at their country seat will be of very short duration, unless I should abandon the plan of going at the end of next week to Birmingham to hear some good music. Oh, how much I would enjoy this beautiful evening if near your kind Mamma and you. With what pleasure I would see the little robin pick from the plate before the window a few grains for his supper, or look on the thrushes hiding themselves, their bills furnished with a tray of mulberries, or listen to the sweet sounds [played] by my friends John and Henry Chorley, or take a full pinch of snuff from Mr. Austin's box, and again perhaps from your brother Richard's or the "Intelligent Swiss's." None of this can I enjoy. Therefore I will think doubly of the kind privilege you have allowed me to write to you.

My little son John Woodhouse enclosed me from America a couple of small [drawing] essays of his on rice paper. I have taken the liberty to put one in this, with hopes that perhaps you would give it a place in the little red portfolio. I hope sincerely that he may have the honor of thanking you himself for such acceptance. I will not apologize for the want of merit in the drawing. John is only twelve years old[12] and is *my son*.

The sun is now set, I see you all at tea, kind to each other as ever you were. I alone am speaking with my pen only. I have just drank a glass of wine to the health and continual happiness of all the inhabitants of "Green Bank." Many, many such will I wish again if a longer life is granted me. I shall not breakfast with my "Intelligent [Swiss"] friend tomorrow. Neither will I listen to a French sermon. Indeed I can scarce now tell to what church I will go. Had I not my beloved wife's letters to read and read again tomorrow, it would be dull indeed, although I have to go to Mr. Heywood's to dine, and that I dread still more than the dullness of Manchester itself.

My letter is composed of different effects of feeling. Please to excuse it. But, between the pleasure of having heard from home and the disagreeable sensation of being 38 miles from you, it would be impossible for me just now to collect one better deserving your attention.

I wrote to your brother William last evening. Please to remember me to both his family and Mrs. Rathbone's of "Woodcroft," to whom I will take the liberty of writing next. Do not *forget* to write your name in full in my blank book, I beg of you. Believe me, with the sincerest sentiments of highest respect, my dear Miss Rathbone,

forever your truly
obedient servant,
J. J. AUDUBON

12. Actually John would be fourteen on November 30.

I know not why I have not received my trunk, &c., from Mr. Munro. I thought he promised to send it, to the care of the Misses Greg.

Manchester   September 16th, 1826

This morning, my Lucy, I received thy two letters of May 28th and June 3rd. Oh how much relieved my anxieties were. I recollect daily our last parting, and my blood often congealed at the idea that perhaps I might never see thee again. Thanks, thanks to thee, my dear wife, for thy kindness to me!!

It is not worth while to say here what I did this day in the way of writing. The copies of my letters to Miss Rathbone, and to Thomas Sully, are sufficient. Then, to the day:

Early this morning I visited a charity school instituted about two hundred years ago in a building created nearly four hundred years past. The antique gothicity of the structure was quite new to me. Some boys dressed in large gowns of coarse blue cloth, their heads close-sheared, feet kept from the damp by large shoes ornamented with large brass buckles, exhibited the curiosities contained here and in a nasal sing-song key explained, quite aloud I assure thee, the meaning or name of all the stranger saw. The library is immense, but so old that many of the books appeared better fit for food for worms than men. The boys are eighty in number. I understood the teacher principal was unwell. The kitchen, of immense size, was particularly neat and the servant attendant very polite. The bread room, as it was called, contained many large loaves, in substance much like those distributed to soldiers on their marches.

I spent nearly all my time at my Exhibition Room. Saw some ladies who spoke a good deal to me. But my cold rendered me still very uncomfortable. I read thy letters frequently. Mr. Tanetti, an Italian who has a large establishment of paintings and fancy objects on sale, gave me advice about my exhibition and told me that if well managed it must [mean] a fortune. May God grant it.

How often I wished for an impossible thing this day; that is, to be at work in America and have my drawings exhibiting there. I conceived the idea of having my son Victor here to attend to it, and [of myself] returning to America to draw more and on a handsomer plan still. For what is my life intended, if not to [chart] for my sons the way to industry and consequently to happiness. I thought of writing to N. Berthoud on that subject and [getting] his ideas about it.

I retired early, and wrote late, and late wished thee good night, my sweet beloved wife.

Manchester Sept. 17th, 1826 Sunday

Having closed my letters to thee, to Thomas Sully, to De Witt Clinton and Henry Clay, I shaved, washed, dressed myself, and heard the town clock strike 2, [with] apprehension that I might be too late at Mr. Heywood's for dinner. However, I walked gently down Bridge Street and followed the Great Road toward Liverpool. I was much pleased with my walk. For nearly a mile [out of] Manchester the road lays on an elevation, apparently made up mostly of earth [and] giving an extensive as well as an interesting view of the country for many miles. A small creek ornaments the foreground, and the vast number of pretty English women bound to afternoon church service fed my eyes amply, although my stomach grumbled all the while at my lingering [along the way] towards "Claremont." I followed the new [branch] of the old road and thereby arrived at the younger Mr. Heywood's.

I was about to suffer an "Hey ho!" to escape when the gatekeeper, or porter, or sentinel, (for the person might be called by all or any of those names), told me that I might "walk through the grounds, turn to the left, and reach the old gentleman's seat."[13] My stomach thanked the man with a very indecent sort of a grumbling noise, I thought, and I hurried on, leaped over an English five-bar gate, and was in the presence of—who does thou think, Lucy? Not Waterton's snake, nor his alligators, no indeed.[14] It was the elder Miss Heywood, I guess, because one older could not exist and be a Miss. My steps at once became balanced. They could have been counted a mile off without a

13. Much of this entry's penmanship suggests that Audubon's carafe was handy.
14. Waterton attacked Audubon's paper on the rattlesnake. Yet his *Wanderings* . . . contains at least one tall snake story, later challenged by John Bachman.

telescope. My face cooled also, and my speech was adapted to the *tournure* of Miss Heywood.

"This way, Sir," [I heard, and] jumped to open another five-bar gate. "You have seen many Indians, I daresay, Sir."

Now Lucy, I daresay that I *have!*

"Pray, Sir, are there not very many snakes in America?"

I was so near laughing that I *daresay* Miss Heywood saw my situation and spoke of her brother. But Lucy, as I am fond of ladies, read here two descriptions.

Mrs. Hedge, my landlady, is low, and Miss Heywood is high. Mrs. Hedge is fatter than Miss Heywood. Both do not weigh more than 450 pounds *avoir du poids*. My landlady's hams, if *cured well*, would turn out the more extraordinary bacon. My Mrs. Hedge borders on fifty years, and the maid of "Claremont" has set seventy springs aside, without enumerating those that now creak most vehemently in her well set corset. The woman of King Street is kind. So is the lady of "Claremont." The former charges me two shillings for a dinner. To dine with the other I must wear three shillings worth of boots.

"Stop, stop," thou sayest, "for goodness sake stop. Why my LaForest, this is most tiresome and absurd. I cannot bear it."

Well, well, I have reached a beautiful garden, and far in the distance Mr. Heywood and one of his nephews are perceived. We meet and shake hands. The fat maid leaves us and we are talking about *American bugs!!!* Fine conversation to be sure. I would like to know what the entomologist *Thomas Say*, Esq., Academician, &c., &c., &c., &c., &c., &c., would say on such an occasion. American bugs!!! Waterton only saw *one*—I have seen millions. And Thomas Say[15] has described the same species over and over again, probably hundreds of times. "Mr. Audubon, this is a most destructive insect. It kills all my beech trees," [I can fairly hear Mrs. Percy of "Beech Woods" saying]. I look and imagine I see the little beautifully white flies that [fill] our beech woods, here before me, and wish myself in America.

The grounds of "Claremont" are fine, and on a much larger scale than those of "Green Bank," but the style is utterly differ-

---

15. Thomas Say (1787–1834), *American Entomology*, 3 vols. (Begun in 1817, completed in 1824–28, New Harmony, Indiana).

ent. The house is too large ever to be *filled with friends*. However, I was received as kindly as any other man as well recommended would have been. Mr. Heywood seems to feel the great weight of his purse, yet he talks plainly and put me at my ease in a few moments. There was no company from abroad, two nephews, Miss Heywood, and another Miss, perhaps. I am quite as old [as] were all that sat round the table with me. The dinner was plain, much more so than at "Green Bank." The wine was not handed me with Hannah Rathbone's kindness. No, it was poured here in each person's glass by the waiters. The ladies left us early, and we the gentlemen soon afterward left the table. We talked of America again and principally of the Battle of New Orleans, [which] seems yet to be a great rough bone in their throat.[16]

In the library where we had sat before dinner we retired to drink tea, and Miss Heywood's portfolio of drawings of birds shewed itself to me as I entered and said quite aloud to my senses, "Audubon, be merciful." Who would not be when looking at beautiful drawings finished under the fair hands of a fair female? Stuffed, by Washington! Yes, stuffed specimens, and the drawings *stuff* also!

"What do you think of them, Mr. Audubon?" [I hear].

No my Lucy, if kindness ever entered thy heart, if the disconsolate brought on involuntary tears to thy eye, if thou ever hast pitied the culprit as he passed thee with downcast looks of agony, take pity on thy husband and answer for him.

I took up the drawing, looked at it sideways, brought it close to my eye, glanced [from] the proper distance to [judge] the effect—and—well—shall I tell thee what I said? Upon my word I do not recollect what I said. I passed drawings, one after another to the last, and my heart was glad [and] my eyes were relieved when several sheets of blank paper appeared together without drawings. The book [was] closed, and I will close the subject of the trifling observation that I [would] address to parents generally:

If you please, good friends all, do not tease the stranger's eye

---

16. Battle of New Orleans, January 8, 1815. Won by Americans under Jackson, before word of peace treaty crossed the sea. British losses 2,000, American, 8.

with the daubs that parents' conceit [reckons] equal to Raphael's designs. Be not deluded at first, and you will not find out the truth when too late to repent.

I took my coffee, and answered to all the questions put to me about snakes, Indians, Mr. Waterton, John Hunter,[17] and myself until, perceiving that my good host Mr. Heywood had fell asleep, I felt inclined to do the same, and as gently as possible bade the circle good night.

The moon was high, the clouds large, dark, and portentous of a stormy night. I knew the navigator was preparing to reef all sails and to double the helm at sea. The dull dashes of lightning in the north only augmented the growing horrors of the expected scene of death. Here the people, pressing forward each on each, hurried towards Manchester to escape the rain that fell heavy on the ground, drop by drop, each [drop] raising a little cloud of dust. As I walked faster than those good citizens, I could plainly hear the heaving breasts of the fair maids through the rustling of their silky gowns, and as they leaned and hung for support on the arm of their lovers, their looks were most interesting.

Where is my Lucy now? Is there a storm about her, or is she herself alone?—calm!—serene!—beautiful and happy!!

I am inside, and in a few moments will blow my light. The storm has passed over, merely as a ruffled, angry thought the countenance of man. Now all Nature is beautiful and calm again. Such is the weather of Manchester. Now my Lucy, good night.

MANCHESTER, Sept. 17th, 1826. Sunday

MY DEAREST FRIEND,

I at last received two letters from thee yesterday morning, and although they both are of extremely old date—the 28th of May and 3rd of June—they have relieved me from much anxiety. Thank thee, dearest Lucy, for them and their contents.

I have wrote now very frequently to thee since my arrival. Indeed this is the third time during one week, but I

---

17. Sir John Dunn Hunter, father of Mrs. Basil Hall. Author. Murdered by Cherokee Indians in east Texas in 1827.

will nearly repeat all that I mentioned in all of them in substance in this one. I have been most kindly received at Liverpool by all those to whom I was introduced either by letters from America or subsequent means, and I feel that the name of Audubon has left no disgrace behind him. There are at Liverpool three families of the name Rathbone, to all of whom I am particularly indebted, and towards whom I never can cease to feel the highest sentiments of gratitude. Through them I formed the acquaintance of all the best families, and by their recommendations abroad I cannot fail to continue to be received with all the kind hospitality that renders a stranger happy when far from his friends and relations. To Dr. Thomas S. Traill, the President of the Royal Institution of Liverpool, and Mr. Roscoe, a most eminent person now known over all the world, I also owe a great portion of my success.

My drawings were exhibited for four weeks without a cent of expense to myself, and produced me £100. My time was spent the while at painting and drawing, to present pieces of my work as slender works of my gratitude. I gave to the Institution a large piece of a "Wild Turkey Cock," to Mrs. Richard Rathbone one of the "Otter in a Trap," to Mr. Roscoe a "Robin," and to each of my other friends also a drawing.

Mrs. Rathbone, the mother of all these friends of mine, a most venerable lady [Mrs. William Rathbone III[18]], having invited me to her house, I spent two weeks there enjoying all that can be enjoyed far from thee, my Lucy. When I left Liverpool, now one week ago precisely, the President sent the Curator of the Institution to wait on me and help me here to arrange my collection for exhibition. I am again known by the most distinguished persons here in Manchester and its environs.

My plans will be now fixed, unless altered by accidents or circumstances, as follows. It is my intention to travel through England and Scotland very slowly, exhibiting

18. For a good description of Mrs. William Rathbone III ("the Queen Bee"), see Hewlett's . . . *Memoirs of Henry Fothergill Chorley (1808–72)* (London, 1874).

my work until the first of March next, when I wish to reach London and there exhibit on a larger scale and for a long time.

During my travels I am determined to apply [myself to] painting in oil and to drawing pieces of large birds and quadrupeds to make part of my exhibition. Should I, on the contrary, discover that my exhibition does not continue to produce as much as I conceive it ought—say, four times the amount of my expenses—I will go to Paris or London sooner, and publish my work and establish myself under the patronage of some person of importance. It would be difficult for me at present to say more of my movements.

Now my beloved wife I would wish thee, at the end of thy time at the "Beech Woods," to remove either to Nicholas Berthoud's at Shippingport or to New York City. The latter I would greatly prefer, viewing the quickness of communication with this country. Or the thing still more preferable [would be] for thee to come over with John only, and travel with me, or remain with me either in London or Paris where I think I may reside a long time. If thou were remaining at New York or any other part of the United States that thou wouldst prefer, I would remit [to] thee punctually amounts sufficient to keep thee well [and] comfortable; but in such a case our son John must come to me, as, situated as I will be, I wish him to make rapid strides in the world. If I succeed even as I have done, I can afford you all, all the comfort that I hope would be thought sufficient, and through my friends in Liverpool I would be able in course of time to procure a good situation for our Victor, should he prefer being nearer his father and mother. I have always afforded thee the following of thy wishes in all things, and I again entreat thee to do nought but thy pleasure respecting the offers now adverted to. In the meantime, I earnestly entreat thee to *speak French* and *think in French* if possible. I also entreat thee that my son John should spend a great portion of his time at drawing from *Nature only*, all the size of life, and to scrupulously keep every drawing he makes. And if it is possible for thee or him to remember what plants, or birds, snakes, fishes, or insects, &c., &c., that I have not drawn, to attend more particularly to those, but to draw all he can. Do also insist on his taking lessons of music from thee on the piano. I wish I had brought him and thee also along with me.

I certainly have brought with me my collection that is considered as the best of the kind in existence, but I wish I had remained two more years at close work in the woods of my beloved America.[19]

I shall take thy advice respecting the "Beech Woods," I assure thee. Yes, should I return to America and to Louisiana, I would go to my good friend Bourgeat's with great pleasure, without trespassing one foot north of his line.[20]

The letter enclosed in thine that thou ought to have opened is from Mr. [Thomas] Sully, who says that he sent me one directed to New Orleans for Sir Thomas Lawrence. I would like to receive it. I have wrote to him this day. Thy watch is gone long ago by way of New York. I have sent thee and N. Berthoud packs of newspapers, and will continue to do so. I think it not worth while to send thee any other things until my future life is more ascertained, or thy own plans known to me.

Now farewell, my dear Lucy, my beloved wife. Write often. Kiss my dear John for me. It is very doubtful if I do call on Miss Gifford[21] at all. I may, however, see her, should I be presented to the Duke of Devonshire, [to] whose domain she goes sometimes. Farewell, God bless thee and grant thee happiness. I have seen very little of thy sister Ann. They see no company and I have been in a constant round of it. Again, God bless thee. Thine friend and husband,

J. J. AUDUBON

---

19. Audubon returned to America in spring of 1829 to redraw some birds and to draw others for the first time.

20. Audubon and Mrs. Percy had an altercation over his portraits of her daughters. She ordered him off the plantation, relenting only during his convalescence from yellow fever in Natchez, and for one year until his sailing on the *Delos*.

21. Euphemia Gifford, wealthy Derbyshire first cousin of William Bakewell, the father-in-law of Audubon.

Charles Middlemist's wife shall receive her money as soon as I reach London, he may rest assured. I have wrote to H. Clay for a letter of introduction, especially to General Lafayette. I *wish thee* to write to him also, and ask him to send me one to the care of the *Minister at London.*

MY DEAR BELOVED SON, JOHN,

I am truly glad to receive the two watch papers you sent me in Mamma's letter. Do continue to improve. Draw, my dear boy, and study music. You will soon now be able to assist your father very much in rendering our good friend your Mamma quite comfortable. Oh what pleasure you will feel then. Copy this letter, and send as much of it as Mamma may wish, to your brother Victor. I['ll] send you some chalks and colors in a few weeks. God bless you. Affectionately your father,

J. J. A.

Manchester Sept. 18th, 1826 Monday

The weather being beautiful, I took a good walk. Had to-day more persons than usual at my rooms. A Mr. Railston of Feltonfold, Cheatham Hill, who brought a handsome wife and three sweet children, spent a good deal of time. Giving me a card [he] invited me extremely kindly to his cottage to spend either the day or the night, whenever it would be agreeable or convenient. I know not Mr. Railston any other way than through this mark of extreme politeness, and will try to make some return. A party from Mr. Heywood's also came; and Miss Heywood, I hope, saw some *Drawings of Birds.*

I received my trunk, &c., from Liverpool, and a packet of letters from Richard Rathbone, [including] a note of invitation from Mr. Samuel Greg to go and spend some time at "Quarry Bank," fourteen miles from [here].

The invitation I had from Mr. Sergeant[22] was not forgotten, and he came for me at half past 3, to shew me the way to his house. Let me tell thee that before that I had the pleasure of

22. E. W. Sergeant appears in Audubon's *Letters* . . . (Cambridge, 1930), I, 101. The Weyhe Gallery, New York City, owns drawings sold by Audubon to Sergeant.

meeting Mr. Murray at my rooms, and he was very kind to me also.

I have been delighted with the acquaintance of Mr. Sergeant, and his house, his books and his pictures, his guns and his dogs, and very much so with a friend of his from London who also dined with us. We chatted very friendly, made experiments with percussion pieces, and drank some good wine until half past 10. I offered him Harlan's "Fauna," and he promised me a good blooded pointer. He gave me a small box of brass containing brass medals of all the great victories of England.

Amongst the letters that came for me [was] one of thanks from the Secretary of the Liverpool Royal Institution for my [painting of the] Wild Turkey.

Receiving no letters from Mr. Alexander Gordon, I wrote the following to him. I felt some anxiety to see how he would express himself towards me in his recommendations.

A. Gordon, Esq., Liverpool
My Dear Sir,

I have now been here a week, and after constant and strict enquiries I am forced to conclude that your intended visit must have been postponed. The good people of Manchester have received me with great marks of attention, and I am going on much as I did when at Liverpool. From this place I will go to Birmingham, Oxford, &c., as I told you when last I had the pleasure of seeing you, and as I do not at all like travelling entirely through this country without the letters that you promised me, I ask you again for some.

Please remember me to Mrs. Gordon and Miss Donathan, and believe, &c., &c., &c.

J. J. A.

It now becomes quite necessary to inform thee, my beloved wife, that the portion of my wardrobe not infrequently called shirts is fast giving way. Therefore I looked at some linens this day, and probably will buy some tomorrow. God bless thee. Good night, my love. It is raining now like fury.

Manchester   September 19th, 1826   Tuesday

I saw Mr. Melly this morning at the Exchange. He had just arrived from Liverpool. He had gone to my doorkeeper, and, having examined the *book of income,* he told me when we met that he was very sorry and displeased at my want of success and that my exhibition would never do. He advised me, as he always has done before, to go either to London or Paris, but to Paris in preference, and return to Liverpool first and see my friends there and [obtain] more letters. Altogether he so much reduced my spirits that I felt sick and I am sure must have changed my countenance extremely. He wished me to go and dine with him at Mr. George Murray's with some French persons of his acquaintance, but when I told him that I contemplated going out at 4 to "Quarry Bank," to pass the night, he urged me by all means to do so. We parted for a short while, for at 4, whilst I was taking a cup of coffee with Miss [Ellen] Greg in Fountain Street, in came my "Intelligent" friend, who turned quite pale [on] meeting the very fair and amiable companion I was with. The fair maid did not turn pale, no. She blushed as if a blooming rose, and for a while her dark eyelashes robbed both the "Intelligent Swiss" and I from the pleasure of looking at her eyes. Now the query is, does he or [she] love the other most? That they both love, *I* have not the least doubt, and may God bless them!

Mr. Samuel Greg, the father of the large family, came in and met me as if he had known me fifty years. The brothers [his sons] Samuel and William also came. The carriage was ordered and I was soon seated precisely in front of the fair maid. Her father was next to her, and off we went, pushing for the country as if moving off from evil spirits. I think that on moderate calculation I looked at the objects *before me* one hundred times more than I did on any about the country we traversed, and had we not crossed a river nearly fifty feet wide I would have looked one more time in the same [interval]. But this river I did look at and positively stared when I was told that it was a stream of great importance. [Its] name I have forgotten,[23] but I know it to be several miles from Manchester on the way to Derbyshire. The

---

23. The Irwell River.

land, I remarked, is improved by an immense quantity of [lime], to grow wheat principally. The aspect of the country improved extremely, and many of the buildings really beautiful. We at last turned quickly to the right and moved slowly down a declivity, when I saw "Quarry Bank," a most enchanting spot situated on the edge of the same river we had crossed, the grounds truly picturesque, and improved as much as improvements can be.

I was introduced to three ladies that I met drawing, reading and writing. The misses Mary Ann, &c., &c., and I kissed the second daughter of my friend William Rathbone. We had tea, and the drawing being continued, I made a sketch in black chalk of a dog, and rubbed it with cork to give an idea to the ladies of the improvement over the common stumps usually used.

Then I accompanied the two brothers (who had come home on horseback) to a discussion club instituted on their premises for the advancement of their workmen. Going there we passed the chapel [and] a long line of cottages for the working people, and at last entered the schoolroom where about twenty men had assembled and were awaiting the arrival of their young masters. The question presented consisted of ascertaining the superior advantages between the discovery of the *compass* or the art of *printing*. Had our Franklin been there, he could have told something, on both sides of the question, well worth relating, but the illustrious man lies at the corner of Fourth and Mulberry Streets in Philadelphia. We did without him. I, Lucy, delivered a lecture this evening! Now do not laugh so. I assure thee I understood the subject well, and that is more than one half of the lecturers can assert with a clear conscience. I spoke of Birds, Alligators, Beavers, and Indians.

Marched back to the company of the ladies at nearly 10 o'clock, took a glass of white wine, looked at Miss [Ellen], bid the three other sisters good night, shook hands with the father and the sons, entered a room for me that night, undressed in a thrice, and bid thee at leisure good night. My thoughts were very gloomy, uncertain of the future, undetermined because uncertain. I turned over and over in search of—thee, my Lucy, but all in vain, and at last I closed my eyes, impatient to see the next day.

"Quarry Bank," 12 Miles from Manchester
Sept. 20th   Wednesday

The clock from Mr. Greg's mills made me think of arising, and although the weather was bad, cloudy and rainy I took an immense walk down and up the river, through the gardens, along the ponds, about the woods, the fields and the meadows. Saw a fine flock of Partridges, some Jays, &c., and at half past 8 I had nearly finished daubing a picture of an Esquimaux drawn in a sleigh by four dogs. The conversation of the ladies during the morning was extremely animated and interesting. We all talked about the primitive state of nature in our kind, and discussed, if or no, it was preferable to the present stage of [man's behavior]. I know that I astonished the ladies with my odd ways and my curious expressions, but all this could not be helped, and I enjoyed *them* most certainly.

The sight of the Partridges in the morning and of those that were on the dinner table made me [propose] a shooting party for the afternoon. I expressed my wish to see some Pheasants and to draw some. All was arranged, and the pleasure was augmented by the arrival of Mr. Shaw, Lord Stamford's[24] principal gamekeeper, who obligingly [offered] to show us many birds (thus Partridges are called]. Here we were, with guns no longer than my arms, two good dogs, and plenty of land before us. Pheasants are not to be touched until October 1, in this land of freedom, and I dare venture to say that, had we seen none, we would not have infringed on the laws of the goodly country. But somehow or other (as a Kentuckian would say) I positively saw one, tilt over tail after head, until down to the earth he came, as dead, I believe, as if shot any time next month. Beautiful creature, his eye was yet all life, his crest all crimson, his coat all brilliance. Presently another was brought down. Indeed I had so completely forgotten to think of October that every bird that flew brought the gun to my eye; and I would have played the Pheasants a bad trick had not the gamekeeper interfered in their behalf.

---

24. Lord Stamford was a descendant of Henry Grey, first Earl of Stamford (*c.* 1599–1673).

We had a fine walk and a fine hunt, killed some Partridges and saw the hills in Derbyshire, the hills amongst which my Lucy was born.[25] How I thought of thee, of Matlock; thy birthplace; of England; of thee, and the hills before me, forty miles from where my Lucy received light and breath!! Mr. Shaw pocketed five shillings and we [took] the Pheasants and Partridges. Thus I have hunted once on British grounds, on Lord Stamford's domains, where every tree that we would scarcely call a sapling is marked and numbered, and for all that I know [costs] a tax to [the] government or a tithe to the parish. A Partridge that crosses the river, or a road, or a hedge, and alights on other grounds than those of Lord Stamford are as safe from his attacks as if it were in Guinea.

We returned to "Quarry Bank," well fatigued, and enjoyed our tea drinking well, I assure thee. The evening was beautiful. Of course thou seest that it has rained and cleared up fine. I got up. We talked much about Mr. Sim's views of the interior of this earth. The whole company were much interested; and the rapid improvements of our country also a subject brought forward. I again looked at Miss [Ellen] very much. I could not help it. She is so very attractive of looks and manners, and so polite, and so—God bless thee, my Lucy, good night.

Manchester   Sept. 21st, 1826   Thursday

About 6 o'clock I sat to drink some cocoa, eat some bread and butter, and then packed my male pheasant snugly to take it to Manchester to draw it. I was soon mounted on Dicky the pony and moving slowly toward town again, holding the basket in my hand and kicking Dicky to force him to trot. And he trotted and I jumped, for Dicky trotted hard and I would not ride à l'anglaise. Of course my posterior was sadly *hurt*, at my stubbornness. But Dicky, after three hours of consideration, took me direct to his stable in Chancery Lane, not by chance but by solid *raisonnement*. He was glad of being relieved from my weight, I daresay, and I was glad to be on foot again.

25. Some lines later Audubon gives the true birthplace of Lucy, Burton-upon-Trent, Staffordshire. Her family lived near Crich village, not far from Matlock, Derbyshire, before moving to America. Her own long adherence to "1788" notwithstanding, Lucy was born on January 18, 1787.

I reached my Exhibition Room and received miserable accounts. I saw plainly that my expenses in Manchester would not be repaid, and of course that I must move shortly. I wished to draw the Pheasant but my hands refused to act, and therefore I put my brains at work. I called on Dr. Holme and represented my situation. I told him that my expenses were enormous and my returns did not meet them. He walked to the Academy of Natural History and ordered a committee to meet on Saturday to see if a room could not be provided for me gratis. Mr. Hindley,[26] to whom Mr. Shepherd had given me letters, promised me his assistance. I hunted for another room to remove my drawings to, should I not succeed with the academicians, and should I conclude to try, sometime longer, in this place. This employment did me some good. I took tea at Mr. Bentley's, who has a fine daughter also. Lucy, remark that I do not miss a miss, if fair, wherever I go. He gave me some wires in a board for me to fix my pheasant,[27] and I came to my lodgings in better humor than I left them this morning.

I have mounted my bird. All is ready for work tomorrow. Will my works answer my intentions or will they not? Oh my Lucy, how dull I feel without thee. Good night.

Manchester   September 22nd, 1826   Friday

I have drawn all day and am fatigued. I have had only twenty people to see my Birds. Sad work, this. The Consul Mr. Brookes came to see me and invited me to dine at the banker Mr. Loyd's at 1 next Sunday. He advised me also to have a subscription book for my work, &c., &c. It is easy to have advice, but to strike a good one is very difficult indeed. I am fatigued as I told thee before, and too low in spirits to write answering thoughts tonight. Then farewell, God bless thee, good night.

Manchester   Sept. 23rd, 1826   Saturday

I could not write last evening because I felt fatigued and was rather low of spirit. Therefore I went to bed early, perhaps 9 o'clock. However, a gentle rap at my door made me bid, "Come

---

26. John Haddon Hindley (?) (1765–1827), orientalist, scholar.
27. See "My Method of Drawing Birds," in *Edinburgh Journal of Science*, Vol. VIII (1828). Reissued.

in." And through the dark I recognized the voice of Mr. Bentley, called for a light, and was up in a moment. We chatted a while, read some, drank some; and as he went down the stairs, bound home, I entered my bedroom bound to bed for the second time, and the last time this night, barring *all accidents*.

My drawing moved rapidly this morning, and by 11 o'clock I was ready to dress myself. I walked to the Exchange and met Dr. Holme with several other friends who told me that the Committee had voted unanimously to grant me a room in this Institution, *gratis*, to exhibit my Birds. Of course I thanked them, as it lessened my expenses thirteen shillings per week. I saw Mr. Samuel Greg, Sr., and three of the daughters. Miss Sarah was amongst them. I had many ladies and I felt more gratified than I had been previously this week. I went to dine with the family Greg in Fountain Street. I had sent the Pheasant, killed last Wednesday, to Mr. Robert Greg's countinghouse and saw him at the lodgings of his father. I gave the Misses Greg two dozen black chalks and two dozen six-inch corks to draw with, for which I paid the extraordinary price of %—more than four times as much as in Philadelphia. England is so [overburdened] with duty that it is almost past the power of anyone in it to do his duty much longer. And I feel inclined to think that some period hence will bring forth combustion. But as I said, I felt in better spirits and I hoped that my changing rooms would be of some good result to me, the more so because I determined to do with one person instead of two for my exhibition hereafter.

Now then, that I feel fully at par with the weather that for a wonder is fairer than usual, like myself, *for this world*, let me give thee slight descriptions of the remarkable objects a man may see in England.

Primo, a small man, an Englishman, bearing under his left arm a large setter spaniel and [under his] right a nosegay not quite so sizeable as the dog. On his legs and over a pair of red breeches [he wears] buff-colored chamois gaiters that so completely serve to bog down this little man that an American woodsman would conceive the whole a caricature of our species, [going along his way] with a fairer specimen of the canine creation, and [with] a fairer specimen still of the stores of the goddess Flora. Now Lucy, just look at the red, potato-nosed little man and his sugar-loaf-[shaped] hat, and listen to the inch-[thick] wooden soles of his brass-buckled shoes on the pavement, kept in a nearly constant state of cleanliness by the square flaps of a coachman's "*surtout*," and thou wilt have the fairest picture of one of thy countrymen I can give.

From this [spectacle] I jump into Piccadilly, and turning into Murray's street enter Mr. George Murray's cotton mills, where fifteen hundred souls are kept not only from a state of pure starvation but also from dissolute and extravagant outrages when without either food or employment. Rather natural circumstances. These mills consist of a complete square area of about eight acres with five, six or seven story houses. In the center of this square is a large basin of water from the canal that flows through the tower. Two engines of forty and forty-five horse-power are kept agoing from 6 to 8 o'clock each day and are condensed from the basin mentioned. Mr. Murray himself accompanied me about, and I saw a general blacksmith shop, the turning and spinning of threads of cotton that grew in Louisiana, for Numbers 200 and 250. I saw the gas[-making?] furnace, the processing machines for the cotton hanks, and all that Mr. Murray dare show me when he discovered that I knew something of mechanics.[28] This is the largest establishment owned by one single individual in Manchester. Some others belonging to friends, or co-partnerships of several, have as many as 2,500 working hands—as poor, miserable, abject wretches as ever worked the mines of Golconda.[29] But Lucy, Mr. Greg's mills at "Quarry Bank" are rendered more comfortable. I have been assured that during the time of need and scarcity Mr. Greg kept his hands *paid*, if not employed; and may God give him credit for so doing. Whilst I am speaking of Mr. Greg's mills, Lucy, let me also say something about his manners. He addresses his children in the most patriarchal style I ever heard, and with a kindness only equalled by my friends of "Green Bank." His son Robert, a man married and who has at least one child, dined with us, and the old Mr. Greg scarcely ever spoke to him with-

28. Audubon had owned a saw and grist mill in Henderson, Kentucky.
29. Golconda, the city of Hyderabad, India, was a diamond mine center.

out calling him "My love." He asked his eldest daughter Mary
Ann to drink a glass of wine with him as if with all the anxiety
[of] receiving the boon of a mistress. And when she refused he
appeared quite chagrined, and feared that she was not well. Yet
there is a bluntness in his speech at times; regularly, however, a
complete gentleman. I prefer the bluntness to any of the false,
hypocritical phrases of the fops as much as a beggar prefers a
good dinner to starvation.

I was asked to go and spend next Monday night at Mr. Robert
Hyde Greg's, the son that he called his *love*, "Summer Place,"
Higher Hardwick, but as I had been previously offered a ticket
for a concert for the same night it is doubtful if I will go. I felt
inclined to write much when I begun, and I see that I have really
spun it out pretty well. Yet, I have not done. I took tea at Mr.
Bentley's again and promised to write to thee on his behalf for
the bones of an alligator of a good size. Now we will see if he
gets one as quickly as Dr. Harlan did.[30]

I concluded to-day to have a book of subscriptions, open to
receive the names of all persons inclined to have the *best American illustrations of birds of that country ever yet transmitted to pos-
terity*. And *I* will do so. I have also thought of a plan to procure
lookers-on by putting up a few drawings of mine in the most
conspicuous shops here, to invite the public to call upon me,
with each their shillings, and perhaps out of twenty [win] a
name for my support in publication. Indeed I feel as inclined, if
not more so, to do all in my power to push forward at a round
pace and prove the test of my value, from the penny's worth to
the capital now in the Bank of England!! Now my sweet wife,
God bless thee, good night.

Manchester   Sept. 24th, 1826   Sunday

I drew at my Pheasant until precisely eleven o'clock. The
weather cloudy and the wind much like rain.

Mr. Bentley came in and sat with me perhaps an hour. Then I
had that most disagreeable and fatiguing job to perform, shaving, washing, brushing coat, brushing pantaloons, combing and

---

30. ". . . Alligator," *Edinburgh New Philosophical Journal*, Vol. II (1826–27), 270–80.
Account of hunt for specimen for Richard Harlan, of Philadelphia.

cleaning my long locks, and in fact making ready to walk to Mr. Loyd the banker's. I performed the whole of this in twenty minutes and marched out of King Street, through St. Ann Square, past the Exchange, up fish market, the old church, and Cheatham Hill, [with] my cane in one hand and the other holding both my gloves, as clean, I will say, as any man in England. I passed a turnpike gate where, having given a sixpence, I received back five again and a small ticket, my full title to go through on my return. This is a way in this country that prevents cheating to an eminent degree, and no doubt improves the [efficiency] of the keeper very considerably.

I then proceeded along this turnpike a good two miles, having, however, only a very imperfect view of the country surrounding me. The servant maids and men waiters were most plentifully in view, all neatly dressed, rosy cheeked, and gay in all their movements. Nature, however, seems to be inclined to change her verdant dress, and I remarked that the foliage was deeply colored with autumnal tints. The season is finer, and longer summer, than usual, and I may say with safety that I am viewing England in her best garb.

I have just passed the second gate, and stopped as I told thee some ten days ago, on the right of the road, and entered the house of our Consul, [Samuel] Brookes, Esqr., where the first object after [this man himself] was a plaster cast of an eminently marked cranium possessed of all the faculties belonging to our race, either from the bad, the indifferent, or good perspective. We talked a little on craniology and comparative anatomy, and walked a few hundred yards to Mr. Loyd's house, also close by the turnpike and still on the right side of the way.

Before I enter this house let me tell thee, my Lucy, that Mr. Loyd is a banker worth the comfortable amount of 400,000 pounds sterling—only two millions of dollars, quite a trifle in this country, and less still with Columbus when he discovered America, but an amount very scarce, I assure thee even in England except with a banker like Mr. Loyd.

The gentleman himself received us most kindly and politely at the entrance, and we sat for a short while in a delightful room where I saw a chair made in London that would be, or might be, called a sofa anywhere else. Did I know what it cost I would tell thee, but really I do not, [and] of course will abandon the task. Please follow me into the grounds, the gardens and the hot houses.

The grounds are laid on a declivity affording a far view of agreeable landscapes. The gardens are most beautifully managed and provided with all the commodities that this wonderful *islet* affords. The hot houses contain abundant supplies of exotic flowers, fruits and shrubs. The coffee tree was bearing. The bananas were ripening under the juicy grapes of Spain and Italy, the little sensitive [plant] of Kentucky shrank humbly at my touch, and the multifloras were mingled overhead with cucumbers and other rampant growth, mixing all perfumes together. How thou wouldst enjoy this! How much I wished my Victor with me, or our dear John! Art here supersedes, nay I might say, helps Nature to produce her richest treasures at will, and in England man may be called the God of the present day. Flowers upon flowers, were plucked for me, and I again remarked how very much our superiors Englishmen are in those simple attentions to strangers that can make them feel at once contented, and defiant of national prejudices, should any exist.

A bell is heard. It is the summons for dinner. We have been joined by Mr. Thomas Loyd and Mr. Hindley and we move towards the house again. For the second time I see Mrs. Loyd, another lady, and two daughters of the banker. Books lie about the table. All is rich, comfortable, pleasing to the eye, to the mind, to the body. A second summons to dinner gives Mr. Brookes an opportunity of taking the two daughters under his arms, to Mr. Hindley that of feeling the weight of Mrs. Loyd, and to thy husband that of escorting the fair unknown. [This entry, from here to the end, is "under the influence."[31]]

I have rather a [notion] to describe, tonight. So here comes dinner. Please sit down and partake. Three servants, all male, I believe, dressed in livery trimmed with red on a white ground, more like killdeer. The American visitor is next to Mrs. Loyd and Mr. Hindley opposite him. Next the woodsman [Audubon]

---

31. Although penned "under the influence," these lines do not prove Audubon a habitual tippler. He could not, by his own admission, even take wine without effect; by 1840 he found it necessary to take particular care.

is a Miss Loyd and the Consul next. Mr. Thomas Loyd faces him, &c., &c. Some eat soup, and I eat *soul.* Mr. Loyd offers a glass of wine to thy husband and we each bow respectfully to each other without a word and drink the wine. This in England is quite a signal; and challenge follows challenge with the quickness of communication given by telegraphy. I ought to have asked Mrs. Loyd to drink with me; this would have been *bon ton.* However, I did in [due] course, and, after her, every other person round the table.

At such dinners the waiters perform every duty. No individual attempts to help anyone directly. And although I was next to Mrs. Loyd, my plate was always handed most carefully by the waiter [beside] her, who also put the stopper on the decanter, &c., &c. We have at such dinners three services, all abundant, and choice of their kind. Conviviality moves round and round the table with the wines, until the ladies rise and retire. Lucy, their health is drank, and thine also. Perhaps I take a pear or a few grapes, and fill my glass with madeira as regularly as the bottles go their rounds. No more "healths" however, unless someone should absent [himself] (through necessity), when invariably his health is drank whilst he is doing all in his power to improve it in the next room, from which he reappears, quite relieved and improved, and ready to receive again from Bacchus a full benison. Now politics, or localities, or of other countries we talk, of America for instance, and as I like it best as a *subject* and am American, I rather swell my tone and enjoy the conversation. The waiters have retired. We are a multiplied *tête à tête,* and they only come in to bring old wines in fresh bottles. However, it is quite dark, and we have been no less than five hours at this dinner. We rise, we XXXX, and are in the library with the ladies, who, no doubt, know all the last proceedings of this closed door business as well as any of the members.

Coffee and tea and books and talk, and after another hour a good night is bid to all, and brings me arm in arm with Thomas Loyd, Esqr., on the turnpike again, following the Consul to his house where we part from him. The "Flora," a coach newly instituted, called for Mr. Hindley. We are in Manchester once more, and Mr. Loyd has just left me to rap most desperately five or six times at Mrs. Edge's door. Thus has been spent this Sunday: without going to church, but not without praying my God to grant thee happiness and comfort.

I heard some singular accounts of the wonderful fortunes accumulated in this country, by men beginning with no more than industry could bring forth, some really wonderful. But my Lucy, I must go to bed and bid thee good night again with all my heart.

Manchester   Sept. 25, 1826   Monday

Who should come into my room this morning about seven, whilst I was busily finishing the ground of my male Pheasant? A handsome Quaker, perhaps twenty years of age and very neatly dressed. "My friends are going out of Manchester before thee opens thy exhibition rooms," he [declares]. "Can we see thy collection at 9 o'clock?" I ask the stranger to set, answer yes to all he asks, and shew him my drawings. Now were all the people in this good land of England Quakers I might perhaps have some encouragement, but really, my Lucy, my times are dull, heavy, painful, and harass my mind almost too much.

Five minutes before 9 I was standing waiting for the Quaker and his friends in the lobby of the Exchange, where two persons [were] also standing and holding the following discourse.

"Pray, have you seen Mr. Audubon's collection of Birds? I am told it is well worth a shilling. Suppose we go now."

"Puh, it's all a hoax. Save your shillings for better use. I have seen them. Why the fellow ought to be drummed out of town."

Did I blush, Lucy? No I turned pale and dared not raise my eyes lest I might be known. But depend upon it, I wished myself in America again.

The Quakers, however, made up [for it] again, for they praised my drawings so much that I *blushed then* in spite of my old age.[32] Now, Lucy, in come two cards of invitation for the concert, one from Dr. Holme, the second from Mr. Loyd the banker. I also received a short letter from Mr. Edward Roscoe, all about drawing. But I am rather, indeed I will say a good deal surprised that

---

32. Despite repeated contradictions over the years, Audubon, who was now forty-one, knew his birth date.

I have not a word from either Miss Hannah Rathbone or Mr. Gordon, and that I have not heard a word from my album.

I took my drawing of the Pheasant to Mr. Tanetti's shop and had it put in a good light, to prove to the good people of Manchester that I really did wish to see more of them.

Then, Lucy, I purchased twenty-five yards of good linen for £4.3.3., being three and four pence per yard. And I will have, in ten days, a fresh supply of comfortables.

The old dog that attends the rooms of the Exchange gave me due notice that my time was out and that I must clear my Birds because an exhibition of Deaf and Dumbs must take place. I have no objection, far from it. I have already made arrangements for my new place in King Street and hope to do better there next week. At five I took down 240 drawings and packed them, ready for removal in less than one hour. I am quite sure that a stranger might have thought I was about [to] escape to save really being drummed out of Manchester.

Now for the concert. It was 6 o'clock and raining very agreeably when I left my room for Fountain Street, where carriage and people on foot were already accumulated to a great number. By elbowing I arrived at the entrance and presented my ticket. I was asked if I am a stranger and requested to write my name and residence on the back. Again, no objections, and "J. J. Audubon, Louisiana, America" is wrote just as handsomely as Napoleon himself would have done it when pressed by time.

The room is full of red, white, blue and green turbans well fitted to the handsome heads of the ladies that already are seated, all attention. I glide modestly to one side and settle myself where I conceive that my heart, my eye, and my intellect may be well satisfied and supplied without being myself observed. But no, it would not do. My long hair seen, and bearer pointed at in such [a] ridiculing manner, that I needed to recollect that I was an honest, plain man and ranked as high as any other in the eye of God. [I] therefore stood the brunt and listened to the music. It was fine but it sank my spirits, and could I have left the assembly I would certainly have done so.

Many ladies were richly beautiful. Several old dames "twiged" [?] at me with their lorgnettes, and in unison with themselves on that score I wished them younger. But a remarkably elegant woman who set on the bench [in front of] me turned round [so] frequently to examine (I suppose) the shape of my nose that I took [it] between my fingers several times to torment this fair one. I have passed many uncomfortable evenings in company and this one may be added. At last "God Save the King" came and I went, squeezing myself sideways, pocket handkerchief in side pocket, coat buttoned, one hand on my watch and the other ready to seize any rascal who might dare to attempt to steal from me.

I soon reached home, with the headache, and have wrote this. Tomorrow, this time, I intend being at Liverpool again. So my sweet wife, good night.

"Quarry Bank" Sept. 26th, 1826 Tuesday

Well my Lucy, [the] date here above clearly proves to thee that I am not about taking my rest for the night in Liverpool, and the reason is just in the sequel. Whilst very engaged at putting up my drawings in my newly granted apartment, two of Mr. Greg's sons entered, and after a hearty and friendly shake of the hand gave me the following kind note from their mother:

> MY DEAR SIR,
> We are all very solicitous to see you as early in the week as possible, on *many accounts*, but more especially because we shall lose Mr. Professor Smyth[33] before the end of it.—he talks of leaving us entirely on Saturday.
> It will make us all very happy to be able to render "Quarry Bank" comfortable or agreeable to you, as often as you can favor us with your company during your abode in Lancashire. Yours very sincerely,
> H. GREG
> (Hannah)

> My husband and children desire to unite me in kind regards. Monday night, 25th Sepr.

Now Lucy, the call of a lady was always heard by thy husband, and if the lady be such as Mrs. Greg, neither water, fire, nor propitious loss could stop me a moment. Again Professor Smyth ran into my brains as a deep, cool, immensely powerful

---

33. William Smyth (1765–1849) was a Cambridge history professor and poet.

stream of knowledge, benevolence, real goodness, and above all liberality. Again the beautiful dark eyes of [Ellen] Greg again——. Again the delightful enjoyment of the company of all the sisters, muselike——. And again the brothers and the good old pair themselves, all were irresistible temptation. The coach [to Liverpool] is forgotten. I am ready to dine again in Fountain Street, and after having listened, with many large-mouthed yawns on the way, to a Mr. Ashton, a great cotton weaver, I again seated myself precisely [in front of] the fair [Ellen] of "Quarry Bank." Her father slept, by the way, but I did not, no. I kept up a vivid conversation about my own beloved country, *our progress* in all points tending to improvement, and at last felt the hands of Mrs. Greg welcoming me to her house. The tears flew from her eyes as she kissed her husband, and he Lucy, acted loverlike!!!

Once more I am surrounded by peaceable gentleness, and am presently forced to remark more dark eyes, more dark eyebrows, a darker complexion, which ended at last in my speaking to an Italian lady. But mark, Lucy, here comes the stranger, tall, fresh, ruddy, complete gentleman, [who] walks in and with an ease only known [to] gentlemen [he] bows and meets first the ladies and then thy husband. Yes, it is he, the professor of Cambridge, all about him knowledge accompanied with agreeable gaiety. What a leap from the Council Bluffs[34] on the Missouri to "Quarry Bank." What contrast between him and the natives of either country! There, the Red Man, with nought but [his] simple nature, is lying, spread upon the earth; and seeing the stranger without courtesy, he yet affords him security, warranted by the mere presentation of his pipe. Here, the powerfully [brained] man, nearly dressed in silk, gives his hand and his eye and gradually his heart with affection, with regard, with esteem, and in course is quite as powerful a friend. Pray, where does the difference lay?

We dine, the professor opposite the "woodsman," the father between his eldest and youngest elm. The mother divides both knowledge and courteous affection [between] the professor and

---

34. Audubon did not see Council Bluffs, Iowa, until 1843. He may have been momentarily identifying with his heroes George Rogers Clark and William Clark.

thy husband, an oblique glance giving me a correct view of the fair Italian female, and sons and daughters intervening, who fill the round table. Again America [is] the subject. Englishmen, and I may say ladies also, are fond of hearing of it, and I fonder still of praising it—of giving it [in] true light. Our Washington and the Napoleon of France are weighed (as they ought to be) in very different scales. Our habits and those of Europe come next and vary in value quite as much. And after many witty *pros* and *cons* (from the professor, recollect), we rise to go and see the ladies that have prepared tea for us.

This professor, Lucy, is a happy man. He possesses the extraordinary talent of teaching comfort and pleasure as he goes, wherever he stops; and I may safely say that our evening spent with him and the fair, kind circle at the "Quarry Bank" is worth a hundred concerts such as I heard last evening.

Lucy, when I related our [country's] receiving our noble and worthy General Lafayette both in New York and Philadelphia, I saw the tears trickle down the cheeks of the good Mr. Greg with a weight of feeling better understood by me than easy of description. Those tears, Lucy, proved to me that many men were born alike and might have been Washingtons! Mr. Greg, my dear wife, is a lover still of wife, of children, and of friends!!! I saw and kissed the eldest daughter of my good friend William Rathbone.

Tonight, my Lucy, my bed was narrow but comfortable. I was led into my room by one of the sons, and whilst I undressed myself I listened to the heavy dripping of the rain with sorrow, thinking that my early morning's walk would be less comfortable by far than the evening I had just spent. Wife, and son, and friends, God bless you all. Good night.

Manchester   Sept. 27th, 1826   Wednesday

My walk was long, wet, fair, rains again, all in a 120 minutes lapse. Strange state of atmosphere. Worse than Louisiana by half. My return to the house at about 8 brought me into the company of four of the sisters, all drawing in the library that in this country is called the setting room. Then the Italian of the well-arched eyebrows, then the professor, then 10 o'clock, and we all arose and went to breakfast. Aye, four hours later than we used to do at Natchez. What odd!! Again I heard, "Mr. Audubon is the most abstemious man I ever saw." I answered that the Ohio had risen sixty feet at the foot of the Falls of that river, and everyone wondered, and yet how true. Then [I talked] of duels with us [in America], of my friend [Henry] Clay and of crazy [John] Randolph, of wearing daggers, and of the murdering son of the governor of Kentucky. [35]

My Lucy, all is known here about our country but known imperfectly, so much so, indeed, that I dread to talk about it, for the English themselves say that *truth is not creditable*.

Now Lucy, I am advising about drawing, and I am quite sure that my old master, David, [36] never [knew] an easier task. But I, Lucy, foolish, conceited, yet anxious to please (my only apology in a case of this kind) attempted a sketch of the professor, and made one of Mr. Priestley [37] instead—fatal error. Yet better off than those who work altogether in vain. I think my luck is that if I had not imitated [the features of] one great man I had at least revived [the method] of a far distant one.

We eat a lunch. The pony Dick is again ready. Mrs. Greg has said *in English* to the fair Italian that a bunch of grapes will be given her for a walk through the garden. I have in my pocket all the notes for Liverpool, press all hands that press mine, mount the saddle, [turn] around, and with a whip trot off towards the smoky city again. Dick is a pony of knowledge, and of course wishes to improve others. Of course he brings me by a new road, quite, to Manchester again, and here I am.

Positively [I am] bound to Liverpool tomorrow and have paid

---

35. Clay dueled with John Randolph in Washington, D.C., in 1826. Isaac Desha, son of Governor Joseph Desha, murdered Francis Baker on November 2, 1824. He went free until he killed a man years later.

36. The name of David—like similar allusions in Audubon's writings, such as "Admiral" for Audubon *père*, who on retirement was promoted to *Lieutenant de Vaisseau*, a step lower than official Captain, which he had often been called on commissioned merchant ships under his command—was mentioned in the journal to offset old feelings of academic inadequacy. The Rathbone ladies often read it. To repeat, the claim of tuition with David seems wholly unfounded.

37. Audubon could have met the son and namesake of Joseph Priestley, but not Priestley, who died on February 6, 1804, in western Pennsylvania, and who paid his fourth and last visit to Philadelphia in February–March, 1803, before Audubon reached America (Edgar Fahs Smith, *Priestley in America* [Philadelphia, 1920]).

my fare on top the coach, because my companion Mr. Bentley is not an American and prefers the inside seats. Yes, tomorrow I hope most sincerely to be thirty-eight miles nearer to thee, and most probably in the company of the benevolent family Rathbone.

I must look for clean linen, pack up, have all ready, and then, my Lucy, I will wish thee, as I hope I may always be able to do, a good night.

IV

Liverpool, A Return

"Green Bank" *Sept. 28th, 1826* *Thursday*

AT PERHAPS 5 THIS MORNING I left Manchester and all its smoke behind me, but I also left there the labours of about ten years of my life, fully one half of my collection. I had had my place inside the coach held by young William Greg. Finding the weather fine, and an English gentleman being very solicitous of making sure of the weather and of the relative comfort of being outside on top, or in, this prevailed on my feelings so much that I gave up my inside place and took his. The weather, however, proved that I was still in the vicinity of the manufacturing town. It rained hard and the wind followed us. I soon found my skin wet, and although I wrapped my great coat well up about me, and held my umbrella strongly, I could not save my ears, and sometimes my eyes, and frequently my neck, from being very disagreeably tickled with the gatherings of the umbrellas that surrounded me. The condition was uncomfortable, but I felt too much foolish pride within me to recall my inside seat, and the good gentleman [was] too snug in his situation to have the least idea of disturbing himself.

I saw nothing of the country and very little of my fellow travellers, none of whom seemed the least inclined to chat but looked very inclined to cry. Thus, Lucy, I was brought to bright Liverpool again, and as I bounced onto the pavement I felt not as if being in a land of strangers but on that of friends, and good friends! Stop a moment, let me tell thee that the Englishman or English gentleman did not even offer thy husband the difference of price that I paid for the inside seat, a trifle of five shillings only. But I must remark that I thought it rather a strange occurrence, and again that perhaps another time an *English gentleman* would not meet the like courtesy from me.

I am [soon] at the Institution. Mr. Munro is glad to see me, and I am pleased to meet William Rathbone, Esqr., Mr. John Foster[1] and Mr. Pillet,[2] who all welcome me as if glad to see thy husband again. The streets of Liverpool looked very wide, very clean, very well lined with very handsome buildings, and although I was completely drenched by rain I felt it not, so glad was I at being in Liverpool again.

Breakfasted at the Institution, dressed there, and marched towards St. Ann Street, meeting [along] the way Dr. Rutter and then the two young Chorleys who ran out from their house and shook hands as if [my] brothers. I received from them an invitation to some music tomorrow, and as I well know that my hair will not be ridiculed I believe I will go.

I find Dr. Traill at home, and all the family are well. What shakes of hands! The sleeves of my coat tapped my wrists with the rapidity of one of the cutting machines of Manchester. My being at Liverpool is soon explained. The doctor refers me to William Roscoe, Esqr., and after a good talk and the promise of breakfasting with him tomorrow I am off toward Lodge Lane— ah, Lodge Lane, on the very way to "Green Bank," with hope of seeing my good friend Richard Rathbone and his beautiful wife and sweet little Basil. I am quite, quite sure that I was not walking slowly when Miss Donathan came across the street with a smile on her lips, her fair arm extended, to ask me how long [it

---

1. John Foster (1787–1846) was an outstanding Liverpool architect.
2. Michel-Fréderic Pillet (b. 1781) was a Paris banker and a member of the French Royal Academy and Legion of Honor.

is] since [I arrived] again in Liverpool, if I am well, &c. What a pleasure for me to be so remembered. I pressed her hand gently and my feet felt not the pavement. Abercromby Square is deserted by Mr. Rathbone's family, [who] are all at "Green Bank." But the "Intelligent Swiss," I am told, may be found here, [I look for him] only to hear, soon after, "Not at home."

[On I go to] the Botanic Garden, to learn, "Mr. Shepherd is not in, Sir." [Finally, I reach] Lodge Lane, Mr. Roscoe's. Even the maid that opens the door smiles and answers to my wishes. Once more I see that venerable, generous, good man at study and at work; and his large eyebrows bent over his mild eyes are once more before me. In an instant I hear him speak. [A] good man, the noblest work of God, God bless him. My business is brought forth and [he says that] he will attend my wishes. I see Miss Jane. We dine, and talk of Manchester,[?] and of Professor Smyth, and bye and bye I ask for my album. It is given me, not blank now, no Lucy—the name of Roscoe will lead it through worlds of time; and those of many, many more friends, I hope, will color it for thee to peruse.

Now toward "Green Bank." I can hardly discern the new residence of good Richard, [but] I soon have before me and seated by my side his amiable consort. I had not the pleasure of seeing my friend Richard, and the sweet little Basil would not kiss me. Again I am [on my way], and am positively at "Green Bank." Yes, my Lucy, I have the consolation that, if [far] from thee and from my own home, I have a home at Mr. Rathbone's. The evening is spent as usual. Mrs. William Rathbone is forming [the] paths of [the] constellations for the *Bazaar*. I read [to] them [about] part of my time at Manchester. William Rathbone reads fine poetry for my pleasure, and the remarkable "Queen Bee" needles a well colored carpet.

Again I am in the Prophet's chamber and in bed—God bless thee. Good night, my sweet wife.

"Green Bank" Sept. 29th, 1826 Friday

I did not tell thee, my Lucy, how surprised I was during the course of last evening at seeing that gentle being, Hannah Rathbone, after a short absence from the library, return with a beautiful frame of rosewood and a drawing, asking me to arrange them each to the other. I looked at a drawing that I had entirely forgotten, a good likeness of thy husband, and I framed it. Surrounded by his new *habillements* of English manufacture, he looked well and I am sure that thou wilt be glad to hear it.

It rained during the night and nearly all the early portion of this morning. The Curator of the Botanic Garden, Mr. Shepherd, came in early. I breakfasted by the side of Hannah Rathbone, although I had promised to be at Dr. Traill's by half past 9 and to call on Mr. William Roscoe on my way. William Rathbone took me to the latter's house in his gig. There I was told that nothing could be done in the way of forming a Prospectus for my work without more knowledge of what it could be brought out for. I was referred to Dr. Traill again, and there I went.

It happened that a Mr. Bohn[3] from London, an immense bookseller, not a publisher, was in Liverpool. Being a man to be depended on, an excellent person from whom truth and truth only might be expected, also a very particular friend of Dr. Traill, the latter had invited him to meet for the purpose of giving me light and advice respecting my publication.

I was introduced to this mighty book warehouse man who has 200,000 volumes as a regular stock, and saw a handsome, well formed young gentleman, possessing all the ease and good manners requisite to render him fit for his situation. His advices to me were as follows:

To proceed at once to London and through my introductions to form the acquaintance of the principal naturalists of the day, and by their advices to see the best engraving, lithography, colorists, printers, paper merchants, &c., &c., and with a memorandum book note down on the spot all required to give a tolerably fair idea of what could be expected.

Then to go immediately to Paris through Bruxelles, and at Paris to proceed with the assistance of good letters in the same manner, and thereby become able to judge of the advantages and disadvantages attached to either country.

To determine myself where, when, and how the work would be undertaken and begun.

3. H. G. Bohn (1796–1884) was a noted London bookseller.

To be announced, during this lapse of time, to the world, through the medium of those able and connected correspondents of scientific societies in some of the most read periodical publications.

"Then, Mr. Audubon," he said, "issue a Prospectus, and bring forth a Number of your ornithology, and I think that you will succeed and do well. But remember my observations respecting the size of your book, and be biased by the fact that, at present, productions of taste are purchased with delight by persons who receive company, particularly, and that to have your book be laid on the table as a pastime piece of entertainment is the principal use [to be] made of it, and that, if in compass it needs so much room as to bring shame on other works or encumber the table, it will not be purchased by the set of people who now are the very life of the trade. If large public institutions, only, and only a few noblemen, will have it, perhaps not exceeding one hundred will find their way out of the shops of my brothers in business, instead of a thousand copies that may be sold if small.

"The size ought to be suitable to the *English market*" (such was his expression), "[and] ought not to exceed double that of Wilson's [*American Ornithology*]."

This conversation, Lucy, all took place in the presence of Dr. Traill. I repeated it to my good friends here, and all are convinced that it will be prudent to follow this plan. Mr. Bohn told Dr. Traill in my presence that my exhibiting my drawings would not do well, that I might be in London twelve months before I would be known at all there, but that through scientific, periodic monthly productions I would be well known all over Europe in the same time, when probably my first Number [of five engravings] would have found its way even to America. As to [the] number of copies, he said that Paris would take 100, London 250, Holland 100, Russia 100, America 450—in all, 1,000.

Although he strongly advised me to have the work all published and finished in Paris, where he thinks it is best for me to undertake it, [he said] to [bring] over to England, say, 250 copies to receive its form and to have its title page printed, to be issued to the world of England as a genuine English production, an astonishing advantage in matters of this kind. He said to do the same with all other portions of the number of copies, and that although the undertaking was greatly laborious I may rest assured that success would ultimately crown my undertakings, my drawings being so very superior.

Then, my beloved wife, I will follow this plan and no other until I find it impossible to succeed, and I will follow it with the same perseverance that, since twenty-five years, [about sixteen] I have continued to wish to come at the completion of it; and for thee, and for our children's ultimate good, may it succeed, and *God's will be done.* [Audubon was to follow his own intuition and judgment, mainly.]

Having determined thus, I will return to Manchester after a few more days spent with those dear good friends from whom it is sorrowful to part; visit thy native Matlock; gaze on the tomb of the friend of thy youth, Darwin; lose my steps amongst thy cherished former paths of Derby's wilds; and enter into London with a head humbly bent but with a heart intently determined to conquer or die.

I was anxious to meet the "Intelligent Swiss," to afford him the pleasure due to a person by whom I have been so kindly treated, to assure him that now, in full unison with all other friends, I was going to do what *he first* wished. But he had left for Manchester—nay, not Manchester—I hope he is enjoying the company of "Quarry Bank," and has seen the sweet Helen that so richly ornaments that lovely spot.

I called on thy sister Ann and dined with her and drank thy health. Mr. Gordon, I was told, is extremely engaged and will leave for the Continent in a few days.

In returning to this abode of peace and repose I was overtaken by a gentleman (who was not on foot, thou knowest well, but in a gig) unknown to me quite, but who offered me a seat by his side. I thanked him, accepted, and very shortly learned him to be Mr. Dearman—not so dear a man, Lucy, as the English one who took my seat inside the coach, was he to my pocket, no. And yet I assure thee he was a much dearer man to me altogether.

Mr. Shepherd was still at "Green Bank." I thought the venerable lady enjoyed a good portion of good spirits. The evening come, truly like at home at Henderson, Kentucky. Each [person was] busily employed and conversing with mildness [and] learning, and [with] that spirit sufficient to bring the American to a pause of thoughts and to a contemplative mood, delightful and necessary to relax the bent bow of his morning's abstracted business. We were joined by Mrs. Rathbone and her husband Richard, and I again admired the warm, well lighted picture of friendship, benevolence, and real merit that laid before me!

Now Lucy, dear friend, good night.

"Woodcroft"   Richard Rathbone's   Sept. 30th, 1826

I bid that God might grant thee rest and happiness, from under the roof of Richard Rathbone, the most lively example of what is known [as] the true English gentleman, and [who, I] am quite sure, is thy friend although thou art yet unknown to him.

I did not leave "Green Bank" this morning until nearly 12. I was extremely anxious to possess a few lines from the very pen and hand of Mrs. [Wm] Rathbone, [Sr.,] the "Queen Bee," and something also from each member of the family. It required Audubon, my Lucy, to have this [wish] granted, and now that I possess this gem in my book, more persons will write in it, more will be honored by having their productions in the company of this truly wonderful lady. Mrs. [R.] Rathbone wrote, but I could not prevail on my Miss Hannah. She turned her wishes another way and [made] a cover [for] the book to save all its contents. I then took it to Dr. Traill who promised to add to it this day, but [having] a great deal of other things to attend, he did not remember the album. I tried to meet Mrs. Edward Roscoe. She was absent, and I must be contented that I kissed her lovely child.

I visited the Institution and was glad to see the American hills in the background of [my] "Wild Turkey" [painting]. But my Lucy, I felt an extra fatigue about my body. My head felt heavy and the bones of my legs ached. I was not well, and the idea of being ill far from thee tormented me dreadfully.

However, I went and dined with Dr. Traill, [who] had only [his] family and a Mr. Finney. Dr. Traill entertained me very much. Indeed a man of [such] extensive knowledge of all things cannot fail to be agreeable if he will only talk. Having previously declared that my wish was to go to "Woodcroft," [I] was taken there about 8 by the doctor's son in a gig at a round rate.

Soon I was with Mrs. Richard Rathbone and three Quakers, two of whom were females. The conversation was [of] natural history, and the ladies were all versed in such matters. My friend's wife produced a beautiful and good microscope, and through it the Diamond Beetle shone in all its splendor. My good friend Richard did not join us until ten; [he was] fatigued from his Saturday's labours. We set chatting after the Quakers left us until 12. I was sorry to discover that he did not know how to swim, and still more so that I could not have the pleasure of teaching him a thing so rapidly done in one hour's time. My good friend, with manners quite beyond my powers to describe, accompanied me to my chamber, felt if the bed would be comfortable, and pressed my hand with a pressure felt at heart. We parted. His wife was in the next apartment, and thou, my beloved Lucy, wert fully 6,000 miles from Liverpool. I, notwithstanding, wished thee, quite *aloud*, good night.

"Green Bank"   Oct. 1st, 1826   Sunday

I slept more than usual, and although the morning was bright and fair I did not leave my friend's house until nearly 6. The air felt more rarified and I filled my lungs with pleasure. I reached this sweet spot in a few minutes and wrote in the library, whilst the mirth of the young Rathbones above indicated their gamboling about the nursery.

I soon returned to "Woodcroft" to breakfast and did not see my friends here. I had the pleasure of riding to Liverpool by the side of Mrs. Richard Rathbone, most amiable, interesting lady.

Dr. Traill had not wrote in the album, and I went to the Institution where I wrote the letter to thee annexed before this sheet. Visited Mrs. Edward Roscoe and found her as usual devoted to study and anxious to improve. She promised to put something in my book also, and I came then to "Green Bank" to enjoy during this afternoon that silentness and quiet connected with devotion.

Speaking of America the immensity of the waters, the numerous steamboats, immense trade and traffic, I told William Rathbone that N. Berthoud kept an account of the whole, and that, if he desired it, I would write to our Victor for a copy. He wished it and I wrote. The same gentleman asked if I should wish to [be] a corresponding member of their Philosophical Society, and to that I answered yes. But Lucy, the strangest and most curious event of this evening was that, after service had been read and supper [was] over, and bidding good nights was passed, I found Mrs. Rathbone leaning on her children in the lobby, waiting apparently for me. And with a smile that I never saw before she asked me, with a modesty just as scarce, if I would make a sketch of a Wild Turkey for her, and I felt elated at the thought of presenting her [with] one from the hands of [the engraver] Roskell's best artist. But she smiled again and I then discovered my simplicity, for she begged that I would give her the sketch only. Then *she*, Lucy, wished to give me the seal, and I thanked her with all my heart. Who could not wish to admire such a kindly, delicate, worthy woman?

My night was bad, my cough very rough, and I thought that I had caught the whooping disease. I scarcely slept, and I thought of thee, dearest wife, until day.

LIVERPOOL, Oct. 1, ROYAL INSTITUTION, 1826

MY DEAREST BELOVED,

I returned here from Manchester a few days since on the advice of my friends and learned acquaintances, with a view to conferring with them respecting my publication of the Birds of America. For that purpose the president of the Institution, Dr. Thomas S. Traill, invited me to breakfast at his house to meet a Mr. [Henry G.] Bohn of London, perhaps the most extensive *bookseller* (not publisher) in that immense city. This person has on hand a stock of 200,000 volumes; travels constantly through this country and the Continent, is well versed in all matters relative to the subject, and exceptionable for veracity and candor, so much so that Dr. Traill assured me that I might, with great confidence, disclose all my views, ask all questions, and expect answers full of truths.

His advices have been amply given, and so full of prudence, care and knowledge have I found that gentleman to be possessed of that I now will proceed with a firm resolution to attempt *being an author.* It is a terrible thing to me, far better fitted to study and delineate in the forests than to arrange phrases with sensible grammarian skill. However, my efforts will only equal my faculties, and with this I must and will be satisfied, if remunerated sufficiently to enhance thy comfort and that of our dear boys.

Then, my dear friend, my exhibiting my work publicly will be laid aside for a while at least. *I* hope forever.

I visit next week, or early the week following that, thy dear native spot, and kiss and bless that earth that bore thy sweet form, youthful, gay, lovely, and destitute of care. I can hardly yet tell thee if it will be mostly a jaunt of pleasure or a pilgrimage of sorrow, but I long to feel either under the happy round of circumstances that, after a knowledge of thee, full twenty-five years have passed and filled me with that sense of gratitude towards thee that [makes me] hope our God will enable me to feel and enjoy until we meet, *never to part again.* Yes, I will see thy Matlock, thy Derby, thy hills, dales, mountains, cataracts and valleys, and see amid the morning dews the light [trace] of thy steps and see thee, my Lucy, as *I love thee!*

I will visit our cousins Gifford and Bakewell,[4] and through them make an effort to see and speak to the Duke of Devonshire, pass through Oxford, and reach the metropolis sometime this month. There, Lucy, from street to street will I move, and examine all objects connected with my views, make regular memorandums, and try *once more* to become a *man of business.* I must [learn] from the engravers and lithographers their price and executive powers, [and]

---

4. Reference to Miss Euphemia Gifford, of Derby vicinity, and to Robert Bakewell, geologist of Hampstead (London).

the same from the printers, paper-makers, &c., &c., all I can discover. I must try to become acquainted with men of eminence as naturalists and of standing in society, sound all and each, and every night weigh well the different parcels of advices, and judge for myself at last. What a task, my Lucy? How difficult to please one's self and yet how much more so to please many.

With my book of memorandums made all on the spot and time, I will leave *la belle Angleterre* and go to Paris to compare the advantages of those two mighty countries. I feel, however, a certain predilection beyond my venerable mother, my kind sister and their family circle, I shall not like France as I now do England. And I certainly hope that this country will deserve the preference that by interested motives I must ultimately give to the one best suited to meet my endeavors at doing well. Then I will enter my own old garden on the Loire and with trembling steps reach my mother! Our mother, my Lucy—ah——then we must part. May it be to *meet again.*

As between this day and the time I will determine, at Paris, what will be considered left to be done, I hope to be able regularly to write to thee again and again. I will now bid thee farewell. And I will speak of my good friends here. My letter of the second of last month said that I *wished thee* to have cut and forwarded to New Orleans as soon as possible six segments of one magnolia, one yellow poplar, one beech tree, one bottom wood or sycamore, one sassfras, one oak, each of about seven or eight inches in thickness of the largest diameters that can be procured in the woods about thee. Try to have them all average six feet. Of course six segments only are wanted. Have each segment carefully handled to save the bark, and names painted in oil neatly on one face with the height of the tree given. Direct them to the care of whom thou may think will be most attentive to have them shipped as soon as possible, all directed to and for the Liverpool Royal Institution, care of Messrs. Rathbone Brothers & Company here. *I wish thee, my dear wife, to be at some trouble and expense to bring this to a good conclusion.*

It is probable that Dr. Pope would feel a pleasure at doing this, being favorable to scientific pursuits, or our good friend Judge Mathews, to both of whom I beg thou wilt remember me. As the least [costly] carriage by land will be best. Perhaps some might be found at the Bayou near the Mississippi, or on the very bank, and floated to the steamboat, where [a] particular request must be made to the captain that they are not to be barked or injured in any way. Recollect that those are troubles that I give thee so as to repay troubles that I have given in exchange to others. Advise me as soon as possible. I conceive the whole can be managed in one week with a little attention, and John could see about it. Kiss him, my Lucy, and remember me to all about thee. I will see Mr. Middlemist's wife as soon as I reach London. God bless thee and protect thee forever, thine husband and friend.

J. J. A.

The freight from America here will be *paid here*. Cotton is rising in value, and business bears a better face. Give this news to Mrs. Percy and my good friend Bourgeat, who perhaps will help with the segment business, if [their cotton is] not already shipped.

"Green Bank"　Oct. 2nd, 1826　Monday

My cough, as I told thee, was bad. I did not rise until late and had scarcely time to write a page before my sweet, kind friend Hannah made her appearance, and with a smile and the gentle pressure of her hand bid me good morning.

My principal objects to-day were to attend on Mr. Richard Rathbone and to sketch the Wild Turkey. I rode to Liverpool with William Rathbone, Esq., and went again to Dr. Traill for my book. I waited a short while, on the way to Mrs. Chorley, the mother of my young friends John and Henry. Saw their sisters and their portraits. Had my book from Dr. Traill, and walked to the Institution very slowly with John Chorley, who gave me some kindly advices, and spoke much of the habits of his countrymen.

I sat opposite the twenty-three hours picture [of the "Wild Turkey,"] and sketched it the size of my thumb nail in less than twenty-three minutes. If the engraver does his duty, the scal will be beautiful, and in such a case the "Wild Turkey" will revisit America, his country.

I sent my album to Mr. Edward Roscoe and walked to "Wood-croft." The sweet children were all a little indisposed except my little darling, Basil. I gave a lesson of drawing and received one with pleasure. My acquaintance in this kind family has for-tunately been of so propitious a nature that we can talk of our feelings without fear, risk or danger. I dined, and [occupied] my friend Richard's seat, a thing I disliked even at my own home. Whilst dessert was on the table, the calls of a younger little one reached the mother's ear (and heart I daresay), and *sans* cere-mony she bid me farewell and went to nurse her sweet little Benson. Once more, my Lucy, I had at hand the sweetest of pleasures. I attended on four little ones, divided pears and peeled them, gave them the fruit and kissed them.

I left this little group and reached "Green Bank," where, it being pudding time, I sat to table again to receive from Hannah a glass of wine and from her mother a bunch of grapes. I gave [her] the "Wild Turkey" [sketch], and, as they please to admire all I do, they admired that also.

It was nearly 5 when I walked to Liverpool, reached the In-stitution, saw Mr. Munro who is so good [as] to see that the little quantum of linen that I brought from Manchester will suf-fice, and reached my friends the Chorleys in good time to have a good deal of chat with [John's] mother, sister and brothers be-fore the flutes and the piano were brought to unison.

I saw the son of Mr. [John] Gilpin of Brandy Wine Creek, America. My father had been well acquainted with his.[5] I had seen this young gentleman at Dr. Mease's[6] in the company of

5. John Gilpin, neighbor of Mill Grove, whose lead veins he is said to have dis-covered, was host to Lafayette at the time of the Battle of Brandywine; his house, used as headquarters, is now a national shrine. The 1827 journal of Audubon men-tions the Joshua Gilpin paper mill.

6. James Mease (1771–1846) was a doctor, agriculturalist, historian, and Phila-

[Charles] Bonaparte in Philadelphia in 1824, and I felt quite gratified to be known by my own countryman. The evening passed
most agreeably. I told them how shockingly annoyed I had
been, the last concert I had been at, and they all were sorry for
it. Mrs. Rathbone's servant and gig arrived for me, and against
all entreaties I left about 9, the evening clear but quite cold, the
frost falling in heavy dew. The servant was surprised that I
would not make any use of a great-coat brought for me. How
little he knew how often I have laid to rest wet, hungry, harrassed and full of sorrow, with millions of mosquitoes buzzing
me awake, listening to the Chuck Will's Widow, the Horned
Owl, and the roaring Bull-frogs, impatiently waiting for the return of day to enable me to hunt the forests and feed my eyes on
their beautiful inhabitants. I thought of all this, and then moved
the scene to the hunting cabin [where], again wet, harrassed
and hungry, [I] felt the sudden warmth of "Welcome stranger!";
saw the busy wife unhook dry clothes from the side of the
logged hut, untie my moccasins, unleash my Indian deerskin
dress, and give me a warm draft of whiskey with looks that insured my life free from danger; and bid me expect more comfort. I saw the athletic husband wipe my guns, clean the locks,
hang the whole over the abundant fire, call his eldest son to rise
to see about more wood, some eggs, and some venison, whilst
my ears were greeted with the sounds of the handmill crushing
the coffee that was to enliven my spirits. I saw, dear Lucy, many
little ones, roused by the stranger's arrival, peeping from under
the robe of the Buffalo and turning over on the Black Bear's skin
to resume their rest.[7] I saw all this, my dear wife, and arrived at
"Green Bank" to see much the same on a larger scale. The squatter is rough and true, my friends here [are] polished, amiable,
benevolent. The first gives all he has, freely. Here the stranger
has about him all he wants, and he who, during the comfortless

delphia civic leader who introduced Audubon there in 1824, when he urged a haircut. But for the mission abroad Mease apparently favored the "woodsman" style, a
length recalling that of Franklin while in Paris. Mease was a friend of William
Bakewell, father of Mrs. Audubon. He knew Priestley, Cuvier, and many other no-
tables. His son Pierce Butler married actress Frances Anne Kemble. Butler had
changed his name from Mease for reasons of inheritance.

7. Theme of an episode in *Ornithological Biography*.

Audubon's second sketch for the "Wild Turkey" seal, magnified. The seal made from the original sketch is in the Audubon Memorial Museum, Henderson, Kentucky.

storms of life, can reach either such spot may say, before he dies, that he felt happiness during the while.

Sweet friend, God bless thee. My Lucy, good night.

"Green Bank" Oct. 3rd, 1826 Tuesday

I have been to the jail of Liverpool to-day, my Lucy, and will try to give thee some partial description, both of its building and [the] manners within. The situation is fine, placed at or near the mouth of the estuary that here is called the River Mersey. From its walls an extensive view of the Irish Channel may be had, drawing the eye to the country and mountains of Wales. The area altogether occupied by the institutions consists of about eight acres, and the arrangements within the walls are— but permit me, I think a slight sketch will describe faster and better than my poor pen.

[At this point appears a small pen-and-ink plan.]

A is a large handsome building in front, forming a court house of quarterly sessions with all the conveniences appertaining.
B is the general entrance for strangers of all descriptions ever for those, my Lucy, who go there to receive sentence of everlasting banishment.
C is a large entry lined on both sides with the offices of the Governor, Assistant Governor, and different turnkeys that are well secured from communication from the culprits, should they attempt escaping.
D and all the plain grounds are used as walks but only by visitors and members, properly speaking, of the institution.
E a piece of water with the three, emblematic of sorrow, in its center.
F an office of distribution, and guard house.
G chapel able to contain 450 persons.
T a connecting iron bridge
4H gardens
2L tread mills
12I open cells or walking yards for culprits.
K connecting corridors

Besides these marks, my Lucy, imagine the cells for sleeping, one to each individual female, but sometimes one to two or three males. *I did not ask why so.* There are large apartments for cooking, washing, &c., council rooms, store rooms, &c., &c. I end this with: the institution, as far as [its being] comfortable if [one is] at rest [is concerned], is fine. I will try, at least, to enter its meritorious intentions, [while confessing that] I consider the treadmill infamous. Conceive of a wild squirrel within a round wheel, moving himself without progress. The labour is too severe, and the true motive of correction destroyed, as there are no mental resources attached to this laborious engine of shame only, if viewed by strangers. Why should each individual not be taught different trades enabling them, when thrown again on the vile world, to support themselves more honestly, and save them from the temptations that, through necessity, they must ultimately resort to (knowing nought but walking up hill), and be dragged again and again to the treadmill's transportation or to despair? Trades would be more profitable to the institution, fourfold, than the mere grinding [of] flour that is done here, and the principle would be more honourable and more worthy [of] the true intention of such a [place]. Thus I do condemn the treadmills not only as machines of labour without benefit either general or personal, but also as extremely prejudicial to health. Think of those poor miserable beings, obliged either to weigh heavily on one paddle or raise their own weight to the next, which is the same labour as walking up a steep hill constantly for four or six hours, or averaging five, whilst the man [doing this] might [instead] make a good pair of shoes, cut nails, be a hatter or a watchmaker, or [work at] any other useful business.

The wheel is only six feet in diameter. Therefore the motion is accelerated, and each step must be performed in quick succession. And as I know that a quick, short step is more fatiguing than a long one and soon destroys the ultimate power of the general frame, I say it is conducive to destruction. The sallow, withered, emaciated, thin visages and bodies of the men at work proved this to my eyes as well as to my powers of calculation. The wheel forces thirty steps to a rotation, and, as I say, these are steps going up hill more than equal in length and labour to those on level ground. I will calculate them at two and a half feet for each, and as the wheel goes round once per minute I will call the single movement seventy-five feet, the hour, 4,500, the labour 22,500. This repeated twice per day gives 45,000.

Lucy, the circulation of free air is wanted. Each man receives the breath of his neighbour in exchange for his [own], and, as this is accompanied by the most debased conversations, both the body and the mind suffer. I would write more, but I am not William Roscoe. Therefore I close the subject. I was sorry to find the female deportment [is] more difficult to manage than that of the men. And to give thee an idea of the force of habits kept in this place, suffice it to say that through the want of tobacco the *ladies* there smoke their *petticoats.* Yes, when I entered the rooms the smoke was [thick] and most disagreeably so. Each female hid the cause in her bosom. Lucy, did nature intend the female bosom [to be] the receptacle of a filthy pipe? Come—no answer, eh—.

Lucy, I felt glad when, after writing my name in the Governor's book, I issued with my companion from this abode of misery. Now that I am as free as ever, [I shall mention] that my companion's name is *Mary Hodgson,* a Quaker of great benevolence, smartness and solid understanding, [one] of a committee that attends every day and week, [so as] to superintend the institution's purchases and to disperse all articles necessary or for sale, &c., &c.

I dined with her and her sister who is a poet, and with her brother [Adam] who is a merchant in partnership with Messrs. Benson Cropper & Company.

I took a long walk with friend John Chorley. Had seen Mrs. Richard Rathbone a moment this morning, also Mrs. William Roscoe. Had seen the engraver of the Wild Turkey [seal,] had thought of thee so often and so much that I forgot to call on Mr. Roscoe, who will think me rude. And after all this [I] reached "Green Bank" to enjoy handsome prints, handsome ladies, good wine and good conversation, and bid thee good night, dearest friend.

"Green Bank" Oct. 4th, 1826 Wednesday

I heard last night that perhaps the "Intelligent Swiss" would be with us to breakfast, but he came not. I called several times at his office, but no Mr. Melly.

I visited Mr. Foster, Mr. Lawson, the family Chorley, &c., &c., bidding my farewells as diligently as possible. I called on

Mr. Gordon who invited me to both dinner and breakfast for tomorrow, and as the latter generally comes first, I accepted the opportunity to see thy sister once more, Lucy.

I saw the engraver of the Turkey [seal]. I saw Mr. Munro and spent [some] time at the Institution. I took a long walk with John Chorley, spoke of the *Bataille* of Tippecanoe, and my being a midshipman when a boy.[8] I gave a long lesson of drawing to my friend Richard R.'s lady. Called on Mr. Roscoe whom I feared would be offended, having been so stupid as not to go near him since the second day after my return to Liverpool. I received a present of a *snuff box*.

"Why my LaForest thou astonished me. Not going to suffer a vile habit to encroach on thee, I hope?"

No, my Lucy. John Chorley presented me with a snuff box to hand to my friend snuff takers, and I assure thee I have some worthies among them. I, Lucy, will not take much, I assure thee.

I called for my album at William Roscoe, Jr.'s, but it had been forwarded to Mr. Foster, and I must go there for it.

There are various ways of begging in England, but the following deserves thy notice. A man of middle age sat on the edge of the street-walk and wrote with a beautiful hand that he is "a poor man, out of employment, turned away from the Manchester mills on account of the hard time," and solicited charity of the passersby. He had a few pamphlets for sale. I gave him the value of one, and as I proceeded faster I saw through a window very many efforts of the pencil, several dozen small attempts at portraiture, all miserable, under which was wrote in immensely large characters, "Apprentices are Wanted." As I walked, I wished the person had been in need of masters instead of apprentices, [he being more in need of the former].

I returned early, felt very fatigued, spent a most agreeable evening, saw the signatures of many great men, and retired early. Sweet wife, good night.

8. Audubon was a cabin boy, first class, rather than a midshipman. He was assigned to the Arsenal riggings at Rochefort-sur-Mer from August 18, 1796, to January 19, 1797; in 1798 he did port duty; and in September 20, 1799, he applied to the School of Hydrography for training toward second grade but failed candidacy tests before March 1800 when he returned to Nantes.

"Green Bank"   Oct. 5th, 1826   *Thursday*

I felt extremely fatigued when I returned here this afternoon, but seeing Hannah reading this book to her sister, Mrs. William R., gave me pleasure, and refreshed me quite as much as the wine that was handed me. I read to them [from my journal] until the company arrived for dinner and—but, my Lucy, I am rather forgetting myself.

I breakfasted with thy sister this morning. She and her husband gave me some letters and a commission to purchase for them ten guineas worth of engravings in France.

I called on Mr. William Laneson, Upper Islington No. 53, and saw some wonderful paintings by Wouvermans,[9] &c., &c., &c., and I think the finest oil landscapes I ever saw from the pencil of a Liverpool lady, whose name I regret I have forgotten. This gentleman was unusually polite and I spent full two hours with him. His travels over the European continent enable him to amuse and interest the visitor to a very gratifying degree. I can only regret that I did not see as much of him as I wished.

I also outlined the Turkey [seal] completely for Mr. Gifford, the engraver, on the very pebble itself. I felt more satisfied about it. Although Mr. G. certainly engraves well, his knowledge of the birds is not quite so extensive as mine.

I walked in the *Bazaar* of the *Fair of Charity* but it was too crowded. I saw very little and the air was quite disagreeable. I spoke a few words to Mrs. Traill and some other ladies who knew me better than I did them. I had [already] bid farewell to Dr. Traill, [and] to John Chorley toward whom, and his whole family, I felt a great attachment. I had received my album from Mrs. Maria Foster, the wife of John Foster, Esqr., to whom I wrote a few farewell lines.

I visited the Institution once more and, accompanied by the good Munro, I [set] sail for this spot. Mr. Roscoe, his daughter Jane, Mr. Pillet of Paris, and the son of another banker of the same city dined with us. I was not very prepossessed with the latter, because he opened the conversation at table on horse races, whilst Mr. Roscoe and I were talking of the miseries of the

---

9. Phillip Wouvermans (1619–68), Dutch painter of battle pieces and hunting scenes.

treadmills, another kind of race quite as disgusting in its effects, but toward the abolition of which, Mr. Roscoe and I were intent, whilst the banker's son seemed willing [that] the continuation of the first should be improved. This gentleman gradually changed his grounds, however, and I liked him better. I gave some particular details of the navigation of the Mississippi, &c., &c., after the ladies had retired (amongst whom my good friend Mrs. Rathbone did not make her appearance). Richard Rathbone and his lady came, and the evening was quite cheerful. William Rathbone thinks much of the cleverness of his wife and she in return is very good to him. They have three interesting little children here now, the youngest a fair simile of a rosebud.

I bid adieu to Richard Rathbone and his lady with a feeling of uncomfort more than disagreeable. I could not accompany them to their carriage. About 12 o'clock the ladies bid us good night. Mr. Saravey, the banker's son, wrote a letter to his father[10] and giving it [to] me said that I would receive at his house all the hospitality that I had met with in England. I thought this a good deal in a few words, but recollected that he was a Frenchman. I have no wish, my Lucy, to infer that Frenchmen are not very kind. I merely say that *generally* their kindness is more transient, and that I prefer a *growing acquaintance*, one that improves as it

---

10. Translation: "LIVERPOOL, October 5, 1826
"MY DEAR PAPA,

"Well received as I am on every side in England thanks to good introductions, the least I can do is seek to gain a like advantage for some of those people whom I am meeting here. That has already happened for some Scotsmen and Englishmen whom I have directed with recommendations. Now here comes a Frenchman, born in St. Domingue, brought up in our country, and established for twenty years in the United States, M. Audubon, who is to visit Paris with a very beautiful collection of paintings of flowers, &c., of very great interest, in hopes of finding means to publish there. Naturally he needs to know our scientific personnages—Cuvier, Humbold [sic], &c. He has letters to them, but a bit of help will be useful to him, and I think that cousin will procure for us introductions and directions in case of need. Make him also form the acquaintance of M. Pithou who will be agreeable and indeed interesting to him. In a word, try to render him a share of what I am experiencing here among excellent people (Mr. Rathbone—the patron of Pillet—and his family) at whose home I met him. He seems to me a trifle sad to be separated from his family: that recommends him all the more to your attention.

"I embrace you in haste, as well as all the family, and Mamma to whom the tales (*récits*) of one whom I am recommending will give great pleasure.
"Your loving son,
"C. A. SARAVEY"
(Beinecke Library,
Yale University)

grows, and, like the live oak, stands the storms of life through all kinds of circumstances.

The venerable Roscoe was extremely kind to me. He requested I should write to him often, and depend on it I shall, and never will forget him and his attentions to me.

Lucy, tomorrow I go again to Manchester. I would anticipate the journey and write more but I must bid thee good night.

V

Manchester Revisited

Manchester   Oct. 6th, 1826   Friday

I COULD NOT BEAR THE IDEA of leaving either this place or Liverpool without first having seen the "Intelligent Swiss." I knew how generously he had acted during my exhibition at the Royal Institution; and many pounds sterling had been added by him to the regular amount received in concert with some other friends, whose names I will not speak now. And I felt as if I saw that he had a peculiar interest toward me.

Well then, with all this before me, and the daylight scarcely sufficient to see to dress myself, I issued from my bed where I had been not more than four hours, arranged my clothes about me as snug as opportunity would allow, and again, with my boots in one hand, I turned the latch gently and on tiptoe moved along the passage down the stairs and out of doors, finally in the sight of waking Nature.

It was one of those mornings when not sufficiently cold for frost. The dew lay in large masses on all objects, weighing down the points of every leaf, of every blade of grass, and ran in startling streamlets about the larger objects. The heavens were

251

cloudless. All breezes were hushed, and the only intervening twitterings of the Red-breasted Warbler broke on the silence that Nature, at this spot, seemed willing to enjoy. I cast my eyes around, perceived the Blackbird mounted on the tall larch, waiting anxiously, wishing to salute the reddening horizon with his mellow notes. The Thrush stood on the grass and by the mulberry tree, quite erect, well spotted, her cunning large eye watching the movements of one she knew was a stranger. And the Lark, unwilling to bid farewell to the last days of summer, had sprung and risen up and with a swelled throat was trying to recall the pleasures of spring. Lucy, I had risen early, and this sight of magnificence and peace made me wish to recall my youthful days, to see again in reality the pleasures of our early life, and again to grow up once more together. The bright light of the sun colored the upper foliage of the trees. The sheep walked underneath them and eat the fallen fruit. The Rook's voice joined that of the Magpie. I saw a Stock Pigeon swiftly pass over me, and recollected my errand to Liverpool.

I walked swiftly and never met a person until I reached Abercromby Square, and that person neither thee nor any other person would know a word of, was I not about to tell thee. After having closely examined every name on the doors of Chatham Street and other surrounding buildings, I was forced to procure information by knocking at the house of William Rathbone to know where "the Swiss" resided since his removal. Lucy, the person that I met first this morning was a young female, scarcely dressed, with rosy cheeks, and eyes that had not been made to sleep forever for nothing. I begged her pardon, gave her my name, and at a quarter of 6, the sun, brightly risen, enabled me to see the head of Mr. Pillet who from an upper window was giving me notice that he had heard my repeated pulls of the bell.

I would not have wrote so much about a morning, the like of which I have had for full thirty years, but I had nothing else to do. And to have been idle might have created evil wishes, ending probably by hanging myself, as many a man has certainly done for want of much better employment. Mr. Melly opened his eyes as I opened his chamber door, and with his usual "Eh bien, Papa," received [me] with great cordiality, although as I sat on his bedside I felt fully convinced that I had been the cause of the headache of which he complained during the conversation by disturbing him before his accustomed time. What powers habit gives! But what powers does not habit destroy? His partner was better, but still very ill; and as I might forget the [latter's] name, know, my Lucy, that it is *Schmidt*.

On my return I met Mr. William Roscoe, Jr., with a straw hat, taking, he said, an early walk. The straw hat struck me more than the walk; for several days past, the last swallows have been flying toward the South, several frosts [had] altered the primitive tints of foliage, and this morning's chillness engaged me to rub my hands and fingers together frequently as I walked along. There habit exhibited herself, rather against me, I must say. "A fine warm morning this, Mr. Audubon," [young Roscoe said]. "Yes," I answered, "just such as brings on half a cord of wood to the squatter's fire in Latitude 32°." We parted, I walking fast to warm myself, and he slowly to enjoy the effects of an English October morning. It is not to be wondered at, if Englishmen with so much warm blood about them are *warm hearted.*

At "Green Bank" all was still yet, except the maid that gives light to the house by opening it first in the morning when I am not there. I had done much this early time, had walked five miles, seen my friend, had a book in hand, and listened for the seven [strokes] of the clock, anxious for my breakfast. Soon the little ones came down to kiss me, and then ran after flowers to their own garden. I felt as if I only wanted thy presence and a kiss from thy lips to afford me all the bliss this earth can produce. But only that kiss was wanted, and all the bliss with it, and I reclined on the sofa.

I saw William Rathbone and his clever wife and amiable and benevolent mother. We breakfasted. The carriages drew up. The first pair and their children bid us all adieu. Our turn came, and by 11 o'clock we were on the road toward Manchester. I looked at "Green Bank," unknowing if it was for the last time, but wishing all its inhabitants well and happy. Hannah sat next to me, her mother beyond, and, thus compactly arranged, three on the seat of the chaise, we passed through *Wavertree*. Silence prevailed the while, each of us thinking, no doubt, of their most immediate concerns, friends and relations. Judging for myself, this must have been the case. However, conversation soon found its way; and [going] from one topic to another, either by change of objects in view or in recollection, [we] passed the time most agreeably. Hannah had requested that this, my poor book, be given her, and from time to time she opened and read in it.

We changed horses perhaps twelve miles from "Green Bank." It was done in a moment. A new postilion mounted and again we proceeded. Did I ever, when in the forests of America, dream or think of travelling in the chaise of one of the best ladies of England at her particular request, accompanied by her kind, amiable daughter, both feeding me with the most obliging and unremitting attentions merely because I brought a single letter of introduction from [Nolte] a friend of mine from New Orleans, and after an acquaintance of only a few weeks? No, that I never did. I can scarcely now realize it. It is all wonderful to me, and whatever receptions, no matter how different, my countrymen have had in this land, I can only say that mine far surpassed all my most sanguine hopes. May God forbid that I should ever be ungrateful, and may he bless those who have so kindly received the naturalist of Louisiana.

But my Lucy I have almost forgotten that I was travelling towards Manchester. We frequently spoke of thee, of our children, and suddenly my venerable friend said that she had an inclination to be hungry! Each of us had our little table, made of our knees, each a little cloth, little plate, knives and plenty of provisions. The wine was handed round, and although it seemed as if anxious to escape the glass before reaching the lip, it at last produced the effect intended. Our dessert, Lucy, consisted of a melon and some grapes and some pears and some apples, and I at last [wondered] if coffee [were] not coming. We were all gay. I never saw Miss Hannah more so. Her dark eyes were more beautiful than ever, and the smile around her mother's lips proved to me how much can be felt when the heart is at peace with the mind.

Thus we rolled, and reached the smoky Manchester, gradually passing from street to street. Hatless at the door of the Academy of Natural History, [I] pressed the hands of my good friends, and thrusting myself into the building felt at an end of my pleasure. How changing the scene! Again in worldly engagements! My doorkeeper proved insane; he certainly had an oversupply of spirit within him. I do not wish to pun, Lucy; the man had positively taken too much Irish whiskey to look with care on American Birds. Seldom in my life have I felt more vexed. However, I cooly begged of him to come to my lodgings, where I balanced accounts with him, and opening the door quite broad gave him a full opportunity of breathing at leisure, of cooling himself, and of looking for a new situation for the next day.

I returned to my Birds and looked at them very closely. They were fresh and as gay in appearance as their originals in our woods. I determined to have only the young son of Mr. Wilson to take charge of them and pushed through the streets again to seek Mr. Bentley. I saw him. I received my income that was rather slender, and in time retired to my apartment. There, my Lucy, in the world and yet completely divided from it, I thought of thee, of the time spent in England since my arrival, of the acquaintances I have formed, of the many kind attentions I have received, of the probabilities of my ultimate success.

My good friends had proceeded to Mr. Dockray's, about one mile distant. I thought of them. I was not fatigued, yet I felt the wish to sleep quickly. I felt as if my situation was not suited to enliven the dullness of my present ideas, and after my supper and glass of wine dranked in desire that thy health might be good and thy happiness complete, I wished thee again, again, and again, good night!

"Quarry Bank"   October 7th, 1826   Saturday

I arranged many letters this morning for my good friend Mrs. Rathbone, and having promised her one of thine I gave her thine of the ninth of May, dated "Beech Woods." I had also promised one of Charles Bonaparte's to her daughter-in-law Mrs. William Rathbone, and this I also put by for her. My time was spent walking, visiting my acquaintances with a wish to procure more letters of introduction; and whilst I was setting in front of my drawings at the Academy, giving some idea of the habits of some birds to some lady who seemed to possess a good knowledge of ornithology, Mr. Robert Greg and his mother came to me, and with so much openness and friendly manners desired that I should accompany them this evening to their country seat that, although I had rather obligated myself to spend the evening with Mrs. Rathbone at Mr. Dockray's I could not refuse this invitation. Thanks to this good lady I will be peaceably in the country again tonight and tomorrow.

I arranged colors, chalks, paper and linen sufficient, and walked to Fountain Street at three of the afternoon. Conceive my astonishment and momentary disappointment and confusion when told at the door that the carriage was gone. Yes, gone. With my colors, chalks, &c., I made for the office of the son, and being told there that Mrs. Greg expected me at the Dockrays' I pushed toward Piccadilly to procure a coach. It is not every man who knows where Piccadilly lays in this smoky town of Manchester. Therefore I applied to the first man that I thought could instruct the woodsman.

"Sir," [I was told], "I am walking that very way myself and will do myself the pleasure of conducting you to the place."

This, Lucy, would have been true English politeness had not my present companion been *guided* himself by interested motives. I had my new coat shaped and named after Lafayette. Never until now had I dared to wear it, and it was quite as new to the gentleman by my side, almost, as to me. He saw with a connoisseur's eye that *I* was not a Manchester man, asked me what countryman I was with all the ease of one of our brave Yankees, and for my answer begged to know if I wished to purchase umbrellas for America!

The weather certainly did look as if one might be wanted, and although mine was again snug at my lodgings I smiled and told him that I dealt not in the articles generally.

"No offense, Sir, I hope," [he said]. "If you follow this street, turn to the right, then to the left. Anybody will show you the way to Piccadilly."

Thus, Lucy, from an umbrella maker or merchant to a [one-time] cotton dealer [turned] fop. I collected all information needed to bring me, in a few minutes more, opposite a coach just at the entrance of Piccadilly. "Take me to Mr. Dockray, Hard-wick," I said. "A Quaker, Sir?" "Yes."

Up the driver jumped and turning his horses round, he brought me in a moment [to] Mr. Dockray's. There my friends were, all yes all. I cannot help calling them all friends, who are so truly kind to me. I was chided for not having come to dinner, or to breakfast. And between the three parties it was difficult to tell with whom I would spend the time to come. I saw the lady Abigail [Dockray] with nine children of different ages, all lovely. But, my dear wife, Mrs. Rathbone's reception of me perhaps exceeded all I had ever experienced from her. She positively appeared to think that I was one of her own sons. I could not help feeling rather disagreeable for a while. The more I saw, the more surprised I was. I really think I was asked three distinct and different times if I had dined, and although I certainly had I could not refuse a glass of wine brought to me by kind Hannah.

Mrs. Rathbone spoke of going to *Matlock* with me in such a manner that I thought it [*might*] be, and oh how I did wish it. We soon bid adieu. I handed Mrs. Greg into the carriage. Her husband filled the further seat. And after the last nod of adieu we rolled most easily snug.

We reached "Summer Place," the [country] seat of Robert Greg, Esqr., where, whilst I was admiring a "Laughing Girl" of Sir Joshua Reynolds and some fine drawings of Vernet, a tall female figure entered the room and gave me a powerful idea of the inferiority of art to beautiful Nature. I forgot Reynolds and his girl, left Vernet at the Field of Moscow, and after a timid glance [ahead I saw] the well featured Mrs. R. Greg, and at last I made a bow most awkward I have no doubt. She, Lucy, has blue eyes and is very amiable and I doubt not very clever, but I really like the fair [Ellen] of "Quarry Bank" better, and the dark eyes of Miss Hannah also.

This house is agreeably situated about two miles from Manchester. From it a very extensive view is obtained and a circulation of air that assures health and pleasure.

Again in the carriage. Mr. Greg soon went to sleep, and Mrs. Greg helped me to a good quantity of most agreeable conversation. Lucy, Mrs. Greg is one of those rare examples of the superior powers of thy sex over ours when education and circumstances are combined. She is most amiable, smart, quick, witty, positively learned, with an incomparable memory and as benevolent as woman can be. Her and her husband form the finest picture of devoted, tender and faithful attachment I ever met with, and I have looked on them and their *family circle* as being probably as happy as would be found in all America, for instance. Well, Mr. Greg awoke; I gave him a pinch of snuff, and we turned again quite short to the right, then moved slowly down the hill. Presently I was leading Mrs. Greg to her house. Thus from "Green Bank" to "Quarry Bank" and from one pleasure to another, not like a butterfly that skips from flower to flower and merely sees their beauties, but more, I hope, as a bee gathering honied knowledge for older times!

I am soon among that flock of females, the daughters of my kind *Irish gentleman*. Therefore I am soon at ease. One academician would stupefy me whilst twenty such fair objects as surrounded me have no other tendency than to augment the ease I am so fond of. The Italian made her appearance. She is more magnetic. Her eyebrow is more regular, darker, her nose more angular, but her voice is delightfully sweet. Her expressions glide into the remotest intercourse of the mind and give a good idea of the superiority of language adapted for conversation.

My cold was really disagreeable and I sneezed so constantly that it was no joke to me, I assure thee. And had I followed the kind advice of the family I would have felt still more like sneezing the next day, for they wished me to "*do something for it,*" that is to say to take some physic. This I never do, thou well knowest, unless quite ill. Our conversation was animated respecting the superiority of women over our sex, and Miss Ann Mary (I believe) proved the superiority of her knowledge, understanding and eloquence in a very few minutes. Dispersed about the room as we were, some singly, others by twos, I looked at the whole when Mr. Greg, with a smile that reached the eyes that were on his lips, pointed to his lady and pronounced her his superior also. The ladies all worked at light things. I looked at them all, and my eyes returned, always with more satisfaction, to the fair [Ellen].

I went to rest early. I had been obliged to open this book to shew a sketch of the Flying Fish. All eyes were fixed on the drawing for a while, and when, after I had answered their question that it was my journal they said that no doubt it must contain some "curious things." The hint was not like to take, however. I remember well my promise to thee, and the observations of some other friends, and shut it quietly.

Now, my love, good night.

"Quarry Bank" Oct. 9th, 1826 Monday

As soon as possible this day a male Chaffinch was procured, and I sat to draw it to give an idea of the style, as the artist calls it, of my work. With a smile that would penetrate cold marble, [Ellen] Greg asked me for a pin, and as I had none about me, she presented me with a little cushion made for the waistcoat pocket, well [supplied], and hoped I would not refuse it. Refuse it, no, I would just as soon think of dranking poison. Refuse it, not I. I snugged it in my waistcoat and thanked the fair maid with a *good portion* of my heart, Lucy.

The Chaffinch was outlined, daubed with water colors, and nearly finished in *my style*, when two youths made their appearance. They were introduced but I scarcely saw them. They were some lord or other's relations, and as the language they used was *exceedingly exquisite* I kept my thoughts confined and my eyes bent on the Chaffinch. The young ladies, I thought, cared not for them. I heard that they had called to pay their respects to the fair Italian; and as she had not appeared since breakfast, the gentlemen, after tapping the fair tops of their boots smartly with their smart whips, arranging their cravats a little, and walking round my seat to view my locks, my coat, and my performance, made an *exceedingly exquisite* bow and departed. May God bless them and help them and render them both rather more simple. Yes simple!

Mr. Greg, not so well aware as William Rathbone that I prefer wine when handed me by a lady, brought me a glass himself. This proves how apt we all are to do contrary to our likings. I am quite persuaded that Mr. Greg himself is blessed with the same wish [to be] helped to such things *as wine* for instance by a lady as ever I was or ever will be.

Dr. Holland[1] came in. I was pleased with him, and although I am neither a physiognomist nor a craniologist, the moment he talked I pronounced him within myself a good man. We dined most cheerfully. I was glad that Dr. Holland had come. It gave me the opportunity of sitting opposite my favorite, [Ellen], and of seeing her wild eyes moving as if they loved and yet feared all. The doctor had come to see Miss Greg. She had a cold also. The doctor no doubt will cure [it] with time; time will cure me without the doctor, and as I dislike to trouble more individuals than is really necessary I am glad to confide entirely in the latter's ability.

The gamekeeper from Lord Stamford's was again waiting for the young gentlemen and me, and to my great regret we left the table and company to enter the fields and commit murder. We had a long walk. The grass was very wet. I killed a pheasant and a hare, and Mr. S. Greg killed a hare also. This walk did me much good. The weather and drawing had kept me close within the walls of "Quarry Bank" and I needed exercise as well as time to cure my cold. It was with difficulty that I escaped the physic intended for me in the evening. Mr. Greg said that wine was bad for me and I must not touch it. I pleaded that it would warm my cold, and swallowed a glass with quite as much pleasure as ever.

This evening was delightful. Mr. Greg was in high spirits. So was his lady. And all the stars shewn brightly also. Much entertaining poetry was read and repeated. We had a little music and a great deal of interesting conversation. The map of the U.S. was laid before me, and they all were astonished to discover how little the particularity of that country has been mentioned by writers. I wished I could write. I would delight giving my country fair play. Well Lucy, I went to bed and did not forget to bid thee good night.

Mr. Dockray's, near Manchester   Oct. 10th, 1826   Tuesday

The ladies were all up at "Quarry Bank" very early. The weather was sad. I worked at some oak leaves for the Misses Greg, much in a hurry. I gave my fair pupil my brushes and she

---

1. George Calvert Holland (1808–65) was a craniologist versed in phrenology.

gave me some excellent India ink and Chinese white. But Lucy, I positively forgot the little pin cushion, a full proof of the difference between loving, as I do, Miss [Ellen], or loving as I do thee. Mr. Greg generally goes to Manchester every Tuesday. I wished to return with him, anxious, if the weather alters tomorrow, to visit Matlock. I packed up half my chalks, anxious the ladies should try to work with the other half. And after an early breakfast I found myself close on the right side of Miss [Ellen], who divided me from her father.

Slowly ascending the hill that leads from "Quarry Bank," and thinking of Manchester, I cleaned my nose and took a pinch of snuff, moved sideways not to encumber the fair companion, and opened the conversation on cotton, corn laws, taxes here and in America. I begged Miss [Ellen] to send me the little pin cushion, and arrived in Fountain Street at 11.

I soon reached my Birds and all well. I found a card from Mr. Bohn on my table, saw my good friends Mrs. and Hannah Rathbone, the family Dockray with whom I promised to dine, and pushed out to discover Mr. Bohn's [whereabouts]. I found him at the hotel with the help of Mr. Bentley who, I may say, has been of great service to me in Manchester. We returned to the Academy together, and after examining my drawings a long time he advised me to publish them, full size of life, and that they must pay well. May God grant it. Mr. Bohn advised me strongly to [clear out] of Manchester, assuring me that in London I would be cherished by the nobility and could not but succeed with my talent. He was going to add "and agreeable manners" when I stopped him short by putting a question to him.

Lucy, the boy that attends [to] my exhibition is named John Wilson. When I returned with Mr. Bohn he came and shewed me a sovereign, and said a letter to me this morning had given it to him and said that the amount over the number of her [party] was for him. I did not mention that Mrs. Rathbone had read to me a part of her daughter's letter from Liverpool, but I am very sure that thou hast guessed before this *she is the sovereign lady*. What am I to do, to ever return all the *gifts*, attention and motherly kindness of this good lady?

I reached Mr. Dockray's house about 2, [and this time] was

not directed first to the right and then to the left by the umbrella manufacturer. But I was positively conducted by a good, neatly dressed woman who walked quite as fast as I did without [effort], and would have accompanied me to the very door had I not begged of her not to do so. I felt a great desire to give her a shilling, but again remarking her figure and neat dress I dared not lest I offend her.

Lucy, I am not able to describe Mrs. Dockray beyond this, that she is a Quaker, a lady, and a most kind and benevolent woman, [with] a large, interesting family and a husband resembling William Penn. My letters were returned to me, but [in] a portfolio, made by one of the daughters to keep them safer from [tearing]. I read a few short passages of this book at the request of my good friend Mrs. Rathbone. Showed how to rub the chalks. Sketched an Egret[2] for one, a wild Turkey for another, spoke of America, wrote with my left hand, drank I think rather too much wine, enjoyed my Miss Hannah's dazzling eyes, and at 11 o'clock was conducted with many apologies to a nice small chamber where, after praying for our sakes and that of *all our species*, I lay to sleep *and bid thee good night*, dearest friend.

Bakewell   Oct. 11th, 1826   Wednesday

I am at last, my beloved wife, at the spot that has been honored with thy ancestors' name. I am at Bakewell, and I can neither describe my feelings nor the place.[3] It is dark, rainy, and all promises a wet tomorrow. I have just returned this moment, fifteen minutes of 9, from a walk in the very churchyard of the village. Singular place to report to, is it not? But being on an errand with Hannah Rathbone, say shopping, she wished me to see some portion of it; and attracted by the ancient Gothic appearance of the church, we gradually approached it and finally walked round it. I positively know very little either about the churchyard or the church, but I am quite sure that I and Hannah [went] around it, she leaning on my arm and I supporting her, neither very happy nor very sad, [I] perhaps feeling a sort of

2. Pencil on paper, owned by Mr. and Mrs. Reynolds Rathbone.
3. Bakewell, named Bath Well by the Romans, a market town in Derbyshire, is believed to be the place of origin of the Bakewell family that spread into Leicestershire and Staffordshire.

Egret. Pencil on paper, actual size. Inscribed "Believe me, Kind Lady all fair objects reflect themselves fairly." "October 10, 1826."

vacancy about me, and undetermination, a kind of restless dreaming, illusion-like, that made me doubt if I lived and walked, or if I saw and felt. If thou were present or not. If the place was called Bakewell or Audubon. But, since I re-entered the Inn and seen my good Lady Rathbone and her niece Mrs. Dockray and listened to the light touches of Hannah Rathbone on the piano I have awakened and know, yes positively know that Audubon possesses a Bakewell!! But I have not come here accidentally, that thou knowest well. It must be some twice ten years since a view of Bakewell was desired. And when I think how frequently, since, my plans have been defeated and my voyage to Europe postponed, it is no great wonder if I should feel more at a loss than usual, when seated here, at finding it difficult to tell thee precisely, or in the most interesting manner, how and under what circumstances I have reached it at last.

Know thee, my beloved wife, that at breakfast this morning Mrs. Rathbone spoke of going to Matlock [and Bakewell] and in a few minutes it was all arranged that her, her daughter and niece, and several of the children would leave in two chaises at 12. The weather was then fair. Earlier I had walked with Mr. Dockray and viewed all his work with elation, perhaps the more so on account of his extreme politeness in giving to my view all the most interesting details. He procures wool rough from the sheep and disposes of the cloth when finished. Between sixty and seventy weavers were at work. The engine made its returns silently and smoothly. I saw the dyeing apparatus, &c., &c., and walked to dirty Manchester to put up my Birds. I [decided], however, the limited time did not permit me to do this, and I only packed some to shew Mr. Gifford [the Liverpool engraver] and others willing to view them.

I saw Mr. Rathbone who invited me, extremely kindly, to his house. Dr. Holme appeared disappointed that my Prospectus was yet to be prepared. I begged of Mr. Bentley to see to my drawings. The coach being [outside] with Mr. Dockray waiting, I thrust my body, my bundle, my book and my thoughts into it, and off we whirled to Hardwick.

My Lucy, it was decided, [as I have said], that I should have the pleasure and honor of riding to Matlock with my good friends.—To Matlock where Dr. Darwin[4] nursed thee on his knee. What I should be in body or mind when I reached the *bijoux* of England, I knew not.

[Picture] seven of us in two chaises, our servant and two postilions, peeping to the right and left, hungry with curiosity, passing objects one after the other, finding the one before us always the most interesting perhaps because the newest, until we reached Stockport on Wellington North Road, a manufacturing town between two elongated hills, where we entered Cheshire. We changed horses. Again at Chapel En-la-Frith, twenty miles from the point of departure [the horses were changed]. I had by this time taken my station on the dicky seat behind, and had for companion the younger daughter, Sarah Dockray, who entertained me very much with her innocent, well regulated observations, [and whose place was taken later] by the eldest [girl], who spoke much to my satisfaction on many subjects.

I saw a good deal of thy England, which I admired very much. The railways were new to me. Many buildings resembled those of Pennsylvania, but the approach [to] the mountains dampened my spirits. The aridity of the soil, the want of hedges of course, of course of birds, of course of good music, the scarcity of cattle, and the super-abundance of shackling stone walls cutting the hills in all kinds of distorted ways, tended quite too [much] to recall me America, and probably made me a very unsociable sort of companion to Miss Rachel!

When we arrived here I was pleased to see how comfortable we were at the Inn. The room where tea and supper were drank and eat [was] ornamented with many good prints, and thou knowest a piano was there. Our circle was all gaiety, and [our] being so contiguous to Bakewell raised our spirits, and I, with the help of several glasses of wine, feel quite as inclined to wish thee a good, happy, blessed night as I ever did since I knew thee, either by the name of Bakewell or that of Audubon. So may God bless thee, Dearest Friend, my sweet wife. Good night.

Stop. Only conceive how foolish I found myself when about a

---

4. Erasmus Darwin (1731–1802), grandfather of Charles Darwin, was a physician, botanist, and author of a botanical text in verse entitled *The Loves of the Plants*. He was at times the Bakewell family physician.

mile from Mr. Dockray's I discovered that I had forgotten my letters from [Miss] Gifford.[5] And moreover, instead of Matlock being, as I thought it, thy birthplace, I looked at thy memorandum and plainly saw that it was Burton-upon-Trent in Staffordshire! And why all this stir? Because I was bound towards thy native spot!

Matlock, Derbyshire   Oct. 12th, 1826

I certainly slept well last night. I felt comfortable although very far from thee. My bed was sweetly clean, and the name of Bakewell was so connected with all about me that I laid my head on the pillow, contented, imagining thee well and most certainly wishing thee so. Day made its appearance, [and] my eyelids, consciously opened, [were] aware of it. I sprang up, anxious to see all about this delightful country. I called my young companion, David Dockray; his youth, the peace of his heart, and the tenderness of his body all joined [me with] reluctance, and it was not until I had warned him several times that it was quite [day-] light, that he slipped from his slumbers and dressed quickly after my example.

Again I saw and walked around the church, remarked its decaying state and that of all the thatch roofs of the humble cottages that surround this religious asylum. The sky was cloudless. We might easily have believed that all above us was silently admiring Nature's opening and the morning twilight. I saw, I thought, close by my side, a little child, a female, cheeks dimpled, smiling with loveliness, light-footed, lightly moving, gazing with that anxiety that nothing but youth can genuinely enjoy, beckon to me and bid me follow path after path, and turn and wind from lane to lane, and imperceptibly lead me through this village [Bakewell] called after thy name. I watched the bewitching child, and the more I saw of her the more I saw in her my sweet little Lucy—so young, so beautiful, so joyfully gamboling through the Bakewell grounds. So well persuaded did I at

---

5. Miss Euphemia Gifford (1765–1853) was the daughter of Richard Gifford, Anglican vicar of Duffield near Derby, and of Elizabeth Woodhouse, great-aunt of Mrs. Audubon. With the Duke of Devonshire and Sir Richard Arkwright the heiress shared in the Crich mines. In his boyhood her cousin Benjamin Bakewell (Mrs. Audubon's uncle) was the orphaned ward of the Balliol-educated vicar.

last believe thee near me that I concluded to have had thee most especially for this day's guide, and [with thee would] I now go and ramble from this spot through Matlock.

As I have come here under the beneficial escort of benevolence, friendship and amiable sweetness, let me introduce thee to my good friends Mrs. Rathbone and her Hannah, Mrs. Dockray and her Rachael, and the two younger children. Come and walk with Hannah, Rachael and David, and let us take our course over the bridge that crosses the winding river. Ascend with us the hills that look upon the village with complacency. From the bridge, look and see the sprightly trout, how gaily it leaps at the skipping fly. Look now, how sweetly the old church emerges from the smoke to receive the rays of the morning sun, and see how playfully the villas are arranged amongst the hills and along the ornamented valley. Now that we have ascended quite to [the top of] the sunniest, see the sun's light, how it clears the horizon for us. See the road that we followed last night, and the one that we will survey to-day. Did thou ever taste of the water of this spring, or pluck the violets that growed under these hedges? Hast thou ever rambled through this shrubbery and seen the beautiful sights up the river before us?

Let us return to the Rutland Arms Inn. Hast thou rested in it with thy good father and thy botanical friend [Erasmus Darwin]? And seen and felt the comfort that along with good friends one can enjoy there? It is nearly 7 o'clock, the time appointed for us to proceed. Young as thou art, walk by thyself, [Lucy], but I pray thee be close at my elbow whilst I help our friend Hannah. Pretty place this, my Lucy, very quiet, peaceable and happy-looking. No Manchester this, no hammerings, no heavy blows either to the heart or the eye! Come this way, and let us walk up and make ready.

Now we are arranged, and we go. The weather is fretful. I doubt if it will be fair all day. Ah, here is Haddon Hall—beautiful! It looks still better [as] we approach it. The road is really very good and this valley truly charming. How contented those pheasants appear by the side of that wood, how safe from all but the will of the Lord!

[A faint but large pencil sketch, a landscape, follows.]

Hey day, what have we here? The very Duke of Devonshire's groom. What whiskers, mustachios and strange looking spotted horses, going tandem, too! At what a rate he goes. This gentleman's [country] seat is pretty, that cypress large and well-leafed. Ah Lucy, what beautiful brakes and high hills, delightful turns, well-shaded little streams. Surely we must be nearing some enchanted fairy boudoir.

"Ha, what now?" What now, my friend? Matlock, opening before thy wistful eye in all its beauty. Seest thou the mountains dotted nearly all over with the sweetest cottages, [as well as] a gentleman's country seat? The autumnal tints diversify the landscape and enrich bountiful Nature. How pretty, yet how grand. Is it not very much like thy America on the clear Juniata river? Watch, remark the cleanliness. Here is the old path, the museum, the little shop that disposes of the sparry productions. In that pond they wash the post horses. Now that we have left the course of the river, we are rising slowly and gently approaching the new baths, where thy friends wish to spend the day.

Remark the large Newfoundland dog. His name is Neptune. Quite a comfortable house, this. How well its [occupants] do look. I cannot help remarking their anxiety to please! Mr. Saxton is our landlord, it seems. Here is breakfast, ready.

Well, it will not do to be idle, looking at our empty coffee cups. On with bonnets, and umbrellas, and let us proceed. As thou hast visited all this so frequently, [Lucy], fly to America and look at our dear sons. I myself will visit all, and compare notes with thee when we meet again. Farewell, be happy.

"My dear Miss Hannah, which way?" I ask. "Let us go and visit the museum first. I am anxious to gather a little assortment to send to America, and will thank you for your tasteful judgment."

[To the shopkeeper I say,] "I will take these boxes and smelling bottles and this vase, and I would like to have this beautiful inkstand."

[Miss Hannah says to me,] "Pray accept of this little box for little John. Matlock is nicely engraved on it. Send it to him."

"Thank you" [I reply].

Here is another shop, cheaper to be sure but not quite so well [stocked]. [I tell myself] that I will buy sixteen shillings worth here, and eleven here, and—will not buy any more.

"Let us take a good long walk," [I suggest], "and ascend those hills, and as a man is offering to take us into a curious cave, let us follow him."

My Lucy, we walked slowly up a very steep hill. On turning to view the delightful scenery I saw either a good husband, or a good brother, or a well compensated lover bearing in his arms either his wife, his sister, or his young mistress as heartily as I have done, myself, hundreds of times: with my wife, my sister, or my lovely mistress. The weather had [by] now become quite rainy. We reached the entrance of the cave. Hannah was fatigued. I dried a portion of a bench, spread a portion of my umbrella and my handkerchief for her to set [on,] but her genuine politeness on seeing the female stranger made her bid me to offer the seat prepared for her. I did so. The lady accepted. But in a moment we were all under way towards our visitation into the earth's bowels. Hannah went in only a short distance, [turned back], and walked [through] the door [to wait] for our emergence.

We proceeded, each of us with a light in his hand, and saw all the different caves containing most rich minerals and spars that the country affords. From one natural chamber we [proceeded] to another, and I squeezed myself into the last and lowest with the guide only, scarce able to maintain my hold and expecting that [each] stone that I [touched] might give way with me. I found the bottom faster than I was willing. That chamber was, however, superb. It all shone like burnished steel and dazzled my eyes completely. Again outside, I bid the fair stranger good-bye, bowed to her sinewy partner, and leading one group we walked [on up] and saw all the views that render this enchanted Matlock so desired by every traveller. We again felt our steps lengthening, and went down hill after hill until we found ourselves on the first level.

A single door and a single woman troubled us. The first could not be passed without a toll of sixpence each, we having passed through private grounds, and the latter would not give us guiding without a shilling. Again at the Inn, my bountiful friend having heard me mention the black spar inkstand, requested Hannah to purchase it for thee, and [so] it was. Now Lucy, how much art thou in debt to this wonderful woman? I saw the turning of spar from the crude state and was rather astonished at the very great alteration perceptible when any portion is put under the influence of *red heat*.

I thought of gathering leaves, plants and all other such trifles as might give thee a moment's pleasure by [their] reaching America.

Something that my ears probably met with the most pleasure was the repeated notes of the Jackdaws that constantly flew from hole to hole along the stupendous declevities of the rocks about us. The wind blew fresh. Each tree turned each leaf as if anxious to shew thy husband positively all about Matlock.

I will not dwell upon our dinner. I have not time when the country so much calls on my attention, and so reminds me of thy youth and thy loveliness. Our dinner, my dinner, Lucy, was good. Trout, mutton and rabbits, vegetables, and many hearty healths were drank and eat.

Now my Lucy, we all did wish to ride on the *Derwent*. We all set out from the inn for that purpose, but the rain [having begun] to fall again, the aunt and niece returned and we, the remainder, seated [ourselves] in a boat rowed by thy husband and went down the pretty river stream as well as down that of our lives! We reached a dam and a falls, landed, looked at the falls, walked through the woods, gradually reached to hilltops again, gathered all kinds of mosses for thee, saw some hares, heard a Kestrell just as if in America, entered our boat again and rowed up the stream, reached our inn, eat and drink, and enjoyed a most lively evening. Saw my sweet friend Hannah quite happy, all about me quite happy, wished thee quite happy, and bid thee good night, quite happy!!!

Matlock, Derbyshire   Oct. 13th, 1826   Friday

The rain did not put a barrier before my inquisitive desires. We got up early and walked down the river. I saw a particularly handsome spot, affording just the making of such a sketch as I thought would give fresh ideas of the vale of Matlock. During the morning I made it very slightly, on a card for Hannah Rathbone, and here [in these pages] closely drawn for thee.[6] We entered part of the grounds of Sir Thomas Arkwright,[7] saw his castle, his church and his meadows. The Rooks and Jackdaws were over our heads by the hundreds. The steep rocks that here border the right side of the valley, following the course of the Derwent [river] were pleasantly [intermingled] with clumps of shrubby trees. The large castle is on the left on a fine elevation, and [too] regular to be called, by me [at any rate, suited] to the rich scenery about it. We passed along a canal by a large manufactory's coal yard, and returned to breakfast [by way of] *Crumford.*

Nearly the whole of my day was employed at drawing. I purchased more spars for thee. Having reached the *Heights of Abraham* I seated myself in full [view] of the whole of Matlock, [its] hills and vale and river below, and then I made a general sketch. David Dockray took that of the castle, and his sister followed me and worked by my side. I found her a very interesting child. Dinner over, I returned quickly to the spot with David, and between him and I [the sketch] was finished about sunset.

Rachael Dockray accompanied me through the Rutland Cave. I was highly gratified. It surpassed all my expectations. The natural chambers sparkled with brilliancy, and to enhance the value of the sight, lights were raised to the very summit to reflect the richness of the place. The way into all the parts was easy. I saw there some little fishes that had not seen daylight for three years, and yet quite sprightly. A certain part of the roof represented a very good head of a large tiger. We were going out, intent on returning to David Dockray, when our good friends Mrs. Rathbone, her daughter Hannah, and Abigail presented themselves to our view. They went in also. I soon fol-

6. In *Art News* (May, 1965), this drawing, *Matlock,* is illustrated and declared to be the "only known landscape" by Audubon. Its companion piece is illustrated here. *View of Natchez,* a large oil on canvas painted in 1823 and first published by F. H. Herrick in 1917, is the pride of Melrose plantation near Natchez, and it ranks as Audubon's oldest existing and best landscape. *Audubon and His Journals* (1897) has a pencil sketch of 1843, *Three Mamelles.* His large oils, *Suave Qui Peut* and *Black Grouse,* have impressive landscape backgrounds. There is more to be said on the subject of Audubon landscapes.

7. Richard Arkwright (1732–92) was knighted for his spinning mill inventions.

Landscape. Matlock, Derbyshire. Pencil sketch.

"*October 12, 1826 . . . taken from the window of our Inn. New Baths. Saxton's. The little houses are shops for sparrs and other notional curiosities.*"

lowed, and imitated the owl's cry and the Indian yell. The latter music never pleased my fancy much, and I well know the effects it produces previous to an attack, during an attack, and whilst the scalping knife is at work.[8]

We had a pleasant walk back to the inn. The moon shone brightly. The evening was quite calm, and Matlock and my friends were all purity. Our tea was soon over and the night so truly inviting that we made for the river in a body, entered a boat and seated ourselves to contemplate the placitude around us. I rowed and I sung, up, down, and up the Derwent again. Again [we were] on shore, again at the Saxton's baths. I had all thy wares nicely packed up, and, fearing that I might forget the contents, I will now put down the whole:

1 fruit bowl	£1.6.0
1 bell vase	1.0.0
5 boxes, 4 bought by me	16.0
1 wafer box	2.0
19 smelling bottles	19.0
10 lockets	10.0
1 inkstand given thee	
1 salt stand, &c., &c.	
	£4.13.0

We have now eat our supper, and talked of our departure tomorrow. I have seen thy Matlock and repeat, it is most beautiful!! God bless thee. Good night, my dear wife.

I have no wish to forget that I bathed in the waters of Matlock. The baths are situated immediately under our setting-room—that is, the east one, with a large bow window through which we could see the stupendous rocks across the river. The baths are built of white marble and vaulted. I thought them completely secure from noise and splashes, but when I returned to the company I was told that I was heard all over the house. A great proof indeed that walls are no safeguard for secrecy.

Our lady hostess [of the inn] came last night to bid us all farewell, and thanked Mrs. Rathbone very gentlewomanly. I liked this.

---

8. Audubon knew from hearsay only.

Manchester   Oct. 14th, 1826   Saturday

Several times last night I wished to get up, dress, and ramble through the hills of Matlock, but the frost was too severe [for me] to enjoy such walks alone, and I patiently waited until I thought I might wake my little friend David.

By 5 o'clock we were running down along the Derwent. Nature was positively enclosed in a veil of sparkling, congealed dew. The rising fog only permitted us to see its waters, where they rolled against a rock [and] formed a ripple. The vale was all mist, and had we not known our positive situation and heard the notes and the wings of the Jackdaws above us, we might easily have conceived ourselves travelling through a large subterranean avenue. The strength of daylight gradually abated the filthy curtain. Gradually the tops of the tallest trees, the castle turrets, and the church [spire] pierced through and stood before our eyes, as if suspended and detached from their lower members. All was calm and pure until a bell struck [upon] our ear, and we soon saw the long files of little girls, sisters and mothers moving in a procession towards the mills of Arkwright. We had but little time allowed us, and I returned to the inn to write a few lines in these sheets [about] yesterday. [See pages 273 and 277 for illustrations of Audubon's impressions of Matlock.]

Judge of my dismay when, after a close search for my little knife, I could not find it. Pockets, baskets, walks, last night's boat, all were searched over and over in vain. I knew that I had mended this very pen with it during the writing of this book, and that was all, alas, that I could [recall] of it. In such a cold, disinterested manner Hannah Rathbone said that it was not worth pining after that I felt quite irritated, and again sorry, fearing she might think that I ought to have been more careful. The knife was lost, and I very much regretted it.

We were all under way by 7. I passed the last cottage of Matlock, thinking of thy younger days, of the sweetness of the spot, and of the great pleasure we would have had if thou hadst been *more positively* of the party. Anxious [for a good view] I and Sarah Dockray mounted the dicky [seat] but regretted it. The cold was too severe for me, and notwithstanding the beauty of the scenery that accompanied us I was heartily glad when we

Landscape. Matlock, Derbyshire. Pencil sketch.

"Matlock . . . October 13, 1826 . . . I saw a particularly handsome spot, affording just the making of such a sketch as I thought would give fresh ideas of the value of Matlock. I made it very slightly on a card for Hannah Rathbone, and here, closely drawn, for thee. . . . Having reached the Heights of Abraham I seated myself in full [view] of the whole of Matlock, hills and vale and river below, and then I made a general sketch."

Matlock from the Highland of Abraham
Oct — 1A B 1826 A P
Matlock [?] — [?]
Oct — 14 — 1826 — 7 day — [?]

reached Bakewell, and still more so when we entered the well furnished, well warmed room of the Rutland Arms. There a good breakfast soon [revived] us all. Had I had my little knife in my pocket I would have felt quite well. I felt toward that knife a kind of sentimental attachment. Indeed I always prefer such objects given by a sweet female friend than all that money can purchase out of my own pocket.

Travelling again through Bakewell I still liked its ancient look, its peaceable quietness, and the simplicity of its cottages crowded together as if needing the support of each other. The ivy, the wall flowers and the little boxes of *reseda* before the little leaden glazed windows made me wish to reside under their mossy roofs to feel the happiness of the owners. We changed our route and made for the well known watering place of Buxton, still in Derbyshire, the principal portion of which belongs to *his grace* the Duke of Devonshire. The country here is barren and rocky but so picturesque that the want of trees is well balanced by the grand beauty of Nature displayed along the [entire] road, winding along a very narrow valley for several miles and affording a vast variety of detached bits of scenery extremely agreeable. The natural scantiness of vegetable matter forces the vagrant cattle to risk much to obtain their food, and now and then, when seeing a bull kneeling with stretched neck and putting [forth] his tongue to nibble the few grasses hanging over the precipices made me dread for their safety.

Here the Hawk sails in vain. After many repeated rounds he is forced to abandon the dreary steep, having only espied the swift Kingfisher that in full security gives chase to the little minnows of the deep-seated rivulet. [At one point] the view is quite close. A high wall of shattered rocks seems to put an end to our journey, and yet the chaise runs swiftly down the hill and suddenly, [rounding] a sharp [bend], affords delight to our eyes by opening a new prospect, quite as wild and diversified as any before [it].

We all alighted and leisurely walked for a better view of the beauties around us. We examined the mosses, and gathered the finest.

[Presently, moving on,] we saw before us the pretty village of

Buxton and its large building properly called the Crescent. [There] we met our friend the American Consul, Maury. We visited all the baths in his company. [But] his age does not admit of his moving at the anxious rate that is needed on such occasions when curiosity forces the body and mind onward with all its power, [so] I felt anxious to be alone. My kind friend Hannah knew this and procured an opportunity by advising me to accompany David Dockray to the bath, and I flew on the wings of ecstasy toward the Crescent again. [Here], for one shilling, a man [can have] the comfort of cleanliness in the public baths; for three [shillings], a private one; and for two [shillings], two persons can have a room that admits of no greater number. They are all commodious, clean and well attended, but I found the heat of the atmosphere uncomfortable for the want of circulating air. Mr. Maury has visited this place regularly each year for the past twenty-five, and during that lapse has spent just two full years of his time at Buxton. I saw his lady. The beauty of this place is not a Nature that interests me; one day here and twelve months at Matlock would suit me. I heard the Duke was gone to Russia to pay his respects to the Emperor. Thus God knows if I will ever meet him.

We had what travellers usually call a luncheon. I thought it an excellent dinner. We left at 2.

Since reaching Bakewell I noticed that we had gradually been descending. I had the pleasure of Hannah's company in the dicky until the drizzle usually felt on these hills made us exchange our seats and we parted, I to enter the carriage of her Mamma, and her that in which Mr. Dockray was. This good Hannah gave me most excellent conversation and some advice. She desired me particularly to see Mr. George Barclay when in London.

As we again drew near Manchester the air became gradually thick with coal smoke. The population increased. The carts, coaches, and horsemen gradually filled the road. The female faces became less clean, less rosy. And the children had none of that liveness found amongst those of the Derbyshire hills. Involuntarily I felt the general difference operate and gain on my thoughts, and regretfully I felt the carriage turning into Hardwick again, [and] the loss of Matlock and my little knife, and the approaching moment when I must leave these excellent friends about me. Lucy, during this most agreeable excursion I became more intimate in two days with the amiable family Dockray than ever I have done with any other in so short a time. I called the eldest daughter "the little lady" and spoke to her as I do to thee. The mother, I assure thee, is one of the *fairest* specimens of English female and most amiable and kind. To view the groups I have been in is enough to refresh [one] from years of labour.

I wished to go and see how my Birds were. Mrs. Dockray put *comfortables* of her knitting around my neck and wrists, and presented them to me in a way that admitted not of a refusal. Am I not fortunate, my Lucy, to possess such friends in England? Manchester is not *altogether* an umbrella man manufactory, and it is easier to find the house of the Dockrays than to leave it when found.

My drawings all safe, I returned here. My friends in Liverpool were all well. The good mother had heard from all her children. The kind Hannah mended my gloves most neatly, and during the while I finished for her the little sketch I had began on a card yesterday. We were all happy. Mr. Dockray enjoyed our return. We supped, and I wish thee a happy good night, my Lucy.

Manchester   Oct. 15th, 1826   Sunday

I went to the Unitarian Chapel in Moseley Street for the purpose of hearing a good sermon delivered by the Reverend John Taylor. However, he was gone into Derbyshire and I was obliged to content myself with one from Mr. Carpenter, but it was not quite as *practical* a sermon as I am fond of. I saw Mrs. Taylor who with a smile invited me to see her at her house, [saying] that she would give me letters from Edinburgh, &c. I also saw Mr. Ewart and family. Mr. Maury invited me to go and spend the evening with him, but I felt no inclination. I did not like perhaps to have to wait until quite too late to return to my friends at Hardwick.

I returned to my lodgings, inquired for parcels, &c., but was sadly disappointed. My hopes that a letter from thee would

Visiting Card. Pencil sketch, actual size, 3½ × 2⅖ inches.
Inscribed "Mr. John J. [or L.] Audubon. About one mile from
Matlock going down the right side of the Derwent." Presented
to Miss Hannah Mary Rathbone.

have been there were ended. I reached Mr. Bentley's and dined with him and family, and was glad to find him and all about him so kind to me and to [one another].

When I reached Hardwick, Mr. Robert Greg was there and he told me that he had sent two parcels for me to my room and that they were from Liverpool. I pushed for town, inquired again at my room, [and] at Mr. Bentley's, in vain. I had no hopes of seeing the parcels until tomorrow. I returned with my little friend David to Hardwick quite sick at heart, and whatever figure I made this evening amongst my friends I cannot well tell, but frequently I felt as if tears were rushing from my eyes, and a lowness of spirits so overcame me that I scarcely spoke to anyone. My having so few letters from thee is very trying at this great distance. I went to bed early, scarcely heard what was read at prayers. I thought of my little penknife over and over, and concluded that even amidst my kind friends, sorrow made its way to me in spite of all their best endeavours. Yet my Lucy, I bid thee good night.

Manchester   Oct. 16th, 1826   Monday

I left Mr. Dockray early this morning, intent on getting the longed for parcels. I went to the Exhibition Room and found, instead of letters from thee, my album with a note from Mrs. William Rathbone and another from Miss Agnes Greg. I felt myself fainting at the disappointment, and to force my sorrows again I determined to do a great deal of work by calling on almost everyone I knew, to ask for letters. I was very fortunate at this and walked so much that it relieved me very considerably. I was vexed that one of the printers who had inserted some advertisements for me about my Birds had called during my absence several times without receiving his pay. I have no doubt the poor fellow wanted it bad enough.

I had promised to dine at Hardwick to see my good Mrs. Rathbone and her Hannah before their going to "Quarry Bank." I read the notes from Mrs. William Rathbone and Miss [Ellen] Greg that, through disappointment and sorrow, I had [earlier] put in my pocket without scarcely glancing at either of them. They were kind notes, and the little pin cushion from the fair

[Ellen] was carefully put up in my pocketbook, [lest] it share the misfortune of my sweet Hannah's little knife but that constantly came across my thoughts and all I did.

Whilst walking the streets this morning I saw her twice but she did not see me. I was busy as she was herself. I bid goodbye to her mother, to all around the table, and herself, and moved towards the door with Mr. Dockray. Hannah rose from her seat, and coming to me, asked if my knife had been found. I felt a blush, answered no, and was going to bow again to her when she gave me another knife, my Lucy. I took it, scarcely looked at her, and walked off, not even making the intended bow. But Lucy, as I went I looked at the knife and if I have it not when ever I meet her I agree now never to use a knife again.

I reached Mr. Bentley's by 4 of the afternoon. It had been agreed that he would accompany me to the Reverend John Clowes at Broughton Hall, three miles from Manchester on the Cheatham Hill Road. We entered a coach known here by the name of the "Flora" and were going along, chatting together pretty generally, when the coach stopped. The steps were thrown down and a tall figure of a *flora* with a child in her arms came in and seated herself opposite me, and the child was put by my side. Her light-colored hair hung more loosely about her forehead and neck than is generally seen now. The fairness of her complexion and the placid blue of her eyes attracted my eyes and my thoughts. I dared not look at her again, and had not Mr. Bentley been there I would no doubt not have opened my lips. The lady arranged herself comfortably in her seat and the rustling of her deep purple silk gown almost electrified me. Mr. Bentley talked, however, and I answered him. The conversation brought on many names of persons about and in Manchester. [I] having said to Mr. B. how much I admired the family Greg, the lady asked me with an angelic voice if I was personally acquainted with the Misses Greg. I bowed in affirmation when she again spoke and told us that she had been a schoolmate. She spoke of their [fine] qualities, of the father, of the cleverness of their mother in such a delightful manner that I felt as great a desire to thank her for expressing herself so much to my wishes as I ever did on such an occasion.

I gave the little child by my side a few pomfrets and dared ask if the lady had seen Mr. Audubon's drawings. She replied no, but that she had a great desire to do so. Then Lucy, [like] a Manchester man, I composedly took out of my pocketbook and handed the lady one of my cards. She read my name, but her whole face so reddened that I dreaded having committed a very rude and impertinent action. I was soon relieved from my apprehensions when she said she was very happy to have the opportunity of seeing me, and she paid me so many compliments that at last, through different motives from the first, I wished my card in my pocket and my name unknown.

The coach stopped opposite her door. She told me her name, and I wrote it down in my tablet, "Mrs. Laing, Cheatham Hill." A man servant in livery took the child and I lost sight of both in a moment. Her curtsey as well as her language proved to me that she was an accomplished lady altogether.

We soon reached the lodge of Broughton Hall, ordered the coachman to call at 7, and went into the lodge. It rained and I had no wish that my portfolio should feel the dampness. Everything here was snug and clean. Chairs were handed us, umbrellas looked for, whilst I watched the bubbling tea kettle overflowing its spout. The weather is so changeable here that by this time it was quite cleared up, and we walked towards the hall, entered a garden, saw a swan, and an eagle; and at the entrance door the thermometer marked 53° Fahrenheit. The master had walked out and had not yet returned.

Good paintings ornamented the lobby and the setting-room. A little table was richly prepared for the master's dinner. We seated ourselves on a sofa where I thought quite at leisure of the astonishing distinctions amongst men of fortune, talent, power and the miserable wretches that pine through the world in want of nourishment. How much, for instance, this gentlem[a]n might spare to help others! How much pleasure he could feel in doing so. But Lucy, a man six feet high with a square-set body [and] a large hooked nose covering a good portion of an angular red face came in, and I was introduced to the Reverend J. Clowes of Broughton Hall.

"I am not much of a Frenchman, ha, ha, ha."

"A blustery evening this, Sir, ha, ha, ha, ha."

"Let us take a walk in the garden. Talk English, heh, heh, heh."

"Fine eagle this."

"No water this season, heh, heh, he, he."

I looked at this wonderful laughing man until I became so very furious that I walked by his side more like an automaton than a living friend of Nature.

"I'll have dinner, he, he, he, he, I'll to dinner, he, he. Walk about and come in bye and bye. I'll to dinner, he, he, he, he."

I now thought this still more wonderful. Had I come alone to Broughton Hall, had I not had an invitation from the Reverend J. Clowes, I would have turned about face and reached Piccadilly, I am sure, without asking the way, notwithstanding the politeness [one can] expect from the umbrella manufacturers. So here we were, gazing around.

I could not help remarking the structure of the old hall, the rookery, the puddle. I even visited the stable, where I found more fat, on two horses ribs, than could be seen on those of a hundred of the spinners of Manchester. We re-entered the hall, much against my will. The gentleman bid us take seats, with a well fed set of "ha, ha, ha's," and offered us wine and fruit. I drank, and I listened. I saw and I thought. I fairly shut up myself within myself, wondering at the strange personage before me. Sometimes I met his sharp, fine eye. I saw his glance penetrate, and his whole head signified much, within, of knowledge. He spoke cleverly, is a good botanist, and knows something of birds, but it would puzzle him to guess what I thought of him. He told me he had no acquaintances anywhere particularly, that he made friends as he moved along through the world. I was on the point of saying that until this evening I myself had been as fortunate, but my tongue fortunately laid quiet and cool and I did not offend him. He saw Clay's letter; De Witt Clinton he knew not. He read aloud a few words of [Charles] Bonaparte's letter [written] to Baron Temminck,[9] and, probably perceiving the extreme composure and coldness of my manners, put an end to his fits of laughter and met my eye more frequently.

---

9. Coenraad Jacob Temminick (c. 1778–1858), Dutch naturalist.

I at last heard 7 and bid him well. He did not ask me to call again; and, depend on it, I will know more of a hall before I enter one hereafter. Why should he have been so anxious to see me, and receive me in this way? With thy knowledge of the world, my dear Lucy, answer me.

The bugle call sounded but we reached the gates too late. The "Flora" had gone, and I realized the great superiority of manners between Lady Laing and the wonderful new species of clergyman. We walked, and talked of our reception. Mr. Bentley was disappointed but as he knows the Reverend J. Clowes better than I ever will, he alone pleaded his defense. I reached Manchester, supped with Mr. Bentley, and retired to my little room early. I turned my ideas over and over, and could not conclude which of the [two], the Reverend Sir or thy husband, had appeared the most original to the very kind Mr. Bentley.

Manchester   Oct. 17th, 1826   Tuesday

I had my trunk repaired completely this day, purchased a neat box of razors, and had a neat comb neatly arranged in a case, to be able not to borrow wherever I go. I wrote a letter of thanks to the consul, Samuel R. Brookes, and prepared myself to go to Mr. Robert Greg's to spend the night. I intended going to "Quarry Bank" tomorrow. I was told that a gentleman was waiting to speak to me at Dr. Holme's. I went, and himself proved to be the person. He invited me in such a lively manner, so very kindly, to dine with many of his friends, all invited on my account, that I concluded to accept his offer and to write an apology to "Quarry Bank." Addressing my generous, good friend Mrs. Rathbone I wrote the following:

My Dear Madam,

I intended fulfilling my promise of seeing you, your kind daughter, and the amiable family at "Quarry Bank" tomorrow, but an express invitation from Dr. Holme, that I would meet and dine with several of his friends, will force me to remit the pleasure to Thursday. As you are best able to frame and offer an apology in my behalf, will you please to do so for me to Mrs. and Mr. Greg? to present my remembrances to the general circle, and to believe me, my dear Madam, forever your most obliged and most humble, obedient servant.

J. J. AUDUBON

Mrs. Rathbone, "Quarry Bank."

I had scarcely finished this when I found that I was engaged to go and spend the evening with the *Buxton gentleman*, who had been at some trouble to procure some musical friends to amuse me. What was to be done? I know not the *Buxton gentleman*, but he is very polite. I wish to go, and yet how shamefully I will treat Mr. Greg whom I have now disappointed several times.

I took a shilling out of my pocket, and whirling it up in the air I left it to chance, giving Mr. Greg the face of the King and the Buxton gentleman the arms of England, [which] came uppermost. Now, Lucy, what will Mr. Greg think, who, I am very certain, knows nothing of all this?

I had excellent music, vocal and instrumental, enjoyed the evening extremely, and went off at half past 12, just thinking of Mr. Molineux's party at Liverpool, of the difference between this evening and that of [yesterday] and of Mr. Greg, and went to beg a bed at Mr. Bentley's, sure that my lodgings must be shut up. His large family and his little house were, I knew, just fitted to meet their number, but I know him so good that I dreaded not giving him the extra trouble. All was arranged in a few moments and he and I laid in the same bed. I told him that I prayed aloud every night, and bid thee good night aloud also. What he thought of this I do not know, but without any further ceremony I bid thee good night, my love.

Yesterday, my love, Mr. Bentley presented me with a beautiful specimen of art and persevering patience. He gave me for our dear Johnny a beautiful model of a seventy-four-gun ship completely rigged, mounted with guns, under full sail, encased in a glass three inches long and about two broad. It was obtained at a lottery for the benefit of a poor French officer at the cessation of the last war, and was then valued at thirty guineas. I hope it will sail safely across the ocean and remind Johnny if he ever visits England that this land produces many good men, truly benevolent and kind to strangers who behave as good men of all nations ought to do. Again sweet wife, God bless thee.

Manchester   Oct. 18th, 1826   Wednesday

I breakfasted at Mrs. Dockray's. Having much writing to bring up, the quietness of the place attracted me. I wrote until about 1 o'clock whilst her daughter and son drew by my side. I returned to Manchester where, with the assistance of Mr. Bentley, I accomplished many small undertakings. I reached Dr. Holme's at 4 but was so surprised to find the setting-room filled with ladies and gentlemen that I felt awkward for a moment. I offered to shew them some drawings. About half past 5 we proceeded to the dining room, each male [accompanying] a female. The novel way of taking a lady under the arm is by no means disagreeable. She frequently sets next to you and you feel a mutual desire to please that brings always a relaxation from the custom of being stiff, unsociably careful in the use of words, and that always makes me believe I am before a big tribunal of justice instead of at a table to partake of good food and good cheer.

Amongst the name of those [I met], I recollect only that of the brother of Professor *Smyth,* his wife, his daughter and a Miss Harrison. Miss Smyth is extremely good looking, and the young gentleman who sat next to her knew this fact quite as well as myself or anybody present. I thought that the ladies next and beyond her did not gaze at her with quite so much pleasure. We had already dined, the ladies had retired and the wine and wit was slowly going round when a servant entered and told me that three parcels had just arrived from Liverpool. Thinking of scarcely anything but thee, I hoped to have letters from thee, made a *gentille* excuse, and went to my lodgings.

The first parcel was directed for Mr. Rathbone, the second contained four flannel shirts for thy husband, and the third the box of spars that I purchased at Matlock for thee. My arms crossed each other insensibly; and, my eyes cast on the last parcel. I wished myself a spar ornament to be forwarded and bound to thee. I could not return to Dr. Holme's. I had no wish for company. I went to bed very early. But before I bid thee goodnight I must not omit to transmit the best act, no doubt, I did this day. Whilst I was writing at Mrs. Dockray's a poor woman, no doubt a constant visitor, called and soon made her errand good. I saw with great pleasure the mother ask the daughter, who was *porte* bearer that day, to come to the entry. With a shaking, quick beating pulsation at my heart I heard the jingling of the shillings [and] the honest giving without pomp. I also, Lucy, gave, and I returned to my writings much better pleased than I was before. I will put up my old clothes and send them to my good friend Abigail Dockray, and she will give them to this poor woman.

Now, with a good heart, sweet Lucy good night.

"Quarry Bank," 12 miles from Manchester
Oct. 19th, 1826   Thursday

At 6, my cane in hand, and a small bundle under my arm, I made my way from Manchester, bound and on foot [for] "Quarry Bank." The morning was pleasant. I enjoyed my walk very much until I found myself quite out of the way [that] leads to the spot I wished to reach. Therefore, instead of twelve miles, I measured sixteen. When I arrived I was warm and hungry. Several of the family were still at breakfast. It was 10. I shook hands all round the long table, but as I always have done I felt pain that my venerable friend, Mrs. Rathbone, as well as the rest, should get up from her seat.

My Hannah was well, the fair Ellen and *La Belle Étrangère* also. Indeed all were well. Mr. Greg was making love to his lady as usual, and as usual received me very kindly. I longed for a walk with Hannah. I wished to talk to her alone, but the weather altered. It rained and I rambled by myself after a beautiful rose that [later] died on her bosom.

I was soon put in requisition at drawing, and drew the whole day. Those days spent amid such female groups always bring a calm to my mind, delightful to enjoy. I wish the parting at night might not come at all.

A nephew of Mr. Greg arrived from Ireland in time for dinner, a tall, firm-built youth of about twenty. The afternoon was spent first at sketching a portrait of Mr. Greg. Mrs. Rathbone and his lady sat opposite him. The chalk moved fast and I was quite satisfied [with] my work. But it was not so with everybody else. Faults were found, and I enjoyed the criticism very much. However, it was to be finished the next day.

The weather fair, a walk took place. I entered an English cottage, sweetly clean and arranged—the dairy especially, a short distance from the house. It was the [home] of a poor silk weaver. However, all was comfortable. I saw there for the first time since I left France the weaving going on. We returned quite in the dark, but enjoyed the evening exceedingly.

The ladies read and wrote poetry for me, and I drew for them. *La Belle* Madame Grabant of Leghorn retired early. She had received a mandate from her husband to join him at a short distance, and all regretted her approaching departure. I gave Mr. Greg an account of the planting of cotton, and wrote for him the names of many of our best planters. I was induced to remain the night, finding myself so happy and comfortable, and very desirous of finishing the sketch of Mr. Greg for his amiable daughter, Mrs. William Rathbone. I was then accompanied into my little chamber, bid thee good night, and slept well.

"Quarry Bank" Oct. 20th, 1826 Friday

This day [I] was mostly employed again at drawing, but Lucy, I was most surprised at being presented with a beautiful pen knife of eight blades by Mrs. Greg, and almost immediately another from Miss Agnes, and a beautiful pin cushion with a large parcel of pins for thee from the fair [Ellen]. Another gave me a little book of riddles and I at last found my pockets literally filled with different articles. The pretty little plants pressed on this sheet[10] were given me by the sweet child of William Rathbone, her name Elizabeth. Mrs. Rathbone was mortified that she had not the Turkey seal for me yet.

We had a long walk and again visited a beautiful cottage where to my great surprise I saw two cases of well stuffed birds. I had the kind Hannah under my arm nearly all the morning, and also Miss Anna Mary Greg, a clever lady, I assure thee, possessing a commanding eye and a benevolent heart. Fair [Ellen] had led me in the morning before breakfast, with her sister Agnes, to their farm, where I saw the finest dairy and handsomest cattle I have yet met with in England.

I finished Mr. Greg's [portrait] sketch quite to my satisfaction.

---

10. Traces remain on the journal page.

It was shewn to many of the servants, work people, &c., and the observations of many of whom I felt exceedingly pleased by. *La Belle Italienne* had left us, was accompanied to her carriage by all present. Her beautiful dark eyes wept with gratitude, and those of the young ladies with sorrow. The young nephew gave me his card and a pressing invitation that I should call upon him if ever I was led to visit Ireland. He lives near Belfast. His name is Samuel Greg. Young William Greg had wrote a pretty piece in my album, and bid farewell to the family and my generous kind friend Mrs. Rathbone. Hannah promised to walk with me on the road to Manchester again, and Miss Agnes promised to accompany her. I retired to my room quite late and bid thee as usual good night.

Manchester   Oct. 21st, 1826   Saturday

As soon as I had swallowed two cups of warm coffee and a few slices of buttered bread I left "Quarry Bank." The two fair companions had already preceded me. I found them after a few hundred yards from the vale, and with one under each arm, three roses in the upper buttonhole of my coat, we walked lightly on.

The weather was pleasantly warm. The rich-tinted leaves fell languid to the earth. The clouds had much of wildness in their distributions, and the sun was as bright as in Louisiana. Perhaps three miles had been [traversed] when my friend spoke of parting. Miss Agnes bid me well and happy and shook my arm with friendship's ardor. I turned to Hannah, met her brilliant black eyes, felt my heart swell, pressed her hand fervently, and fervently said, "May God bless you." We parted. She wished me well, I am sure. Good girl, how I admire her. How kind she has been to me. Dear Hannah, may thou be forever happy, and thy mother, thy friends and all about thee!

I buttoned close, put on my gloves, sunk my hat deeper on my head, and hurried towards Manchester. I breakfasted fast; called on Mr. Bentley; paid for my trunk's repair, two pounds and fourteen shillings; called on Mr. Heywood, took my money from his bank, and [received] from him a letter to Professor Jameson of Edinburgh. Called on Dr. Holme who wrote three

more to different persons. Paid twenty visits. And dined with
Mr. Bentley. With his assistance packed up my birds safe and
snug, walked to twenty more places, and felt so uncommonly
fatigued that I determined to go to Hardwick to stay the night
with the Dockray family. I found them all well. I paid £2.10.4 for
my flannel shirts, and was again surprised at receiving a large
book purchased for me and presented to me by my generous
Lady Rathbone. Will this good friend adopt me for one of her
sons, I wonder? For positively there is no end to her generosity.
I was thinking of what I have just wrote, and what was to be
written, when suddenly I recollected how mortified I was to-
day, when a letter from Edward Roscoe was brought to me from
Mr. Greg's office, to find that a small paper was inside it with a
bill of postage. I immediately sent [a boy] with a sovereign, and
was brought a receipt of seventeen shillings four pence. But I
felt mortified that Mr. Greg should have *a clerk* that was so far
from possessing the feelings of his employer.

Mr. Bentley to whom, I repeat, I am under many obligations
presented me with a nice foot rule for the pocket, my name engraved on it by the side of his. Lucy, Mr. Bentley is a brother
Mason!! I received at his house, from a gentleman who saw me
exhibit my little pack of penknives, a most superb one, the most
beautiful I ever saw and as good as can be manufactured. The
handle [is] made of cocoanut shell, the whole strong and made
for service. We chatted a good deal. "The little lady" thanked me
for the silver point crayon I had given her. I drank several glasses
of wine with the good Quaker Dockray, his wife and Benjamin
Waterhouse, and went to bed in a superb room where, if I mistake not, my friends Mrs. and Miss Rathbone slept whilst there.
I prayed for thy health, bid thee good night, and went to sleep
without remorse at heart.

Manchester   Oct. 22nd, 1826   Sunday

I have been writing all day. My eyes ache. I forwarded letters
to Richard Rathbone and enclosed five pounds [for] him. But I
have not the strength [for] copying the note. I forwarded the
letter for Charles Bonaparte to William Rathbone. I took tea
at Mr. Bentley's. Dined at Mrs. Dockray's, but I really cannot
say more.

Sweet, dearest friend, good night.

MANCHESTER   Oct. 22nd, 1826

MY BELOVED WIFE,

I leave tomorrow for Edinburgh. My time at Manchester has not been productive.

I visited to Matlock in the company of my generous friend Mrs. Rathbone who made a party purposely on my account, took me in her carriage, and showered me with kindness. Matlock is beautiful, truly. We were there two full days, passed and repassed through Bakewell, and returned by Buxton. I have some sketches for thee, and send thee now a box of beautiful spars, some plants collected about they favorite hills, and an inkstand presented thee by Mrs. Hannah Mary Rathbone. The little black box marked Matlock is especially for Johnny from Miss Rathbone, to whom I request he will send as quick as possible a *very small beautiful drawing*. I forward him all my chalks. I hope he will use them fast. The ship is for him and is beautiful. It is a present from Mr. Bentley, who has been uncommonly kind to me. He will write to Johnny, and I hope Johnny will meet his view. It may turn out quite an advantageous thing for John. The plaster head is that of William Roscoe. The pyramid is of the Rock of Gibraltar. The pins and little cushion [are] from Miss [Ellen] Greg, the gooseberries from the Botanic Garden, Liverpool.

I will write to thee a long letter a few days after I reach the great seat of learning. No letters from thee, my dearest friend, and I cannot conceive why. I hope thy watch has reached thee by this. The white pitcher is from my friend Miss Hannah Rathbone. I would like thee to write Mrs. Rathbone, for my sake, a kind letter of thanks for her attentions to me. Remember that the family is of the first distinction, and extremely amiable and learned. Mrs. R. is particularly desirous of knowing thee. The services she has rendered me can never be repaid. Direct care of her sons, Messrs. Rathbone Brothers & Company, Liverpool, and if thou canst accompany thy letter with dried plants, or a small keg of good nuts, acorns, seeds, &c., she will receive these most gratefully.

Farewell, my beloved Lucy, be happy, be well, and believe me forever thine,

J. J. AUDUBON

Remember me to Mr. Bourgeat, Mrs. Percy's family, &c., &c. I will be in London in a fortnight from now.

Oct. 22, 1826

To Charles Lucien Bonaparte
MY DEAR SIR:

Will you permit me to honor my list of subscribers with your name, and ask of your father-in-law [Joseph Bonaparte, erstwhile King of Spain] if I may also have his? I hope you will not feel offended. I have no wish to call as a mercenary, but positively for the honor of enriching my list with these names. I have some hopes of forwarding my first Number (size of life, [5] engravings) in about four months. You would oblige me much if you will send me a copy of all your observations on the *Birds* of Wilson, your synopsis, &c., and a copy of your second volume. Should you please to do so, direct the whole to Messrs. Rathbone Brothers & Company, Liverpool.

Pray remember me to *our* friends of Philadelphia, and believe me, my dear Sir,

Your truly obliged, obedient servant,
J. J. AUDUBON

[Audubon wrote beneath the above copy:]
"The same, nearly, to De Witt Clinton, Henry Clay, General Andrew Jackson, General William Clark."

A. Dockray's. HARDWICK, Sunday [Oct.] 22nd, 1826
[To Mrs. William Rathbone, Sr.]:
MY DEAR MRS. RATHBONE,

I write to you now not only with a wish to thank you for the useful book that I found here for me, but for all your kind attentions—at your hands, under your roof, and through your introductions. I have now felt in England all that generous hospitality, benevolence and warmest friendship can bestow. I speak from the heart. Never have I felt more. Never did I expect it. So strong and powerful is the reality impressed on the whole of my feelings that I blush lest I may never sufficiently feel grateful to you and to all of your family.

I arrived at Manchester after a delightful walk, dressed my "family" in their red coats, buttoned them all tightly and put over them a good slip of well oiled silk to preserve them from wet.

I paid all my visits, and I hope all my debts, but felt so fatigued that I concluded coming here to rest and to write the whole of this day. I felt extremely, yesterday, whilst packing my manuscripts, when my eyes accidentally glanced over that portion of the work mentioning the flight of birds and the astonishing mistake I made when I wrote down their velocity for you. Please to destroy the memorandum and instead accept it more correctly now: Swallows, 2½ miles per minute; Wild Pigeons when travelling, 2 miles per minute; Swans, 2 miles per minute; Wild turkeys, 1¾ miles.

My body feels now quite a *superficial* degree of warmth.

The family Dockray is all well. Pray remember me to your sons and daughters. Again accept my thanks, and believe me forever with highest consideration and esteem,

Your most humbly obliged and obedient servant,

JOHN J. AUDUBON

[MANCHESTER] Oct. 22, 1826

To John [Rutter] Chorley,
Liverpool
MY DEAR FRIEND,

I could not bear the thoughts of leaving this dirty smoky town and removing to Edinburgh without letting you know that, since I left you, I have enjoyed life in the most agreeable, congenial manner possible. My journey to sweet Matlock with good friends, the ladies Rathbone and Dockray, is yet like a dream of enchantment. *One more female* would have made it home to me quite.

Then, my dear friend, the time since spent at "Quarry Bank" has been no less interesting. I left that last place with a pocket literally filled with penknives given me not to sever friendship but to mend pens. Permit me to mend mine now, and take a pinch of "Number 37."

Now I want from John Chorley a little poem about these same penknives. They are in one pocket, all claiming supremacy and desirous to prove how much one might be preferred [to the] other. Hannah Rathbone's gift has powerful demands on my feelings. It has two blades and is mounted in silver bright. "Quarry Bank" is engraved on another and came to me from Agnes; it has two blades also. But a round mass containing eight, the former property of Mr. Greg, swears that it will cut and slash most cruelly if not suffered to have [its] way first. Another modest one, [with a] cocoanut handle, large, useful, firm and elegant, says that [it] is not, in [its] opinion, quite a *gentleman*, [as it] would demand the first calling of my goose quill. Now what is to be done is best known to you. So set to, stir up the brains in the pan on your shoulders, and send me soon the desired [verse].

The silver [engraved] pheasant, as if discontented, attempted to fly the other day, positively started from his ground but fell immediately, and I luckily caught him. I cannot think that he ever will again try such a prank. I positively had him nailed through the body to hold him faster then ever [to my snuff box].

Remember me to friends, all—to mother, to sister, to uncles and brothers, and rest assured that with esteem I am and hope to be forever,

Your most attached friend,
J. J. AUDUBON

Manchester   Oct. 23rd, 1826   Monday

This day was absolutely spent at packing and making all ready. The great confusion of my letters and papers required some time to put them again under a systematic order. Mr. Bentley, with whom I breakfasted, was of great service at such work. My box of spars, &c., was also well packed and directed to Mr. Munro to be forwarded from Liverpool through the care of the Rathbone brothers. Then my trunk and all my effects were arranged, [and] my seat in the coach taken and paid (£3.15.0) to Edinburgh. I intended calling on the Dockray family but I found it impossible and I merely wrote a note of thanks and apology.

Having found in my trunk two of the Damask sword beans, I thought the best present use that could be made of them would be to present them, enclosed, to the Reverend J. Clowes, whom I thought had received me so very civilly that no one else would be better entitled. I paid all my debts, I believe; my bill at Mrs. Hedge's was £5.2.0. I had only eat a [scant] breakfast then. Poor woman was sadly sorry at losing me, for I discovered that my bill had maintained her and her children.

I spent my evening with Mr. Bentley and family, gave the young ladies each a handsome pin cushion, and they in turn gave me a knife just one inch long and young night thoughts.

The coach is leaving before 5 tomorrow. I went to sleep at the inn, to be called at the moment, thinking all done. I have only to regret that I [leave] Manchester much poorer than when I first entered it. May my friends in it and about it be happy. Sweet wife, good night.

Carlisle, England   Oct. 24th, 1826   Tuesday

At 5 I had left Manchester. The morning was clear and beautiful, but as no dependence can be placed on the weather in this country I thought but little of it. I was rather amused by the observations made about my Folio at the stage office. A clerk there laughed almost as much as the Reverend J. Clowes, but the poor fellow lived *in Manchester* and consequently had not heard of either the owner or his works. I was alone on the inside of the carriage (truly, coaches in England are very good) and had been there for some time, lamenting myself and feeling much dissatisfied at having no company, when a very tall gentleman came in from the top and said that he wished to sleep. He turned on his side, and I looked at him and envied his condition. Could I have slept also I would certainly have preferred this to being the companion of a drowsy man.

We rolled on, however, and arrived at the village of Preston, where breakfast was swallowed as quickly and with as much avidity as our Kentuckians usually do. Coaches were exchanged, passage transferred, &c., and I entered the carriage to meet two new gentlemen. Their appearance was goodly, and to break the silence I offered both of them a pinch of "Number 37." It was taken by one and smelled at by the other. The chat begun and in less than ten minutes we all had travelled through America, part of India, crossed the ocean in New York packets, discussed the emancipation of slavery and the corn law, and reached the point of political starvation of the poor in England and Ireland. [As we went] tranquilly along I peeped frequently through each window. I saw little girls running alongside the coach with nosegays loosely fastened to a long stick and offered to passengers for a penny. I took one for a sixpence and again resumed the chat.

At a little village where the horses were changed, it was discovered that a shocking smell existed on the top of the coach. The man who is called the guard spoke of it and told us that he could not keep his seat. I felt anxious to view the country, and got out to mount up and behind, but the smell was so insufferable and the appearance of the man near whom I had seat myself so far from being pleasing that I immediately jumped down to take my inside seat. Judge of my dismay, Lucy, when I was asked if *my trunk* belonged to me, and if it did not contain a dead body intended for dissection at Edinburgh. I answered no, thou may be sure. The guard smiled as if quite sure my trunk contained such a thing, and told my companions that he would inform against me at Lancaster. I bore all this very well. I was innocent! I offered to open my trunk and would have certainly done so at Lancaster; but, whilst we were proceeding, the guard came to the door and made an apology. [He] said the smell had been removed, and that it was positively *attached to the inside parts of the man's breeches* who was on the seat by him. This caused much laughter and many coarse jokes.

My subject was a source of conversation when everything else failed. I became quite pleased with all my companions. My being a stranger was sufficient to be well treated by them. And indeed what better mark of superior politeness is it not over all other countrymen? The English gentlemen are gentlemen at all points and in all circumstances.

The approach to Lancaster is beautiful. The view of the well planted castle is commanding. The sea seen from [here] was also agreeable, as it is bounded by picturesque shores. We dined at Kendal, having passed through Bolton and Burton. But, before we dined, my companions, who had been left behind after the changing of our horses at a stage [stop], had to run for nearly a mile to overtake the coach. This caused many altercations between the gentlemen and the driver and guard. One of the proprietors, a Mr. Saunders, who interfered and who was unfortunately *rather* drunk, made matters much worse. A complaint was lodged against the driver, and he received no more shillings from my companions. I saw and heard all very peaceably. Mr. Walton, the tall gentleman who had slept so well during the morning was extremely attentive to me. But the Messrs. Pattison[11] from *Cornwall* were still more so. The father kindly gave me his card and begged that I would call on him if ever I travelled in the south of England.

We now entered a most dreary country, poor beyond conception. Immense hills rolled in constant succession, spotted here and there with miserable cotts, the residence of poor shepherds. No game was seen. The weather was bleak and rainy, and I cannot say that I enjoyed the ride at all beyond the conversation of my companions. We passed through Penrith and arrived at Carlisle at half past 9, having rode 122 miles. I was told that in hard winters the road becomes at times impassable, choked with snow, and that when not entirely obstructed it was necessary to [look for] posts placed every 100 yards and painted black at the top as [guides].

We had a miserable supper but good beds, and I enjoyed mine for I felt very wearied, my cold and cough having [been]

11. Dr. Granville S. Pattison, prominent Edinburgh physician.

very much increased by having rode some twenty miles outside to view the country. I was praying and wishing thee well when two female voices struck my ears and I discovered that the noise was close by my door. A conversation was kept low and indistinguishable for some minutes, when one of the persons began weeping and continued increasingly until it became most piteously hideous. I felt a strong inclination to rise, open my door, and inquire into the cause when I recollected that it could not be about me and that consequently it was not my business to interfere, a part of conduct in man that I will always strongly recommend to our beloved sons. The females at last retired into a room next to me, and the noise subsided. I felt fatigued and bid thee good night, full of thoughts of apprehension for the future.

Edinburgh, Scotland Oct. 25th, 1826 Wednesday

We breakfasted this morning at Carlisle. Left there at 8. But I was sadly vexed that I had to pay twelve shillings for my trunk and portfolio, as I had been positively assured at the coach office at Manchester that no further charge would be made. I paid it, however.

For perhaps ten miles we passed through an uncommonly flat country, meandering a while along a river, passed through a village called Longtown and entered Scotland at ten minutes before 10. I was then just six miles from the spot where runaway matches are rendered lawful. The country changed its aspect, became suddenly quite woody. We ran along, and four times across, a beautiful stream quite a miniature of the Mohawk. Many little rapids are formed in its abrupt windings. The foliage was about to die and looked much as it does along our majestic streams of the West. This lasted, however, only one stage of perhaps twelve miles and again we came to the same dreariness of yesterday. Now and then a tolerable landscape of nakedness was opened before us, but the want of objects besides mere burnt mountains was very uninteresting. The number of sheep grazing on the hills was very great, and they all looked well, although of a very small species, many of them with black heads and legs, with all the body white [and] without horns. Another species [had] horns and some color; and a [third] very small kind is called here the Cheviot. The shepherds were poor, wrapped up in a thin piece of plaid and possessed none of that nobility of race so well painted by Walter Scott.

I saw the sea again to-day. We dined at Hawick on excellent sea fish, then for the first time in my life I drank Scotch whiskey. I suspected young Pattison wished to surprise me and make me drunk. I told him of this and the father replied that probably it was to try if I would be, in such a case, as good natured as I was without. I thought this quite a good compliment and forgave the son, but soon discovered that Scotch whiskey was too powerful for my weak head. I felt it for some time afterward. I found the taste extremely agreeable. Some Scotchmen who were at table with us drank glasses of it pure, as if water—so much, again, for habit. We passed through Selkirk, having travelled, during nearly the whole day, through the dominions and estates of the Duke of [Buccleuch], a young man about twenty who passes his days shooting black game and his nights—indeed I really do not know how! He has something like 200,000 pounds per annum. Some of the poor shepherds on this astonishing estate have probably not more than 200 pounds of oat meal. Miserable contrast, man's moral and physical perdition—will [it be] thus endured long?

But Lucy, I passed so near Sir Walter Scott's place or seat that I raised from my seat and stretched my neck some inches to see it, but it was all in vain and I did not see it, and who knows if ever I will. We passed a few miles from Melrose. I had a great wish to see the old chapel and the gentleman to whom Dr. Rutter had given me a letter, but the coach rolled on and at 11 o'clock I entered the Splendid City.

I have seen yet but a very small portion of it, and that by gaslight, yet I call it Splendid City. This is not the time to say why. The coach stopped at the Black Bull Hotel, [which] was so filled with travellers that no bed could be procured. We had our baggage taken to the Starr. The clerk, the guard, the driver all swore at my baggage and said that had we not paid at Carlisle he would have charged me, particularly, ten times as much as I had given. Now it is true that my trunk is large and heavy, and so is the portfolio I carry with me; but to give thee an idea of the charges and impositions connected with those coach owners and attendants remark that, *primo*, I paid £3.15.0; at Carlisle for baggage, 12 shillings and during yesterday and to-day, to guards and drivers, 18 shillings sixpence; making £5.5.6, for two days travelling from Manchester to Edinburgh. It is not so much the general amount, although I am sure it is quite enough for 212 miles, but the beggarly manners used to obtain nearly one half of it. To see a fellow with a decent coat on, who calls himself an independent, free-born Englishman, open the door to the coach every ten or twelve miles, and beg for a shilling each time is detestable and quite an abuse. But this is not all. They never are satisfied, and if you have the appearance of wealth about you, they hang on and ask for more.

The porters here were porters indeed, carrying all on their backs, the first of the kind I have seen since I [reached] this island. At the Starr we had a good supper, chatted a good deal. The Messrs. Pattison were with me but Mr. Walton had made another course, perhaps never to be met again. It was more than 1 o'clock before I went to bed. I thought so much of the multitude of learned men that abound in this place that I dreaded the delivering my letters tomorrow. I wished that thou hadst known at this very moment that I was positively bidding thee good night in Edinburgh.

VI

Edinburgh

George Street, Edinburgh   Oct. 26th   Thursday

IT WAS 10 O'CLOCK WHEN I BREAKFASTED, because I wished to do so with the Messrs. Pattison, being so much pleased with their company. During breakfast I could not help observing the bombast and impudence of some of the persons who were seated and walking in different parts of the room. Some blowed their noses violently to attract others to view them. Another whistled, whilst two more laughed to burst their lungs; and another again with an acquired phlegmatic air stirred a lump of sugar in a large tumbler of water, each pleased and proud of himself I have no doubt, all keeping the waiters skipping about with all the nimbleness of a dormouse. But to business.

My companions, who knew all about Edinburgh, offered to accompany me in search of decent lodgings, and we proceeded, soon turning and entering the second door in George Street, (perhaps the most beautiful street here) and in a moment made a bargain with Mrs. Dickie for a fine bedroom and a fine, well furnished setting-room. I am to pay her one guinea per week. I considered it very low. The situation is fine. I can see from where I now am writing the Firth and the steamboats plying about. I had my baggage brought here by a man with a tremendous beard who imposed on me most impudently by bringing a brass shilling which he said he would swear I had given him. I gave him another, threw the counterfeit in the fire, and promised myself to pay some attention hereafter what kind of money I received or gave away.

I walked to Professor Jameson's in the Circus; not at home. James Hall,[1] advocate, 128 George Street, absent in the country. Dr. [William] Charles Henry[2] of the Royal Infirmary was sought after in vain. Dr. Thompson was out also, and Professor Duncan could not be seen until 5 o'clock. I only saw Dr. Knox[3] in Surgeon's Square, and Professor Jameson[4] at the College. I thought the latter received me lightly. He said that Sir Walter Scott was now quite a recluse, much engaged with a novel and the life of Napoleon, and that probably I would not see him. Not see Walter Scott, thought I—by Washington I shall, if I have to crawl on all fours for a mile![5] But I was a good deal surprised when he added that it would be several days before he could pay me a visit, that his business was great and must be attended to. I could not complain. I was precisely bent on doing the same toward myself, and why should I expect any other line of conduct? Why, my Lucy, because the world goes all against the streams, and, besides, very cranksided, each needing help, and more anxious to receive than to give. Yet not so with all. Look at my friends the Rathbones, the benevolent family, how I have been treated by them all!

Dr. Knox came to me with only one eye, dressed with an over

1. Sir James Hall (1761–1832), father of Basil Hall.

2. William Charles Henry (1774–1836) was a chemist and a prominent member of the Manchester Literary and Philosophical Society.

3. Robert Knox was an anatomist, and a descendant of John Knox, the Reformationist.

4. Robert Jameson (1774–1854), foremost University of Edinburgh professor of the day; founder of scientific Wernerian Society and of *Edinburgh New Philosophical Journal*.

5. Not until January 22 did Audubon meet Sir Walter Scott, the novelist who secretly admired his manner and appearance more than his art. Scott MS journal, Pierpont Morgan Library, New York City, does not support thesis of one researcher that Scott introduced Audubon to his copyist J. B. Kidd who, almost certainly, was

gown, and bloody fingers. He bowed, washed and wiped his hands, read Dr. Traill's letter, and wishing me well, promised all in his power, appointed tomorrow to see me and my drawings, and said he would bring some good friends of science to be introduced. My opinion is that Dr. Knox is a physician of great merit, and Mr. Jameson a professor of great merit also, but that they act on different principles I am quite sure. The former does not deal in birds, but the latter does, *I guess*, although his principal study is mineralogy, I am told. But I perhaps met him at a bad moment. I will draw no further conclusions until I know more, positively more, of him.

I walked a good deal and admired this city very much, the great breadth of the streets, their good pavement and foot ways, the beautiful uniformity of the buildings, their natural grey coloring and wonderful cleanliness of the [whole] was felt perhaps more powerfully, [after my] coming direct from dirty Manchester. But the picturesque *tout ensemble* here is wonderful. A high castle here, another there, a bridge looking at a second city below, here a rugged mountain and there beautiful public grounds, monuments, the sea, the landscape around, all wonderfully managed indeed. It would require fifty different good views of it, at least, or of its parts, to give thee a true idea; but I will try, day after day, in my humble way of writing, to describe more particularly all that I may see either in the old or new part of this town.

I could not spend the day without having a peep at my own handiwork. I disengaged my Birds and looked at them with pleasure and yet with a considerable degree of fear that they never would be published. I felt very much alone again, and longed for someone to [whom I could] dispose of my ideas. How much, whilst at my dinner, I thought of the country that I have left behind, and of thee particularly. Some dark thoughts came across my mind. I feared thee sick, perhaps lost forever to me, and felt deathly sick. My dinner was there, cooling fast, whilst each part I swallowed went down slowly as if choking [me]. I felt tears frequently about my eyes, and I forced myself

introduced by W. H. Lizars. Was not "Key" of the 1827 journal, November 27, in fact Kidd? Audubon continually garbled and forgot names.

out of the room to destroy this painful gloom that I dread at all times and that sometimes I fear may do more.

After a good walk I returned rather more at ease and looked at the pair of stuffed pheasants on the large buffet that ornaments my present setting-room, at the sweetly scented geraniums opposite them, at the black hair sofa, the arm chairs, the little studying cherubs on the mantelpiece, the painted landscape on my right, the print exhibiting Charity well appropriated by Free Masons, and at last my own face in the mirror. I saw in it not only my own face but such a powerful resemblance to that of my venerable father that I almost imagined it was him that I saw.[6] The thought of my mother flew about me, my sister was also present, my younger days, those I have enjoyed with thee and those I have spent, miserable, from thee. All were alternately at hand, and yet how far away. Ah how far is even the last moment that is never to return again. But my Lucy, such reflexions will not do. I must close my book, think of tomorrow, yes of the future that always, as we reach it, evaporates and becomes a mere yesterday, not thought of but with regret, [whether] passed rightly or wrong.

My sweet beloved Lucy, God forever bless thee. Good night.

Edinburgh   Oct. 27th, 1826   Friday

I visited the market this morning, but to go to it I first crossed from the new town into the beginning of the old, over the north bridge, [and] went down many flights of winding steps, at last reaching the desired spot. I was then positively under the bridge that no doubt was built to save the trouble of descending and mounting from one side of Edinburgh to another. [The city] is built mostly on the slopes of two long ranges of high broken hills. The vegetable markets are well arranged and look well, as well as the fruits and meats, but the low situation and narrow kind of booths in which the whole is exhibited is not agreeable, and compared with the famous new market of Liverpool it is nothing.

I ascended the stairs leading to the new town, and facing me,

---

6. Audubon had made an oath to his father to keep secret the fact that he was his father's natural son. He did not yet know that his "mother" died in 1821.

after I turned a little to the right, the monument in honor of Nelson. I walked towards it and reached it. Its elevated situation, [and] the broken rocks along which I went, made it very picturesque. But a tremendous shower of rain accompanied by a heavy gust of cold wind made me hurry from the spot without being quite satisfied, and I returned home to breakfast.

I was struck with the relative appearance of the woman of the lower class with our Indian squaws of the West. Their walk is precisely the same, and their mode of carrying burthens also. They have a leather strap passed over and poised on the forehead attached to large baskets without covers, and waddle through the streets with toes inward, just as the Shawanees for instance. Their complexions, if fair, is beyond rosy, partaking indeed of purple, cold and disagreeable. If dark they are dark indeed. Many of the men wear long whiskers and beards, are extremely uncouth of manners, and still more so of language.

I had eat my breakfast when Messrs. Pattison came to see my drawings and brought with them a Miss Ewart whom Mr. P. senior said drew *uncommonly beautifully.* I thought that according to Johnson this must, if well applied, mean a great deal, and I opened my book with a certain portion of reluctance. I thought I could soon discover if she *thought so herself.* Several drawings were looked at. She remained mute. Mr. P. pronounced them surpassing all he had ever seen. I watched the lady's eyes and the coloring of her fair cheeks. She looked closer and said with a smile that it seemed America would certainly surpass all other countries in points of arts and sciences in less than another century. I shall not be alive then, neither my name recollected; I still longed for acquiescence from the mouth of the fair stranger. I thought that perhaps a picture of lovers would bring my wish to bear. I turned until I found my Doves[7] and held them in good light.

"How beautiful, exquisitely beautiful! How delighted Sir Walter Scott will be to see your magnificent collection!" [she said].

---

7. Folio Plate XVII: *Mourning Dove.* The catalog of an exhibition, *Audubon Watercolors and Drawings,* held at the Pierpont Morgan Library, New York City, in 1965, states that lacquer was used on this and all twenty-five of the original studies shown, from the Folio, *The Birds of America.* However, the substance used for sheen was egg white only.

Now that I found the steam was high, that perhaps some explosion might be produced, I exhibited the "Rattlesnake attacked by the Mocking Birds."[8] This had the desired effect. The lady was pleased and I was satisfied that she drew well.

Mr. P. said that Mr. [Prideaux John] Selby never would publish another *Birds*, was he to see mine. We parted, all friends, I having begged of each of them to bring or send any of their friends to view my work any morning from 10 until 12.

I called again at Dr. Thompson's, but Monsieur T. not being at home I left the letter and my card. The same at professor Duncan's. I walked to Fish Market Close, High Street, old town, where I found Patrick Neill, Esq., at his desk, after having passed between two long files of printers at their work.[9] At first the gentleman (if I mistake not) believed that the letter I had handed him was an advertisement for insertion. But after having read it he shook hands cordially, offered me his services, and proved to me in a few words that he was a gentleman and a very clever one, gave [me] his home address, promised to come and see me, and accompanied me to the street, begging of me not to visit the Museum until Professor Jameson had sent me a general ticket of admittance. He said the Professor would feel hurt at my paying for it. I felt toward Mr. Neill a great deal of esteem. It was by now 1 o'clock. I returned to my rooms, eat a lunch, drank a tumbler of Scotch grog, and, determined to see a good deal, proceeded toward the port of Leith, distant not quite three miles. [After losing] my way I reached the Firth of Forth at Trinity, a small village on that bay, where I could see the German Ocean's waters. Opposite me on the shore of Fife, about seven miles distant, looked naked and hilly. (Fife happened to be the name of my landlady in New York in 1823.)[10] During my walk I frequently turned round to view the beautiful city back of me, rising gradually [like an] amphitheatre most sublimely and backed by mountainous clouds that improved the whole really superbly. The wind was high. The waters beat the shores vio-

8. Folio Plate XXI: *Mockingbird*.
9. Patrick Neill (1776–1851), printer, naturalist, and Wernerian.
10. Actually 1824.

lently. The vessels pitched [at] anchor. All was grand! On inquiry I found that this was no longer an admiral's station, and that in a few more weeks the steamboats that ply between this [port] and London and other parts of the northwest of this island would stop their voyages, the ocean here being too rough during the winter season.

I followed along the shores and reached Leith in about twenty minutes. I saw a very pretty, iron, suspended jetty with three arches, at the extremity of which steam vessels and others land their passengers and freight. Leith is a large village apparently mostly connected with Hamburg and other sea ports of Holland. Much business was going on. I saw there a great number of herring boats and the nets for capturing the fishes, also some curious drags for oysters, clams, and other shell fish. The docks are small and contained mostly Dutch vessels of small size. An old one is appropriated as a chapel [for] mariners.

New Haven, [the next village, was] not that New Haven planted on the shores of the Connecticut river ornamented with diversified colored buildings of wood, where thou first put thy foot on the happy continent of America, and gamboled around its famous college and through its extensive salt marshes—not the New Haven where thy father lost his large brewery by fire, and where each youthful girl has cheeks better colored than even the peach blossom.[11] No, my Lucy. It was only a place bearing the same name but possessed of not one of its embellishments, a small village only, of white stones, and not very clean, built there, one would think, to remind the traveller that he will not always meet with such a place as Edinburgh or the sweet village on the Sound [of Long Island].

I approached Edinburgh and was walking slow, viewing the scenery around when a woman, extremely well dressed, accosted me, and with good language and a soft voice told me that she was very poor and much in need, offered to do anything for me for a little money. I thought this a stranger way of craving charity than anything I had seen yet. I told her that being a per-

---

11. The Bakewells lived briefly in New Haven, Connecticut, before moving to their plantation, Fatland Ford, near Norristown, Pennsylvania, in 1803.

fect stranger and without change I begged she would not either stop nor follow me, and went away fast. Yet not quick enough, for I heard her *damn me* as plainly as could be. This is a lesson I shall not forget, depend on it. I, after this, knew well what sort of woman this wretch was, and how guarded I must be in my generosities.

The sun set. I returned to my lodgings to inform my landlady that I was going to the theatre and that I wish not to be shut out. She answered politely that she would wait my convenience. Having left my purse, my watch, my pocketbook and even my pocket handkerchief, I took my sword-cane and off I went to see "Rob Roy." The theatre not to open until half past 6 precisely, I entered a bookseller's shop, asked for prints to look at, and purchased for thee a map of this town ornamented with eighteen views of the principal and most interesting objects about and in it. I gave an order on Mrs. Dickie for five shillings and forwarded it to her. I read an account of the Palace and Chapel of Holyrood, and also of Roslyn Castle, and was at the door of the pit at the lawful instant. It was crowded by gentlemen and ladies, for, my dear Lucy, ladies of the second class go to the pit, the superior class to the boxes, and those of neither, unfit to be classified, way above.

The house is very small but well lighted. Many handsome females ornamented it. "God Save the King" was the overture, and everyone rose, uncovered. I wish we always had "Hail Columbia, Happy Land" with us, or "Washington's March," on such occasions; it would almost daily impress [on] the mind of our citizens our noble institutional Constitution. But to "Rob Roy," it was represented as if positively in the Highlands. The characters were good and natural, the scenery perfectly adapted, the dress, the manners and language quite true. I may safely say that I saw as good [a] picture of the great outlaw, of his Ellen, and of his unrelenting Dougal as ever could be given. I would, were it possible, always see "Rob Roy" in Edinburgh, "Le Tartuffe" in Paris, and "She Stoops to Conquer" in London. The first, [as] exhibited in America, is quite a burlesque. We do not even know how the hardy mountaineer of this rigid country throws on his plaid or wears his cap, or his front piece beautifully made of several tails of the red Deer. Neither can we render the shrill tone of the horn bugle that hangs at his side; the merry bagpipe is also wanting, and also the scenery. I would just as well be punished with the second in broken French by a strolling company, as to see the first again as I have seen it in Kentucky for instance. It is almost to be regretted that each country does not keep to its own productions. To do otherwise is only infatuation, and leads to enforce on minds ideas as far different from truth as day is [from] darkness.

I did not stay to see Rosina. Although I liked Miss Stephens[12] pretty well, she is by no means equal to Miss Foote. Her appearance is too attempted; her voice is not sweet but much affected, and I left her and the house at half past 10, extremely pleased with "Rob Roy," his Ellen, his Dougal, the magistrate and his Matté.

It is now late and very cold. My landlady has brought me some warm water to make a glass of grog again. She says it will do my cough good. God knows. Dearest friend, good night.

Edinburgh   Oct. 28th, 1826   Saturday

I have just time to copy the following before I go to deliver it to the dread of all writers, the famous Francis Jeffrey,[13] Esqr.:

45 YORK PLACE, 28 Oct., 1826

My Dear Sir,
   I take the liberty of introducing to you Mr. Audubon, who has come to Europe with a most magnificent and truly scientific collection of drawings of the Birds of North America. His letters of introduction are of the strongest description, and from what I have observed he seems deserving of them. I have no doubt that you and your friends will be highly gratified by seeing the productions of his pencil.
                    I remain yours most truly,
                            ANDREW DUNCAN, JR.

---

12. Jane Stephens (1808–1850), popular actress.
13. Francis Jeffrey (1775–1850), the essayist and critic, was a Scottish Lord. Andrew Duncan, Jr. (1774–1832) was the son of the more eminent Dr. Duncan. The connoisseur was related to the Knox family.

EDINBURGH, Oct. 28th, 1826

MY DEAR JOHN,[14] [son]

I now write to you from the place where I wished most you could have been educated. It is a most beautiful city, perhaps the most so I ever have seen. Its situation is delightful, not far from the sea, running on two parallel hills, ornamented with highly finished monuments and guarded by perhaps impregnable castles. The streets are all laid at right angles in that portion of it that is called the new town, are built with fine houses of four, five, six or seven stories. [They] are clean and well paved and all lighted by gas lamps.

I have been here now three days. I came from Manchester in a public coach that carried four inside passengers and ten outside or rather on the top, besides a guard and a driver and all the luggage of the parties. I sometimes stayed in, and sometimes rode outside to have better views of the country I travelled through. Now and then I saw some fine English Pheasants that you would delight in killing; and some curious small Sheep with black head and feet, the remainder only being white; and those pretty little ponies that you are so fond of. I wish I could send you one.

Before I left Manchester I visited Matlock, Bakewell and Buxton, all watering places, in the carriage and company of an old lady named Rathbone and her daughters and several others, all Quakers and extremely kind to me. The daughter of Mrs. Rathbone purchased and sends you a beautiful little black box of Matlock marble or sparr, and her mother a beautiful inkstand of the same materials for your good Mamma. I forwarded them with [a] great many others and also different things for you both, the day before I left Manchester, to the care of Messrs. Gordon and Forstall, New Orleans.

I was very much pleased with all the places I saw, and wished very much that you and Mamma had been with us

14. Son, aged fourteen.

to enjoy the journey. We all spoke frequently of you both and brother Victor.

To-day I have visited the Royal Palace of Holyrood completely. Was in Queen Mary of Scots' rooms and saw her bed, chairs, tables, &c. I looked at my face in the mirror that once was hers, and I was in the little room where the murder was committed. It is very curious. I also saw the Chapel where the Queen was married and the spot where she prayed; also paintings of all the kings and families of Scotland; the apartments where the present King of France resided during his exile; and the fine rooms where the King of England, George IV, was four years ago when he visited this country. The women of the low class who labour hard for their living here carry burthens just as our squaws do in Louisiana, in a large basket behind and a leather strap coming from it to their foreheads.

I bought for you and Mamma eighteen views of different parts of this city that I will send when I make up another box from London. In a day or two I will see Roslyn's Castle, and afterwards go to Melrose to see the chapel there and call on Sir Walter Scott the great novelist.

I hope you will be good to your dear Mamma and do all she bids. Draw a great deal and study music also, for men of talent are welcome all over the world. Talk about all your little affairs when you write to me, and send me a long letter, and tell Mamma she does not write often enough. I have only received two letters from her since I landed in England. Mr. Bentley of Manchester will write to you to send him bird skins, &c.; if you do it well, he will send you whatever you please to write for, either books or anything else.

Remember me to all the young ladies, little Charles, Bourgeat, &c., &c., and believe me forever

Yours most affectionately, father and friend,

J. J. A.

And thou, my sweet wife, I hope thou are well and happy. I will write to thee as soon as I have seen more of my learned acquaintances here. Forever thine, and may God bless thee. Thy husband and friend,

J. J. A.

I will send them my journal up to my arrival at London. It will be, there, interesting. I have, moreover, asked if I might, or not, write to Mrs. Percy. Keep directing to Messrs. Rathbone Brothers, & Co., Liverpool.

EDINBURGH, October 28th, 1826

Mrs. [Richard] Rathbone,
Woodcroft
MY DEAR MADAM,

As I stood this evening, quite late, silently, and lonely, looking from within at the shattered remnants of Holyrood Chapel I could not help remembering my pleasure I felt at Liverpool when guided by you and your kind husband. I saw there the powerful beauties that pencils, well tutored, can render. I compared the efforts of the arts of Free Masons at their early age with those of the painters of the present day, and lost myself in a labyrinth of uncertainty, not knowing to whom I ought to give preference, either as regards taste, powers of comprehension, or those of execution. Those thoughts carried me back instantly to "Woodcroft," reminded me of how much I was indebted to you and your husband, and the pleasure I would feel by thanking you this evening for the pretty black chalk sheets you have been so good as to send me in the album. The album, again, convinced me that I ought to have wrote especially to thank my good friend Mr. Rathbone for the many useful hints contained in his piece. Please assure him for me that

"England, although once unjust to my Country,
"England has not been unjust to me—"

will never be forgotten. Then I again looked at the little boy praying, and thought how well you would draw, could a mother's attentions to a lively brood be put aside a short while daily.

I have found Edinburgh far more beautiful than I expected. (Having seen sweet Matlock I thought that this island was covered only by smoky towns.) Its cleanliness almost equals that of our Philadelphia, and its picturesque site far surpasses it. I always was fond of plain appearances and the greyish, *Friendly* [pun on Quaker] color of the buildings here is very much more congenial to my feelings than either the red painted bricks, or the sooty overcast that hangs about Manchester for instance. There is a wildness expressed in all its component parts as well as its *tout ensemble* that agrees precisely with the ideas of a man of the woods. I can ramble here in company with grand Nature, and cast an eye of admiration on the powers of man so very alternatively that more pleasure accompanies me in my excursions, in and about this city than ever I yet had felt on like occasions. It brings to view many groups of different figures, so well managed in one large picture that you are pleased at each of them, attracting singly as well as when, with a cool judgment, no fault can on the whole be found.

'Tis no wonder indeed that the Scotch kings sought the spot. None other could be better suited either to protect them or afford them repose. And how the round monarchs of France must have fattened on the sweet black-headed sheep that ramble on the heath!

[Deleted by J. J. A.: "But I have been tormenting you with details."]

I was also very much delighted when on my way here from Manchester and about fifteen miles from Carlisle I entered Scotland, following the meanderings of a complete miniature of our Mohawk river. Many little rapids ornament its abrupt windings; and the foliage, about to die, looked much as along our majestic streams of the West. It reminded me of the most agreeable tour your generous Mamma procured me, about and from Matlock. I was admiring Nature here, and the goodness of her heart in her every movement when suddenly, entering amongst high, bleak, naked hills, I found myself quite alone, rolling fast away from the best friend I ever had away from home. Two amiable gentlemen of the name of Pattison from Cornwall, one accompanying the other (his son) to this place, were polite and very kind to me both in the coach and whenever we stopped. We soon understood each other, and since here they have rendered me valuable services. But this reminds me that I ought to tell you that near Lancaster I was on the eve of being arrested, and my trunk was opened and examined on the suspicion that it contained a dead subject for anatomical researches, going to the learned of Edinburgh. My poor *chevelures* so went against me that everyone said I was an eminent foreign physician. I offered to open my trunk, but, one of the [outside] passengers having left us shortly after this, the insufferable odor complained of went with him, and apologies were made me.

I liked the appearance of the Castle at Lancaster, and [it] best fits those within. On the whole my journey has been sufficiently agreeable. The colleges will soon be in *full bloom*. Students were arriving from all parts of the world, and in a few weeks this town will be seen at her best in point of society. I must acknowledge I would prefer the atmosphere warmer by thirty degrees than it will be either then or now. For although wrapped up as carefully as a suffering infant, the cold enters me at every pore.

I am extremely agreeably lodged at No. 2 George Street where some of the first people here have already visited the Birds of America. Unfortunately for me, however, a letter from my good friend Dr. Traill proves to be addressed to an eminent man who is himself engaged in a publication of an ornithological nature, and *consequently* (I am told) received me not very warmly. Indeed I fear that he will not even call to see my drawings. Yet I never made them with a view to offending anyone, but with a great wish to please all. (Such a hand I do write that notwithstanding a complete assortment of beautiful knives not a pen can I make that will mark legibly.)

The pleasure of writing to you, or, as you were pleased to say, to *"womankind"* has kept me at it until I fear your patience will suffer.

Then, my dear Madam, permit me to beg of you to present my sincerest and most kind remembrances to your good husband, to your Mamma, your sister Hannah, and Mrs. [W.] Rathbone, to your brother Mr. William Rathbone, and to Mr. Theodore Rathbone my good wishes. The pleasure you all must have felt at his arrival I can partly conceive; and that [pleasure] of his conversation I would like to enjoy in company with you all. If you please ever to grant me the honor of an answer, will you remember that I once bid to expect a joint one from sweet little Basil. [He] and all his little relations are, I hope, quite well.

Wishing you and yours, my dear Madam, health, prosperity and a continuation of the sociable pleasures I have seen you all enjoy. I remain forever, most respectfully, your much obliged and very obedient, humble servant,

J. J. A.

EDINBURGH, October 28th, 1826

Dr. Thomas S. Traill, Liverpool
MY DEAR GOOD SIR,

I do not write to you because I have much matter on hand, but because I began feeling ashamed of not having done so before.

When at Manchester I saw Mr. Bohn and he examined my drawings closely. What will you think and say when you read here that he is of opinion now that the work ought (if at all) to come forward, *the Size of Life?* He said more, for he offered to publish it himself if no one else would undertake it, but as I *need the needful* I did not jump at his offer. He again desired that I should see him in London, and I certainly shall.

I am anxious, and will try very much to have a few lines from Sir Walter Scott to some one of note in the Metropolis, and will be there after having spent a few days with Mr. Selby. Professor Jameson is, I find, engaged with this gentleman and others in a large publication. And Mr. Edward Roscoe, to whom I will write this morning, advises me to connect myself with them. Will you write me immediately and give me your views on this subject? I must acknowledge that my independent spirit does not brook the idea with any degree of pleasure, and that I think that if my work deserves the attention of the public it will stand on its own legs as firm as if joined to those of men who are no doubt far my superior, in point of education and literary acquirements, but not so in the actual course of observations of Nature at her best—in her wilds!—as I positively have done. Yet as I am but an infant entering the Great World of Man, I wish to be submissive to its ways and not stubbornly raise mountains between my connections with it and my own interests. It is for that very reason that I beg your opinion as one that I look upon as extremely valuable. Please present my humblest and best respects to Mrs. Traill and family. Remember me to our good friend William Roscoe, the family Rathbone, and all others who have been so very kind to me, and believe me, my dear Sir,

Your much obliged friend and obedient servant,

J. J. A.

Please direct me care of Patrick Neill, Esq.

EDINBURGH, Oct. 28, 1826

Mr. W. H. Bentley, St. Mary's Gate, Manchester

MY DEAR MR. BENTLEY,

Although I have positively but little to say, I set to, to write this, more to fulfill my promise and to have the pleasure of inquiring how you all are than persuaded of its being either very agreeable or advantageous to yourself.

My journey here was pleasant. I had good company in the coach and fared well. I was pleased with some portions of the country, but since in this island I have seen nothing to compare with this beautiful Edinburgh. I have done nothing yet in any way of business, and although I regularly delivered all my letters, only one of the persons has called on me, lectures, &c., rendering all the professors too busy to come and see only the Birds of America.

I now send you a list of such birds as I think my son John can procure for you. Pray remember me kindly to your young ladies and Mrs. Bentley, and believe sincerely,

Your truly obliged friend,

JOHN J. A.

[EDINBURGH, October 29, 1826]

To Victor Audubon
Falls of the Ohio
My Dear Victor,[15]

Where I am now for some four days is the most beautiful, picturesque, and romantic city probably in the world, I am delighted with every portion of it. But as I am a very poor describer I will refer you to Morse's *Gazeteer* for a general outline, and tell you only that its streets are broad and clean and well lighted with gas, its public squares regular in all their shapes, differing from *squares* by their being octagons, hexagons, full circles, crescents, pentagons, &c. The monuments are many and well erected. The especial one to Nelson is superb, mounted on a rock commanding a fine view of the German Ocean. The Castle I should conceive impregnable; two sides of it are protected naturally by an almost perpendicular rock 300 feet high. It looks like an eagle perched on a bold naked cypress ready to fall and crush all about below. The two hills that run parallel, one of which is covered by the old town and the other by the new, are connected by immense bridges under which a third city may be said to exist. To reach this, stairs are made, winding easily from either side the declivities, and lead from different parts of the great street verging the two principal towers.

The public buildings are immense. As the whole city is made of fine, well cut stones it has a modest, chaste appearance quite agreeable to the traveller's eye. The Palace of Holyrood and its decaying chapel are objects deserving the attention of all strangers. The ancient furniture and beds of Queen Mary of Scotland are real curiosities, and I sought in her mirrors for traces of her beautiful visage with anxiety and concerns, as I knew how tormented her life was. The little table and room wherein she supped the night of the murder are perhaps in best repair. The armour of the conspirators I saw. And I went down the staircase that helped the introduction of the villains. The paintings of all

15. Fifteen years of age. Born 1809.

the different families of the Stuarts are decaying fast. The rooms that were inhabited by Louis XVIII during his exile here are in good order, yet not to be compared with the apartments kept for the King of England who visited the Palace some years ago [and] laid the foundation stone for a new cathedral at the same time that he ordered the rebuilding of Holyrood Chapel.

The markets are extensive and well supplied, their contiguity to the sea very advantageous. But my dear Victor, Scotland generally is a barren, poor-looking tract. The mountains are merely covered with earth, and the shepherds the most abject beings I ever saw. None but the rich here seem to enjoy life, and was it not my interest to remain some weeks to form a close acquaintance with all the great men of this portion of the world, I would leave its rigid climate and poverty behind me tomorrow.

Since I left Liverpool I remained at Manchester and its environs about four weeks, formed there very interesting connections, particularly with a family of the name of Greg twelve miles distant, at a seat called "Quarry Bank," where I enjoyed a circle of amiable young females with the company of a most happy father and wife. Courted for my talents, my time was uncommonly agreeable. There my friends' mother, Mrs. Rathbone of Liverpool, who had brought me in her carriage with her daughter to Manchester, gave me again a most delightful ride of 120 miles to Bakewell, Matlock, and Buxton. The whole of that family has treated me with a kindness never before experienced by me under any circumstance, for which I am debtor to my friend Vincent Nolte who never suffered either opulence or poverty to prey upon his generous feelings.

My time at Liverpool was wonderfully spent. I can safely say my pocket was furnished and my body fed most luxuriantly.

Tomorrow I will visit Roslyn Castle where I have an excellent friend in Mrs. Fletcher, a scientific lady. Afterward I will go to Melrose to see the Chapel there and present my introductions and myself to Sir Walter Scott. Then I shall go into the highlands, after having seen Glasgow and Inverness. I am forced to travel a great deal to open the gates of renown to my Work that now proves superior to anything of the kind in existence. I never, before this, knew what the feel of pride was, but I am confident that I no longer fear to shew my head or my drawings. That all this may end well and that I may return to my Beloved America with rich stores of wealth and fame is to be hoped. I shall spare neither time nor attention or preference to reach my ends, I assure you.

In the course of next month I will pass through London, Bruxelles, Valenciennes, Paris, and reach my mother's house in Nantes, and may God grant me the favor of kissing her once more. [Here a line and a quarter are blacked out by a pen that appears to have been Audubon's own, rather than Maria Audubon's, a supposition based on the unusually faded appearance of the ink.]

I expected long ere this to have had at least one letter from your Uncle Berthoud and also from you. Certainly time is not so scarce with you. *I* do wish four hours sleep and keep now a great correspondence, yet copy all my letters myself, even this one; and my journal keeps a pace with all, and my letterpress for my Birds is almost ready. My boy, pray read the "Discontented Pendulum" from Dr. [Benjamin] Franklin or someone else (for the world is at odds about the authorship) and see how much can be done if time is not squandered. It would give me much pleasure to receive from you some token of your still thinking about drawing or music, or [of] your natural talent for poetry. Talents will lay dormant in man if he does not, by exercise, cultivate them, and hide his faults, unaware.

I have an album that contains many beautiful pieces from very eminent men, and as I travel I gather!

I was at the theater the other night, and saw "Rob Roy."

What I thought [of it may be read in my journal] a few sheets previous [to my copy of this letter].

This reminds me that the labouring class here carry their burthens just as our squaws do; and was I to judge by the present appearances here, fashion will soon put aside razors and scissors that you know I seldom use myself when away from your mother. But my son, amongst people of solid understanding, outward appearances have no weight, and my locks are not even here sneered at. I find myself in company where persons from all parts of the globe [are] all attired differently, and yet all reasoning very much to the purpose. In fact it is not the coat, but either the mind or the heart, that connects man to man.

I sent a fine assortment of colored chalks to John. Should you feel inclined to draw in my style (and for your own sake you ought to do so) request him to forward you an exact half. Correct, measured outlines, precise tints, and a little life given, makes a picture. My works in oil are now no more despicable, and a few lessons from Thomas Lawrence will enable me to send you my own portrait worth the remembrance. [Of two blacked-out lines only this is discernible: "Whilst I walked tonight I . . . the thought of seeing a painter."]

During my publication I will visit Spain, Italy, Holland, Germany, of course Switzerland where I have at Geneva a most powerful friend in the Baron of Sismondi, who [will] introduce me to Baron [von] Humboldt, also in Mr. Melly, the agreeable companion of my [Liverpool visit]. My letters for Paris are good, and if I safely depend upon it, [there] will not be want of stock and cash on hand.

I have heard that your Aunt Sarah [Bakewell] was married. To whom, pray? At her age she would better not have done so (if I may give my allowance of advice).[16] Your Aunt Ann, whom I saw in Liverpool, said that my sweet sister Eliza had proved a mother again! Your Uncle T. W. Bakewell is now a citizen of Cincinnati, if not a Cincinnatan. Pray inform me how the world "busies" about you. Is your Uncle[17] the Duck Killer married yet? I thought when I saw him that his eyes glittered with affection for some fair one unknown to me. Has my sweet little Mary grown well?

---

16. To Alexander Anderson. His brother Theodore was a prominent Baltimorean.
17. William Gifford Bakewell, brother of Mrs. Audubon.

And what has been done with friend Gibbs, who also, I heard, has some ideas of kneeling to the goddess of love? Is poor Bainbrough still alive? At this distance, a step in thought but thousands of miles in measurement, all details are agreeable, and were you to set to with your uncle and write to me for one week I would thank you both. Now may God bless you, keep you well and happy, and convince you that I am, and forever will be, yours most affectionately, father and friend,

J. J. A.

I forwarded this letter in one to William Rathbone, Esqr., to whom I spoke about the sketch of Mr. Greg, on the 20th of Oct., 1826. Too much fatigued to copy it, it being 2 o'clock at night.

Edinburgh   Oct. 29th, 1826   Sunday

It is very perceivable, my beloved wife, that as I copy almost every scrap of letters or notes that I write, purely for thy own sake when absent from thee, that as my correspondence increases, so must my manual labours. It is now Sunday night, and [with] the exception of a few minutes walk taken to carry my letters to the Post Office, I have been as busy as a bee all day.

Yesterday at ten, Messrs. Pattison brought twelve ladies and the Messrs. Thomas and John Todd of this city to see my drawings. They remained with me a full two hours. Professor Duncan came in during the *interim* and is truly a kind friend. Mr. Pattison proved that I was right about Professor Jameson, for this latter is most positively engaged, and connected with many others, with ornithological publications. Nonetheless, I will have fair play if I deserve it, for although there exists heavy taxes on windows in this country, still I, being a free man, will have my share of the sun when [it is] shining.

After my company had left and I had been promised several letters for Walter Scott, I took a walk and entered a public garden where I soon found myself a prisoner, and from where, had I not found a pretty maid who took pity on my *étourderie* and praised my curled locks, and called me The Handsome Stranger, I certainly would have felt very awkward, as I had neither pocketbook nor any letter to shew. This proved to me that women were most undoubtedly intended for the comfort of men and in that instance again superior, for this one had the key that gave me liberty!

I then went in search of the richest Scotch pebble that could be found, but saw none sufficiently superior to be bought for thee. One for an instant attracted my fancy, but a child in the shop said his father could *make another* still handsomer. I opened my eyes and made way toward the street. I wanted not pebbles made by man. I wanted them the result of Time and Natural Invention. As I was going off, the [shopkeeper] went out also. I watched him turning a corner and returned to the [place] to inquire how handsome pebbles were made. Without hesitation the boy answered, "*By fire heat.*" Whilst the pores of the pebbles are open, colored infusions are impregnated frequently with a surprising effect. What will man not do to deceive his brother?

This account of the pebble maker made me forget to say that Mr. Jeffrey was not in, that he comes from his hall two and a half miles off every day from 2 to 4 o'clock of the afternoon. Therefore I entered his *sancto sanctorum*, sealed the letter, and wrote on my card that I would be happy to see him. What a mess of books, papers, letters, portfolios and dirt, beautiful paintings, engravings and casts, with such parcels of unopened packets, all direct, "Francis Jeffrey, Esqr." Why Lucy, the people are crazy when they say that I have done wonders to produce so many drawings. And what have I done compared with what this man has [done] and has to do! I much long to see that famous critic, to watch his penetrating eye measure the depth of my understanding. All knowledge now seems tending to the knowledge of the head, by outward appearances of the composition within. I wish more philosophers would examine hearts and try to judge of and improve them.

My letter to John shows that I visited the Palace of Holyrood, its every room and antechamber. What a round of different causes have brought king after king to that spot, what honors have been [conferred] there! The general structure is not of a defensive nature. It lays in a valley dividing the old from the new town, and has simply its walls to guard it. I was much surprised that the small stairs by which the conspirators arrived at the little chamber where the murder was committed communicated at once with the open country and without any means of defense. Could it have been merely to afford the queen opportunity to receive friends at once to her immediate bed chamber? Or give her free admittance to walk abroad? I was also surprised to see that her mirrors were positively much superior to any of the present day in point of intrinsic purity of reflexion; the plate cannot be much less than three quarters of an inch in thickness. The furniture is all decaying fast as well as the paintings that are all encrusted into the walls. The great room for the King's audiences contains a throne by no means corresponding with the ideas of the *luxe* that I thought moved along with his majesty wherever he goes. The whole, however, being hung in bright scarlet cloth, had a very warm effect, and I thought more than once during my stay that it would be a capital room for my drawings to be exhibited!!!

From there, where I paid five shillings to five ladies who attended me and called out names of every article I saw, I ascended a long high hill until I had a splendid general view of the whole city, country, and sea around for miles. The more I look on Edinburgh the better I like it. On returning, I ransacked much of the old town where the colleges, museums, &c., are, and where the great portion of business is done.

Today (Sunday 29th), as I told thee before, I have been at my room constantly. Received this morning Dr. Knox and a friend of his who pronounced my drawings the finest in the world (it is no trifling praise, this). I wish it was worth £10,000, but unfortunately it is only a light puff. However, they promised to see that I should be presented to the Wernerian Society, and talked very scientifically indeed—quite too much so for the poor man of the woods. They assured me that the work on ornithology now about to be published by Messrs. Selby, Jameson, Sir Somebody & Co., was a job book. It is really amusing and distressing at the same time to see how inimical to each other men of science are, and why are they so? I will not further trouble thee.

Good night, friend of my heart.

Edinburgh   Oct. 30th, 1826   Monday

I waited most impatiently to-day until 1 o'clock, getting up from my chair and looking down in the street through my window to see someone coming to view my work. But all my anxiety and my ill humour availed not, and to vent it I took my umbrella and marched direct, rather stiffened, to Fish Market Close, and passed the files of printers in Mr. Neill's office as if the world was about being convulsed. I reached the owner of the establishment and all my pomposity evaporated and dispersed like a morning's mist before the sun. I became at once as quiet as a lamb, and merely told him that I regretted very much my not deserving the attentions of those for whom I had letters, and that, if so, I must off to London. He gave me good words and in such a calculated cool manner that none but an ass could have resisted his *raisonnement*.

He accompanied me instantly to one of the most scientific men who, after looking at me as I look at the eye of a bird as it loses its brilliancy and I fear to lose its character, he noted down name and residence, and promised to send amateurs. Mr. Neill, not satisfied any more than myself, took me to a Mr. [William Home] Lizars[18] in St. James Square, the engraver of Mr. Selby's Birds, who at once followed me to see my work. He talked of nothing else (as he walked along under the same umbrella) besides the astounding talent of his employer [Selby], how quick he drew, and how well, had I seen the work, &c., &c., until, having ascended the stairs of my lodgings and entered my room, his eye fell on my portfolio and gave him some other thoughts I am quite sure. It is a doubt with me if I opened my lips at all during all this. I slowly unbuckled the straps, and putting a chair for him to set, without uttering a word, I turned up a drawing! Now Lucy, poor Mr. Selby was the sufferer by that movement. Mr. Lizars, quite surprised, exclaimed, "My God, I never saw anything like this before!" Now Lucy, Lawson,[19] the Philadelphia brute, never gave an inch, and to this day swears

18. William Home Lizars (1788–1859) aquatinted the first ten plates of *The Birds of America*, completed by R. Havell & Son. However, platemarks for the ten vary.

19. Alexander Lawson (1772–1846) was the Scotsborn engraver of Wilson's *American Ornithology*. In 1824 he belittled the fresh style of Audubon, who had nettled him by criticizing the traditional, profile drawings of birds by Wilson.

that I know nothing about drawing, that [Alexander] Wilson did more with one bird than I ever will with thousands!

Mr. Lizars was so astonished that he said Sir Somebody [Sir William Jardine] must see them, that he would write immediately, (and so did he), that Mr. Selby must see them and to him also he wrote. And, going as it grew dark, he called, it seems, on a Mr. W. Heath,[20] a great artist from London, who came immediately to see me. I had, however, made my exit in search of a handsome pebble for thee, and missed him then. I called at the Post Office but it was not open—shocking arrangement for a traveller [who,] if in town for a few hours only, cannot be told if, or not, there are letters for him. I found it the same case in England.

I returned and found two lines from Mr. Heath, and not knowing who he was I posted to go and see who he might be— No. 4 St. James Street. Up three pairs of stairs (*à l'artisan*), met a very dark brunette who acknowledged herself to be the better half of her husband, who, in a moment, shewed me two enormous mustachios on his upper lip, and a great many, various drawings and etchings. I will not say that they were without fault, as thou knowest there are faults in everything. I thought some of them good. He will come tomorrow.

I met accidentally this day my third companion from Manchester, Mr. Walton. I was glad to see him and he reciprocated my feeling very amicably. Tomorrow he also comes.

Edinburgh, Scotland   Oct. 31st, 1826   Tuesday

So at last Professor Jameson has called on me! That warm-hearted Mr. Lizars brought him this morning just as I was closing my letter to Victor. He was kind to me, very kind, and yet I do not understand the man clearly. He has a look quite above my reach, I must acknowledge, but I am to breakfast with him tomorrow at 9. He says he will announce my work to the world with my permission, bring his lady and daughters, &c., &c., and who knows after all if I, myself, am not mistaken and if *he* may not prove an excellent friend! But really, he and Mr. Lizars did praise my drawings so highly, so astonishingly so, so much

---

20. Charles Heath (1784–1848). The engraver? If so, he was not "great."

above all I ever heard that I cannot help thinking yet that [there is] some question about the affair and the *entretien*.

Dr. Thompson's sons came in, tall, slender and well looking, made a decent apology for the father, and invited me to breakfast at 9 Thursday next. Young Dr. Henry also came and wrote [a note of introduction for me] to Dr. Thomas Allen: ". . . Audubon, artist of great ability. . . ." and having again called this evening when [I was] absent [he] left his card and a note of invitation to Professor H. Hibbert to breakfast tomorrow. This I cannot do. A Mr. Symes who lives [at] 63 Great King Street, and who, besides, is called Patrick, but who I am quite sure is a learned Scotchman, was with me a long time and entertained me very much.

My morning was indeed quite an agreeable one within, although it rained and the thermometer never rose up to 35° this day. I called at the Post Office. All fudge. And again, my Lucy, Edinburgh is surprising, grand, beautiful, most picturesque and romantic!! I eat fish for dinner to-day because my landlady (may God Bless her) said that she heard me cough last night and that light food was best for me. God knows. I never heard myself cough, nor am I very sure about light food being so very advantageous. But women being men's superiors, I will not meddle in contradiction with them, for although they suffer us to hold the reins they will forever lead the way for us!

I have looked on thy likeness, sweet wife, very intently to-day and felt such an inclination to kiss it that my lips became burning hot and————oh sweet wife when will we meet again?————

I called again this evening on Mr. Lizars, who seems very favorable to me. He shewed me some of his work, and judge how abashed I felt when I discovered him to be a most wonderful artist. He has invited me to call on him at 8 to spend the *evening* with him. Now I call it much more, as if going to spend the night there. His wife is lively, very affable, and has fine, large eyes well colored with burnt umber, or perhaps Vandyke brown. Yet they may be [a] better color; I am not quite sure as it was just during that twilight when I saw her, and eyes then render objects not always as they really are. On the [whole], however, I cannot commit any mistake by saying that she is beautiful! And she is the first lady to whose house I have yet been, and received kindly. I will, hereafter, call her Lady No. 1. Remember this, my beloved wife.

Now my Lucy, I have just returned from Mr. Lizars. It is just 11 o'clock. His young brother accompanied me, of course. I came without any risk or danger. My evening has been extremely pleasant. I have had many good advices given me. I have seen Mr. Selby's *original drawings*, and *Sir William Jardine's*,[21] and as I conceive my Johnny can do as good I am quite proud. Lady No. 1 had a sister of hers there, a very agreeable woman; another brother; a good doctor; all wished me well. All together we drank thy good health all around. I hate late hours. I have to be up, Lucy, long before day to write, and so may God forever bless thee, dearest Lucy, my love. Good night.

Edinburgh   November 1st, 1826   Wednesday

Well, my good lovely wife, I breakfasted with *Professor Jameson!* A most splendid house, splendid everything, a good breakfast to boot. The professor wears his hair [in] three distinct, different courses, [so that] when he sits fronting the south, for instance, those on the upper forehead are bent westwardly, towards the east, those that cover both ears are inclined; and the very short sheared portion behind mounts directly upward, perhaps somewhat like the sister quills of the "fretful porcupine." But dearest Lucy, notwithstanding all this curious economy of the outward ornamental appendages of his skull, the sense within is great, and if I mistake not it feels the suavity of a kind generous heart. Professor Jameson is to-day no more the man I took him to be. He accosted me most friendly, chatted with an uncommon degree of cordiality, and promised me his powerful assistance so forcibly, convincingly, that I am quite sure I can depend upon him. I left him and his sister at 10, as we both have a good deal to do besides drink hot, well creamed coffee.

The separation, however, was short, for when the clock struck

---

21. The superb originals, indifferently engraved and printed, have never received fair recognition.

12 he entered my room (then filled with fair females), accompanying a notable baronet and perhaps a couple more gentlemen. *He*, [Jameson] Lucy, made them praise my work, said he would call again, and I saw him pull my door after him, quite sorry, for as I said just now, Professor Jameson is quite the man for me now. Ah, and Mr. Neill also, and Mr. Lizars, and Dr. Hibbert, and Dr. Henry, and Dr. Knox, and for all I know a full score double twice.

At 4 o'clock I was still very patiently turning one drawing after the other, holding the larger ones at full arms length, and pushing the small ones quite under the delicate beauties' noses to give their fair eyes all kinds of opposition. (And yet, God knows how all this will end.) I felt very fatigued. My left arm, once I thought, had some idea of revolutionizing. I thought once that my left fist was about to assail my own so well formed nose. I took the hint and saved both.

I walked out and was looked at by many. As I passed one, I could hear, "That's a German physician, I know." I answered *low*, "Fudge!" Another [said] "That's a French nobleman." I answered *low*, "Bah!" Took plenty of needed exercise, inquired in vain after chalks, called in vain at the Post Office. Thought often of my good friends of "Green Bank" and of thee, and at last pushed in at Mr. Lizars's just as he was about supping several cups of tea into his supping-in place—well, I could not remain quite a blank the while. Mr. Lizars uncorked a bottle of warmed London porter. Lady No. 1 handed it me with a smile, and I handed it to my mouth with thanks! Whilst down in his counting room I expressed the wish to purchase a set of views of *superb Edinburgh*. The book was brought upstairs for me to look at. He asked me to draw a vignette for him and wrote on the first sheet of his book the exact following transfer of properties in fee simple thus:

> To John J. Audubon as a very imperfect expression of the regard entertained for his abilities as an artist, and for his worth as a friend by
> WILL H. LIZARS, Engraver of the
> Views of Edinburgh

Any Kentucky lawyer who would pretend not to acknowledge

the whole *un bona fide* I would knock down. But as our advocates are all of the *good Clay kind*, I neither fear the contestation nor that of being conquered by physical power in such an encounter.

We walked and purchased chalks. Yes, for three pounds and one shilling and eight pence I took home three boxes of crayons, two brushes of sable hair, and two handles of God knows [what] genera or species of wood. I had seen some artists of Mr. Lizars coloring by gas light, printing on copper, &c., &c., for the first time in my life!

Well, I went to bed [to read,] until I was so pleased with the book that I put it under my head to dream about it like children are wont to do at Christmas Eve, I believe. However, my senses all operated another way. I dreamed of the "Beech Woods," of a house there! Of a female there; Of—!

God bless thee, sweetest friend. Good night.

Edinburgh   Nov. 2nd, 1826   Thursday

As punctual as an *artist* I drew the bell of the door at No. 80 George Street just as the great bell of St. Andrew's Church slowly struck 9.

Whilst I was blowing my nose and taking off my gloves, I examined how well the name of Dr. Thompson was engraved on a well polished and well brightened piece of brass eight by five. Not feet, Lucy, the more common measurements of *extraordinary paintings*. No, inches. Well, the Scotch waiter came and introduced me to his Scotch master, a good, and very good-looking man. Kind, extremely kind, he said to his wife, "Mr. Audubon, my dear." Happy man who can thus, to-day at breakfast, welcome a stranger and present him to a sweet wife, whose company he has enjoyed ever since, and every day since I, as a poor exile departed from American shores [and] can only *remember* that I also have had the pleasure of doing the same. Ah my Lucy, every woman brings me [to] more [unity] with thy good qualities. The more amiable they, the more amiable thee!

We sat to breakfast. A daughter entered. Then [came] the son of the other day's [call on me], then another young gentleman. And when my second cup of coffee, held carefully, ah and gracefully by its delicate handle, was ascending in its perfumed steam, a certain Dr. Fox[22] entered also, and sat to like an old acquaintance. Fine young man. Speaks well. Has been seventeen years in France, of course speaks [French] well also. Wishes to see my Birds. Most willingly.

After having talked somewhat about the scrubbiness of the timber here, and its lofty majestic [aspect] in my dear country, I left them to come and shake hands with Lady *No.* 1, who came in as tall and as lovely as ever, with her husband and some other persons. Mr. Lizars had not seen one of my largest drawings. He had been enamoured with the "Mocking Bird and Rattlesnake," but Lucy, the "Turkey"—her brood—the "Cock Turkey"—the "Hawk" pouncing on seventeen Partridges—the "Whooping Crane" devouring alligators newly born—all were, he said, wonderful productions.[23] According to his say so, I was a most wonderful compositor. He wished to engrave the "Partridges," but when the "Great-footed Hawks" came with bloody rage at their beak's ends and with cruel delight in the glance of their daring eyes, he stopped mute for perhaps an instant. His arms fell (if so, he was not squeezing me), then he said, "I will engrave and publish this."

We were then too numerous in the room to *transfer* business, and the subject was adjourned. A gentleman offered to pay me a certain amount for the use of my drawings for exhibition; but more of this bye and bye. At 4, fatigued again, I walked and paid my respects to young Dr. Henry at the Royal Infirmary, a nice young man.

At 5 or thereabouts I was positively again in the presence of Lady *No.* 1, and her good husband first gave me a glass of good wine, and let me *see* one, two, yes three, glasses of warm Scotch whiskey toddy. I requested him to advise as to the size for a picture of "Turkeys" in oil. We spoke of the exhibition, when [I] mentioned how kind and generous the Institutions of Liverpool and Manchester had been, and that I had a letter of thanks containing the order and invitation of the committees. He started

22. Not to be confused with the eminent Dr. Charles James Fox, whose son he could not have been.
23. All appear in first fascicule of *The Birds of America,* Folio.

Virginian Partridges Attacked by Hawk. *[Bob-White, Folio Plate LXXVI]. Oil on canvas, copy of water-color study for* The Birds of America. *Brought from Audubon by Benson Rathbone, the painting went eventually to the Royal Institution, Liverpool.*

with me at once, and we marched arm in arm to Mrs. Dickie's. He read the letter, and off he went to Professor Jameson. Then he returned again, after having given my letter to the professor (he said) to make good use of it. Shewed many, many letters of recommendation, and he said to me, "Mr. Audubon, the people here don't know who you are at all. But depend on it, they shall know." We talked of the engraving of the "Hawks," and it seems they will be done.

Then Fame, expand thy unwearied pinions, and far, far and high, high soar away! Yet smoothly circle about me wherever I go, and call out with musical mellowness the name of this child of Nature, her humble but true admirer. Call out, call out, call out—LOUD, LOUD, *LOUD, AUDUBON!!!!* Sweet wife, should this lady positively put it into her head, by putting the mouth of her trumpet into her mouth, to name Audubon as worthy of public patronage, depend on it, Audubon's industry and perseverance would soon be able to procure the needful. Yet that dirty trash, money. "But why thus anxious?" [thee asks?] Anxious? Why! Do I not love thee and my children? Have I not the most ardent desire to give them a good and more formal education than I ever will have? Do I not wish the comfort of you all? Yes by heavens, I do! Then must I, as the world goes, have this trash called most judiciously and with most accurate veracity, the Needful. I'll try so much to dream about it that perhaps Dames Fame and Fortune may think it pleasant to lay under my pillow a good many scores of long, strong, worsted hope of ample dimensions, filled with gold, amethysts, rubies, diamonds and—what now shall I wish for? Wish, aye—*UNE PRUNE!!!*

Edinburgh   Nov. 3rd, 1826   Friday

Instead of *une prune* this morning, I had most positively two boiled eggs for my breakfast. I was not very much surprised at the difference. November is not a month for plums, it is too late then for my expectations *this* year. Perhaps next June, in Paris, I may be supplied: because better prepared and because more seasonably *a propos*.

My Birds were visited by many persons this day, amongst

were several female artists of fine features and good taste. And amongst the numerous males was a Mr. Professor James Wilson,[24] a naturalist of pretensions, an agreeable man who invited me to dine at his cottage next week. I received a letter from Mr. Bentley of Manchester, informing me that thy box of spars, letters, &c., had been received at the Royal Institution, Liverpool. But I must say that I am quite surprised at not hearing from Mr. Munro or any of my Liverpool friends. Mr. Lizars who certainly is here *mon bon cheval de bataille,* is exerting himself in my behalf most manfully. At half past 3, good Mr. Neill came whilst I was dressing, and we soon walked together toward his little hermitage. Sweet spot, quite out of town, nice garden, house, with exotics, and house walls peopled by thousands of sparrows secured in the luxuriant masses of ivy that only here and there suffer the eye to see that the habitat is of stone. The Heron's sharp lance laid on his downy breast, his shoulders surmounting his watchful eye, and he stood silently, motionlessly, balanced on one leg. The Kua [Kittiwake] Gull yelped for food. The Cormorant greedily swallowed. Whilst the waddling Gannet welcomed her master by biting his foot. The little Bantams and the great Cock leaped for the bread held out. The faithful Pigeon cooed to his timid mate, and the great watch [dog] rubbed against his master with joy! We entered the house, the library, the parlour, all neat and gracefully systematic.

[Gradually the company of] friends increased. I counted amongst them Bridges,[25] Combe, Lizars, Syme and others, and full of gaiety we all set to a sumptuous dinner. The wine augmented the fecundity of wit. The eyes around sparkled with knowledge and sense, and the health of Audubon [was] drank in unison—then thine, sweet Lucy—then our noble host's and then "Peace forever!" Mr. Combe has a head quite like our Henry Clay's, and is an extremely fine man. My neighbor Bridges is all

---

24. James Wilson (1795–1856), *Illustrations of Zoology* (1828). James introduced William MacGillivray to Audubon, whose scientific and general editor MacGillivray became, for *Ornithological Biography.* He was a brother of "Christopher North" (John Wilson).

25. David Bridges was an Edinburgh newspaper editor. George Combe (1788–1856) followed the phrenologist Kaspar Spurzheim, whose theories were eventually discredited.

life and the pleasantest companion I ever met. But Lucy, after a few observations concerning the birds of our woods, *he* retired to let the world know that many of them have "arrived" in Scotland.

What thinkst thou when it is unanimously agreed that I must set for my portrait to Mr. Syme, and that friend Lizars must engrave it to be distributed abroad?[26] Even so. And next week there will be two Audubons in Edinburgh. I wish for my sake that one of them was named Lucy! Well my love, this is the way, much *à la Liverpool,* and if I mistake not it will end well. Four [of us] linked together, I was accompanied to my lodgings. Have brought some native bread for thee, and chestnuts and walnuts and pears and apples, all native and rather bigger than green peas!

Tomorrow I am to see Lord Somebody and Miss Stephens. She was called such a *delicious* actress so frequently by my learned friends that I reverse my judgment, or at least will suspend it until I see more of *hers.* Wife and friend of my heart, God bless thee, good night.

Edinburgh   Nov. 4th, 1826   Saturday

Had I the inexpressible faculties of my good friend Mr. Bridges, and therefore the ability to write all that I feel toward him and the good people of the romantic Edina's academic halls, I would set to, and post up most marvelous accounts of what I have enjoyed this day. But alas, poor me can only scratch a few words next to unintelligible, and very sincerely say that I know that they are good, great and friendly!

Full [was] my little room all day with noblest individuals. Exhibiting my wondrous works (as they are called). I am quite wearied tonight. So sweet wife, only know as quick as possible, for it be now half past 1, that if I *dined* at home I supped abroad—yes, abroad—most deliciously at Dr. Lizars, where

26. John Syme (1795–1861), R.S.A., was a pupil of Raeburn. The portrait of Audubon, an oil on canvas long believed lost, was recently acquired for the White House Collection, Washington, D.C. Charles Wands, rather than Lizars, engraved it; it was first published *c.* 1833 by Brown and Lauder in their plagiaristic *Miscellany of Natural History.*

music, beauties, wines and conviviality joined all in hand to proclaim, health to thee! To America, health and peace, and by thy husband, the *"spirit of noble Scotland."* Lady No. 1 and her husband *supported* me here. I felt the warmth of her arm and thought of thine.

I received a delightful letter from John R. Chorley and the poem on knives, and—yes, and—went to bed praying for thee and our dear ones!

Edinburgh   Nov. 5th, 1826   Sunday

I begun painting very early this morning with hopes that I would go deep into my picture of Wild Turkeys. But no. By 10 o'clock my room was full of visitors. Friend Bridges, I will please to call him, came and stayed a long, good time. Miss *Stephens* the actress and her brother also paid me a visit. The lady who, I am told, bears well in the respectable world, had my album sent her, and I am to have in it some produce of her fair hand. The day passed but I did little on my [picture], for friend Bridges having invited me to dine with him, I walked to his house at 4 and never perceived that I was in my slippers until I reached the port of destination. A Mr. Harvey dined with us. Mrs. Bridges is one of those stately good featured ladies. We had quite a dinner *de famille* that pleased me exceedingly. I saw quite a stock of paintings, well selected by my knowing friend. I returned home early, found a note from Mr. John Greg, and waited anxiously their coming. They brought me a *scrubby* letter from Charles Waterton, the alligator *maquignon*, and a sweet little sketch from fair [Ellen] of "Quarry Bank." I was very glad to see [the Gregs.] [It] seemed like old times to me. They were desirous that I should go to Mrs. Fletcher's with them, but as I cannot leave town, I wrote a note to that lady, promising to call on her next week, and must try to do so.[27] I am by no means in spirit to write. It seems to me as if thou hadst entirely forgotten that poor Audubon *who* never ceases to think of thee. Ah my

---

27. Mrs. Archibald Fletcher (*née* Eliza Dawson) (1770–1858), later famed for her *Autobiography* (1874). Her daughter married naturalist Sir John Richardson, whom Audubon later met but who resisted close co-operation.

Lucy, this is severe indeed, and how long it will continue I cannot even guess. Yet I cannot go to rest without wishing thee as much as ever a good, happy contented night.

Edinburgh   Nov. 6th, 1826   Monday

The same today—very little work and a great deal of trouble. I was glad, however, to see those who came. I had a *Lieutenant Colonel* Faithfull, extremely interesting. Mr. Walton, my coach companion from Manchester, also called and invited me in a very friendly manner to see him often. It snowed this morning, [and] it was quite new to me for I had not seen any for about five years, I think.

I do not feel well, my Lucy. I am quite dispirited about thy silence, or better say at my not receiving the letters that I know thou must certainly have wrote.

The papers give such accounts of my drawings and of myself that I am quite ashamed to walk the streets. I would not be very surprised if I exhibit my drawings here again.

EDINBURGH, November 8th, 1826

Messrs. William and Richard Rathbone
Liverpool
MY DEAR SIRS,

Please to accept my sincerest thanks for your generous reception of me on the outset of my entering in a world that I may truly say was quite new to me. Your kind attentions have been powerfully felt—never can I for *a day* (even in the most distant portions of the world to where my avocations may lead me) lay my head to receive repose without thinking of you and the whole of your families. Never will I cease to pray for your health and happiness. Never will I cease to be your most truly devoted,

obedient servant, friend,
JOHN J. AUDUBON

P.S. The bill enclosed will repay Mr. William Rathbone £5.7.6, advanced for me for colored chalks. The residue please memorandum to the credit of the expenses you will be at, (I hope), paying postages for me from America or elsewhere.

J. J. A.

Edinburgh   Nov. 19th, 1826   Sunday

I do not know when I have thus pitilessly put away writing day after day for just two weeks. My head could not admit of it, I am sure, and that is the only excuse I can now bring forth. I must try to *memorandum* all I have seen—what I have felt and feel at this present moment is quite too much for me to write down. Yet, my beloved wife, not a night has been spent without praying for thy health and happiness, and may God forever bless thee!

Every day I kept exhibiting my drawings to all who came recommended. I had noblemen, amongst whom Sir Patrick Walker, and innumerable numbers of ladies and artists, and I daresay, of critics. At last the Royal Institution through the astonishing perseverance of some unknown friends, invited me to exhibit publicly in the rooms gratis. Then *I was no longer at home.* My book was shut and I painted from day to night closely and perhaps more attentively than I ever have done before. The picture was large, contained a Turkey cock, a hen, and nine young, all the size of life.[28]

Mr. Lizars and his amiable wife visited me often. I often spent the evenings with them. Mr. David Bridges, Mr. Cameron and several others had regular admittance and they all saw the progress of my work. All apparently admired it. I dined at many houses, was everywhere kindly received, and certainly enjoyed the time happily as far as my isolated situation could admit. It was settled by Mr. Lizars that he would undertake the publication of the first Number of my Birds of America and that was enough to put all my powers of acting and of thinking in a high paroxysm of fever. The papers also began to be eulogists of the merits of myself and productions, and I felt quite dazzled with uncertainties of hope and of fear.

I received letters from Miss Greg, Mrs. William Rathbone,

---

28. The oil is now at Harvard University, Cambridge, Massachusetts, Museum of Comparative Zoology. Also the drawing illustrated on page 341.

Miss M. H. [Mary Hannah] Rathbone, and one most precious from the wonderful "Queen Bee" of "Green Bank," accompanied by the beautiful seal of the Wild Turkey Cock surrounded with "America, My Country"! I saw Miss Fletcher and liked her very much. The young Misses Greg visited me often and at last my exhibition was opened. The professors of all denominations saw my Birds and spoke well of them. (I forwarded by the penny post seventy-five tickets of free admission to the principal persons who had been kind to me and to those also from whom I needed further assistance, and to *all the artists of Edinburgh!*

I sat once for my picture, but *my* picture—[of Turkeys]—kept me at home afterwards. I *saw, dined,* and dined again with Sir William Jardine, Bart., became acquainted with him and like him very much. He visited me frequently and sat and stood looking at my paintings during his stay in the city.

The famous phrenologist, George Combe, visited me also, spoke much of the illustrating powers exhibited about my poor skull, of the truth of his theory, begged that I would suffer a cast of my head to be taken, &c., &c., sent me a card of admission to his lectures for the winter. The famous Professor [John] Wilson,[29] the *author* [sic] of Blackwood's Magazine, visited me also, and was quite kind to me. Indeed Lucy, everyone was kind, most truly so. How proud I felt that in Edinburgh, the very vitals of science, learning and solidity of judgment, thy husband was liked, well thought of, and thus treated and received most kindly. How much I wished thee to see all this, to partake of it; that our dear sons should also have enjoyed it all would have rendered each moment an age of pleasure. I wished to write to thee, to Victor, to N. Berthoud, to William Roscoe most especially, and yet nothing of the kind could I conclude to send after I read what was done. I burned four letters, all for thee, because they did not please me, and wished to see more of my way before I could set to in real earnest.

I have now determined to remain here until my first Number is completed, when I shall go to Liverpool again to procure sub-

---

29. John Wilson, "Christopher North" of Blackwood's Magazine (1785–1854), was to hail the appearance of *The Birds of America*.

Audubon's pencil study for Wild Turkey Hen
and Chicks, *Folio Plate No. VI.*

scribers with *proofs in hand*. I will forward a Number to John Quincy Adams, to H. Clay, James Barbour, Andrew Jackson, Joseph Bonaparte, the King of England, Sir Walter Scott, the King of France, Emperor of Russia and young Napoleon, and two to thee, dearest beloved. I will keep painting here the while, and watching the progress of my engravers and colorists. Two drawings are now under the gravers, and God grant me success for thy sake and that of our beloved children.

I have not written to my dear Miss Hannah once since I pressed her gentle hand at "Quarry Bank." I will try to find time to go and spend one week at Jardine Hall and some days at Mrs. Fletcher's, and write to all my friends this coming week.

Edinburgh   Nov. 20th, 1826   Monday

Whilst my breakfast was preparing and day light improving, I sat to at my little table to write a notice of descriptive import about my painting of the Wild Turkeys that now leaned against the wall of my room *finished!* My breakfast came in but my pen carried me on the Arkansas river, and so much did I feel of my beloved country that not a morsel could I swallow; and for the first time since I am in England 9 o'clock had come, and I was neither shaved nor cleaned. But still I wrote. Mr. Bridges who generally pays me a daily visit, happened to come in just then. I read my composition and told him my intention to have it written down in a neat hand, to lay on the table of the exhibition room for the use of the public. He advised me to go to the Professor Wilson to have it put in [good] English, and taking my hat, slippers—undressed as I was—I pushed to his residence. I thought of the fine dwellings I passed, of a multitude of learned beings they contained, wished for knowledge also, and reached the door of the author of *Blackwood's Magazine* about 10.

I did not ask if the Professor was in, no. I ordered the man waiting to tell his master that Mr. Audubon from America wished to speak to him. In a moment this person returned and conducted me in a room where I wished that all that ever was written in it was my own. I did not [wait] long before a sweet child, no doubt a happy daughter of this great man, with her hair all yet confined in fairly white paper, begged that I should go upstairs, [saying] that her Papa would be with me in a moment. Could I have gone upstairs? Could I have intruded, undressed and in slippers, into the heart of such a family? Not I. I shrunk, I am sure, very considerably, from my usual size and apologized very awkwardly. I had scarce done speaking, and the fair child [had] scarce turned away from me, when the Professor came in with freedom and kindness [in his] hand, life in his eye, and benevolence at heart. My case was soon explained. He took my paper, read it, and said he would send [it to] me in good time.

Off again to my lodgings, hungry by this time, or rather say, cooled after walking. I breakfasted most heartily. And now let me say I wrote to thee last night after all, and sent thee several copies of the puffs contained in the newspapers about my drawings, as well as one of my cards of admission to my own exhibition. I then felt much relieved.

My paintings finished, I dressed and walked to the Royal Institution and was pleased at seeing there a good deal of company. [The exhibition] produced today £6.3.0, and seventeen shillings [worth] of catalogues sold. Young William Greg was at my room when the ticket box arrived, and he complimented me on my success. But my Lucy, the most disagreeable part of my day is yet untouched.

I had to go to dine at Professor Graham's,[30] No. 62 Great King Street. It was 6 o'clock when I reached there. Ladies after ladies came in, and each brought with her a gentleman. My outlandish name was called out and I entered the salon also. I was introduced only to Mr. Graham, and I bowed to the rest of the company. Then Lucy, I stood up, yes stood up motionless as if a Heron, and gazed about me [as much as] I dared to all that surrounded me. Still I stood, and thought of the concert at Manchester, for I saw many fair [pairs] of eyes cast upon me—not, however, rudely, no. I felt better here. I knew that I was in perfectly polite company and waited more patiently for a change of situation. The change came. A woman, aye an angel, spoke to me in such a way that I walked at once towards her and sat at her

---

30. Probably Robert Graham (1786–1845), who was professor of botany, University of Edinburgh.

side. As I spoke, or rather answered her I could not help think-ing how much her little foot was shaped like thine, and how like thine it rested in a well fitted enclosure of blue satin. She moved it up and down a little, then sideways, just as females do when they talk with interest, or, when not so kind, they exhibit a little of what is usually termed temper. In five minutes more I was at ease. The shrill ringing of a bell ordered us to dinner. I accom-panied the blue satin lady (for her name I may never know), and sat by her opposite another young daughter of Venus.

The sumptuous dinners of this country are quite too much for me. This is not [as] with friend Bourgeat on the Flat Lake, roasting the orange-fleshed Ibis and a few Sun Perch; neither is it on the heated banks of Thompson Creek on the Fourth of July, where the roasted eggs of the large Soft-shelled Turtle are quickly swallowed. Neither was it [as] when, with my Lucy at Henderson [in Kentucky] at good Dr. Rankins,[31] [I] listened to the howlings of the wolves while eating well roasted and jellied venison in full security. No, alas, [I] was far from all those dear spots, in *No.* 62 Great King Street at Dr. Graham's, professor of botany, &c., &c., &c., by the side of the blue satin lady. Most sumptuous dinner, well eat.

I found here an acquaintance of our Dr. Dowe of New Or-leans. I would have stayed late no doubt, if I had wished, but I longed to rest one good night, quite thoughtless if possible, and I bid the party all good night at 10 o'clock. I reached my destina-tion, safe. Edinburgh I find much clearer of those servile wretches that infest both Liverpool and Manchester at those hours. And I bid thee good night, longing to hear from thee and still more so to press thee to my heart. God bless thee.

[On November 24, Audubon wrote the following letters:]

EDINBURGH, Nov. 24th, 1826

William Rathbone, Esqr.
Abercromby Square, Liverpool

---

31. Adam Rankin, first true physician of Henderson, Kentucky, employed Mrs. Audubon as tutor of his children at Meadow Brook farm where the Audubons spent more than two years.

My Dear Good Friend,

I have just this instant received your favour of the 21st instant, and, engaged and harassed as I am, I know that the present moment is the best to answer to it.

I am really happy and very much relieved from such anxiety at seeing that your dear little ones are all on the recovery and quite safe from alternate dangers.

I have indeed received the seal from your kind benevolent mother. I am certainly pleased with the powers of the impression. But my dear Mr. Rathbone, the short note that accompanied it—the very handwriting of that excellent friend of ours is far, far more valuable to me. The golden present is and always will be precious, but the note is a gem not to be purchased. One I begged for but never expected is now placed in the first sheet of my album. I felt inclined to write to your good mother, and sat to do it twice, but my heart failed me. All I wrote was trash, and I destroyed it. But it is my duty to thank her personally, and I shall certainly do so in a few days. Pray tell her so, and beg of her to excuse me for having deferred daring doing it.

I must now enter on a subject that I assure you is perhaps of more consequence to me than any event save my marriage that ever has happened me. It is, positively, the publication of my enormously gigantic Work. But to do this I must lead you gradually back to my arrival here, and give you several of the most circumstantial details that have brought [me] to the present moment, connected with that mighty business. The first three days after my arrival here were spent dismally and quite by myself. The different letters I delivered were, I thought, of no use, and I had determined to leave Edinburgh for London *uncalled upon*, when a friend of Dr. Traill, Patrick Neill, Esqr., on whom I *called again*, left his business to see about mine, and introduced me to Mr. Lizars, the gentleman who is now occupied at publishing my first Number. He came to see my drawings, (not without some small degree of reluctance), but was so very pleased with them that to him I may safely say I owe the vast many attentions bestowed on me since I sent person after person to view them, until some of those to whom I had delivered letters showed a little of their Scottish fearlessness and also came, and since have proved good solid substantial friends.

The Royal Institution offered me their magnificent rooms to exhibit my drawings, and the newspapers all resounded their praises. The exhibition itself has been doing well, averaging about five pounds per day clear of expenses.

Mr. Lizars gradually evinced a wish to publish my Work, and my anxiety to see it proceed has made me acceed to his offers. I would have sent you a Prospectus sooner, but I really felt awkward about it, fearing that you should think yourself bound to subscribe your name to it through a friendly way of acting. Your letter has, however, relieved me, and I now enclose one with great pleasure. It is not fully represented as I intend to have one become, but sufficiently so, I hope, to obtain subscribers. My plan is to publish one Number at my own expense and risk, and travel with it under my arm, and *beg my way*. If I can procure three hundred good substantial names of persons, or bodies, or institutions, I cannot fail [to] do well for my family, although I must abandon my life to its success, and undergo many sad perplexities and perhaps never see again my own beloved America.

From what I have seen of Mr. Lizars's execution, the work will be equal to anything in the world at present. My vanity and wish to do better might prompt me to say that it will surprise all, and I think it is best to let the world judge for itself. However, I shall superintend it myself, both engraving and colouring and bringing up, and I hope my industry will be kept in good repair thereby. In about six weeks some members will be ready to leave this place to diffuse themselves, and the very first will go to my own beloved wife with a wish that the whole may succeed and render her happier still. In the meantime I will certainly beg of you to procure me as many subscribers as you can. [Distribute] the enclosed Prospectus as you please for the same purpose. I would be pleased that Lord Stanley and Sir Thomas should subscribe; and if perhaps the Liverpool Royal Institution may think it fit to do so. Although the whole amount is certainly great the number of years that must elapse before it is ended render it an [no?] easy task. And as I often have thought, I must try—if I do not succeed, I can return to my woods and there in peace and quiet die with the thought that I have done my utmost to be *agreeable* if not useful to the world at large.

Some of my good friends, particularly Dr. Traill, is much against it being the size of life. I must acknowledge it renders it rather bulky, but my heart was always bent on it, and I cannot refrain from attempting it so. I shall publish the letterpress in a separate work, got out the same time with the illustrations, and it is well that you should know that [the] work encompasses many localities and anecdotes connected with my eventful life.

I would beg of you to be so good [as] to instruct me whenever *one* subscriber is procured, and how many numbers over the quantity subscribed I might send to you to be deposited wherever you please for inspection—at the Athenaeum or the Institution.

I have painted a large picture of Wild Turkeys, and can only say that instead of twenty-three hours I spent sixteen days closely at it. It is now at the Royal Institution, where it will probably remain forever. I have formed the acquaintance of all the principle people here and am treated with great honors. Yet never will I forget the dealers in pounds and shillings and pence of other places, no never. Sir William Jardine, who is now at the head of a large publication on general ornithology has spent many hours at my side, seeing me work and inquiring *about my knowledge.* I am to spend some weeks at his hall about eighty miles from this, and probably will be [confronted] with the whole tribe of Scottish ornithologists shortly.

This has been a tolerably long talk, and I will close with wishing you most happy. I have not heard from my Lucy since I left Manchester, and I assure you it [goes] hard with me; and the many immense parties where I go are only dreary reflections of past times. Remember me, pray, to all your family and our friends, and believe me forever your most sincere friend,

J. J. AUDUBON

EDINBURGH, November 24th, 1826

William Roscoe
Liverpool
MY DEAR GOOD SIR,

As you are a man of business and my friend, I therefore will not apologize any farther than saying that with all my good will and great wishes to write to you long since I have deferred it until the present moment, because I disliked to write about nothing. I heard through our kind friend Mr. Rathbone of your disappointment at not going to Allcome at the intended time, but I heard that your health was good and that your spirits were also very good.

My great work is at last under way, but how long it will be able to bear itself up is a matter of much doubt and concern to me. It is publishing, however, here, by Mr. W. H. Lizars, an eminent artist and a man of most excellent character and great personal amiability. It will come out in its best dress only, life size, all coloured and in the very handsomest style. That is promising a good deal in a few words, and perhaps presumptuously, but it is really my wish and intention that it should prove so. I have some hope that I shall not disappoint my friends or the world at large.

My Prospectus is a very humble one, and I send it you now in its nakedness that you may clothe it (if you please) as you may best think fit. To tell you all my feelings would be quite impossible. My head can scarcely be said to be on my shoulders. I never before felt so wild, and at a loss to speak or to act as I do now. I may perhaps become reconciled and habituated to all my present perturbed situation, but I scarce can conceive it possible, and I fear often that the woods only were intended for me to live in. I have wrote a long letter to my friend William Rathbone that I wish you to read, as it contains more than I can possibly say now.

Should you, as chance may happen, procure subscribers for me, will you advise me?

Please assure your son Edward and lady that I am quite ashamed that I could not send them a drawing. I found that shop I intended for them was in London, and have omitted, day after day, writing them so. Remember me kindly to all your amiable family, your daughter Miss Jane particularly, and believe me, my dear sir, forever your most obliged and obedient humble servant,

J. J. AUDUBON

EDINBURGH, Nov. 24th, 1826

Miss Hannah Rathbone

MY DEAR MISS HANNAH,

Night after night my journal has counted an increase of days spent without speaking to you until they have accumulated to precisely thirty. I have wished frequently to write to you, but really my poor head has been so employed with business that I have been forced to relinquish the pleasure one day after another, until shame and the sense that you might think me neglectful brings me now to it. So truly busily engaged have I been that I have not forwarded the letter you gave me to Professor Stuart, because I spared his making an appointment that I must have been forced to decline, as I have not been able to absent myself from this city one hour yet. I have frequently thought of the delightful journey to Matlock, and longed for one of those peaceful nights that I have spent at "Green Bank," often wished that I could walk by your side for a few moments, and enjoy your and your dear good Mamma's conversation. But every time the turmoil that surrounds me calls me off until my poor head aches and I am ready to faint. Will you, until I can summon up myself to do so, thank your benevolent mother for her tokens of esteem? Then please read the following and the long letter I have written to your brother William. Remember me kindly to all about you, and believe me forever your most devotedly and most sincerely attached and obedient humble servant,

J. J. AUDUBON

[P.S.] I have not had the pleasure of seeing Mrs. Fletcher yet. Miss Fletcher was so good as to call on me with the Misses Greg, when I gave them [a sight] of my drawings at my rooms. I have formed the acquaintance of a few extremely agreeable ladies, where I go to relax at evening from the labours of the day. You must know the phrenologists are about having my poor head plastered to take an impression of the extraordinary bumps that are, they say, all about it. My portrait is also just now painted for the good public, and I am told I soon will be a *fellow* of higher rank than I am. At present I am expecting Sir Walter Scott who will be here shortly, and I shall have the pleasure of being presented to him by Professor Wilson, the author of "Blackwood's Magazine," an extremely agreeable man. Would you like to see the different sights of Edinburgh? I have had a superb present made me of fifty-seven engravings in one volume that also contains accounts of this beautiful city. I intend sending it to my Lucy, and would send it to you first with great pleasure; if you wish, only say so. Will you please write to me. I perhaps ask too much, but I cannot well help it, you have been so good and kind to me. May you be forever happy, most respectfully yours,

J. J. A.

Edinburgh   Nov. 25th, 1826

I have been drawing all day at some *Wood Pigeons*[32] as they are emphatically called here, although woods there are none.

Young [William] Greg called upon me as usual. The day was cold, wet and snowy. Mr. Lizars brought me a Dr. [David] Brewster,[33] an eminent man. I expected a visit from Mrs. Fletcher

32. *Wood Pigeons* was presented to the National Galleries of Scotland, Edinburgh, in 1951, by Miss Marion B. H. Rutherford. First published by Ford, *John James Audubon*.

33. David Brewster (b. 1781) was a scientist and writer, and also co-founder of *Edinburgh New Philosophical Journal*.

Sir David Brewster (1781-1868).
From a portrait by W. Bewick, painted in 1824.

and her young ladies but was disappointed, and therefore disappointed my portrait painter, Mr. Syme.

I received a note of invitation from George Combe the phrenologist to sup with him on Monday next. Having also received one from young Dr. Henry, telling me that he could not accompany me to Dr. Munro's[34] *Craiglockhart* near *Slateford*, I had declined going there to dinner. But Mr. Lizars and Dr. Brewster advised me to the contrary, so much so that I dressed and sent for a coach that took me there, two and a half miles from my lodgings for the moderate sum of twelve shillings. As I rolled along quite alone, my thoughts were multiplying fast, and perhaps would have perplexed me still more than I was already, when I found that my purse must again be pulled out of pocket to pay one shilling toll. A dear dinner, this. I arrived, however, and entered a house richly furnished.

Three ladies and four gentlemen [were present], Mrs. Monro, Miss Maria Monro and Mrs. Murray. Amongst the gentlemen I recognized the amiable and learned Staff Surgeon Lyons and was happy to meet [him]. The remainder I knew not, neither will I probably ever know them. Mrs. Murray I found a woman of most extraordinary powers, voluble and most attractive. It is a query with me if her eyes are not quite as brilliant as those of my sweet friend Hannah Rathbone. She sat by me and entertained me much, as well as the whole company very much. I need not tell thee that the dinner was sumptuous, for I meet no other kind here. Dr. Monro was more agreeable than I had anticipated, and his *rosy-dressed* Maria quite an amiable child of five and twenty, a perfect musician, anxious, I thought, that I should look at her. But I could not. I thought too much of home, of thy sweeter self and my beloved boys, quite comfortless at not hearing from thee. The evening passed and I came away alone again in my coach, reached Mrs. Dickie's at 10, and sat to write this, very fatigued and very cold.

Snow lies about all the hills that surround this enchanted city. I was astonished to see to-day all the gas lamps let loose by

34. Alexander Monro, M.D. (1773–1859), was professor of anatomy, University of Edinburgh. Mrs. Monro was a friend of the minor writer, Mrs. Isabella Murray, daughter of Lord Strange and mentioned below and later.

3 o'clock P.M., just as lights gave way, and I was forced to abandon my work. God bless thee, good night.

Edinburgh   Nov. 26th, 1826   Sunday

I had been drawing constantly and I will add assiduously all the morning. Snow laid thick on the ground. All looked forlorn and dismal in my room *except my picture* [*Wood Pigeons*]. I had got up on my chair and put the work on the floor to study the power of effect at a good distance. I had thought a thousand times of thee, and my chagrin was greater than usual. I could not well understand why no tidings from thee reached me. Oh how much I thought of the dear wife, the dear girl, the dear woods, all in America. I walked in thought by thy lovely figure, kissed thee, pressed thee to my bosom, heard, I thought, thy sweet voice. But good God, when I positively looked around me and found myself in Edinburgh, alone, quite alone—without one soul to whom I could open my heart—my head became dizzy and I must have fallen to the floor, for when my senses came again to me I was stretched on the carpet and wet with perspiration, although I felt quite cold and as if recovering from a fit of illness. It was about that time that the interesting figure of Lady No. 1[35] made her appearance in my room. Her husband and herself had come to invite me to dinner with them on roasted sheep's head, a Scotch dish, and I was glad to accept, for I now felt as if afraid to remain alone at my lodgings.

Last November, twice each week, I had my ride to Woodville. But twice each week I could kiss thee and gaze on thy features with delight, run down with thee to the Bayou Sara, and again to the *celebrated* room where many of the Birds of America had been looked at before they flew to this mighty land of Learning and Science.

At 4 I reached James Square [Lizars's] and dined with those good people without pomp or ostentation, found the sheep's head delicious, and spent the evening most agreeably. A letter from Sir William Jardine was read to me. *He* inquired if my "Turkeys" were sold, &c. I told Mr. Lizars that I would prefer selling

---

35. Mrs. William Home Lizars.

them to him for seventy guineas than to any other person for one hundred, which was the case, and Mr. L. wrote him so. I was shewed many beautiful sketches from great masters and two plates of my birds well advanced. At 10 Mr. L. accompanied me home. He was anxious to see my work. He gave me some advice about the ground and I altered it immediately, although in oil. The weather was intensely cold. When turning a corner the wind cut me almost down, and although wrapped up in flannel shirts and drawers, I felt it most acutely. This morning it was scarce light at half past 7, and the lamps were yet all lighted.

God forever bless thee.

Nov. 27th, 1826   Monday

I was at work as soon as up, and finished my drawing [*Wood Pigeons*] quite before breakfast. Mr. Syme came to see me and was not a little surprised to find it *done*. I had also outlined an otter in a trap, my very favourite subject, and that he prized also.

At 12 I went to *stand up* for my picture, and sick enough of it I became by 2. Mrs. Lizars and her husband saw *me* and it in the wolf-skin coat. As it is to be engraved I sincerely hope it will be a strong likeness.

Mr. Lizars brought a Mr. Key [Kidd?],[36] an artist who threw a sky over my drawing, and the gentleman did it in handsome style. I dined at home on herrings, mutton chops, cabbage and fritters. Received £5.11.6 from the money man of my exhibition, saw William Greg a moment, and as I am going out to sup with the famous George Combe, the great phrenologist, I will stop

36. "Key" is not in the lexicons. To repeat: Did Audubon mean J. B. Kidd, whom he mentions not long after, at the start of his 1827 journal? If so, Lizars introduced them. Kenneth Andrews, keeper of prints and drawings at the National Gallery in Edinburgh, where records of painters of any prominence exist, suggests but one other possibility. It seems a dim one, because Alexander Kay, listed in the 1819–43 city directories as an art teacher and landscape painter, did not—if he was Key— turn up again at a time when Audubon was seeking to make and retain helpful connections. Probably Key was actually J. B. Kidd, who in a matter of weeks Audubon was to hire to copy his *Birds* in oil and improvise on some of the backgrounds. The addition of sky, hills, and atmosphere material in some of the copies by Kidd bears comparison with the background of *Wood Pigeons*. Properly introducing him in his 1827 journal, Audubon wrote that Kidd had not seen his *Birds* before; that does not mean, however, that the two had not previously met. (Audubon, notoriously lax about names, had been referring to William Jardine as "Sir Somebody," as will be remarked.)

"Wood Pigeons," *a study in watercolor and oil
on cartridge paper stretched on canvas. Signed
and dated by Audubon, November 25, 1826.*

and write tomorrow morning what I may hear there tonight.

But my dearest friend, Professor Jameson sent me this day a card of admittance to the Museum. I have not seen the professor for three weeks.

I left my room and went to watch the engravers at work at my Birds. I was glad to see how faithfully copied they were done, and scarcely able to conceive the great *adroit* required to form all the lines in a sense contrary to the model before them. I took a cup of coffee with Lady No. 1 and her husband and Daniel Lizars, a brother bookseller. Again I went home to dress and at 9 was again with Mr. Lizars. He was so kind as to accompany me to George Combe in Brower Square, and I entered the dwelling of phrenology! Mr. Scott [not Walter Scott], the president of [the phrenological] society; Mr. Stuart;[37] Mr. Pritchie; Mr. McNalahan; Dr. Combe, and many others were there; and also a German named Charles N. Weiss, a great musician, composer, &c. But Lucy, neither the musician nor myself had been seen before by President Scott. George Combe asked before [Scott] entered if we had any objection to having our heads *looked* at by the President. Both of us having answered in the negative we were seated on a sofa, and as the President entered, Mr. Combe said, "I have here two men of great talents. Will you please to tell us what their natural powers consist in?"

The President came up, bowed, and looking at Mr. Weiss pronounced him possessed of the musical faculties. He then looked at my forehead and said, "There cannot exist a moment of doubt that this gentleman is a great painter, compositor, colorist, and I would add a very amiable man, but he might take this as a compliment!" There's Phrenology for thee, sweet wife! Our heads were then gently touched; the company was highly gratified.

We had supper. A Miss Scott and a Miss Combe were there, neither of them by any means handsome. Mr. Weiss played most sweetly on the flute, Mr. Scott sung Scotch airs, and at 1 o'clock Music and Painting, locked arm in arm, together left the company. I soon reached my lodgings. Mr. W. gave me a

---

37. Dugald Stewart (1753–1828) was a writer, and a professor of moral philosophy.

card for his concert, and left me at the corner of Rose Street. Mrs. Dickie, who had sat up waiting for me, said she had good news for me, and brought me a ship letter which she hoped was from home. Ah my Lucy, how I did hope it, myself. But alas, no. It was from Governor De Witt Clinton, enclosing one of introduction to General Lafayette. It was dated just thirty days from Albany, and as it came in care of my friends at Liverpool I expect some from thee shortly. I am quite mad of disappointment. Yet may God grant thee a good night. God forever bless thee.

Nov. 28th, 1826   Tuesday

This morning, as soon as I could see to write, (say 9 o'clock on account of the damp fog), I forwarded five newspapers, each one to W. Rathbone, Richard Rathbone, Mr. [Roscoe], Dr. Traill and [Alexander] Gordon, with the wish that they should all go to America. I put the drawing of the Wood Pigeons [Ring Dove or Wood Pigeon (*Columba palumbus*)] in the Institution, superbly framed, and they looked well I thought. Very little company there this day, being quite too dark.

I sat for my portrait two dreadfully long hours, but it improved and I hope to see it a good one. Whilst yet in my hunting dress word [came] that Sir Walter Scott was in the rooms of the Royal Institution and wished to see me. Thou may depend on it, I was not long measuring the distance and reached the building quite out of breath. It was to no purpose, however. Walter Scott had gone to preside upstairs, and [it] being now quite dark, he could neither see my work nor my drawing, and I abandoned the thought of seeing him this day.

I dined with Mr. Lizars and Lady No. 1, and saw, my dearest wife, the first proof impression of one of my drawings. It looked pretty well, and as I had procured one subscriber, Dr. Meikleham of Trinidad, I felt well contented. Immediately after my good dinner I wrote the following note to Mr. Professor Wilson:

My Dear Sir,

It is full fifteen years since I first felt a great anxiety to shake the hand of the great, Scotch, Well Known. I have heard this afternoon of his being in the city, and my heart has been positively acting with apprehension. Will I or can I have the honor and pleasure of being introduced to him? Will *you* provide the means of such a meeting? Appoint whatever time or place you like and you will confer a very great favor, I assure you, on your most humble, obedient, servant,

J. J. AUDUBON

Mr. Lizars also wrote to Mr. Professor Jameson about my notice of the "Wild Turkey," intimating that I was not so hard run for support as to beg for such an account to be inserted in a Journal without its being asked for. Then, sweet wife, we all walked a long distance, to Gilbert Street and a Mr. Moule where we spent the evening extremely agreeably. I saw their two young boys, as beautiful as I ever saw. The little wife is also extremely interesting, *particularly at this period when ladies are at their best.* Mr. Moule is a man of good information. We talked much of America. I learned there that Mr. Professor Jameson was jealous and extremely shy of communication. It was 12 when we left, and it is now half past 1.

God bless thee, good night.

Nov. 29th, 1826   Thursday

The day was cloudy. I received no answer from Mr. Professor Wilson, and was not a little surprised at this. I hope I did not hurt his feelings by asking a favor that perhaps I am not entitled to. Setting for my portrait has become quite an arduous piece of business. I was positively in "durance vile" for two and a half hours, and *pour surcroît de malheur.* Mrs. Fletcher sent for me just as I was setting to my dinner. Ladies, however, having the right to command, I went immediately and saw a woman not handsome but good looking, more characterful in her features than women are generally. Her eyes were penetrating and her words powerful. I was struck with the strength of all she said, although nothing seemed to be studied. It certainly was and is the fruit of a long, well fed round of general information. She, of course, praised my works but I scarce thought her candid. Her eyes reached my very soul, and I feared her presence. I know that at one glance she had discovered my great inferiority. The group of children she had with her were all *gentil* looking but not so properly subordinate as those of the beautiful Mrs. [Richard] Rathbone of "Woodcroft." She asked me kindly to go to her house near Roslyn, but her carriage was not offered as that of the delightful Mrs. [Samuel] Greg.

Lucy, I feared her probably too much to like her. I felt her elevated mind bearing on my feeble intelligence more and more forcibly, the longer I tried to steal a glance at her face. But this was not permitted. She positively riveted me to my blushes, and never before have I felt more stupid. I was glad I had met with her, and yet still better pleased that I was at liberty to go.

The doctor from Trinidad relieved me. His fair wife and, I suppose, the wife's sister, opened a conversation with me not so scientific but more pleasant, and I pressed their beautiful hands as they went off with more warmth than I did that of the female Maecenas. I returned to my dinner and swallowed it down in a hurry. Then I went to Mr. Lizars to talk and take a cup of coffee. I forwarded from his house newspapers for thee, Victor and Governor [De Witt] Clinton. Wrote a letter to my friend William Rathbone and heard that the doctor from Trinidad had a wish that I should draw 400 birds for him for publication of the Birds of the West Indies.

I reached home early and wrote a long letter to my good friend Mrs. Rathbone of "Green Bank." But Lucy, before this, I received, answered, and received again, a note from Mrs. Isabella Murray, insisting I go and see her and some fine engravings at her house, and I shall do so on Friday. I went to bed late and bid thee good night at about 1 o'clock, very distracted about not hearing from thee.

EDINBURGH, Nov. 29th, 1826
[To Mrs. William Rathbone III, "Queen Bee"]
MY DEAR GOOD MRS. RATHBONE,

I have postponed writing to you day after day in hopes that I could do it as I longed to do, I mean much better than I am able, and more as I thought the occasion required. But it is all a vain attempt, and I am at last reduced to thank you in humble words for the beautiful "token of esteem" you have sent me. Yes, I most sincerely thank you in humble words for the beautiful "token" and the "esteem" that you have so kindly expressed towards me in your precious note. Those favours neither can nor ever will be forgotten, and, if you will permit me, suffer that I should say with all my heart: warmest wishes, may God bless you.

The first impression of the seal was sent to my beloved wife the very night I received it from the hands of Professor Duncan, and it has given me much pleasure to hear some of the learned acquaintances here praise the workmanship and the donor. It is not, I assure you, of little consequence to me, here, that the knowledge of the kind attentions received by you has been diffused through the medium of unknown friends of mine. Wherever I go I am told, "You became acquainted with the family Rathbone at Liverpool, Mr. Audubon." But my dear Madam, I dare not say any more. I know your gentle temper too well, and I will remove to other subjects.

I supped on Monday last at George Combe, Esq., a renowned phrenologist, and to give you some idea of the authenticity of that gentleman in the pursuit of his ideal science I will copy you the time as spent there from my journal . . . [Here follows J. J. A.'s visit with Combe, as given in the journal: Nov. 27, 1826.]

On the whole the company at George Combe's was fully convinced that Mr. Weiss could blow the flute and I quite able to soil brushes. I am not very fully convinced that Mr. Scott did not know previously who we were. Neither can I ever be convinced of the truth of his assertions as far as I am connected with them, but if those men have positive proof to support what I call only a theory, away goes my ideas concerning the very existence of—[Here a word was not deciphered by J. J. A.'s copyist.] Mr. Combe says that my poor skull is a greater exemplification of evidence of the truth of the system than any he has seen except Napoleon, Molière, Garrick, &c., &c., and positively I have been so tormented about the exuberances of my head that my brains are now, I am sure, very nearly out of sorts. But this is not all. My eyes will have to be closed for about one hour, my face and hair oiled over, and plaster of Paris poured over my nose to form a mold of the whole; then a bust will be made, and there, my dear Mrs. Rathbone will be, as I hope always to be, only "simple and intelligent Audubon," as your good son Richard was pleased to call me. And on the other side the artists, quite as crazy and silly-inclined, have said that my head was a perfect Van Dyck's; and, to establish that fact, my portrait is now growing under the pencil of the ablest advocate of the science [of portrait painting] here. It is now a strange looking figure, with gun, strap and buckles, and eyes that to me are more those of an enraged eagle than mine. Yet it is to be engraved, and, that being the case, I shall take the earliest opportunity of letting you be judge of the whole for yourself.

I have been thrown into a constant round of parties, suppers and dinners ever since my Birds were seen, which, bye the bye, was not until three days after my arrival. But the late hours it forces me to keep are distressful and very wearisome. Yet I paint during every moment I can steal from company, and have done much work. I have been [received] in a very friendly way by several of the nobility. Sir Walter Scott arrived yesterday from Paris. He saw my drawings for a moment, and I hope to dine with him tomorrow, with the committee of the Antiquarian Society at the Waterloo Hotel where an annual feast is given.

My work is proceeding in a very good and superb style. Proof impressions have already been struck, and in a couple of days coloured plates will be at the exhibition rooms and the different booksellers' shops. I, this day, had a subscriber from Trinidad. Mrs. Fletcher on whom I never yet had time to call came to see me herself. I [was] very much pleased with the interview, and also with a short visit I received from her daughter. But with all this bustle and hopes to succeed, my heart is heavy, yes very heavy—I do not hear from my dear friend my wife, and cannot imagine the reason or the cause. Could it be possible that letters should be now at London for me?

I will not be ready to leave this place until I receive the necessary lessons for cording and hanging up the plates so as to be able afterwards to [do so] myself. I have undertaken the [publication] at my own risk, but have calculated closely, and if, in twelve months from this date I can procure 300 subscribers I will do well for my children, although I will probably have to bid eternal adieu to my Beloved America, the very thought of which just now fills my eyes with bitter tears. My exhibition has been thus far attended quite beyond my expectations, and the papers have been all constantly supporting the man of the woods. I have taken the freedom of forwarding some to you and will continue to do so if you have no objection from time to time, from wherever I may chance to go. I will be glad after you have read them that they should be forwarded to my Lucy or my son Victor.

I have been very much afraid that our good friend William Roscoe has felt offended at my not writing sooner to him than I have done. But really to write to such a man is not easy, and I am foolish enough to feel anxious not to be laughed at for the want of knowledge in such matters. If he is at all offended, pray capitulate in my favour with him on any terms that will bring back his kind wishes for me.

The weather here is dull, moist, and disagreeably cold at times. The short duration of daylight here is shocking. The lamps are lighted at half past 3 o'clock P.M. and are yet burning at half past 9. And as I never can enjoy walking or staying in bed, I have to sit moping by my fire until breakfast time. I am agreeably lodged in a street called George at No. 2, at a Mrs. Dickie's, a good sort of a woman who is extremely attentive and kind in her way. An American lady called Campbell also lodges in the same house and is pleased to chat with me sometimes. A Mrs. Murray, called Isabella besides, who has visited the European continent frequently, is also extremely kind to me. The families of Professors Wilson, Monro, Brown, Jameson, Dr. Thompson and many others have afforded me much pleasure. Yet since here I have thought a thousand times at least of "Green Bank," of "Wood Croft," Abercromby Square, Lodge Lane, Matlock, "Quarry Bank," the Dockrays, Amelia, my kind friend Miss Hannah, little cherub Basil, and all others connected with you. I long to see you all again, and am anxious that my first Number should be finished to afford me that pleasure, for then, in two days, I will be rolling towards Liverpool and walking to "Green Bank," and pressing your hands, and enjoying your sight, and feeling happy!

Farewell, my dear Madam. May God grant you health and pleasure. Remember me to all about you, and believe me forever your much attached, devoted and respectful friend and humble servant,

J. J. Audubon

Edinburgh   Nov. 30th, 1826

My portrait was at last finished to-day. I cannot say that I thought it a very good resemblance, but it was a fine picture and the public the best judge as to the other part.

The weather being fair, the exhibition was well filled. I did not feel quite well this morning. My head ached a good deal. However, it went. To be ill far from thee would be dreadful. Who would nurse me with thy kind care, kiss me to repose, and do more for me in a day than all the doctors in Christendom can in a twelvemonth? I visited my [exhibition] rooms for a few minutes. I would like to go there oftener but really to be gazed at by a crowd is of all things the most detestable to me.

William Greg called on me at 4 o'clock, and in a few minutes, he having told me that his money had run out, I offered him some and went for a bundle of bank notes [in] my trunk. However, he would only accept five pounds.

Mr. Bridges and an acquaintance of the famous *Alligator rider* [Waterton] came, and I was told that Joseph Bonaparte imitated his brother Napoleon's manners and habits constantly. That is much more than I know or saw.[38]

38. Although Audubon knew Charles L. Bonaparte well, he seems to have met

My invitation to dine with the Antiquarians of this city was not forgotten. I was at Mr. Lizars's at 5 when, having already found Mr. Moule, we proceeded to the Waterloo hotel. The setting room was soon filled. I met many that I knew, and a few minutes after the Earl of Elgin had made his entry I was presented to him by Mr. Innes of Stow. He shook hands with me and spoke in very kind terms, complimenting me at the same time about my pencil's production. At [about] 6 we walked in couples to the dining room. I had the arm of my good friend P. Neill. Mr. Lizars sat on one side of me, and Mr. N. on the other, and then I was helped to a sumptuous dinner indeed. It at first consisted entirely of Scotch messes of old fashion, such as marrow bones, codfish heads stuffed with oatmeal and garlic, black puddings, sheep's heads, tracheas of the same, and I do not know what all.

Then a second dinner was served, quite à l'anglaise. I finished with a nice bit of grouse. Then, my Lucy, came the toasts. Lord Elgin, being president and provided with an auctioneering mallet, brought all the company to order by rapping smartly on the table with this instrument. He rose and simply said, "The King, four times four." Everyone rose, drank to the monarch's health and the president's saying, "Ip, ip, ip!" Sixteen cheers were loudly called out. The Dukes of York, of Clarence, and many others had their health [drunk], then Sir Walter Scott who, to my great discomfiture, was not present. Then one, and then another, until my Lucy thy husband's health was proposed by Mr. Skene[39] the First Secretary to the Royal Institution of the Antiquarian Society, &c., &c. Whilst he was engaged in a handsome panegyric the sweat ran down me. I thought I would faint, and I was seated in that situation when everybody rose, and the Earl President called out, "Mr. Audubon." I had seen each toasted individual rise and deliver a speech. That being the case could I remain speechless like a fool? No, I summoned resolution and for the first time in my life addressed a large assembly thus:

Joseph Bonaparte only once—near Battery Park, New York City, in August, 1824. He directed numerous letters to their estate, Point Breeze, near Bordentown, but is not known to have visited there.

39. William Forbes Skene (1782–1850), Scottish historian and antiquarian.

"Gentlemen, my powers of voice are as humble as those of the Birds now hanging on the walls of the Institution. I am truly obliged for your favor. Permit me to say, may God bless you all, and may this Society prosper."

I felt my hands and they were positively covered with perspiration. I felt it running down along my legs, and Mr. Lizars, seeing how I was, poured out a glass of wine and said "Bravo, take this." The company went on toasting. A delightful old Scotch song was granted us by Mr. Innes. The refrain was "Put On Thy Cloak About Thee." Then Mr. Donald gave us another. William Allan, Esq.,[40] the famous painter, told a beautiful story, then rose and imitated the buzzing of a bumble bee confined in a room, and followed it as if flying off from him, beating it down with his handkerchief, &c., most admirably. At 10 the Earl rose and bid us well. At half past 10 I proposed to Mr. Lizars to go, and we did.

I was much pleased of my having been there, particularly as Lord Elgin[41] expressed a wish to see me again. I went to Mr. Lizars where I took some Scotch grog, and returned home well. The lad that copied my letter to Mrs. Rathbone [into my journal] was yet at work. He took the letter to the office and I took myself to bed. It is again 1 o'clock, sweet wife, and another day has elapsed without a word from thee. God bless thee, good night.

I forgot to say that I visited Mr. Allan the artist in the morning, and saw there a most superb picture [from] his own pencil.

Edinburgh   Dec. 1st, 1826

My portrait was at last hung up in the exhibition rooms. I preferred *it* to be gazed at [rather] than the *original* from whom it was taken. Mr. Lizars thought [it] pretty good.

The day was shockingly bad, wet and slippery. I had to visit Lord Clancarty and his lady at 12 o'clock.[42] Therefore I went. I met Mrs. Murray, her children, and the eldest daughter of Dr. Monro. Mrs. Murray began a speech about her grandfather

40. William Allan, R.A. (1777–1841), a historical painter, was later knighted.

41. Thomas Bruce (1777–1841) was Lord Elgin, seventh Earl.

42. Richard Le Poer Trench, second Earl of Clancarty, first Viscount Clancarty (1767–1837), and diplomatist.

Lord Strange, the famous engraver, and strange to tell the speech continued for half an hour. The details of the Stuart family and the Kings of England to this present day were all introduced in rotation, and I would probably be there yet, standing motionless like a Heron, merely saying *yes* from time to time to help my breathing, if a lucky message that the Earl of Elgin desired to see me at the Institution had not come. But it did so happen; and bidding Lord Clancarty and his black-eyed Isabella a good morning I trotted off, remarking how tall and well formed Miss Monro was.

I soon reached the Institution, for the Lord I had just left resides in Charlotte Square at No. 17. I cast my eyes on the immense and singularly situated rock on which stands the Castle, and reached the Institution in a jiff. I met Lord Elgin in the Academy of Arts room, in company with Mr. Secretary Skene and Mr. Hall the advocate, nephew of Lady Douglas. My interview was extremely pleasant, and although I never said *Lord* to the noble Earl, he spoke to me with all the kindness imaginable. We spoke of my travels, my work, my drawings, and he complimented me much indeed.

But Lucy, perhaps the best thing to relate to thee is my breakfast at and with that wonderful man, David Bridges. I was at his house, No. 27 Dundar Street, at a quarter before 9. A daughter was practising the piano. The son was reading. The wife was well dressed and sewing. The little girl played with my watch seals, and I stood with *my front from the fire,* looking on the pictures about the room. Thus was I looking and thinking when my friend came, *en robe de chambre,* shook my hands, and taking his pocket handkerchief out of its usual abode he began wiping chimney mantel, tables, desks, &c., to my utter annoyance. For I felt for the wife, whose fault was thus expressed, and felt much for it brought me home to thee. I saw thee, so sweetly clean, and all about us through thy constant care so delightfully, sweetly clean that I kissed thee in imagination, and blessed my God for having such an angel for a wife!

We walked to see my picture and to criticize it. Both Mr. Lizars and Mr. Bridges are capital connoisseurs. I dined at home, took coffee with Lady No. 1, visited Mr. Howe the editor of

*John James Audubon (1785–1851), oil on canvas by John Syme.
Size 27½×35½ inches. Engraved by Charles Wands in 1833, the
oil was only lately recovered from supposed oblivion. From a
daughter of zoologist James Wilson it went finally to her descendant,
Miss Marianne C. Russell of Edinburgh.*

"The Courant," and having received an invitation again from Mr. Bridges to go to the theatre to see [Wairner] perform "Tyke" in "The School of Reform," I went to meet him at the Rainbow Tavern, where he and his son were enjoying a glass of punch. The theater was thinly attended, but I was delighted with the piece and the performance.

At nine we left the house and went to Weiss's concert in the Assembly Rooms in George Street, a couple of squares from my lodgings. Very fine indeed. Saw and spoke to Mr. Innes of Stow and several others. The flute player was admirable both in point of execution and softness of tone. We returned to Mrs. Dickie's at half past 10, and Mr. Bridges supped with me. It is now again 1 o'clock. I am quite worn out. I wish I could spend some time with thy sweet self in the country, to rest my poor head on thy bosom and enjoy that sweet composing repose that I never can expect anywhere else. Oh my Lucy, God bless thee, good night.

Edinburgh   Dec. 2nd, 1826   Saturday

The weather was a sharp frost until evening, when it rained. Fifteen pounds sterling were collected at my exhibition. I was busy painting an "Otter in a Trap" and never put my foot out of doors until I went to dine at Dr. Brown's,[43] the Professor of Rhetoric.

Mr. Bridges called on me and said that the weather being bad a coach must be taken and that he would be glad if I called on him in time. Of course a coach was taken, and I called for friend Bridges. We travelled together quietly enough. He told me that Professor Wilson had prepared a notice for "Blackwood's Magazine" respecting myself and my work, but that I must keep the secret that Professor Wilson had read it [to] him in confidence. I said, quite elated, that twelve copies must be had, to forward to America; this, my friend thought very proper, and assured me that if I paid his coach fare this night he would amply repay me by purchasing for me the pamphlets at a lower rate than any individual could do. I *swallowed* this as a man thirsty in the wilder-

---

43. The Scottish divine and professor John Brown (1784–1859) was first to use the exegetical method of Scriptural exposition.

ness, forced to drink from the filthiest puddle or perish. And we arrived at last at Dr. Brown's. I think that the servant who called out my name when I entered the saloon must have received a most capital lesson on pronunciation, for seldom in my travels did I hear my name so clearly, audibly and well pronounced. Two Miss Hendersons, Professor of Greek Dunbar and his lady, and a professor of military surgery formed the company, along with the cool, reserved Professor Jameson. We had quite an agreeable time of it. Dr. Brown is one of those most amiable and clever men who possess the talent of making all comfortable about them at once. Such a dinner would be acceptable every day to me. We retired in goodly time, and now that it is the first time for a long time, only half past 10, I will go to rest with hopes of hearing from thee tomorrow. Sweet wife, good night.

I forgot, as I am often apt to do, that Sir James Hall and his brother [Basil], called on me this afternoon. The [latter] wished to receive some information respecting the comfort that may be expected in travelling through my dear country, and said that he would bring a map and write down my observations.

Edinburgh   Dec. 3rd, 1826   Sunday

My good friends Mr. Lizars and Lady No. 1 came to pay their regular visit at half past 1. Mr. Lizars thought more of the Otter painting than of that of the Wild Turkeys. I nearly finished [it] to-day, to the great astonishment of Mr. Syme and Mr. Cameron who came to announce to me the decision of the Institution that the rooms should be mine until the 20th instant. "No man in either England or Scotland could paint that picture in so short a time," [he told me]. Now to me this is all truly wonderful. I came to this Europe fearful, humble, dreading all, scarce daring to hold up my head and meet the glance of the learned, and I am praised so high. It is quite unaccountable and I still fear it will not last. These good people certainly give me more merit than I am entitled to. It is only a mere glance of astonishment or surprise operating on them, becaue my style is new and different from what has preceded me.

I had to dine with Mr. Witham of Yorkshire in *No.* 24 Great King Street, but I did not know him at all. I had mistaken him for Sir Patrick Walker in the street and addressed him as such a man. He had invited me on [that] occasion, and I am ready to experiment on human propensity to please. Mr. Bridges who goes everywhere and knows everybody led me to the house. Dr. Knox, the daughter of my host, his wife and his wife's sister were all [the company]. I determined in an instant that this gentleman was a gentleman indeed, quite wealthy, polite and versed in all courteous ways. We dined, we drank coffee, we supped at 11. At 12 the ladies bid us good night. I wished and longed to retire, but it was impossible. Mr. Bridges talked much. We all talked much, for I believe the good wine of Mr. Witham had a most direct effect. It was determined by Dr. Knox to propose me as an honorary member of the Wernerian Society. Our host said he would second this motion. It was determined that, to satisfy Mr. B. [Bridges], Miss W. [Witham] would set for her portrait to Mr. Watson Gordon. And at half past 1, after having been dubbed a great philosopher and an extraordinary man, my health drank, &c., &c., I retired with Dr. Knox but let Mr. B. [Bridges] and Mr. W. [Witham] at their whiskey toddy.

As we walked together the doctor spoke by no means very favorably of reserved Mr. Jameson. Said he was of the old school and that perhaps he was the only person who might bear against me at the trial for election.

It is now half past 2 o'clock. What hours I do keep. Am I to lead this life long? If I do I must receive from my Maker a new suit of strength and a better constitution, or I shall not be able to stand it.

Lucy, dearest Lucy, good night.

Edinburgh   Dec. 4th, 1826   Monday

I gave early orders to Mrs. Dickie to have a particularly good breakfast ready by 9 o'clock, because Mr. Witham had offered last night to come and partake of such with me. I then took to my brushes and finished my Otter entirely. I had been just thirteen hours at it, and had I laboured thirteen weeks more I could not have bettered it.

Nine and 10 o'clock sounded. No Mr. Witham. The good wine of last evening made bad work with him, I daresay. He was to accompany or rather lead me to Dr. Knox's lecture on anatomy. I was hungry, thou mayest suppose. However, he did come at last, well ballasted with probably much better fare than I could afford [for] him, and allowing me to perform mastication in ten minutes. I gave him some letters to read, and sat to at a round rate. We then walked to the lecture room in the old town. The weather was beautiful but extremely cold. We reached the place, ascended the stairs, and on entering the room where probably 150 students were already assembled, a beating of feet and clapping of hands took place that quite shocked me. We seated ourselves. Each person who entered the room was saluted as we had been, and during the intervals a low beating was kept up, resembling in its great regularity the footsteps of a regiment on a flat pavement. The Doctor came and all was hushed as if silence had been the principal study of all present.

I am not an anatomist, no unfortunately. I know scarce more than nothing. Yet I was much interested in the lecture, and the words larnyx, clavicles, spinal bones, rotulars, came to my ears with pleasure. The lecture lasted three-quarters of an hour. The Doctor felt also the effects of Londons Griffith's claret of 105 pounds [sterling] per 20 [bottles]. He said his head ached most confoundedly, and he was by no means well. I would have liked to have seen friend Bridges this morning. I will be bound he was not up as I was at 6, nor painting at 7, the dawn of the present day. But instead of seeing him I saw the anatomical museum and preparations of Mr. Bell of London. This sight was extremely disagreeable. The venereal subjects were shocking beyond all I ever thought could be. I was glad to leave this charnel and breathe again the salubrious atmosphere of the streets of fair Edina.

I accompanied Mr. Witham to my exhibition. It was well ornamented with ladies. I was much gratified that it so well bore the test of all description of judges. I gave him a ticket for his family and went home.

I was engaged most certainly to dine out, but could not recollect where, and I was sitting, predicamenting, when the Reverend W. J. Bakewell,[44] thy first [second?] cousin, the son of Robert Bakewell the zoologist [geologist?] and famous grazier of Derbyshire, came in to see me and to say how pleased he was at the sight. He was thin and tall; but [for] being a Unitarian, said he was not liked. He told me of having seen Thomas Bakewell when [he was] in England [looking] for glass blowers.[45] He said that his father spoke oftener of thine than of thy Uncle Benjamin of Pittsburgh, and asked me if I had known Dr. Priestley. I remember having seen him at "Fatland Ford"[46] and also that he paid me a visit with thy father at "Mill Grove"[47] before our marriage. He gave me his card, invited me to see him often and to dine with him the next unengaged day, which will be next Monday week.

I saw Mr. and Mrs. Lizars and told them that as I could not remember my engagement I would dine with them, and I did so.

I received a letter from Mr. Munro of the Liverpool Institution in answer to my last. I was glad to hear that he had forwarded the little figures to John and thy box of spars. He also said that he thought I was elected a member of the Literary and Philosophical Society of Liverpool.

My time at Mr. Lizars's is always agreeable. They are both kind to me and both very amiable, and appear to live quite happy together. They were both very much pleased with my portrait. It was concluded that the Wild Turkey cock should be the large bird of my first Number, to prove the necessity of the size of the work. [Plate I.]

I was glad to retire at a goodly hour. I felt fatigued of being up every night until 1 or 2 o'clock. And now that it is a quarter of 10 I will go and lay down, rest and think of thee, of our sons,

44. Reverend William Johnstone Bakewell (b. Wakefield, Yorkshire, 1794, to Robert Bakewell and Apphia Simpson) was minister at Chester, England; St. Mark's Chapel, Edinburgh; and Pittsburgh, where about 1840 he became an Episcopalian, then a Catholic, and finally an Episcopalian. The father of Mrs. Audubon was a first cousin of the minister's father (G. E. Evans, *Vestiges of Protestant Dissent* [1897]; *Bakewell . . .* [Genealogy] [Pittsburgh, 1896]). *Cousin* of geologist; *not* of grazier?

45. Thomas, son of Benjamin Bakewell, of Pittsburgh, was a first cousin of Mrs. Audubon. His father founded the first American flint glass factory, Pittsburgh.

46. The Pennsylvania plantation of the Bakewells, near Mill Grove.

47. To repeat: Audubon could not have seen or met Priestley, the discoverer of oxygen and noted Unitarian.

America, and my very extraordinary situation at present in Edinburg, looked upon with respect, receiving the attentions of the most distinguished characters, and supported by all men of science. It is really wonderful, and am I really deserving of this? God bless thee, sweet wife.

Edinburgh   Dec. 5th, 1826   Tuesday

After I had put my Otter in the exhibition I met Mr. Syme and with him visited Mr. Nicholson,[48] portrait painter. [Besides] his [own] work I saw there a picture from the far famed Snyders, intended [to show] a Bear beset by Dogs of all sorts. The picture had great effect, fine coloring and still finer finishing, but the Bear was no Bear at all and the Dogs were so badly drawn, distorted, and mingled caricatures that I am fully persuaded that Snyders did not draw from specimens put up in real postures in my way. I was quite disappointed, so much had I heard of this man's pictures of quadrupeds. I thought of Dr. Traill who, although well acquainted with Birds, had never remarked that [Alexander Lawson] the engraver of Wilson's work had always put both legs of each individual on the same side. This made me discover how easily man can [have] his better judgment imposed on with artificial beauties. For really this picture so much admired by everyone had no merit in my estimation. Mr. Nicholson *is only an artist*.

We then proceeded to Messrs. Watson. I saw there better work, and one or [two] very handsome pictures. I again proceeded to Miss Patrickson in Great King Street, a good soul I daresay but a pupil of small attainments. Her mother [is] quite a lady!

I returned to the Institution and had the pleasure of meeting Captain Basil Hall[49] of the Royal Navy, his wife, and Lady Hunter. They were extremely kind to me, spoke of the Greg family and my good old friend Mrs. Rathbone in terms that delighted me. The Captain asked if I did not intend to exhibit by gaslight, and I replied that I could not take it upon my self to speak of it. He

48. William Nicholson (1784–1844), the portraitist, was secretary of the Scottish Academy. Frans Snyders (1579–1657), Flemish painter.
49. Captain Basil Hall, R.N. (1788–1844), was an author and traveler.

promised to do so at once, and told me that he would write me the answer of Mr. Skene, the Secretary. I received their cards and must, of course, call upon them soon. I dined at home, Lucy, for, after all, I found that I had forgotten again that for this day I had no invitation, and I was heartily glad of it.

I saw the friends Lizars and took my usual cup of coffee from the hands of Lady No. 1 as I liked so much to do from those of that delightful girl, Hannah Rathbone, [with] a glass of wine. How much I would like to see her fine eyes just now, or thine, or hear thee or her talk and her dear mother, or my Johnny, or Victor, or thy sweet, lovely sister Eliza. Ah nothing but a deep sigh answers to me, and my poor pen goes on scratching wishes quite in vain, but God bless you all.

I returned home full intent on writing to thee, but my heart is positively giving way, and I must perhaps wait until I hear from thee first. I wrote the history of my picture of the Otter, and sent it to Professor Wilson for correction, [with] a note [to him].

May God grant thee health, Lucy, sweet Lucy, good night.

[Here appears a little pencil sketch of "two cats fighting over a dead squirrel," which Audubon painted in oil for Daniel Lizars. The oil is in the Munson-Williams-Proctor Institute, Utica, N.Y.]

Edinburgh   Dec. 6th, 1826   Wednesday

My breakfast over, I paid a visit to Professor Jameson and proposed to him to give an account of the habits of the Turkey Buzzard instead of the Wild Turkey. He appeared anxious to have either. I spoke to him about the presentation to the Wernerian Society. He then said again it was quite necessary, that it would attach me to the country and that he would give me all his assistance. I visited Captain Hall. He lives at No. 8 Chalon Street, where I had the pleasure of finding him *at home!* As I ascended the staircase I heard distinctly the sweet sounds of a well fingered piano. I entered a room and saw both the Captain and his very interesting lady, the performer on the instrument. Few women ever attracted my notice more forcibly at first sight, although by nature thou knowest well I am dearly fond of amiable ones. But her fine face was [possessed] of something more than [the ordinary] and her [demeanor] had a power that I cannot describe to thee. Her youth and form all unite to [cause] a liking. Her husband received me with great, true politeness and a degree of kindness far differing from the usual on such slight acquaintance. I spent an hour there very agreeably. They spoke of visiting the United States, and I [urged] them strenuously to do so. Captain Hall, a man of extraordinary talents, a great traveller and a rich man professing friendship towards thy husband, was very [receptive] thou mayest be sure. If I am a *phrenologist* at all, they are a most happy couple. I derived this conclusion from the lady telling her husband, as I bid them good morning, to accompany me downstairs, quite low and in such a tone as I am sure she never thought I heard. He told me I would be received an honorary member of the Wernerian Society with acclamation.

I made for friend Neill's establishment in the old town to see by what time my memorandums must be ready for the press. To my astonishment I was told that tomorrow was my last day, and I ran home to scribble.

Professor Monro called on me with a friend, asked me what I would charge to draw skulls for him, &c. Then Mr. Syme brought an engraver to consult with me on the subject of my portrait being immortalized. Young [Wm.] Greg paid me a visit. At last, in a great hurry, I dressed and ran to Mr. Lizars to know the way to Mr. Ritchie's, where I had to go and dine. I saw Mr. L.'s sister [who] had just arrived. Mr. L. gave me a young man to accompany [me] to Great George Square in the old town, and I reached the spot appointed, just one hour and a half too late. I dined, however, and dined well. Mr. Weiss was there, Miss Combe, Miss Scott, and several others, but after wine drinking, [for which] the gentlemen ascended to the tea room, a crowd of ladies and gentlemen not seen before were waiting to see *The Great Unknown* of America. I think, Lucy, I may well call myself thus, just now. We had music and dancing, and I left them at half past 9, all at their pleasures, to come and write more. Dr. Weiss again accompanied me.

I must tell thee that yesterday some *greater Unknown* than myself gave a false note of one pound [sterling] at my exhibition and therefore I paid him well to go and see my Birds. A man who met me to-day at the doors of the Institution, and who was not a *phrenologist*, asked me if they were well worth seeing. Dost thou think I said yes? Not I. I positively said no, and off he went. But a few yards off I saw him stop and talk to another man, and again he returned when I saw him go in, when I daresay he paid his shilling.

Sweet wife, God bless thee, good night.

Edinburgh   Dec. 7th, 1826   Thursday

I wrote as hard as I could until 12 o'clock when I finished copying the letter to Professor Jameson on the habits of the Vulture.[50] I went with the last sheet to the printer. Received a short note from Professor Jameson desiring that I should put the University of Edinburgh [down] as a subscriber for my work. I was highly pleased with this, [it] being a powerful leader.

I saw in the day's paper that Charles Bonaparte had arrived in Liverpool in the "*Canada*" from New York. How I longed to see him. Had I been sure of his remaining at Liverpool a few days I certainly would have gone there by the mail. How surprised I am at the same time at having no letters either from thee or anyone in America, not even one from the family Rathbone.

I saw to-day two of my proofs of drawings completed. I was well pleased with one of them, more so than with the first.[51]

My dinner at Mr. Howe's, the editor of the "Courant," was agreeable, but we had no females to render the conversation less rude. Mr. Allan, the artist, came after 9 when his lessons were just ended at the Academy of Arts, an extremely agreeable man, full of gaiety, wit and good sense, a great traveller in Russia, Greece, Turkey, &c., &c. I went to Mr. Lizars's house with him, had there some sweet music from his wife's sister Miss Ann Wilson, took a glass of scotch toddy, and returned home at 11. I am positively quite done, harassed about thee; so apprehensive am I that I cannot enjoy anything, not even a few hours repose at night. God bless thee, Lucy, God bless thee.

---

50. The controversy over its olfactory powers is recounted by Ford, *John James Audubon*.

51. Folio Plate I: *Wild Turkey* never entirely satisfied Audubon, who as late as 1835 considered drawing a second version for his classic.

Edinburgh   Dec. 8th, 1826   Friday

Men and their lives are very like the different growths of our woods. The noble magnolia, all odoriferous, frequently sees the teasing nettle growing so near its large trunk as to be sometimes touched by it. Edinburgh, my sweet wife, contains a Wilson, a Jameson, and with many other, all great men, a Walter Scott. But it contains also many teasing nettles of the genus mammalia, amongst which men hold a very preponderant station. Now I run into one of those curious trial flights of the mind that puzzles thee quite, I know, but as I never was fond of distressing thee long at a time I will go bluntly to work and say that a drawing of mine was *gently purloined* last evening from the rooms of the Royal Institution by someone teasing nettle, who had certainly strong propensities for drawing. So runs the fact, perhaps a few minutes before the closing of the doors, a Somebody in a large cloak paid his shilling, entered the hall, and made his rounds, *watchmanlike*, with great caution, took a drawing from the walls, rolled it up carefully, and walked off, also carefully. The porter and men attending missed it almost immediately, and this morning I was asked if I or Mr. Lizars had taken it to his house to be engraved. No, no such thing. Immediately I informed Mr. Lizars. We inquired for advice of Mr. Bridges, went to court and to Captain Robeson (who, bye the bye, was at the Battle of New Orleans). I issued a warrant against a young man, deaf and dumb, of the name of Ingles[52] who was unfortunately strongly suspected. Mr. Lizars and I had called on a friend of this youth who told us that he would sift the business, and could tell all about it during the day. I went to the exhibition whilst Mr. Lizars and a constable went to a Mr. Henderson in Kilrich [*sic*] Street, and there I met on the stairs a beggar woman with a child in her arms, but passed her without much notice beyond pitying her in her youth, reached my door and seeing a roll of paper there I picked it up, walked in, opened it, and found my drawing of the "Black Poll Warbler." Is this not an interesting tale? The thief, whoever he may be, God grant him pardon, had been terror struck, and had learned we [were taking] steps, and [had]

---

52. Ingles was the illegitimate son of artist Raeburn and the ward of Basil Hall.

taken this method of returning the drawing before detection. I was in time to stop the warrant and the affair was silenced. The wonder of all this is that the lad suspected is the son of Sir Henry Raeburn, [a painter belonging to] a distinguished family.

During the afternoon I was called on twice by Captain Basil Hall, who was so polite as to present me with a copy of his work in two volumes on South America, with a remarkably polite note, and an invitation to dine with him Thursday next at 8 o'clock. His note was this:

8, St. Colm St., Friday E., 3

Dear Sir,

I beg you will do me the favor to accept a copy of a work which I published some time ago on South America. This is a very feeble method which I take to express the admiration I feel for your wonderful collection.

I remain your most ob. svt.,

Basil Hall

[P.S.] You will not forget to come to us at eight o'clock Thursday the 14th.

Now it happened that Captain Hall was the supporter of young Ingles and was heartily pleased that the affair had had no further effect. But I assure thee that the *effect* it had on *me* was tremendous. I ran about to and fro to proceed to business, became wet to the skin, fretted to my very heart, and wished the business, of the drawing and the nettle at the————what? What the devil, to be sure.

The weather was miserable and I had only thirty persons at the exhibition. But another very strange thing took place. I was invited to dinner by Mr. Bridges, who was to call on me to accompany me, but he came not, and I, at last reduced to all extremities, eat in the house, where nothing is provided for me when I say that I [am] dining out. I spent my evening pleasantly at Mr. Lizars, and now have come to bid thee well, happy, and a good night, my love.

Edinburgh   Dec. 9th, 1826   Saturday

The principal incident of this day was that I purchased cloth for a coat from Mr. Bridges, and wrote closely during all the morning from 6 o'clock until 12, without either having washed, combed, or taken away my nightcap, for Lucy I wear such things now. My landlady was frightened for my health's sake that I wore no cap, and I, to save her from falling into a swoon about it, told her to procure two for me, which [she] did for six shillings. I was thus writing and fretting because I had no news from thee when Mr. Hall came and handed a note from Lady Hunter, requesting the honor of my company on Saturday next to dine at 6. He looked at me with surprise, and thought, I daresay, that I was the strangest looking author of the day.

I had much running about with Professor Jameson, to the printer, &c. Took my Ms. to Mr. Lizars who took it to Professor Brewster. We visited the Museum together, called on a Mr. Wilson where I saw a most beautiful dead pheasant that I longed to have, to paint. Went to Dr. John Lizars's lecture on anatomy and saw him operate on a beautiful dead body of a female, quite fresh. But afterward I went to the dissecting rooms where such horrible stench existed that I thought I would suffocate. I soon made my escape, I assure thee, and went home.

The day was extremely wet, yet I had upwards of 100 people to see my Birds. Therefore to-day paid the expenses of the week which has not been so good as the preceding one. I spent my evening at Mr. Lizars, talking on all sorts of subjects. We heard that Mr. Selby would be here on Monday night next. Now my love, God bless thee, I shall write to thee a long letter tomorrow that I hope will reach thee, well and quite happy.

Edinburgh   Dec. 10th, 1826   Sunday

I wrote and copied a long letter to-day, but I felt as if I was writing in vain. I saw thy form move about me in such sickly appearance that I again was almost afraid to remain alone in my room, so distracted was I with the idea that some most shocking accident had befallen thee or one of our dear boys. Oh my God, destroy that suspense—let me know if my sweet Lucy is well—for thy sake amen.

I wrote also to Mr. Rathbone and to Charles Bonaparte under cover of the Professor Drapier of Bruxelles, and was not a little surprised that I was charged four shillings and sixpence sterling for the inland postage of this last. Young Greg called on me. He was as much astonished at not hearing from home as I was at not receiving a word from Liverpool. I spent my evening at Mr. Lizars, talking on our mutual business. But my eyes were heavy as my heart, and I came home early to bid thee a good night.

EDINBURGH, Dec. 10th, 1826. Sunday

MY BELOVED WIFE,

After postponing, day after day for the last two weeks writing to thee, full of hopes that each new day would bring some tidings of thee or of some one connected with me in America, I am forced to sit and write, filled with fear and sorrow. Many of the vessels I have wrote by have returned from America with full cargoes but nothing from thee. It is the more surprising because, a fortnight since, De Witt Clinton answered a letter of mine dated Manchester, and enclosed one of recommendation to General Lafayette. My situation in Edinburgh borders almost on the miraculous; without education, [and with] scarce one of those qualities necessary to render a man able to pass through the throng of the learned here, I am positively looked on by all the professors and many of the principal persons as a very extraordinary man. I brought from Liverpool thirteen letters of most valuable introduction. After I delivered them and my drawings had been seen by a few of those persons, I requested them to engage all their acquaintances to call on me and see them also. For that purpose I remained each day for a week at my lodgings from 10 till 2, and my room was filled constantly by persons of the first rank in society. After that the Committee of the Royal Institution having met, an order was passed to offer me the Exhibition Rooms *gratis* for some weeks.

My drawings were put up in the splendid room. All the newspapers took notice of them in a very handsome manner and continued to do so constantly, [so that] the rooms have been well attended when the weather has in the least permitted it. Last Saturday I took in fifteen pounds [sterling]. It will continue open to the last of Christmas week, when I will remove the [drawings] to Glasgow, fifty miles from here, where I expect to do well with them.

I have had the pleasure of being introduced to several noblemen here, and have found them extremely kind indeed. About a fortnight since, Sir William Jardine came to spend a few days here, purposely to see me. He was constantly with me. He and Mr. Selby are engaged in a general ornithological work, and, as I find I am a useful man that way, it is most likely that I shall be connected with them with a good share of credit and a good deal of cash. In a few days they will both be in, when this matter will be discussed at length and probably arranged.

It is now a month since my work has been begun by Mr. W. H. Lizars of this city. It is to come out in Numbers of five prints [each,] all the size of life and in the same size paper [as] my largest drawings that is called double elephant. They will be brought up and finished in such superb style as to eclipse all of the kind in existence. The price of each Number is two guineas, and all individuals have the privilege of subscribing for the whole or any portion of it. Two of the plates were finished last week. Some of the engravings, colored, are now put up in my Exhibition Room and are truly beautiful. I think that the middle of January the first Number will be completed and under way to each subscriber. I shall send thee the very first, and I think it will please thee. It consists of the male Turkey,[53] the Cuckoos in the papaws, and three small drawings that I doubt thou dost remember, but when thou seest them I am quite sure thou wilt. The little drawings in the center of those beautiful large sheets have a fine effect and an air of richness and wealth that help insure success in this country. I cannot yet say that I will ultimately succeed but at present all bears a better prospect than I ever expected to see. I think this under the eyes of the most discerning people in the world. I mean Edinburgh. If it takes here, it cannot fail anywhere. It is not the naturalist that I wish to

53. See note 51, Chap. VI, in regard to Audubon's intention to redraw his *Turkey Cock*.

please altogether, I assure thee. It is the wealthy part of the community. The first can only speak well or ill of me but the latter will fill my pockets. The University of Edinburgh having subscribed, I look to the rest of them, eleven in number to follow. I have here strong friends who interest themselves considerably in my success [with] the Work, [and] who will bear me a good hand; but I cannot do wonders at once. I must wait patiently, until the first Number is finished, and exhibit that, for, although my drawings are much admired, if the Work itself was inferior nothing could be done, and until I have it I cannot expect many subscribers. As soon as it is finished I will travel with it over all England, Ireland, and Scotland, and then over the European Continent, taking my collection with me to exhibit it in all principal cities to raise the means of supporting myself well; and [I] would like most dearly to add thyself and my sons also, but can I, or can I not, expect it? Alas it is not in my power to say it does not depend on me, or it would soon be accomplished.

The first professor of the place, Mr. Jameson, the conductor of the *Philosophical Journal*, President of the Wernerian Society, &c., gives a beautiful announcement of my Work in his present number, along with an account of mine of the Turkey Buzzard. Dr. Brewster also announces it with my introductory letter to my Work, and also John Wilson, professor of natural philosophy, in "Blackwood's Magazine." These three journals print upwards of 30,000 copies so that my name will spread quickly enough. I am to deliver lectures on natural history at the Werner [*sic*] Society at each of its meetings whilst here, and I will do the same at all the cities where I will be received an Honorary Member. Professor Jameson, who also is Professor of Natural History, told me that I would soon be a member of all the societies here, and that it would give my Work a great standing throughout Europe. In the event of ultimate success, I must have either my son or some other person to travel for me to see about the collection of payments for the Work and to procure new subscribers constantly, as I con-

ceive my Victor a well fit man for such business, and as it
would at once afford him the means of receiving a most
complete education and a knowledge of Europe surpassing
that of probably any other man. In case, [as] I say, of success, I will write for him immediately, when I hope no
more constraint or opposition will be made to my will.
I am now better aware of the advantages of a family in
unison than ever, and I am quite satisfied that by acting
conjointly and by my advice we can realize a handsome
fortune for each of us. It needs but industry and perseverance. Going to America is [a] mere song, and I now
find that most valuable voyages could be made by procuring such articles as are wanted here, and most plentiful
there. It is now about time to know from thee what thy future intentions are. I wish thee to act according to thy dictates, but wish to know what those dictates are. Think that
we are far divided, and that either sickness or need may
throw one into a most shocking situation without either
friend or help, for as thou sayest thyself, "The world is not
indulgent." Cannot we move together and feel and enjoy
the natural need of each other? Lucy, my friend, think of
all this very seriously. Not a portion of the earth exists but
will support us amply, and we may feel happiness anywhere if careful. When you receive this, sit and consider
well. Consult N. Berthoud, thy son Victor, or such a person as Judge Matthews.[54] Then consult thyself and in a
long, plain, explanatory letter give me thy own heart entire. In this country John can receive an education that
America does not yet afford, and his propensities are such
that, attached to me, he would be left at my death possessor of a talent that would be the means of his support
for life. I earnestly begged of thee in all my letters since I
discovered that I was advancing in the world, to urge him
by all means to set to and begin a collection of drawings of
all he can, and not to destroy one drawing no matter how
indifferent but to take all from nature. I find here that al-

54. Judge George Matthews, planter, father of a pupil of Mrs. Audubon at Beech
Woods.

though I have drawn much I have not drawn half enough. Tell him to employ my method of putting up birds, &c., to draw fishes, reptiles, eggs, trees, landscapes, all, all he can draw. It will be most valuable to him if he be industrious and work well and closely. By the time he comes of age he would be quite able to have a collection that would be a little fortune for him to begin upon.

I was much surprised at hearing of Charles Bonaparte in Liverpool last week. He arrived on the very vessel that took thy watch to New York, the "Canada."

The difference of manners here from those of America are astonishing. The great round of company I am thrown in has become fatiguing to me in the extreme, and does not agree with my early habits. I go to dine out at 6, 7, or 8 o'clock in the evening, and it is 1 or 2 in the morning when the party breaks up. Then [I am] painting all day, until, with my correspondence that increases daily, my head is like a hornet's nest, and my body wearied beyond calculation. Yet it has to be done. I cannot refuse a single invitation. Edinburgh must be the handsomest city in the world—thou wouldst like it, of all things, I think, for a place of residence.

When I send thee the first number of the Birds of America, I will also send a book given [me] containing fifty-one views of this place. In the event of you all removing from America, keep those things, I beg. Finding that I was not going to London for some time, I forwarded the letter I had for Mr. Middlemist from here, and requested he would let me know where Charles's wife resided, that I could have the money paid her through the Secretary of the Legation at London. I have been and am yet most surprised that Charles Middlemist should not answer my letters to him, when I conceive it to be of the very greatest importance to his future welfare. How is he, and what does he do now?

I regret exceedingly not having brought barrels of reptiles of all sorts with me. I could get fine prices, I assure thee, and also for rare bird skins [and] seeds of plants. But I thought I had enough to attend to.

I very frequently spoke to thee respecting the very great kindness I have experienced from the family Rathbone of Liverpool. This kindness they continue to show me so constantly and in such a manner that I feel quite anxious to repay them through our humble means. William R. is one of the principal members of R. Sons of Liverpool, and one of the wealthiest merchants there. I wrote thee from his mother's house dated "Green Bank" to forward [to] him some seeds, flowers, leaves, &c., &c., some segments of the largest trees. I hope that thou wilt attend to these things, for in the event of thy coming to England thou would land and come to their care, and they would be as kind to thee as they have been to me. The [Turkey] seal with which I now close all my principal letters was given me by Mrs. Rathbone, the mother of that excellent family and accompanied by a letter that would honor any man living. Keep always directing thy letters to them, and write to Mrs. R. herself. She will be a most valuable friend to thee. Since I am here I have painted two pictures in oil, now in the exhibition. One contains eleven Turkeys with a landscape. The other is my "Otter in a Trap." My success in oil painting is truly wonderful. I am called an astonishing artist, &c. What different times I see here, courted as I am, from those I spent at the "Beech Woods," where certain people scarcely thought fit to look upon me. I have written to Mr. Bourgeat, Dr. Pope, Judge Matthews, N. Berthoud, Victor, William Bakewell, all to no purpose so far it seems.

I must close this and bid thee adieu for a while. I have to copy it as I do all I write. The task is an arduous one, but the consolation of seeing what I say to thee from time to time compensates amply. I very frequently forward thee the newspapers, each of these contain my name.

I dined at the Antiquarian Society and was toasted by Lord Elgin. Thou wilt see it in the papers I sent thee. I would have forwarded thee books and other objects, but, uncertain if thou wouldst not come to Europe as soon as my plans are solidly fixed, I thought not to do so; but I assure thee I cannot at present conceive failure on my part, and may God grant that it may be true. If I can procure, in the whole of two years, three hundred subscribers, we will be rich indeed. God forever bless thee. Remember me kindly to all about thee. Kiss my son and believe me forever,

Thine husband and friend,

JOHN J. AUDUBON[55]

Edinburgh   December [11], 1826   Monday

I had risen, quite as dull as ever this morning, had walked out to the Institution and gone to see Mr. Lizars without shaving or dressing, and probably would have remained in that uncomfortable way the whole of this day had I not found, on my return to my lodgings, a [London] letter from Mrs. Middlemist,[56] containing two precious ones from thee. How I read them! Perhaps never in my life were letters so well welcome, and they were such sweet letters, my Lucy! Thy being quite well, and anxious that I should be so, was all thy LaForest could wish. To hear that on the fourteenth and twenty-seventh of August, the most sickly time [round] about thee, both John and thy sweet self had escaped illness, rendered me quite happy. I kissed thy name and a hundred times blessed it [along] with thee. I felt a new life, and, braced to encounter any difficulties, I rushed out and ran to announce my pleasure to the family Lizars, who take so much interest [in] thee and our dear boys. I determined to answer thee next Saturday.

My love, thou knowest the great interest I have [in] Charles Bonaparte. Whilst [I was] eating my luncheon, Mr. Stokoe[57] whom I had met in Philadelphia with Charles [Bonaparte] came to my lodgings and told me that he should present [to] me his best remembrances. I was highly pleased at this, although

55. Original letter published in *Letters of John James Audubon* (Boston, 1930). This copy is misdated; it should be December 9, which according to the journal was a Sunday. Posted with date: "December 21, 1826."

56. Charles Middlemist, of London, while a guest of his sister Mrs. Robert Percy at Beech Woods, Louisiana, taught John Woodhouse Audubon painting and drawing.

57. John Stokoe, M.D. (1775–1852), was physician to Napoleon on St. Helena in 1817–19. False testimony went against him when he was court-martialed for showing undue deference to the exiled emperor. He was dismissed and became the agent of Joseph Bonaparte. (Paul Frémeaux, *With Napoleon at St. Helena . . . Memoirs of Dr. John Stokoe . . .* [London, 1902], Translated by Edith S. Stokoe.)

thought [it] rather strange that Charles had [not] wrote direct to me.

Now my Lucy, about my new coat. A tailor who had been spoken to and who was supposed to be an expert came to me to assure me that he could not undertake it. A second, still superior in skill, acknowledged his inefficiency also, but at last a third, a German, was shewn into my room [and] undertook this business, and I hope I shall not trouble about it any more.

I dined at thy cousin the Reverend William J. Bakewell's, and dined well. His wife is [a] very amiable woman with three little ones, the last five weeks old, called Robert. A Dr. Gardner who is a clever man was there. I left at 7, having engaged Mr. Lizars [I would] go with him to the Antiquarian Society. There I met many of my friends. Dr. Russell [invited] me to sup with him on the 18th, at half past 9. I saw a gun barrel found on the sands, after the Spanish Armada, [to which it] had belonged, [and which had] tried to invade England and Scotland in 1527. I heard a very curious and interesting account of that event read by Dr. Hibbert, and saw the Scottish antiquities collected by the Society. Six or seven persons were present, to be received [as] Honorary Members. At half past 9 I was again at Mr. Lizars, where I supped, and [I] left at 11.

Now my Lucy, with feelings utterly different from those of last night, I will go to bed and dream of thee. May God preserve thee and bless thee forever. Good night, my sweet wife.

Edinburgh   Dec. 12th, 1826   Tuesday

Immediately after breakfast, i.e., 10 o'clock, I took one of my manuscripts to Dr. Brewster. I found him writing in a large room where several fine pictures hung around. He received me very politely. In a few minutes, having blown my nose and put my neck in a good attitude to suffer my lungs to operate freely, [I] began reading my letter on the manners of the Carrion Crow, *Vultur attratus*. About mid-way my respiration became encumbered. While I rested a moment to breathe, the doctor took this opportunity to say that it was "very good and interesting." I soon resumed and went through, thank God!

He who all his life has been an auctioneer or brought up in

the Green Room of Covent Garden Theater, for instance, with all his knowledge of business and of man, knows nothing about the feelings that agitate me on such an occasion. Thou art probably, sweet wife, the only one that ever analyzed them as I felt them. A man who never looked into an English grammar and very seldom, unfortunately, into a French or a Spanish one, a man who has always felt awkward and very shy in the presence of a stranger, one habituated to ramble alone with his thoughts, always bent on the beauties of *Nature herself*—this man, *me*, in Edinburgh, seated opposite Dr. Brewster, reading one of my puny efforts at describing habits of birds that none but an Almighty Creator can ever know! was so ridiculously absurd, all the while, in my estimation. Also whilst I felt the riveting looks of observation of the learned personage before me, to say that a cold sweat ran over my body much worse than when I dined with the Antiquarians, and to say this to thee, is only to give thee one of the ten thousand tormenting thoughts that crossed my mind whilst my eyes and mouth were reading.

However, a large black dog, not altogether of the Newfoundland breed, came in, caressed his master, and chased my most dismal agitations. I was afterward introduced through a sliding partition into a large drawing-room and presented to the doctor's lady. Again, I repeat it, the well bred people of this country are uncommonly kind to strangers; and I must add, my Lucy, that thy sex possesses here the most astonishing power of rendering *me*, for instance, quite at my ease in an instant!

I left. A proof sheet was to be sent me tomorrow. I was told that I would be introduced to Sir Walter Scott on Monday next at the Royal Academy. Poor me—*far* from Walter Scott I could talk to him. Hundreds of times have I said quite loud in the woods, as I looked on a silvery streamlet, or the sickly swamp, or the noble Ohio, or on mountain tops losing their peaks in grey mist. ["]Oh Walter Scott, where art thou? Wilt thou not come to my country? Wrestle with mankind and stop their increasing ravages on Nature, and describe her now for the sake of future ages. Neither this little stream, this swamp, this grand sheet of flowing water, nor these mountains will be seen in a century hence as I see them now. Nature will have been robbed of her brilliant charms. The currents will be tormented and turned astray from their primitive courses. The hills will be levelled with the swamp, and probably this very swamp have become covered with a fortress of a thousand guns. Scarce a magnolia will Louisiana possess. The timid Deer will exist no more. Fishes will no longer bask on the surface, the eagle scarce ever alight, and these millions of songsters will be drove away by man. Oh Walter Scott, come, come to America! Set thee hence, look upon her, and see her grandeur. Nature still nurses her, cherishes her. But a tear flows in her eye. Her cheek has already changed from the peach blossom to sallow hue. Her frame inclines to emancipation. Her step is arrested. Without thee, Walter Scott, she must die, unknown to the world.["] Such things I often have repeated, but only the echoes have answered me. Walter Scott did not, does not, never will know this, nor my feelings towards him. But if he did—what more have I to say than a world of others who admire him perhaps more than I do because they are more enlightened and better judges of his worth. Ah, Walter Scott, when I am presented to thee my head will droop, my heart will swell, my limbs will tremble, my lips quiver, my tongue congeal. I shall be mute, and perhaps not even my eyes will dare turn towards thee, Great Man. Nevertheless I will feel elevated that I was permitted to touch thy hand, and I shall bless thee within in spite of all the deadness of my physical faculties. Lucy, Walter Scott resides next door [to] Dr. Brewster in Coats Crescent, No. 11.

My exhibition appeared to have been abandoned, and I ordered the newspapers to say that it would close Saturday next. Mr. Skene had advised me to do so. And he also told me this morning that he would present me as a member to the Antiquarian Society at the next meeting.

I expected to have seen Mr. Selby and Sir William Jardine, but neither came to town.

I went to Dr. Welbank, No. 41 Albany Street to dine with William Greg. Dr. Gardner was there. Mrs. Welbank has a red nose, Lucy. Now when I say red I do not mean to say that it is covered with that soft, downy, velvety, light substance that I often have seen and felt on thine, composed of a bloom of pure white, with the thought of vermillion. Not I. I infer that the strongest decoction of the little insect called *Cochenille* would be only a very poor color compared with the truly red-colored nose of the lady here mentioned. This redness extended from the center of the ridge, off and over the cheeks, the forehead, and the chin in rich profusion; and along with the cap, ribbons and dress I thought that nothing so very red had ever met my eye before. She is amiable, however, and so are her daughters, and so, Lucy, never mind the color!

I had promised to accompany young Greg to a Society where he was going to deliver a lecture on the mental powers of the *animal* Creation. I knew what he meant, because I felt it, and would have gone but I was too old for such a Society. And having great anxiety to see Mr. Selby, I made an apology and left at 7. I arrived at Mr. Lizars. He was busily employed sorting Mr. Selby's plates for eleven numbers. I was glad to see how very industrious he was. An appointment called him from home, and I was left with the ladies. But I became very sleepy. I felt a great contentedness this evening. I thought of thee and was so pleased with thy letters that I begged the [ladies'] pardon and have now come to go to bed, where I think I will sleep better than I have done since in Edinburgh. God bless thee, my wife. Good night, my Lucy.

Edinburgh   Dec. 13th, 1826   Wednesday

Although it is late I am not the least drowsy or sleepy this evening. I have spent the greater portion of this day in the company of Mr. Selby, the ornithologist! Probably thou wilt feel alarmed at my being brought in contact with a man of such genius, but really thou needst not. Mr. Selby is a gentleman naturalist, not in the least resembling the venomous tallow chandler of Philadelphia, [George Ord], possessor of three Greek words, seven of Latin—none belonging to what ought to be his usual language—and describer of objects yet unknown to the Almighty. Mr. Selby is not a man that would say at a large meeting of the Wernerian Society that *he* would be damned rather than give me a favorable vote of election. He is not a man who would say that I knew nothing about drawing, nor the habits of birds.

No, my Lucy, Mr. Selby is not an hypocritical fool, I assure thee. In appearance he resembles Nicholas Berthoud very much indeed, is nearly the same complexion, perhaps a little taller, well formed, plain, polite, clever. But measuring such a person I conceive Mr. Selby to be [such as] I would open my heart to freely, as I did to my benevolent friend Mrs. Rathbone. I was more than two hours with him at the Institution. He was greatly pleased with my drawings, wished to understand the style, and he shall—. I dined with him at Mr. Lizars in company [with] Mr. Daniel Lizars. We talked ornithology. I wish I possessed as much knowledge on the scientific part of that study as he does. I read to the whole my letter on the Buzzard, and [Mr. Selby] was again quite pleased, took it with him to read to Sir William Jardine to whose hall he goes tomorrow to return on Monday next.

About 2 o'clock Lord *Clancarty* and Mr. Murray called on me in their carriage, but [as I was] absent a card was left. [This] has cut [out] for me so much more to perform tomorrow, when it would be impolite not to return the visit. Then Dr. Brewster came and brought me the proof of the Carrion Crow [paper]. He read it himself, and we corrected it together. After having thanked me for it, he told me that it was a question if or not I could be made a member of the Royal Academy, for thirty foreigners only were allotted by law, and they already infringed on [this] and had now thirty-three, but that perhaps this might operate favourably for me. This evening when I returned I found a very kind note from [him], thanking me for my manuscript and giving me intelligence that Sir Walter Scott wished to see me and my drawings, and that he would certainly present me to him on Monday next at the Royal Academy.

Mr. Bridges sent me a few lines to invite me to go and dine with him [at] a Mr. Grime's. But Lucy, Mr. Bridges had promised me a notice in the "Scotsman" which, since a week, has never made its appearance, and I think tomorrow about the invitation. Dr. Thompson wrote, desiring that I be so good as to go and see him at "The Meadows," as he [has] been very ill. And here I am, my Lucy, at 2 George Street, come to bless thee and to wish thee a good night.

Edinburgh   Dec. 14th, 1826   Thursday

I paid my visit to Mrs. Murray this forenoon with little trouble. For the lady, although at home, was not visible to poor Audubon, I hastily put my hand in my left side pocket, took my pocketbook, and out of it a beautiful card on which could be read with much ease, "Mr. Audubon, 2 George Street," gave it to the slender youth who stood before me looking at my hair like an ass [at] a fine thistle, and made off quickly to Dr. Brewster. My business was before him in an instant. I wished not to be introduced to Walter Scott in a crowd, and he promised not to do so. That relieved [me].

I went to the College University to see Dr. Andrew Brown, professor of Rhetoric, who had called [in] turn on me. What a bore it is to be obliged to return calls that are merely fashionable. He also wished that I would write for him the manners of Indians, &c., but writing is very irksome and of no benefit to me whatever. I must think of this before I proceed much further in my authorship. Yet my Lucy, whilst I was speaking thus (to myself, recollect, for the doctor was gone), I arrived at home, and sat down immediately to write a long set of memorandums respecting a journey in America for Captain Basil Hall, and I wrote until my head ached.

I saw Mr. and Mrs. Lizars, thou mayest be sure. Not a day passes without. I heard that Mr. Howe, the gentleman editor of the "Courant," with whom Mr. Lizars and I dined this day week had absconded to the West Indies. This did not signify much to me, but his poor sisters, how dreadful it must be to them, left unsupported, and God knows perhaps without talents to support themselves. Mr. Daniel Lizars procured for me two cats to paint, and invited me to dine with him on Friday at 3 o'clock. That suits me to a "T." Very different from to-day, for it was five minutes past 6 when I reached *No.* 8 St. Colm Street where Captain Hall resides. But my sweet wife, I had on beautiful new pantaloons, new splendid Lafayette coat, and over all this my own face to embellish the whole. The company was precisely what the Captain had promised me. Mrs. Hall, the interesting Mrs. Hall, had her beautiful babe in the room, a rosy, fat, little female urchin. [There were also] a Mr. Hunter and daughter, young Hall the advocate, and Mr. Hall's brother-in-law and wife. Dinner was soon announced and I led a lady to it downstairs. We dined in perfect *bon ton*. I was saved the great trouble of asking anyone to drink wine, a thing in my opinion detestable, quite, a completely foppish art that I cannot bear. I wish everyone was permitted to drink as he likes, and when he likes, and not when he dislikes it.

The ladies having left, the American atlas was put on the table. I read my notes, and the Captain followed the course with a pencil from New York to New Orleans, my Lucy, visiting Niagara, St. Louis, Nashville and a hundred other places. We talked of nothing else but a voyage to America, and Mrs. Hall appears quite delighted with the idea.[58] The Captain wishes to write a book; and he spoke of it, Lucy, with as little concern as I would say "Dearest girl, beloved wife, I will draw that duck." He [urged][59] me to write what I have seen and make a little book. How could I make a little book when I have seen enough to make a dozen large? And in such a case, knowing how badly large books go, I will not write at all. At 11 o'clock the Captain accompanied me to the street door. He said that he was glad [to have] formed my acquaintance. I blessed him within for his good attentions, and walked here. And Mrs. Dickie having complimented me [on] my fine clothes, and my day now wrote down, I kiss thee in thought, pray God to bless thee, and wish thee good night.

Edinburgh   Dec. 15th, 1826   Friday

My sweet wife, I have just returned from the theatre where I saw for the first time, "The Beggar's Opera" and "The Lord of the Manor." They were both badly represented, certainly. Only one female did her part and could sing. It was most truly a beggar's opera. I went to the theatre because I dined at Mr. Daniel Lizars's with his wife's brother, and they were all desirous to see

---

58. The MS journal of Margaret Hunter Hall, wife of Basil Hall, is in the U.S. Library of Congress. See Una Pope-Hennessy, ed., *An Aristocratic Journey* (London and New York, 1931); here are given her impressions of the Berthouds and of Audubon's former haunts.

59. The French *engager* can mean "to urge."

a Mr. St. Clair perform. But I really think that Mr. St. C. had drank too much brandy this day.

Mr. Lizars has been extremely kind [about] procuring cats for a picture that I will try to begin tomorrow. He has a great wish to go to America. He has an amiable Scotch lady for a wife and a daughter six years old who [were] better to my [liking] than all the performers at the theatre tonight.

I did little more than saunter about all this day. I thought I would use it to refresh me from my constant round of hard work I had been at since here.

I visited my exhibition twice. Upwards of two hundred people were there. The idea of its closing tomorrow had roused the dormant curiosity of the public. Mr. Lizars procured a subscriber this morning. I saw him but an instant.

Mr. Stokoe called whilst I was absent and left word that he wished to see me, that he heard from a friend of mine, and I supposed it must be Charles Bonaparte. Mr. Stokoe, Lucy, was formerly a physician of eminence in the British service. When Dr. O'Meara was taken away from St. Helena where he acted [as] physician to Napoleon, this gentleman was sent in lieu, but *would not* answer the views of his barbarous government and was also called off and dismissed [from] the service with a trifling pension. But he was already liked by Napoleon, and when he returned he was employed by Joseph Bonaparte, to attend his daughters from Rome to Philadelphia. I saw him during his stay in America with Charles Bonaparte at Dr. Mease's. So pleased was Joseph with his conduct that he is now one of his *pensionnaires* and his general agent in Europe.

I wrote to-day to Mrs. Middlemist at London, and enclosed a six pound sterling note payable to the order of Mr. Charles Middlemist. But not a word from Liverpool yet. Young Greg, whom I met this morning, has not heard either. It becomes quite a matter of surprise to us both. God bless thee, sweet Lucy. Oh a kiss, my love, and good night.

Edinburgh   Dec. 16th, 1826   Saturday

I have really done much to-day, my Lucy. Just read, and see, and judge for thyself.

At half past 9, after securing a good breakfast to [help me face] the intemperate weather (it rained hard all day), I went to Mr. Stokoe's *No.* 42 Lothian Street, in the old town. I passed over the bridge, looked at the curious portion of the town below, passed by two sides of the college regretting that such [a] memorable and valuable monument was quite buried among the antiquated, dismal houses and narrow streets that surround it. Then I rang the bell at Mr. Robertson's lodgings, and in a minute was admitted to Mr. Stokoe's room, where he was yet snug asleep, so that *I* had enjoyed three and a half hours of life during his extra *quantum* of sleep.

He wished to see me, he said, because Bonaparte had wrote to him again and had commissioned him to mention several particular things to me—that if I wrote, this morning, to the Prince of Musignano at London, care of Messrs. Sampson & Baston, &c., &c., &c., &c., my letter would probably reach him there. I was obliged to Mr. Stokoe, invited him to call on me, and left him to snore longer if he chose.

I returned home, and had began my letter to Charles Bonaparte, when I received one from my friend William Rathbone that, I assure thee, was far from being an agreeable one. He feared my work would not succeed, &c., &c., &c. His mother refused me the pleasure of naming a bird after her.[60] The whole made me feel dismal, but yet, not in the least disheartened about my enterprise. Since Napoleon became, from the ranks, an Emperor, why should not Audubon be able to leave the woods of America a while and publish and sell a *book?* No, no. I will try by heavens until each and every hair about me will have dropped from my body, dead grey from old age!!

I composedly finished my letter to Charles, took both to Mr. Lizars and read them both. He was not dismayed either, and promised me that *he* would see that *I* should not be ruined. I took my letter to the office and wished it Godspeed.

Now to my business—I purchased a tame pigeon, killed it, packed up all my wires and hammer, and at 1 o'clock, having a coach, I was put in it with my *position board* to go to the Wer-

60. Folio Plate LXI: *Rathbone's Warbler.* Probably an immature Yellow Warbler, according to ornithologists.

nerian Society at the University. Lady Morton, however, stopped me for a while. She had sent for me from the Institution. Therefore I ordered the coach [to go] there. Mrs. Skene presented me to a small, handsome woman who addressed me in excellent French, shook hands with me cordially, of course praised my drawings, and told me that Lady Douglas had wrote to her from London about me. She asked my [address], took my card, and I, Lucy, bid her farewell, excusing myself on account of the engagement at the Wernerian Society. She hoped to see me at her hall, &c., &c.

I called for Mr. Lizars, Lucy, and we arrived at the college with all my apparatus. We enter the room of the *Wernerian Society of Edinburgh!* What a name it has in America! The room is a plain oblong square, and two tables, one chimney, many long seats, and a chair for the President were all I saw there with the exception of a stuffed Swordfish on the table for examination that day. Several persons were already present. I unrolled my drawing of the Buzzard for them to look at.[61] Professor Jameson came in. I knew the secretary Patrick Neill, Mr. Witham, Professor Russell, &c. P. Neill read my letter on the Buzzard first, not very well. Professor Jameson rose, made quite a eulogy about it, all my work, and lastly about *myself*. I had the Society's thanks.

I then shewed them my manner of putting up my specimens for drawing birds. This they thought inconceivably ingenious. Professor Jameson then rose and offered me as an Honorary Member to the Society. Everyone clapped hand and stamped the floor [as a] mark of approbation. Then the professor desired that the usual law of suffering the election to be tried for months should be infringed upon and that I be elected at the next meeting. The same acclamations took place, and the Society [adjourned]. I promised to read a letter on the habits of the Alligator at the next meeting.[62]

I returned home in the coach again. I had paid 2 / 6 for going and 1 / 6 for returning. Thus money was refunded to the good people of Edinburgh.

---

61. Folio Plate CLI: *Turkey Buzzard. Ornithological Biography*, II, 96.
62. ". . . *Alligator* . . . , " *Edinburgh New Philosophical Journal*, Vol. II (1826–27), 270–80.

I found a note of invitation from George Combe to dine on Monday next and I answered it immediately.

Now Lucy, my dinner at Lady Hunter's. I dressed [in] all my new [finery] again, and at precisely 6 of the evening I took coach for No. 16 Hope Street. I was shewn upstairs and presented to Lady Mary Clark, who knew both Generals Wolf and Montgomery, a most amiable English woman of eighty-two years of age. [After] Lady Arbuthnot, [Lady] Young, Lady *this*, Sir *that*, Lord *the other*, I reached the interesting Mrs. Hall, with whom I was too stupid not to shake hands. A captain of the [military] post was there, Harvey, young Greg, and [others]. I had the pleasure of leading Mrs. Hall to dinner and was seated next her mother Lady Hunter and Lady Clark. We dined. I did not feel so uncomfortable as usual. This nobility is so uncommonly kind, affable and truly well bred. Lady Hunter and Lady Clark quite nursed me. Captain Hall had the other end of the table. Young Greg was next him. I could see Mrs. Hall quite well from my seat. I took frequent opportunities of doing so. Little wine was drank.

About 9 the ladies rose and Captain Hall *attacked me* about America again. Hundreds of questions were put me by all those noble folks, and I had to answer to all. But as all I said was very plain truths I had no difficulty except of feeling choked from time to time through my natural defect of awkward feelings in company. When we reached the ladies, [at] perhaps 11, I was quite delighted to see Mrs. Hall making tea as simply as I have seen thee do it, without any apparent pomp or fudge. Lady Hunter brought a cup of coffee, [and] a little girl one of tea, saying she knew that "American gentlemen like it." The company had not augmented to a great number, and several were still coming. Miss Monro came in. Mrs. Hall, from whom I begged a little music, played sweetly for me on the piano. Card tables were prepared. Some sat at those. Others played at chess. Some examined prints. Some stood talking in groups, others *tête-à-tête*. And I, Lucy, my head supported by my hand, my elbows on a rich table, was listening to the sounds of the piano, my eyes watching the whole for observation's sake, my heart full of thee, sweet girl. How I longed for thee. This very bustle thou art fond of; it suits thy lively spirits and thy acquirements, but not mine.

I prefer more solitude in the woods by thy side, or at home by the fireside, or in [blank] by thy bosom side. Such are the treats for me.

Well, my love, I left at last with young Greg, but left all the rest behind me, all busily enjoying themselves this rainy Sunday morning, for it is now long, long after 12. And I, Lucy, have come to my lodgings to commit *Murder*. Yes, to commit *Murder*. My canvas was ready and the cats Mr. Daniel Lizars had sent me were ready to be killed! I asked the son of Mrs. Dickie[63] to help me. We hung the poor animals in two minutes each, and I put them up in fighting attitudes, ready for painting when daylight would come.

Now either good night or good morning. It is 2 o'clock. God bless thee. I must have my poor bones a little rested. Good night.

Edinburgh Dec. 17th, 1826 Sunday

I painted all day, my Lucy. That is, during all the time I could see, and I was up at 6 this morning, writing by candlelight that I could not put out until 9. Mr. Bridges called on me for a wonder, for the man is now getting scarce. I dined at home on fried oysters and vinegar, and stewed Scotch herrings. Sent an apology to William Greg and went in preference to Mr. Lizars's. Almost fell asleep there, but washed my head, took some coffee, saw some miserable drawings of birds by the renowned Mr. *Pelletier*,[64] and Mr. Lizars came to see my cats that would have been finished this day had I had four hours more of daylight.

God bless thee, good night.

Edinburgh Dec. 18th, 1826 Monday

My painting, of the cats fighting like two devils for a dead squirrel, I finished at 3 o'clock, having been ten hours at it. This is turning out work of the hands as a journeyman carpenter would do.

---

63. J. B. Kidd to Audubon, a letter in Houghton Library, Harvard University, dated "Edinburgh, November 22, 1832":

"Poor Mrs. Dickie [landlady] fell a victim at last to dissipation. Her household furniture was lately sold off by auction, and your spirited picture of the Cats met the same fate. I believe it sold for £4. This will afford you a laugh!"

64. Auguste Pelletier (active 1816–47) delineated many pages for Thomas Horsfeld in his *Zoological Researches in Java* . . . (1821–24).

I received a delightful letter from my friend Thomas Sully dated the 9th of last month, enclosing one to Sir Thomas Lawrence to introduce me. How strange that Dr. Mease should now advise me not to cut my locks when he was so strenuously desirous to have me do so when in Philadelphia.[65] I dressed and took my painting to Mrs. Lizars to shew it her, as it rained all day and [she] had been prevented from coming to see me. I was at George Combe's at 5, where I dined, [and] the conversation was phrenology. George Combe [was] an extremely agreeable companion and [host].

I left them all at 7, called for Mr. Lizars, and went to the Royal Academy meeting. Two of my [Birds] plates were laid on the table. Dr. Brewster and Mr. Allan wished the Society to subscribe for my work, and the committee retired to act on it and other business, no doubt. The meeting was very [large] and no doubt [a] very learned one. Thou knowest I cannot well say, but according to Mr. Ord, *who is learned and an academician*, I suppose each member here [to be] quite as much so, at least, as *Mr. George Ord.*

Sir William Jardine and Mr. Selby arrived, and came in a little before the seating of the whole. The door of the hall was open, and we all marched in and seated ourselves on well dressed hair-cloth seats. The room, rich and beautiful, is a large oblong, lined with brilliant scarlet paper imitation of morocco. The ceiling is divided in large oblong compartments raised from the ground, painted imitation oak. The windows are immensely large, decorated with borders resembling those of the ceiling and had thin green jalousie [blinds]. Two sets of lamps, each composed of six large globular ground glass, hung from above and lighted with gas, gave a light in every part of the room sufficient to read by. The president sat in an immense red morocco arm chair. After the results of the last meeting were read, a professor gave us a long, tedious, laboured lecture on the origin of languages, their formation, &c. It was a very poor mess, I assure thee, although I who am not an academician ought [not] to say

65. Before submitting to a haircut in 1827, Audubon issued a printed, black-edged card mourning the loss of his "*chevulures*," which, two years later, he again let grow long.

so. My friend Ord would have swallowed it whole with delight no doubt, but I could not make either head or tail of it. A few fossil bones of a Mammoth were offered to view, and thank God we raised the siege. Sir Walter Scott sent Dr. Brewster an apology for not coming this evening. I saw the handwriting but not the contents.

Sir W. Jardine and Mr. Selby had brought birds with them from Jardine Hall, and wish to see my style tomorrow, and tomorrow they shall.

Mr. Witham subscribed to my work. But I went away with Mr. Lizars at 10 without knowing the result from the Committee, who sat much later. I had to go to supper at Dr. and Professor Russell's, in Abercromby Place. I entered a set of two large rooms upstairs, well furnished and much exhibiting the owner's wealth. Some pictures were about the walls (in this country a matter of course, it seems). But Lucy, I entered with as much ease as if I had been going to work at home. I walked about and chatted with several of the academicians that had also come, and was rather surprised to find that many men, although great in [their] way, knew nothing of America beyond her laws or the situation of her principal cities.

We went down to supper at about 11. Everything magnificently rich. I looked on each tart and wished myself by thy side. I felt quite worn out, at work since 6 o'clock, either writing or painting, or thinking hard, dining here, going to the Academy. Supping at this house I felt quite sick of the whole, and when the company rose at half past 12 I was glad to leave and run here. In three minutes I will be in bed, and may God bless thee, good night.

Edinburgh   Dec. 19th, 1826   Tuesday

My writing generally takes me fully two hours every morning, and as soon as I finished this day dressed smart to go to breakfast with Sir W. Jardine and Mr. Selby at Barry's Hotel, Prince Street, where I believe they always take their abode when they visit Edinburgh. It was just 9. The morning was pure and beautiful. The sun was about to rise [above] the line of the old town. The horizon was all like burnished gold. The walls of the castle white in the light, and almost black in the shade, along with many of the buildings in the distance, had a surprising effect on my feelings. I thought of the grandeur of the scene, of the power of the great Creator that formed it all, with a thought of the power of imitative man, and was launched in deepest reflections, when a child, bare-footed, ragged, and apparently on the eve of starvation shook my [consciousness] and altered my [concentration]. I gave him a shilling. The poor child, complained so of want that, [had] I dared I would have taken it to Sir William and made it breakfast at the hotel. But thinking how novel such an act might appear, how little I yet knew Sir W., and how strange the world is, I told the child to come with me. I returned home, took all my clothes from my trunk, and having made an honest parcel of all the linen I had that I resolved at the moment never to wear again, I gave it [to] the child. I gave it five more shillings. I gave it my blessings, and I felt——oh, my Lucy, I felt such pleasure—I felt as if God smiled on me!

I soon reached the hotel and was with my new friends in a moment. They had brought Ducks, Hawks and other birds to draw after my fashion. I breakfasted well; the thoughts of the little mendicant gave me an appetite not felt for some days past. We then came to my lodgings. I shewed the ornithologists how I put my specimens, squared my paper, &c., and had them both intently occupied drawing a little squirrel. They called this a lesson. Is it the first, my beloved wife? It was to me like a dream that I should have come from America to teach men so much my superiors. They work very well indeed, although I perceived at once that Mr. Selby was more enthusiastic and therefore worked faster than Sir W. But this one finished closely as he went, so that on the whole it was difficult to give to either the supremacy. They were delighted. Of course Mr. Selby particularly so. He already cut out much work to himself, for, said he, "I will paint all our own quadrupeds in oil for my own house." They remained with me until we could see no more.

I read them my letter [on] the *Carrion Crow*. But Dr. Brewster had altered it so much that I was quite shocked at it. It made me quite sick. He had improved the style and destroyed the matter.

I dined at Major Dodd's, 19 Pitt Street, with a complete set of military gentry—colonels and captains and majors and generals. There, to my great astonishment, I found young Pattison, my companion in the coach from Manchester here. He was Mrs. Dodd's cousin. Major Dodd is the uncle of John Crawford who was the clerk of Nicholas Berthoud [in Kentucky]. I retired early; I did not like the blustery talk of all those warriors.

I went direct to Mr. Lizars, and having found the ladies by themselves I felt as if enjoying a pleasant bath after a day's march of fifty miles. Miss Anna offered to play on the piano for me. I felt delighted at this mark of kind attention, and I compared her at once to my sweet good friend [Miss Hannah Mary R.] of "Green Bank," from whom I fear I never will have an answer to any of my letters.

Mr. Lizars came in with Sir William and Mr. Selby, and announced that I was elected by acclamation a member of the Society of Arts of this city. Thus I possess one title in foreign lands! [On the page preceding this paragraph, J. J. A. wrote, in large transverse writing, "Elected a member of the Society of Arts of this city this day."]

We talked a great deal about ornithology, my work, their work, &c., and at half past 10 we all three came away, linked closely together until we reached their hotel. I am again at my lodgings and find a kind note of thanks from Captain Basil Hall, enclosing one to Captain Campbell of the Royal Navy at Glasgow.

My beloved wife, I feel extremely anxious to set up all night and write a dozen letters, but then if I do I fear I will suffer tomorrow, and so may God bless thee forever! Good night, my love.

Edinburgh   Dec. 20th, 1826   Wednesday

Phrenology was the order of this morning. I reached Brown Square at 9, and breakfasted most heartily on mutton, ham and good coffee with George Combe. The cloth was left and we proceeded upstairs into his *sancto sanctorum*. A beautiful silver box containing the instruments for measuring was opened. This was a neat present from the ladies who have attended his lectures these last two years.

I was seated facing the light. Dr. Combe acted as secretary; and George Combe, thrusting his fingers about my hair, began to search for miraculous bumps! My skull was measured accurately as I measure the bill or legs of a new individual, and all was duly noted by the scribe. Then with most exquisite sense of touch each protuberance was found, as numbered by phrenologists, and also put down according to their respective sizes. I was astounded when they both said that I must be a strong and constant lover and affectionate father, that I had great veneration for high, talented men, that I would have made a brave general, that music was not to be compared with painting in me, that I was extraordinarily generous, &c. Now I know all [these] to be facts, and how they discovered them to be so is quite a puzzle to me. I was made to sign my name and residence on one copy whilst the other was handed to me. I was asked to have leave to expose this to the first lecture. I consented, and came off full of wonder at the singularity of this science. George Combe gave me a note for a Mr. Simpson the advocate, and I was accompanied to the court by a clerk in search of this gentleman. I saw Mr. Simpson and a hundred other advocates strutting with their raven gowns and powdered, curled wigs. Mr. S. was to introduce me to *Francis Jeffrey*, but he was not in court, and I pushed off.

I called on friend Bridges. He was preparing a *"puff" for me*. Mr. Lizars took me to see Mr. Greville,[66] to [learn] from him the scientific botanical names of some plants. This gentleman is tall and handsome, had a green silk night cap on, and has been unfortunately confined to his house for some time, being asthmatic. He looked at the drawings and searched for names, but I discovered at once that he studied more in his closet than in the woods. He gave me the names wanted, invited us to breakfast on Tuesday next, and we bid him good morning at 3 o'clock A.M.

Neither Sir [William] nor Mr. Selby came to finish their drawings, but Mr. Selby sent me three most beautiful pheasants, and tomorrow I begin a large painting of these Birds attacked by a Fox, for the exhibition in London next March.[67] I received a po-

66. Robert Kaye Greville (1794–1866) wrote on Edinburgh plants.
67. *Suave Qui Peut*, an oil on canvas now owned by the Racquet & Tennis Club, New York City, was later copied by sons Victor Gifford Audubon and John Woodhouse Audubon. The unsigned copy was presented to, and catalogued by, the American Museum of Natural History as the work of Audubon.

lite note from the Earl of Morton to go and spend a day and a night at his hall. His carriage will call for me on Wednesday next, one week hence.

Then, my Lucy, I wrote an apology to young Greg and went to dinner to Mr. Lizars, where I had a most agreeable time of it. The company was made up of bankers, all lively fine fellows. I was between the two sisters, and we all drank thy health, my sweet wife. At 9 I felt an itching to write letters, and I came here for the purpose of setting up all night, but I find I cannot. I am wearied out. I have written two, one to Nicholas Berthoud and the other to Thomas Sully, and now I will go and rest a while. God forever bless thee, good night.

EDINBURGH, December 20th, 1826

MY DEAR NICHOLAS,[68]

That you should not answer my letters is rather strange and most painful to me.

I have been here rather more than a month; my reception far surpasses that of Liverpool. The Royal Institution not only offered me their hall gratis, but the newspapers, the people, the nobility have all greeted me with highest support. My work is now under publication. My subscribers are all of the first rank and include many of the first universities. Were you to see one of my days spent in Edinburgh you would rub your eyes and doubt the astonishing facts connected with my progress through the literary world. Please read the [Edinburgh] Philosophical Journal and others published here. See the different newspapers and think of poor Audubon being elected Honorary Member of the highest Society of science by acclamation, and of hand. Think of Lords sending their carriages to Mr. A. with best compliments, &c., &c., to go to spend days and nights at their hall to see the wonderful locks that hang about his shoulders in full abundance. Think of his portrait being painted to be engraved—of the phrenologists who take casts of a head for resembling Raphael. Think of the same personage selling a Wild Turkey painted in oil for

68. Brother-in-law Nicholas Berthoud, of Shippingport, Kentucky.

Sauve Qui Peut. *Oil on canvas, 57 × 93 inches. Begun in 1826 with a fox;*
finished in London in 1827 with a spaniel dog.

fifty guineas, and you will have a very moderate idea of my success in Edinburgh.

I have wrote to you often, for I am no more lazy now than I was at Shippingport. I regularly do with four hours sleep, and I hope yet to see my family derive the benefit of my labours. Why does not Victor write to me regularly every fortnight? I have heard but twice from Lucy since my landing. Yet letters from De Witt Clinton and Thomas Sully have reached me in answer in forty-two days here. I wish you would send me copies of your daily journal of the weather and water and all kinds of observation, and suffer me to present you, as a corresponding member, to the Philosophical Society of Edinburgh. Make Victor draw, at all leisure hours, anything from Nature, and keep all his work, no matter how indifferent in his eyes or yours.

Collect fossils from the Falls [of the Ohio] for me or for you. I will send you a copy of my first Number and a Prospectus in January. Curious birds preserved in spirits would be valuable to me or to you. Send a copy of this to Lucy. Kiss your lovely children for me. Tell your sweet Eliza that her brother still hopes to see her again. Urge Victor on to business, and reading, music, &c., and believe me forever your friend,

J. J. A.

EDINBURGH, December 20th, 1826

MY DEAR MR. SULLY,[69]

It is quite impossible for me to say how truly delighted I was two days ago at receiving your kind letter of the ninth of November, enclosing the one for Sir Thomas Lawrence dated twentieth of same month.

It is in my present extraordinary situation quite an easy matter to procure letters of introduction not only to the President of the Royal Academy but I believe to any person I wish to see during my present wonderful tour of Europe; but it was the one I now possess from T. Sully I longed for,

---

69. Thomas Sully, portrait painter, whom Audubon met in Philadelphia in 1824.

and I assure you it is the only one I shall present to Sir Thomas Lawrence.

My work is positively now under fair way of publication in all the splendour I have so long wished to see it come forth. I have here valuable friends who have and do take a most earnest interest in its progress, and, I may safely add, my welfare. Edinburgh, this Queen of cities, has greeted me with a welcome far superior to that experienced in Liverpool. The Royal Institution presented me with their magnificent hall to exhibit my drawings. The newspapers, the people, the nobility, all have paid me homage due only to very superior men; and to tell you that I feel greatly elevated is only a slender way of expressing the grateful feelings that swell my heart towards all those good persons with whom I am daily in contact. I am thrown into a vortex of business that I never conceived I could manage and also into a round of most agreeable society. The professors of all classes are pleased to call me a valuable man to society. I am courted by the nobility, and if I do not become a proud fool (and God forbid) I cannot help but succeed.

Think of my painting oil pieces of eleven Wild Turkies estimated at 100 guineas, finished in ten days work. Conceive what my feelings must be when the famous professor Jameson is pleased to request that I should write and furnish the Philosophical Journal with a letter on the habits of some birds; of my portrait being taken to be engraved at their request; of being elected member of different societies by acclamation and *of hand*. What will my friend Ord say to all this when he sees those journals, the papers, and hears of all those wonderful events? Yet with all this, believe me, a dear thought never leaves me a moment. I think constantly of my beloved America and of my friends there—of you most especially who have honored me so much, and in whose company I have felt such delight.

I am truly glad that your amiable daughter [Jane?] has met with *half her match*. May God bless her and her good husband. Why did you not say a word about your daughter, *the artist*, my sweet pupil? [Blanche?] Where is your eldest son now? Believe me, besides hearing that *you* are doing so well, I long to know that each individual of your family is likely to prosper. Present my respects to Dr. Mease. My locks are still flowing, and, I am happy to say, are by no means disagreeable to the eyes of the *learned public* who in all countries pay but little regard to outward appearances. Not even my regular upright collar stops me from being introduced to Walter Scott. As soon as my first Number will be finished, say one month hence, I will forward you a copy. I have to beg of you that you will take the trouble of presenting it in my name to that [Philadelphia] institution who thought me unworthy being one of their members. There is no malice in my heart, and I wish no return from them. I am determined now never to be a Philadelphia member of *that*. Merely let them know (if you please) that humble talents ought to be fostered first in one's own country. I take the privilege of forwarding you from time to time newspapers that I hope cost you nothing, and I shall also write to you from different parts. I wish you would write to my dear wife and have my letters copied. At this distance she cannot write to me too often. She lives at St. Francisville, Bayou Sara, Louisiana. I gave to-day a lesson of drawing birds to the two famous ornithologists of England, Sir William Jardine and Mr. Selby.

May God bless you and yours, and grant you the happiness you deserve. Write to me, pray, I beg, always directed to the care of Messrs. Rathbone Brothers & Co., Liverpool, and believe me for life your friend,

J. J. A.

Remember me to Mr. R. [Reuben] Haines and Titian Peale, &c., and kiss all your children for my sake. I may yet listen to their voices and to your sweet flute.[70]

Edinburgh   Dec. 21st, 1826   Thursday

Weather clear with sharp frost. I thought as I saw it what a

---

70. Reuben Haines was a member of the Academy of Natural Sciences, Philadelphia. Titian Ramsay Peale (1799–1885) who illustrated part of *American Ornithology*, by Charles Lucien Bonaparte, belonged to the famous family of "painting Peales."

number of wild Ducks I could have brought down from their wings with a little powder and plenty shot. But I have other fish to fry. I put up a beautiful male pheasant in attitude, and outlined it on coarse grey paper to *pounce it* in its proper situation on my large canvas. I had Sir William J. and P. Selby, Esqr., drawing in my room a good portion of the day. Mr. Selby finished his piece, but not Sir William. My time being now so taken up, and daylight so short, I engaged Mr. D. Lizars's brother-in-law to copy letters for me, and he also sat in my room at work. Mrs. Lizars and her sister paid me a visit, found us all engaged, and brought a piece of linen for me to look at, and which I took to make me more shirts, for I am frequently obliged to dress twice a day, the greatest bore imaginable to me. The piece cost five pounds.

Dr. Charles Fox came to see me. Poor fellow looked indeed as if he had been in the grave.

Mr. Simpson the advocate who lives at 33 Northumberland Street came twice to see me and invited me and Mr. Selby to a phrenological supper.

Lucy, the morning passed and no canvas came for me. I looked at the beautiful bird before me, admired it much, thou knows. Longed to have him under my pencil and waited most impatiently hour after hour. I went to Mr. Swinton, the seller. It was all vain promises, and I did not receive [the canvas] until half past 8 this evening. So I had lost a most precious day. That is a vast deal in a man's life glass. However, I wrote to William Rathbone, Mrs. Greg, and John Chorley, and when a quarter before 9 had come and brought Mr. Selby we both went to the advocate Simpson. It was really a phrenological party. Nothing else was talked of. Jeffrey's letters and Combe's answers [discussed]. Mr. Simpson compared Selby's head and mine. I had more coloring, he said. But when we had all been seated at table, digesting the long supper, I was attacked on the formation of colors at such a round rate that I let loose and proved to the whole set that if they knew the value of protuberances I did that of prismatic composition.[71] They were not adequate to what they wished to

71. Yet Audubon felt the need of lessons in perspective and background painting while in Edinburgh, such as no bona fide pupil of J.-L. David should at this stage

seek, and I would willingly have abandoned the field, for I was very sleepy. I saw there a brother of David Bridges and his lady, a nice fat bit of English composition. This is quite another sort of pair. At last 12 o'clock came, the company rose in a [body] and proceeded to the street, where I was glad to feel the rarified, pure, frosty air of this fine, starlight night. Mr. Selby and I walked off together. I think him, my Lucy, one of those rare characters that come on the earth only at very distant periods, to prove to mankind how good some of our species may still be found. He invited me in the kindest manner to go to his house, and begged that I would write to him whenever I wanted Pheasants. We parted at my door. I pressed his hand with great pleasure and bid him well and happy from my heart.

Now I have come to my lodgings again, and will go to bed, for the poor girl servant who waits for me at night and will have to rise in four hours to make the fire for me, is not quite so *tough* as I am, and cannot do with as little sleep. Dearest wife, God bless thee. Good night.

Edinburgh   Dec. 22, 1826   Friday

I painted a good portion to-day, although it was quite dark before 3 o'clock this afternoon. Oh how I long for the fair days of May, June, July and August.

My room, this day, was a complete levee. I really thought several times that it was a burlesque kind of quizzing [of] me. However, I received every one as politely as I could, having my nightcap, nightshirt, slippers, and no coat on. I walked with pallet and brushes in my hand, and conducted each in his turn to the door. Thus was I disturbed [at] my work twenty-five times. I shaved and dressed in a hurry as soon as my lights had given way, to escape any more. I was, however, extremely glad to see some of them, and indeed all, for no matter how humble I am I like such attentions as well, I daresay, as if I deserved them more. Sometimes I hope that I deserve what I receive; but again the instant that difficulty arises in my composition, or coloring,

---

have required. Defenders of the David tuition myth are referred to a rare letter recently acquired by Princeton University Library, written during Audubon's 1805–1806 brief return to France. It reveals his confinement to the family villa in Couëron, lest he be conscripted. Rarely did he slip out to hunt and draw.

or finishing, I droop at once and fear that the good people of Edinburgh are not quite awake.

Mr. Stokes came in early to see if I had received a letter from Charles Bonaparte, and I have, my Lucy, a very kind, friendly letter dated London. I wrote this morning to Mrs. Greg, John Chorley and Nicholas Berthoud, and added much to my letter to thee.[72] My young friend Mr. Hamilton was copying for me all day. I supped with Sir William Jardine, Mr. Lizars, and a Mr. Mole, uncle to Sir William, at Barry's Hotel, on oysters cooked and raw. Had much talk about fishes and fishing, for we were all sportsmen. I left at 12 this evening, anxious to rest well, for tomorrow I must paint away. God bless thee. Good night, dearest friend.

EDINBURGH, December 22d, 1826

[To Lucy]:

Thou hast here a copy of my last because it contains much of all sorts, but my sweet friend the very morning that I forwarded thee the original I had the pleasure of receiving two kind letters from thee, forwarded to me here from London by Mrs. Middlemist. I need not say how gratified I was and how happy I felt at knowing thee quite well and our dear sons also. I sincerely hope thou wilt continue thy rides on horseback every fair day and walk a great deal besides in the rich magnolia woods about thee. I never felt so much in my life the want of a glance at our forests as I now do. Could I see thee but a moment there, hear the mellow mock bird, or the wood thrush to me always so pleasing, and be able to give thee a kiss of affection—ah my wife, how happy I would again be.

Since I received thy letters (they are dated August 9th and 27th), I have felt delighted at the idea of thy probably coming to Europe some time next summer. But my Lucy, we must not hurry too much. I wish to sound all well, and be perfectly assured of the general ultimate success of my work. The engravings are proceeding apace and are thought beautiful. My exhibition closes here on Saturday next, and

72. Identical letter appears in a compilation by Howard Corning, ed., *Letters of John James Audubon*, 1826–40, 2 vols. (Cambridge, 1930).

I will remove it either to Glasgow or to New Castle-on-Tyne, but this place will continue my residence until my first Number is quite finished.

I received a kind letter from Sully a few days ago, dated only twenty-nine days back, enclosing one to Sir Thomas Lawrence. I continue to be well, with everybody for an astonishing round of company. I will have copied here for thee some of the invitations I received. It will give thee an idea of the circles I move in. I was elected a member of the Society of Arts and Sciences a few days ago by acclamation. And when I was presented to the Wernerian Society (this is the Natural History Society) for an Honorary Membership I had the same acclamation and no doubt I will be elected next meeting, for the President told the committee that on such occasions the usual time wanted for consideration must be laid aside. I have the honor of being at the Royal Academy meeting. The halls are beautiful indeed. The Great British ornithologists, Sir William Jardine and Mr. Selby, have spent two days with me drawing in my style. I am very much pleased with both and would have gone to Jardine Hall to spend a week but I am really too much engaged at present.

I have forwarded Mrs. Middlemist the thirty dollars of Charles [Middlemist] in a post note payable to her. I wish I could see John to tell him to draw all he can for his and my sake. I expect to hear from thee now very shortly through Messrs. Rathbone at Liverpool, to whom [you should] always direct [letters]. I want to know how thou art pleased with thy watch, &c., and thy Matlock spars. I hope thou wilt like the book I now send thee. It will give thee an idea of the beauty of Edinburgh. Do not forget to collect acorns of *all sorts* and all other kinds of seeds and forward them to Mrs. Rathbone at Liverpool. Send a great quantity, as all the noblemen are pleased to have some, and I will have them sent here. I send thee very frequently parcels of newspapers. They all contain my name somewhere and it will be a pleasure for thee to read them. I wish thou wouldst write every week and enter in any little detail thou likest. Tell friend Bourgeat that I will send him a pair of the best English hounds when I go to Liverpool again in about six weeks. I think John might use my gun, if he would be careful of it and keep it particularly clean. Does he play on the piano now? Send me some of his drawings. I wish to see what Charles Middlemist has made of him; I feared myself that he might not be quite as good a teacher as I wished, and for his own sake hoped he might be.

I will now again bid thee farewell. Do take especial care of thy sweet self for my sake. Thy health is uniformly drank wherever I go, and at Mr. Lizars's it is expressed thus, *"Mr. Audubon, let us drink [to] Mrs. Audubon and the bairns!"*

I have not dined at my lodgings for upwards of a fortnight one single day. My journal would amuse thee. I send thee herein the results of Mr. [George] Combe, the phrenologist, about my skull. It proves to resemble that of Raphael very much, and I have been astounded at the merit of the science through some particular observations that the gentleman and others have made about my propensities and faculties. Mr. Selby will take me to the Duke of Northumberland when I call on him at his house on my way to New Castle. He will, Mr. Selby says, subscribe to my work. The number allotted to *Scotland is now filled,* and I bid fair to have more, but I will take nothing for granted until [it is] within my grasp. I will exert myself much, depend on it, to insure success, and may God grant that I will reach it. I want thee to send me by first opportunity as much of thy hair as will make me a cord for my watch. The silver one that I wear now measures three feet and is about the size of that. [Here Audubon drew a length of braided lines.] But a mere thread in thickness will content me much, as I wear a guard besides. I have come to fine dressing again—silk stockings and pumps; shave every morning; and sometimes dress twice a day. My hairs are now as beautifully long and curly as ever, and, I assure thee, do as much for me as my talent for painting. I began this morning a painting in oil of fourteen Pheasants on the wing, attacked by a fox, that I wish to finish for the exhibition of the Royal Academy at London by March, when I will be there myself. Read this to Johnny for my sake more than once.

["Copies of invitations" were entered in the letter that J. J. A. mailed to Lucy, but not in the journal; they and a postscript may be seen in *Letters of John James Audubon, 1826–40* (Cambridge, 1930), I, 16, 17.]

Edinburgh   Dec. 23rd, 1826   Saturday

I had to grind my own colors this morning. I detested that. It makes me hot and fretful, and, I am convinced, has a bad effect on the mind of any artist. However, I worked close, but the day's are shockingly short. I cannot see before half past 9, and I am forced to stop at 3. However, this is the shortest day of the almanac, and I will be patient.

My exhibition[73] closed this day, and here follows the account:

		Cash received	Catalogues (1,101)
November	14th	£ 3.18	17.6
	15	3.3	12.6
	16	2.6	9.6
	17	3.12	16.6
	18	4.17	15.6
	20	6.3	17.6
	21	5.12	13.6
	22	5.5	15.6
	23	3.3	6.6
	24	4.4	11.6
	25	8."	18.6
	27	4.16	15.6
	28	2.2	7.6
	29	1.18	5.6
	30	6.5	14.6
Decem^r	1	1.1	4.6
	2	13.2	1.12.6
	4	7.7	17.6
	5	4.14	6.6
	6	2.4	2.6
	7	1.0	4.6

---

73. Inclement weather limited attendance to thirty persons.

8	1.10	2.6
9	5.10	4.6
11	2.3	11.6
12	2.5	2.6
13	2.8	3.6
14	4.5	6.6
15	8.2	5.6
16	8.8	1.5.6
18	1.3	19.6
19	2.12	3.6
20	1.8	2.6
21	4.11	8.6
22	2.19	4.6
23	11.2	9.6
	£152.18.0	£20.12.6
	20.12.6	
	£173.10.6	

$770

Thou seest here the amount I am indebted to the good people of this city, a returning memorandum of my past labours. As soon as the amount of expenses has come in I will give it thee. It is heavy, I know, although I paid nothing for the hall. The door-keepers, card bearers and sweepers of the streets expenses during the exhibition has been just 30 pounds [sterling].

Good night. God forever bless thee.

December 24 and 25

The 24th and 25th I remained closely at my work, painting.

On the 24th my drawings were all taken down and my paintings also. I wrote to the president and members of the Royal Institution and presented them my large painting of the Wild Turkeys, and I may say I looked on this as giving them *Something* to remember me by, as I could most certainly have had 100 guineas for it from Gally, the picture dealer. But I was glad to return the politeness of such a body in a handsome manner, and regretted only that the painting given to the Royal Liverpool Institution was so inferior.

I purchased, this morning, a brooch for thee, my Lucy, that I send thee as a Christmas gift. If in return my Christmas gift had been a kiss from thy sweet lips, how happy I would be at this moment. My confinement at work brought a very heavy, sad headache. I felt quite ill all the night, but to-day I went to Mr. D. Lizars's to dine and feel much better now. I get up several hours before daylight to write for Captain Basil Hall, and am glad it is over.[74] I paid seven guineas for the piece I send thee. God bless thee.

Edinburgh   Dec. 26th, 1826   Tuesday

My painting all day so assiduously and my mind agitated by thousands [of] ideas [concerning] my future prospect has brought on me every evening a weariness that I could not surmount or command. This is, I think, the first instance in my whole life when, if needed, I could not rouse myself from sleepiness and jump up, shake myself, and be ready for action in an instant. But it is now as I tell thee, and I will illustrate the fact with this evening's example.

I left work and my room immediately after my dinner.

Captain Hall and his brother had called on me to thank me for my note to him and to invite me to dine with him next Thursday. I had also received a letter from the Secretary of the Royal Institution, acknowledging receipt of mine of yesterday to this body, and thanking me in good words for my painting of the "Wild Turkeys." Then my Lucy, as I said before, I left my room about 5, for I felt a necessity to breathe air from out of the house. The gas lights were dimly shining through the thick, warm, moist fog that filled the atmosphere. I could scarce discern the lights in the old tower, and persons within thirty yards were quite hid from my view. I reached the bustling Princes Street and soon was at No. 3 James Square, where I found Lady No. 1 [Mrs. W. H. Lizars] and her sister Anna busily engaged, cutting out the piece of linen for which I paid five pounds this morning to make me some shirts. Here, after welcomes and

---

74. Where are these letters? Hall went insane in 1844 after completing a novel, *Patchwork* (1841). The American Philosophical Society has a letter written by Audubon for use by Hall.

how-do-you-do's are exchanged, and hands are pressed, I set myself in a large, well-stuffed, black arm chair, lay one hand on each side of me, lean my back to touch the reclining back of the seat, push my feet forward, and, being perfectly at my ease, I ask for some music as I would ask for it of thee.

Bye and bye tea comes. I take coffee. We chat, to supper, eat, drink thy health, and I come to my bed at half past 10. This is all very well and very agreeable, is it not, wife?

"Indeed, my LaForest, it is, and I am glad to hear of this."

But Lucy, this evening I went to sleep, in spite of all my best endeavors, fifteen minutes after my arrival. I took some hot coffee, but it would not answer. The charm was irresistible, and at last I only could beg pardon and make my escape with intention to go to bed at once and rest well, walking, restored and alive again. But when I [reached] home, the drowsiness came on anew. Recollecting that Mr. D. Lizars was to call at 8, I threw myself on the sofa, rolled my cloak about me, and went to sleep giving orders to be awakened at 8. This [hour] came, but no Mr. Lizars. At 9 I went to bed, positively. I was just praying to our God for thy safety and thy happiness when Mr. L. came. I jumped up, dressed at once, and in three minutes was with him. He was holding a candle up to my work, looking at a Pheasant. He said his lady was at the shop. I begged he would go for her. He returns with her and her brother. Things are ordered. We are eating, drinking and chatting again, all very merry. It is 12 o'clock. They are gone, and so is my sleepy fit. Yet I will go now to rest, and rest late in the morning. For was I to go to sleep at the Earl of Morton's tomorrow, what would they say of me? But that would be quite impossible, for I will feel abashed and awkward, and my blood will be all alive, I have no doubt. Sweet wife, God bless thee, good night.

Dalmahoy, the Seat of the Earl of Morton, eight miles from Edinburgh   Dec. 27th, 1826 [75]

There's data for thee, sweet wife! Thy husband has leaped from America to Liverpool, and from thence to Manchester,

---

75. The Audubon Memorial Museum, Henderson, Kentucky, has a Tyler Collection letter of the same date.

Bakewell, Matlock, Buxton, twenty other places besides, then to Edinburgh, and now is seated at a sweet little table in the *yellow bed chamber* at the Earl of Morton![76] But in this fine room, I am quite alone, *I believe,* and will write for thy sake and that of our dear sons regular accounts of this day.

After my breakfast, not anxious to begin another Pheasant, I called on Mr. Lizars, who was much engaged. I saw the ladies and bid them farewell for one day. The morning being *longer than usual,* I called on the Messrs. Syme the painters. One was unwell, and, the other being absent, my visiting extended only to my walks to their doors, and I returned to my lodgings to make ready to pay a visit to an Earl and some Countesses. All this did not go on without thinking of thee a good deal. Indeed I thought of other people besides thee, my good friend. My good friend Mrs. Rathbone was about me in thought, and so [were] her dear Hannah, the "Quarry Bank" family and the Dockrays, [who] all "visited" me whilst my razor was smoothing my chin— but I thought of thee most!

I had to pack a box for thee containing the views of Edinburgh, the brooch, some curious lamps Mr. D. Lizars sent thee, the travels of Captain Hall [and] all the different cards I had received here, with as many newspapers as possible. I did all this assisted by Daniel Lizars and his brother, and I wished it a good voyage to thee. We three had a luncheon, some fried oysters, some drink and some cake, and were still all at work, thus when Mrs. Dickie opened my room door and said, "Lord Morton's carriage, Sir," I was ready. We shook hands all around. My *porte-feuille* was taken off, and I, after having washed my hands and walked downstairs, touched lightly the arm of the waiter who opened the carriage door, and jumped on a large, soft seat lined with purple morocco. The carriage moved. Yes, my Lucy, the carriage moved, but upon my word I never moved in such before. The ship that under easy sail glides slowly on an even sea has more fatiguing motion, and had I not been fully persuaded (being awake) that it was a carriage I was in, I would have thought

---

76. Earl of Morton. See *Burke's Peerage* for this descendant of John, the first lord of Maxwell, who was the son of the third Earl of Morton (*Dictionary of National Biography,* V, 1214–1217).

myself gently wafted through the air in a swinging hammock. It passed the castle, through Charlotte Square, through Coats Crescent, and along the Glasgow road for eight miles, so swiftly, too, that my watch had just changed the hour to another when the porter pushed open the gates of Dalmahoy. I began thinking of my meeting a man who had been great chamberlain to the late Queen Charlotte, for I was not so terrified at meeting the Countess. The day I had seen her at the Royal Institution her eyes spoke softness and amiability of disposition, but the Chamberlain I could not help dreading to encounter.

"And why, my dear? I would not."

No, thou wouldst not because thou art a well bred woman. But I do because I am a fool.

All this did not stop the carriage from proceeding smoothly round a great circle. Neither did it stop my eyes from seeing a large, square half-gothic building with two turrets in front, ornamented with great lions and all the signs of heraldry belonging to the great Lord within. The carriage stopped, opened, and a bell rung. A man in livery [drew aside] a large door, and I walked in, giving my hat and gloves and my American stick (that, bye the bye, never leaves me when I do not leave it myself). I was led through this hall and upstairs, my name was given, and I entered the drawing-room of the Earl of Morton! The Countess ran to me, then returned to her Lord and presented *him* to me, my Lucy. Yes, him to me! I look. I stare. I am astounded that I have not before me another Richard Coeur de Lion. For I had positively expected nothing less. I had formed an idea that a chamberlain and an earl must be a man able to cleave worlds in two—oh my imagination, where dost thou lead me? Why my dear wife, I saw a small slender man, tottering on his feet, weaker than a new hatched Partridge, welcoming me to his hall with tears almost trickling from his eyes. He held one of my hands and attempted speaking, but this was difficult. His good lady was rubbing his other hand. I saw at a glance his situation, and begged he would be seated. This he [did], and I was relieved.

The Countess of Boulcar, [his mother-in-law,] was introduced also, and I at last seated my body on a sofa that I thought would swallow me up as the down swelled around me. I [began] looking fearlessly around. What a room! Full sixty feet by thirty, all hung with immense paintings on a rich purple ground. All was purple about me. The tables were covered with various books and instruments. The Queen of England faced Mary of Scots. A chamberlain was here, a duke there, and in another place I could see a beautiful head of Rembrandt, some Claude Lorrain landscapes. Van Dyck had not been forgotten and Titian gave a luster to the whole. I rose to take a closer view. The Countess explained all to me. But conceive my surprise when, on looking through the middle window, I saw [on] the horizon an object that was no less attractive than anything about me, the castle and city of Edinburgh, a complete miniature eight miles off, making its way to the mind through avenues, and over pieces of water, and fields innumerable!

Now my Lucy, I am told that luncheon is ready. "What," said I to myself, "luncheon again?" I am sure that if my friends complain of not eating much they must, in any event, allow that I eat sufficiently often. Well, to luncheon we go. The Countess of Boulcar rolls Lord Morton in his castored chair, and I give my arm to Lady Morton. We cross a large antechamber and enter a dining-room, also quite rich in paintings, and also in its present sumptuous repast. I eat again and drink again, and in the middle of all this, three gentlemen make their appearance. They were visitors at the hall also—Mr. Hay, Mr. Ramsay, and a young clergyman. This luncheon over, we had to see my drawings.[77]

The Lord was rolled into a good situation for light, and I again unbuckled the great *Book of Nature*. I am not going to repeat praises again, my Lucy, for I am quite sickened at the sound. The drawings seen, we adjourned to the drawing-room again. The Countess desired to receive a lesson in drawing from thy husband tomorrow, and I acquiesced with great satisfaction. The conversation became general. I gradually felt at ease and all went smoothly. The Countess is about *thy age*. Thus I save you

---

77. W. A. Hay, the *Dalmahoy* librarian and antiquarian, was the brother of Robert Williams Hay, Colonial Secretary to India. Audubon may have meant John Ramsay McCulloch (1789–1864), professor of economics; statistician.

both from being called old. You are both quite young enough to delight a husband. She is not what men call handsome, or beautiful, but she is good looking, has a good form, fine clear fresh skin, and eyes that I dared not meet, Lucy, they were so dark! Her conversation is frequently interrupted by a natural impediment, but it gives more spirit to all she says, and she is certainly a very superior woman. As ladies are sometimes concerned about another's dress, I will tell thee the Countess was then enrobed in a rich crimson gown. Her mother was dressed in black satin.

Six o'clock in the afternoon came, Lucy. I had taken a short walk about the grounds with the gentlemen and returned to this hall when I was asked by the Countess if I wished to see my room. I knew that this meant that it was now necessary to dress for dinner, and I followed a gentleman waiter who, on hearing his mistress say "the yellow room," pointed the way. A good fire of wood lighted, my linen was warming in front of it. My shoes had been unpacked as well as my night apparel, and all was snug and delightfully comfortable. I begged to be left alone, and I looked around me. All was truly yellow in this yellow chamber. It might well have been a parlour in some other countries. The bed for me this night was ornamented with crowns, and was large enough to receive four of my size. A sofa was at the foot of it, large arm chairs on each side the fire, a table containing a writing desk with all ready, and everywhere [everything] that I never use. My toilet was soon over, thou knowest, for in my opinion it is a vile loss of time, that spent in arranging a cravat with as much care as a hangman does his knot. And I was down again in a moment.

"Ring the bell, Mr. Hay," said the Countess, who was dressed superbly in white satin and crimson turban. A waiter came and dinner was ordered. It was now 7, and I again led the Countess under my arm, and the Earl was again rolled in his chair. I sat by the mother's side. Mr. Hay officiated as master, and I dined again for the third time this day. The waiters, Lucy, were all powdered and dressed in rich red clothes, all liveried except one who had black clothes on and who gave plates with a neat napkin and positively without touching them. After one hour the ladies and the Lord retired, and we the gentlemen visitors set to talk and drink wine. We talked entirely of antiquities. Mr. Hay is a deeply learned man, an original besides, and quite interesting in his manners.

At 10 we joined the Countess again, but the Earl had retired for the night. After we looked at the signatures of the kings of old, of Mary, Henry, James, &c., &c., and examined a cabinet of ancient coins, and 12 o'clock came, the ladies bid us good night by shaking all our hands. We were then left alone. And to settle the coffee that we had drank, we now drank Madeira wine. What a life—oh my Lucy I could not stand this! I prefer my primitive woods after all. But as I hope this life will enable me to enjoy them at a future period I bear it patiently. I left the gentlemen at their cakes and wine, and I have come to my yellow chamber. Lucy, I have prayed my God on my knees to grant thee well, and I will go to bed. Sweet friend, good night.

————daylight came, my Lucy, and I got up, for a bed, when [one is] awake and without a wife, is very stupid. I opened all the yellow curtains and visited my room by [daylight]. Three doors besides that for entrance were in sight, and the [wish to] seek new adventures prompted me to open one. Singular! A neat little closet lighted by a high narrow slip of a gothic window was before me, and in a moment I discovered its purpose. It was a bathing room. Large porcelain tables, jars of water, drying linens, and all else wanted, lay about. But the color of the whole was quite changed. The carpet was variegated with crimson, and all appeared alike warm. Beautifully contrived. I saw, but touched nothing. I was clean enough. The door opposite led me into another closet *differently intended*, and I merely saw its use. I was going to unlatch the third, yet unknown, when, thinking a moment, I made up my mind not to intrude, for I recollected that it led back towards the interior of the hall.

My chimney piece was decorated with choice shells. I saw myself in the large mirror on it and above it, a painting representing a lovely young female, a true resemblance of Queen Mary. I concluded to venture down. I say venture, for nought but the breeze had yet been heard, but I proceeded, and arrived at the drawing-room where two young women were busily engaged cleaning. *The youngest saw me first, and I* heard her tell her companion, "The American gentleman is down," and they both vanished instantly. I examined quite at leisure, all about me. The paintings were truly beautiful, and the morning was clear, and the lights on them were very good.

The young clergyman came in and a walk was immediately undertaken. The hares all started before our dogs from wood to wood. We arrived at the stables where I saw four truly well formed Abyssinian horses with tails down to the earth and legs of one sinew, no larger than those of an Elk. The riding room was lighted and the training of those animals had been performed that morning. The gamekeeper was unkenneling his dogs. He shewed me a large tame fox, and we proceeded through further woods to the manor, now the habitat of the Great Falconer, *John Anderson*. I saw [him] and his hawks. He had already received orders to come to the hall at 11 to shew me those birds in their full dress.

Next we visited hanging gardens where, to my surprise, roses were blooming most sweetly. I plucked one for my buttonhole. [We] returned to the hall by following the sinuosities of a brook, reaching it by 10.

The ladies were in the drawing-room. A sweet babe was here also, a little nephew of the Countess, rosy with health and gay with the innocence of his age. Messrs. Hay and Ramsay had left for Edinburgh. The Earl came in and we went to breakfast. Neither at this meal nor at luncheon are waiters seen. Now all was bustle about the drawing lesson. I might positively have said that I was about receiving one, for my Lucy, Lady Morton draws much better than I do, believe me. The chalks, the crayons and all wanted was before us in a few minutes, and I sat to give a lesson to one of the first or rather most ancient persons of Scotland as well as of England. Singular fact—yet sometimes, when in the woods, I have rested and anticipated my being introduced to the great nobles of Europe, and I am now gradually proceeding to that effect.

Well, I gave a lesson, taught how to rub with the cork and prepare with water colors. The Earl saw the proceedings and was delighted at my invention. I shewed him many of my drawings. The falconer came, and I saw the falcons ready for the chase. He held them perched on his gloved hand, with bells,— and hood and crest flowing. But the morning was not fit for a flight, and I lost the sight of that pleasure.

During a moment of rest [from the lesson,] the Countess asked for my Subscription Board, and wrote very legibly with a steel pen, "The Countess of Morton." She wished to pay for the first Number now, but this I declined. She promised me letters for England, and I assure thee I was pleased. I conceived a wish to have some fresh Pheasants, and she immediately ordered some to be killed for me.

Luncheon again—after which I walked out to see a flock of full one hundred brown Deer that, like sheep, were feeding within a few hundred paces of the hall. I approach them pretty close. Many had shed their horns. They scampered off at my sight, probably knowing well what a sinning hunter I was.

The carriage had been ordered for me, for I was engaged [for] dinner in Edinburgh at Captain Basil Hall's. I saw it come to the hall, and returned to pay my respects, and did so, but it was agreed by all parties that it should be sent for me next week, to give another lesson and spend another night. I pressed the hands and took my leave. My ride home was soon over. The carriage moved as smooth as before.

I found a packet from the American minister Gallatin, a letter from Charles Bonaparte, some books also from him, and a bill from my tailor. I ran to Mr. Lizars to give an account of my journey, and reached *No.* 8 St. Colm at 6 o'clock. Captain Hall soon spoke of America, and strange to tell, he was a midshipman on board the *"Leander"* when Pierce was killed off New York, and when [I was] on my way from France.[78] Our Captain, seeing the British vessel *"Leander"* moving about round Long Island, reached New York by Hell Gate.

My portfolio was there. After dinner the crowd accumulated. I opened my book for a moment, but soon closed it, for I felt wearied. Lady Hunter came in, and Sir William Hamilton.[79] I

78. Audubon called the *Leander* the *Rattlesnake* in his diary, quoted by Lucy Audubon, *The Life of John James Audubon*.

79. Sir William Hamilton (1788–1856) was a metaphysician, lawyer, and politician.

saw a beautiful sister of Captain Hall, the handsome Mrs. Harvey, and many more, but Lucy I made my escape without bidding adieu except to the Captain. And I reached George Street almost broken down. See what I have again written tonight! But stop—having seen in "Blackwood's Magazine" a curious notice about me, written by Professor Wilson, I wrote him the following note [not copied into the journal by Audubon]. And then, my Lucy, I bid thee a most happy and a most peaceful good night.

Edinburgh   Dec. 29th, 1826   Friday

I painted all day and did this most happily and cheerfully, for I received thy two kind letters of October last, [one being dated] the 14th.

In the evening I went to Captain Hall to shew some drawings to one of his sisters. I returned early, but Messrs. Lizars and [Mr. Hamilton, a brother-in-law], having called on me it was full past midnight when I bid thee well.

[Saturday]

Saturday was much the same as yesterday. I painted constantly, and for a wonder was not disturbed by visitors.

[Sunday, New Year's Eve]

Sunday was also spent at painting as long as light lasted, but I had to go and dine at Captain Hall's again, to be particularly introduced to FRANCIS JEFFREY, the principal writer in the "Edinburgh Review." I reached [there] at 6 o'clock but did not take my watch nor any money, for I was afraid that it might be taken when I returned. I was first at Captain Hall's. [He,] his lady, Lady Hunter and the young babe were all there in the setting room. But Mr. McCulloch, a great writer on political economy soon came in. This is a most extraordinary man, and a plain, amiable character without fudge. Then famous Jeffrey and his wife entered; a small (not to say little) being, with a woman under one arm and his hat in the other. He bowed very seriously indeed, and so much so when he turned toward me that I conceived the personage to be full aware of his weight in so-

ciety. His looks were shrewd, but I thought much cunning resides over the eyes cast about. And the man talked so abun-
dantly that I did not like him at all. But Lucy, this is my first
impression, and *he* may prove better than I now think him. His
American wife was dressy and had a twitch of a nervous nature
that, joined to her uncommon share of *plainness* (for I never
called a woman ugly in my whole life) rendered *her* not extremely interesting. There again I may form very erroneous
ideas, but I like to put *down* my opinions as they come, at once,
fresh from the active mind. If I mistake not, Monsieur Jeffrey
was shy of me, and I was kind enough to return the compliment. Thou must know that this gentleman has used me rather
cavalierly. When I came [to this city] I received a letter of introduction to him. I called on him, and [finding] him absent I left
the letter, my card, and a note of mine which I regret I did not
copy. When my exhibition opened I [sent] Mr. Jeffrey a card of
admittance and my card again. Mr. J. never came near me, and I
never went near him, for if *he* was Jeffrey, *I* was Audubon, and
felt quite as independent as all the tribe of Jeffreys in Scotland,
England and Ireland put together.

This evening he thanked me for what I had done, but I would
not return his compliment for he had done nothing towards me.
And notwithstanding his being a wonderfully great reviewer I
thought he wanted a little of the polish and finished manner of
simpler men. During the dinner the conversation was various. I
liked Captain Hall and his lady the more I saw of them, and I
found Lady Hunter extremely kind. Mrs. Jeffrey sat opposite
me, each close to Captain Hall. Whenever I looked at her, her
eyes were riveted on my whole person; and not finding her
quite so interesting as Mrs. Hall or Mrs. Harvey I turned my
looks more frequently to them. Very little was said about America. I soon discovered that neither the reviewer nor his consort
knew much about it besides their reading, and I thought the
subject was carefully avoided. Captain Hall, notwithstanding,
wished that it should become the topic. We went to tea. I talked
some to Mr. J. and he talked a little to me. A few inquiries were
made about my work. He told me that he was glad to have met
me, and at 10 o'clock I took my leave, having positively seen

the little man that sounds so great abroad—aye, and in Scotland too.

I walked briskly. This was the eve of a new year, and in Edinburgh it is rather a dangerous thing to be late in the streets, for vagabonds are want to commit many errors at this time. Murders and other sinful acts take place. To prevent these, the watch is doubled, and [more than the] usual quantity of gas lights afforded. I reached my lodgings, quite safe. Sat to and outlined a Pheasant, to save daylight [for painting] tomorrow, and was about to go to bed when Mrs. Dickie came in and begged that I would wait [till] past 12 o'clock to take some toddy with Miss Campbell, my American boarding companion, and bid her a Happy New Year. I did so. And had I sat up all night, and wrote or drawn, or sat still by my fire and thought of anything, I would have done as well. For the noise so increased in the streets, and lasted with such confusion until morning that I never closed my eyes a moment. Captain Hall presented me with three volumes of his voyages. I received a note again from the Countess of Morton, requesting that I would go to her on Thursday next when she would send a carriage for me. I received some Pheasants from her.

Account of Expenses Since April 26th, 1826, the day I left the Habitants of the "Beech Woods" near Bayou Sara, Louisiana

paid Negro Toby of Mrs. Percy	$	.50 cts
do. for Mrs. Percy's horse shoes		.50
My passage to New Orleans in Red River		7.50
2 flageolets		5.00
Plants for my Wife		2.00
Crayons for John my son		9.00
Cushion for Lucy to set on		3.50
Barber, theatre &c. up to Wednesday 3 May		2.50
Sirops, lime juice, liquors, &c., pd. Sapinot		16.00
passage to Bayou Sara and down again		18.00
My bill at Sapinot for sundry stores and board		20.00
Bed and bedding with hauling		9.00
My passage to Capt. Joseph Hatch, Ship Delos of Kennebunk to Liverpool		100.00

1 column of Gibraltar Rock   1.50
Cleaning Porpoise jaw Bone   .25

$195.25

[Final entry torn from journal and now privately owned:]

Edinburgh   Dec. [31st], 1826

Sunday Night 12 o'clock—
and Now My Dear book, must I part with thee? Back [to] America, and fed in England and Scotland, and at sea—go to My best Friend. To My Wife, to my Beloved Lucy—yes, go back, return to thy own native soil and give her pleasure a while. *She* will be glad to hold conference with thee now—for she will look on thy sheets as the reflectors of my daily Life. Simple, either in times of Nothing or of wondrous events, and whilst she reads them, she will observe my very gradual advancement into a World yet unknown, and dangerous to be known. A World wherein I may prosper but wherein it is the easiest thing to sink into compleat oblivion. When I open thy sheets again where will *we* be? God only knows, and how happy or miserable shall I be—I will not pretend, at present, to investigate—or torment my brain about [that]—for this simple reason, that God being my Supreme commander I am, and for ever will be, contented to act, to enjoy, to suffer or feel whatever in his Wisdom he may think best fit for me—and so well aware do I think him right in all he does, that happy or miserable, I will enjoy or suffer, perfectly satisfied that it is all for the best at last. Go, that My Wife read this, let my children read it. Let the world know these my heartfelt sentiments, and believe me, my Dear Book, for ever thy most obliged, yes truly obliged Friend.

JOHN J. AUDUBON
—Citizen of the United States of North America

Editorial Afterword

In November, 1826, William Home Lizars, of Edinburgh, began to engrave and color *The Birds of America*. By spring of 1827 he had aquatinted—finished—the first number of five plates, except for the final plate mark details and the coloring of a few impressions.

In April, 1827, Audubon visited London in search of subscribers. The news of election to both the Linnaean and Royal societies lost its tang on word from Lizars that his artisans had struck. A desperate search to replace the shop of defectors led to Robert Havell and his son and namesake. The elder Havell became chief colorist, the younger chief engraver of the Folio. Before long Robert Havell, Jr., was to become sole proprietor of the concern.

On June 20, 1838, the four hundred and thirty-fifth—and last—aquatint was engraved on copper. Only the last fascicles remained to be colored and delivered. The monumental achievement, one of the world's greatest books, represented more than one thousand figures of birds, and birds of hundreds of species, portrayed on or among branches, with flowers and plants, with mollusks, crustaceans or shells, and here and there in juxtaposition with mammals, fishes, and reptiles.

The American subscription of one thousand dollars included customs duties. The full cost to British subscribers was £174.

About 175 sets were completed; or so, according to his niece Maria Rebecca Audubon, Victor Gifford Audubon once estimated. Dropped subscriptions account for the probable existence of many more than that total for various prints from the first two of four volumes. Many sets once owned abroad, and especially in England, eventually found their way to America.

Addenda

[On a loose sheet found within the 1826 journal appear the following entries from the extinct 1828 journal, evidently destroyed by the daughters of John Woodhouse Audubon. The sketch of the lady on the balcony probably accounts for its preservation:]

Paris   Oct. 3d, 1828

Friday.

I wrote to Havell to send the Duc of Orleans sets, &c., and I received a kind letter from Greene. I also had a letter from the Director of the Expenses of the Duke, requesting that I should see him, and I arranged respecting the Duke's subscription. This letter, however, reached me too late to attend to it to-day. My day has been an idle one; my wishes were bent on receiving an order from the Minister, and yet I had no good reason for so doing, as ministers have too much to do to *hurry in anything*. I felt a great desire to write to friend William Rathbone, and yet have not done so, anxious to give him as much good news as possible at once. But if, by Sunday, nothing remarkable takes place I *must* write or he will think that I have forgot all his kindnesses to me, and God forbid. Good night, dearest friend.

Saturday
4th

I called on friend [Swainson] after breakfast and at his request went to the Jardin du Roi to interpret for him. We called afterward on Geoffrey St. Hilaire, and remained some time, and heard some curious facts respecting the habits and conformation of the *Mole*. He gave me a ticket for Doctor Bostock[1] of London to accompany me to the delivery of the prizes at the Institution. On my way back I stopped to look at the giraffe, and saw an elephant employed at uprooting a tree, and I was delighted at the tractability of this noble animal. He seemed to understand the conversation of his conductor or cornac as if a man himself. I now arrived at No. 216 Rue St. Honoré and ascended four of the highest stairs I know of to reach the *cabinet* of M. Pascales, the director of the expenses of S. A. R., the Duke of Orleans. As he was expected in a moment I sat and looked about me. Oh Lucy, what fine arrangement and order in the management of this great house. Different book cases contained the papers belonging to the Forests, Horses, Furniture, Fine Arts, Libraries, Fisheries, &c., &c., and when M. Pascales came in and heard my name————.

[The following fragment differs from the version published in *Audubon and His Journals* by Maria Rebecca Audubon (New York, 1897):]

————at a balcony not far from us a rather well formed lady made her appearance. I judged her to be about 36, well dressed, &c. A table was at her side on which a glass vase was seen. The lady held a glass tube in one hand, leaned on the balcony with the other and—come dearest friend, what was *That Child* doing? As the merry Andrew Matthews said, "You give it up." Hey, dost thou give it up? Well, the child of 36 was blowing soap bubbles

---

[1]Dr. John Bostock, M.D. (1773–1846). Royal Society Fellow. Quit Liverpool for London.

". . . the child of 36 was blowing soap bubbles to the paysans!!" *From a page of Audubon's 1828 Journal.*

to the *paysans!!!* This is the French character, Lucy, light as air and as thoughtless as the lamb who goes bounding at the approach of the storm. I drew her position on my pocket book and I repeat it here with the same pencil for thy own pleasure, when we meet, never to part again.

[Here appears Audubon's sketch of the lady blowing bubbles.]

We have spent an evening as much like the French lady as possible, not to be thought *outré* in France. We in fact have been two hours at a very small theatre to see *Punch* and his gay coadjutors for fifteen sous. And now dearest wife, God bless thee forever. Good night!

[Audubon's writing on front end papers consists of names of persons met in Britain:]
Patrick Syme, 63 Great King Street, Edinburgh,

Oct. 30th, 1826

Staff Surgeon Lyons
D. Stephenson
    13th Lt. Dragoons
Mr. Innes of Stow
Dr. Munro
Mr. Lisbon
J. B. Kenney
    [Writing on front flyleaf (from which a rectangle was cut):
The Residence of My Good Friend A. Hodgson

BRECKFIELD COTTAGE, ERERTON.

13th   21 days

John Crooke—

?

recommended by Mrs. Edge, King Street——

To the Benefit

For Commemoration

My Knife
The Morning—Fog, Walk, &c.
and Start—The Valley—The River—
Bakewell, breakfast—road to Buxton
The River, our Walks—Buxton
Mr. Murray—his account of himself

battrey—The Pony and Driver—our Dinner
ride with Hannah—our arrival
at Manchester—Density of Population
on approaching—Wrk^d & Manchester
Mr. Dockray's present—Evening—

[Penciled writing on next flyleaf:]
The Brig Howard from Britton—from Liverpool (40 days bound
to Havana) spoke to us on the 15th of June off Cuba and 50
miles of Havana. Joel Birney-Master—wished to be reported at
Liverpool.

The Ship Thealia of Philadelphia
Bound to Minorca Mediterranean, Spoke to us on the 21st of
June 1826—Latitude—9 o'clock, P.M.—Sent a Large Petrel to
the Capt. for the Phila.
Society.

Corset laces (motto on seal all's well—)
Trunk. par Excellence—with Thermometer, &c.,—Ink

[Verse (possibly by John Chorley for J. J. A.'s use, judging from
the journal in re poetry, at points) in pencil on flyleaf preceding
the first entry in the journal of 1826:]

"hence-forth may her sorrows cease;
affliction's frown assail her never;
Bless her, kind Heaven, with health and peace,
and Joy attend her steps for ever!

"For she is my supreme delight;
She can fill my heart with pleasure;
She is most precious to my sight;
She is Nature's choicest treasure!—"

[Under the poem are tiny pencil notations, undoubtedly a record of the number of times J. J. A. had written to the following persons at the time he made these notes:]

"Victor 1—   "Lucy 1—

                                                         2—

"Charles Bo. [naparte] 1   1—

[The following lines appear on the first of the end papers in the back of the journal of 1826:]

Samuel Gregg [sic], Junior, Esqr.,
Quarry Bank near Manchester

[The following lines were evidently intended to form part of a letter to Richard Rathbone:]

What *objects* in Nature *now existing* do you look upon as positive exemplification of the reality of the deluge? Knowing *you* a philosophical researcher, I beg an answer. My mind is quite at rest on the subject; and should you wish to know my opinion I will give it to you after you have sent me your own results, as this may lead to many valuable inquiries (to me at least). I hope you will not deny me the pleasure of corresponding with a young gentleman toward whom I never can cease to feel the highest sentiments of esteem, and who, I hope, will permit me to be always, as I wish to be,

his friend and obedient servant,

J. J. A.

I often wished to put the question when under your hospitable roof, but the brilliant eyes of so many superiors to our kind deterred me from it with awe and humility. Please present the whole of your family my best regards and sincerest thanks, and again, my dear sir, believe me, Yours,

Most Sincerely,

J. A.

Please write by your brother William who will send me at 2 George Street—Octr. 29, 1826, Edinburgh.

Pencil sketch on paper, deck scene on the ship Columbia, 1829. *Apparently placed in the journal for safekeeping.*

Index